World History for
Children and Young Adults

LIBRARIES UNLIMITED DATA BOOKS

WORLD HISTORY

An Annotated
Bibliographic
Index

FOR
CHILDREN
AND
YOUNG
ADULTS

Vandelia
VanMeter

A Libraries Unlimited Data Book

1992
LIBRARIES UNLIMITED, INC.
Englewood, Colorado

LIBRARIES UNLIMITED, INC.
P.O. Box 6633
Englewood, CO 80155-6633

Library of Congress Cataloging-in-Publication Data

VanMeter, Vandelia.
    World history for children and young adults : an annotated
bibliographic index / Vandelia VanMeter.
      xvii, 266 p. 22x28 cm. -- (Libraries Unlimited data books)
      Includes index.
      ISBN 0-87287-732-9
      1. History--Indexes. 2. History--Juvenile literature--Indexes.
    I. Title. II. Series.
  Z6201.V28 1992
  [D20]
  909--dc20   91-43521
                                    CIP

To our mothers, with love.

Contents

Libraries Unlimited Data Books

The Libraries Unlimited Data Book series consists of bibliographies and indexes that are issued simultaneously in traditional print format and in one or several computerized databases. (Not every book in this series has an available database. Check with the publisher.) Unlike most CD-ROM products, data books are designed as inexpensive in-house resources to be used with popular database managers used by most libraries, such as Microsoft Works, AppleWorks, or dBase.

Indexes presented in the series provide an innovative idea in indexing for the individual library. Purchasers can tailor the index to their own collections. For example, if the database indexes 300 books and the library owns only 200 of those titles, the 100 titles not owned by the library can be deleted from the database, thus producing an index that matches the library's collection. Titles owned by the library but not indexed can be added to the database as needed. The database can be printed out or consulted by computer as needed by library patrons.

Bibliographies in the series have the advantage of being searched in ways not possible with the printed version. The limitations of these searches are those of the database manager that the librarian uses, that is, the limitations are those of dBase III+, PC File+, Microsoft Works, or any other package used to search the data. The advantage of the bibliography on disk is that it can be modified to suit the needs of local patrons. Local call numbers may be added, new entries may be added by the library, and the publisher can keep the bibliography current between editions of the printed version. Versions for IBM, Macintosh, and the Apple II family are available. Write or call the publisher for details.

Special Needs

Libraries or individuals needing the data in a special computer format or needing parts of the databases are invited to write to the editorial department of Libraries Unlimited for assistance. Include a description of your needs and the format in which you wish the data to be arranged. A price quotation will be provided by return mail.

Users who find errors in the data or who could provide updates to the data are invited to correspond with the editorial department.

Write:

Head,
Editorial Department
Libraries Unlimited, Inc.
P.O. Box 6633
Englewood, CO 80155-6633
Phone: (303) 770-1220

Introduction

World History for Children and Young Adults: An Annotated Bibliographic Index has three purposes: to provide an annotated bibliography of recently recommended nonfiction and fiction trade books relating to world history, arranged by continent and nation, for students grades K-12; to provide a guide to reviews of these books; and to include annotations and a guide to reviews of "old standbys" that are still in print.

The recent titles listed were reviewed between 1980 and 1989 in standard reviewing tools commonly used by school and public libraries. The old standbys are those works found in Seymour Metzner's *World History in Juvenile Books* (H. W. Wilson, 1973), which have remained so popular that they are still in print. In-print items listed in the Metzner bibliography are included because Metzner is still in print in spite of its age, and it is referenced in such standard works as *Elementary School Library Collection* and *Children's Catalog*. Since those individual titles are still in print, frequently in new editions, it is assumed that they have been found to be of value and therefore warrant inclusion in this work. The author regrets that titles published from 1974 to 1979 are not included here. If demand makes it worthwhile to publish a supplement that covers those dates, it will be considered; suggestions are welcome.

Criteria for Selection

The journals searched for reviews are:

Book Report

Booklist

Bulletin for the Center of Children's Books

History Teacher

Horn Book

Library Journal

School Library Journal

Social Education

Voice of Youth Advocates

All items listed in this bibliography have received at least one favorable or mixed review in the sources examined. An effort was made to list all the reviews found in these journals for the titles listed.

Titles were included if they were suitable for students K-12 and their subject matter pertained to the social or political history of any region or nation of the world, other than the United States. The companion volume to *World History*, entitled *American History for Children and Young Adults: An Annotated Bibliographic Index* (Libraries Unlimited, 1990) provides information on titles pertaining to events and persons in U.S. history.

Old standbys listed in the Metzner bibliography were included if they were located in the 1989-1990 issue of *Books in Print*. Where possible, at least one review of the original work or the new edition is listed for the Metzner items.

Scope

The nine periodicals listed above, dated 1980-1989, were searched for appropriate reviews. *World History* lists 2,234 titles, including fiction, nonfiction, and biography, with reference to more than 5,600 reviews. The list includes works on particular historical and political events and movements as well as works of a more general nature. Titles may examine a nation or time period from a particular point of view or provide a feeling for the time through a work of fiction.

Fiction that has a historic setting is included only when it appears from the review that the time and setting are an integral part of, and influence, the action. If the setting appears to be incidental to the story, the title is omitted.

Materials on wars and other events that have involved the United States with other nations are included in this work if the emphasis is on the other nation; if the emphasis is on American activities or the American point of view, then that title will be found in *American History*. Books dealing with the history of science, invention, medicine, and similar topics are not included unless it appears from the reviews that the work relates this specialized history to its impact on the historical development of a given nation or region.

The selection and arrangement of the titles is intended to be of maximum usefulness to the following groups:

1. School and public librarians for collection development

2. Teachers conducting individualized reading programs

3. Teachers, parents, and librarians wishing to provide guidance to students seeking reading materials for personal enjoyment or for school assignments

4. Librarians, teachers, or parents of gifted or remedial students who need materials above or below grade level

5. Authors and publishers who need a ready reference to the availability of recommended literature for students K-12 on specific topics in world history.

Grade level designations included in the citation and the grade level index are valuable features of *World History*. The user who needs material on a particular region or nation may examine appropriate entries in the body of the book. The grade level given in the citation allows the user to determine quickly which books are grade appropriate. If, however, the user's primary interest is grade level, with subject matter a secondary consideration, the grade level index allows the user to approach the search from this point of view. There all of the titles in *World History* are listed according to the beginning grade level given in the reviews.

The inclusion of both old and new titles broadens the usefulness of this book. In addition to the old titles found in Metzner, there are other old titles that were reviewed in the 1980-1989 journals. These may be new editions or they may have been included in a retrospective subject listing. Their inclusion will be helpful to librarians as an additional tool for collection analysis and weeding as well as in selection of new purchases.

Titles whose first reviews appeared in the last two months of 1989 may appear in a future supplement.

Arrangement

The divisions of the work are: General, World War I, World War II, Africa, Asia and Oceania, Europe, North America, and South America.

General articles on world history precede all other articles. These are subdivided as is appropriate, based on subject headings found in *Sears List of Subject Headings*, 13th ed. (H. W. Wilson, 1986). World Wars I and II each have a chapter, with appropriate subdivisions. Other entries are arranged first by continent, then by nation, and then by subdivisions of the nation's history, where appropriate. Materials for most nations are not divided chronologically because there are not enough titles to warrant this. For some nations, however, this division was a necessity. In those cases the chronological divisions suggested in *Sears* were the basis for the divisions used. Other subdivisions are used as they are appropriate, e.g., Biographies, Fiction, Social Life and Customs. Preceding any chronological division for a given nation is a section entitled General, which includes those titles spanning two or more of the chronological divisions.

Decisions concerning names of nations, the inclusion of a nation as a part of a particular continent, or how a dependency, territory, or portion of a country should be listed, were based on the policies followed by *Worldmark Encyclopedia of the Nations* (Wiley, 1986). As a result, Greenland, a Danish dependency, is found in the Europe division, under Denmark—Greenland. Australia is included in the "Asia and Oceania" volume of *Worldmark* and is found under that same division here. An effort was made to provide a cross-reference in the subject index wherever there might be cause for confusion.

A typical entry includes the following information:

Author/Editor. Restrictions of space in the database allowed the entry of the first named author/editor only. The absence of the names of other contributors is regretted.

Title and subtitle.

Series. The name of the series is included in parentheses if it is available through the reviews. Unfortunately, review journals have differing policies on the inclusion of series information, so it is possible that some series names may be omitted.

Publisher/Distributor. All publishers and distributors are given in a recognizable abbreviated form. In the case of small presses, whose addresses may not appear in the usual directories to publishers, the user is referred to the reviews where that information may be found.

Date. For items republished at a much later date than the original, both dates are provided where they are reasonably available through reviews, *OCLC, Book Review Digest*, or other sources. The dates are presented in this format: 1961; 1987.

Cost. All costs are rounded up to the nearest dollar. The price listed is for the trade edition unless specified as paperback (Pb) or library edition (Lib. ed.), insofar as this information could be determined from the reviews. Users are cautioned that the prices listed here should be used only as a general guide because of unpredictable price changes. Even so, it was felt that including the price would be useful as an indication of what the purchaser might expect to pay.

Physical Description. This area includes information on paging, volumes, and illustrations. All illustrations, drawings, photographs, lithographs, maps, and other illustrations are listed under the abbreviation *ill.* unless the review indicates that the only illustrative matter is maps, in which case the word *maps* appears.

Grade Level. If a work received multiple reviews, and if the reviewers recommend varied grade levels, the inclusive range is provided, with ages interpolated as grades. In the event that the reviews do not indicate grade or age, *Books in Print* was consulted. The user will note that on some titles the inclusive grade range given in the reviews is very broad. Those selecting titles for purchase are encouraged to consider this, to check the reviews in their favorite sources, and to make grade level judgments based on their experience with that particular journal. Some items, particularly from *Booklist* and *Library Journal* have been recommended for public libraries and are suitable for advanced or gifted students or for collections more highly developed than the norm. These items are included with the designation *Adult*.

Abbreviations to review sources. The titles of the review sources are abbreviated in this way:

B	*Booklist*
BC	*Bulletin for the Center of Children's Books*
BR	*Book Report*
HB	*Horn Book*
HT	*History Teacher*
LJ	*Library Journal*
SE	*Social Education*
SLJ	*School Library Journal*
VOYA	*Voice of Youth Advocates*

Following the abbreviation for the title of the journal, the volume number and date are given. Preceding the abbreviation for the title of the journal a symbol may appear to indicate a ranking, e.g., * for highly recommended; + − for mixed recommendation; − for negative review. The absence of a symbol indicates a normal recommendation. Items reviewed in *Voice of Youth Advocates (VOYA)* are given an * if VOYA rates an item 5Q or 4Q5P.

In some cases a mixed review shows serious reservations, but in others it may be based on illustrations or some editorial decision that does not negate the value of the content. Thus users interested in the subject matter of an item are encouraged to read the reviews to determine whether it may have value for them. Users are urged to read as many reviews as possible before purchase, especially where mixed or unfavorable reviews are listed.

All titles included received at least a mixed review in at least one of the journals searched, or they appeared in Metzner. As many reviews as possible from the list of review journals are included, but the design of the database limits the number of reviews to seven. If an item is listed in Metzner, this is noted as *Metzner* before other reviews are listed.

Annotations

Brief annotations have been provided to clarify subject matter. All annotations are based on an examination of the reviews listed for that title. Unfavorable comments are not included in annotations since all the reviewers may not agree, but they are indicated by the evaluative symbols mentioned above. If there is a consensus of excellence concerning specific features of the work, this is mentioned as space allows. Once again, users of this book are urged to use it as a reference to the original reviews.

Sample Entry

Great Britain — 1714-1837

1546. Windrow, Martin. British Redcoat of the Napoleonic Wars, The. (Soldier Through the Ages). Watts, 1986. 32 p. ill. $11.

Gr 5-10. BR 5: Jan/Feb 1987. SLJ 33: Nov 1986. * SE 51: Apr/May 1987. Intended for students with some background on the Napoleonic wars, this account of the way of life of the British redcoat includes colorful illustrations, a glossary, and a timeline.

Indexes

World History includes indexes to authors, titles, subjects, series, and grade levels. The subject index includes the names of persons who are the subject of individual biographies and cross-references to names of countries, regions, etc.

Supplements

The author and Libraries Unlimited plan supplements to this book. These supplements will follow the same format and will be announced in Libraries Unlimited's catalogs.

Acknowledgments

The completion of *World History for Children and Young Adults* was made possible by the interest, enthusiasm, critical eye, and hard work of my graduate assistant Jamie Elston. Her loyal support is greatly appreciated.

And then there is Vic. After 36 years he still is interested in the daily events of his wife's work. So he has heard about it all, helped work through conceptual difficulties as they arose, and provided the moral support and encouragement that made the work possible.

Thanks to you both.

General

1. Alotaibi, Muhammad. Bedouin: The Nomads of the Desert. (Original Peoples). Rourke, 1989. 48 p. ill. Lib. ed. $14.

Gr 5-8. B 85: May 15 1989. SLJ 35: Apr 1989. Bedouin history, culture, religion, and way of life are presented, including photos of the people, their homeland, and historical art.

2. Arnold, Guy. Datelines of World History. Warwick; dist. by Watts, 1983. 93 p. ill. $13.

Gr 5+. + - B 80: Dec 1 1983. SLJ 30: Dec 1983. Social and political history are recorded in a timeline that lists simultaneous events around the world. Essays on important topics, illustrations, and a biographical index enhance the work.

3. Carey, John. Eyewitness to History. Harvard University Press, 1988. 701 p. $25.

Gr 9+. B 85: Sep 1 1988. BR 7: Mar/Apr 1989. LJ 113: Oct 15 1988. SLJ 35: Dec 1988. For both browsers and serious readers, this chronological collection includes nearly 400 eyewitness accounts of significant and trivial events from 430 B.C. to 1986.

4. Caselli, Giovanni. Life Through the Ages. (Windows on the World). Grosset, 1987. 64 p. ill. $15.

Gr 5-8. SLJ 34: Mar 1988. This overview of major world events from ancient to modern times is profusely illustrated.

5. Cleveland, Ray L. Middle East and South Asia 1983. (World Today Series). Stryker-Post, 1983. 115 p. ill. Pb $4.

Gr 7+. B 80: Mar 1 1984. This regional overview clarifies the rapidly changing events in the area from 1910 to 1983 using maps. For each nation, history, geography, culture, and economy are covered.

6. Diagram Group. Time Lines on File. Facts on File, 1989. 300 p. ill. $145.

Gr 9+. + - B 85: Jun 15 1989. BR 8: May/Jun 1989. LJ 114: May 1 1989. Suitable for photocopying, these 300 timelines of historic events and lifelines on noted leaders from world history and culture are made accessible through a detailed table of contents and index.

7. Fine, John Christopher. Hunger Road, The. Atheneum, 1988. 148 p. $13.

Gr 6+. B 85: Jan 1 1989. + - BC 42: Nov 1988. SLJ 35: Nov 1988. + - VOYA 11: Dec 1988. Fine discusses the political, social, and climatic causes of hunger around the world. Organizations and other sources of current information are included.

8. Franck, Irene M. To the Ends of the Earth: The Great Travel and Trade Routes of History. Facts on File, 1984. 388 p. ill. $35.

Gr 9+. LJ 109: Dec 1984. The history of over 30 worldwide trails, routes, and pathways is explored, including the silk road followed by Marco Polo, the Appian Way, the Nile River, and the British Great Northern Road.

9. Freeman-Grenville, G. S. P. Chronology of World History: A Calendar of Principal Events from 3000 B.C to A.D. 1973. 2nd ed. Rowman and Littlefield, 1978. 746 p. $40.

Gr 9+. B 76: Jan 1 1980. This outline of principal events and dates from ca. 3000 B.C. through 1976 provides a panorama of contemporaneous events around the world.

10. Gonick, Larry. Cartoon History of the Universe, Book I. Quill, 1978; 1982. 250 p. ill. Pb $7.

Gr 7+. VOYA 6: Feb 1983. A lighthearted but informative overview of world history in comic book format.

11. Grun, Bernard. Timetables of History: A Horizontal Linkage of People and Events. Updated ed. Simon & Schuster, 1979. 676 p. $30.

Gr 9+. B 76: Feb 1 1980. LJ 104: Dec 1 1979. This tabular chronology shows people, events, and trends in politics, culture, science, and the humanities throughout European and American history.

12. Hauptly, Denis J. Journey from the Past: A History of the Western World. Atheneum, 1983. 216 p. $13.

Gr 9+. B 79: Mar 15 1983. - SLJ 30: Sep 1983. * VOYA 6: Dec 1983. This well-indexed overview covers the highlights of 4 million years of human history.

13. Herman, David. Julian Messner Young Readers' Guide to Dates and Events, The. Messner, 1986. 191 p. ill. $10. Pb $7.

Gr 5-9. B 83: Dec 15 1986. SLJ 33: May 1987. Included are a chronology and brief essays on world events from ancient times to 1985, brief biographies on significant people, and a listing of world leaders. Emphasis is on the western world.

14. Lyttle, Richard B. Golden Path: The Lure of Gold Through History. Atheneum, 1983. 162 p. ill. $12.

Gr 9+. B 80: Nov 15 1983. HB 60: Apr 1984. * SE 48: May 1984. SLJ 30: Mar 1984. The author traces the influence of gold on human political, social, economic, and cultural history.

15. McEvedy, Colin. Macmillan World History Factfinder, The. Macmillan, 1985. 208 p. ill. $30.

Gr 9+. B 82: Mar 1 1986. LJ 110: Sep 1 1985. Essays and over 400 colorful illustrations and maps augment date charts that cover events in political and military history, religion, learning, the arts, discoveries, inventions, cities, and social development from ancient times to the 1980s.

16. Monk, Lorraine. Photographs That Changed the World. Doubleday, 1989. 120 p. ill. $30.

Gr 9+. B 86: Sep 15 1989. Monk has gathered familiar photos of significant events and persons in world history since 1860.

17. Mostyn, Trevor. Cambridge Encyclopedia of the Middle East and North Africa, The. Cambridge University Press, 1988. 504 p. ill. $40.

Gr 9+. BR 8: May/Jun 1989. Illustrations and maps supplement balanced and readable essays about the history, culture, economy, politics, religion, and people of North Africa and the Middle East.

18. Phillips, Douglas A. Pacific Rim Region: Emerging Giant. Enslow, 1988. 160 p. ill. $15.

Gr 7+. B 85: Jan 15 1989. BR 7: Jan/Feb 1989. SLJ 35: Jan 1989. * VOYA 12: Feb 1989. All countries bordering the Pacific are presented, including the historic, cultural, political, physical, and economic factors that shape their relations to each other.

19. Pringle, Laurence. Earth Is Flat–And Other Great Mistakes. Morrow, 1983. 72 p. ill. $8. Lib. ed. $8.

Gr 4-7. B 80: Dec 15 1983. BC 37: Jan 1984. HB 60: Feb 1984. Well-known, obscure, humorous, tragic, ancient, and modern mistakes and their causes are covered in a readable text illustrated with humorous cartoons. The events range from the idea that the earth is flat to a missing minus sign that cost taxpayers millions.

20. Quest for the Past. Reader's Digest; dist. by Random, 1984. 320 p. ill. $21.

Gr 9+. B 81: Feb 1 1985. SLJ 31: Feb 1985. Photos and illustrations augmenting this collection of curious facts about people, places, and events from the Stone Age through the Renaissance. Gladiators, the Basques, ancient architecture, brain surgery, explorers, and similar topics will appeal to browsers.

21. Schwartz, Alvin. Gold and Silver: Tales of Hidden Treasure. Farrar, 1988. 128 p. ill. $14.

Gr 4-8. * B 85: Mar 1 1989. BC 42: Jan 1989. SLJ 35: Feb 1989. Historic and legendary accounts of missing treasure around the world are included in this illustrated book about pirates, buried gold, and a cipher that is still unsolved.

22. Silverstein, Herma. Hoaxes That Made Headlines. Messner, 1986. 182 p. ill. $10.

Gr 6+. B 83: Jan 1 1987. + - BC 40: Apr 1987. - SLJ 33: Feb 1987. This brief treatment of over 60 hoaxes throughout history covers such varied fields as art, literature, history, and science.

23. Tapper, Joan. Peoples and Places of the Past: The National Geographic Illustrated Cultural Atlas of the Ancient World. National Geographic Society, 1983. 242 p. ill. $70.

Gr 9+. B 81: Oct 15 1984. This oversized lavishly illustrated work, intended to show cultural and social achievements from ancient times to 1500, includes maps and concise explanations of the illustrations.

24. Trager, James. People's Chronology: A Year-By-Year Record of Human Events from Prehistory to the Present. Holt, 1979. 1206 p. ill. $28.

Gr 9+. B 76: Jul 1 1980. LJ 105: Apr 15 1980. Over 30,000 entries cover topics of general interest including agriculture, disease, food, trade, crime, sports, social justice, education, environment, politics, and military history from ancient times to 1973.

25. Tuchman, Barbara. March of Folly: From Troy to Vietnam. Knopf, 1984. 464 p. ill. $18.

Gr 9+. B 80: Jan 15 1984. LJ 109: Feb 15 1984. Tuchman examines historic errors in judgment that changed the history of the world, including the Greek siege of Troy, the reaction of the papacy to the Reformation, the British loss of the American colonies, and the Vietnamese War.

26. Unstead, R. J. History of the World. A & C Black; dist. by Global Library, 1983. 559 p. ill. $30.

Gr 8+. SLJ 30: May 1984. Over 100 photos and illustrations supplement this readable survey of the major civilizations, persons, and events in world history since ancient times.

27. Van Loon, Hendrik Willem. Story of Mankind, The. Norton, 1985. 610 p. ill. $20.

Gr 5-7. B 81: Aug 1985. An updated and illustrated edition of van Loon's 1921 Newberry Award winner, covering world history from ancient times to the exploration of space.

28. Ventura, Piero. There Once Was a Time. Putnam, 1987. 158 p. ill. $20.

Gr 4-8. B 84: Sep 1 1987. + - BC 41: Sep 1987. SLJ 34: Oct 1987. This lively pictorial history of social and technological change from ancient times to the turn of the 20th century provides a broad overview of farming, housing, dress, inventions, transportation, trade, and similar topics.

29. Wall, C. Edward. Book of Days, 1987: An Encyclopedia of Information Sources on Historical Figures and Events, Keyed to Calendar Dates. Pierian Press, 1986. 786 p. $60.

Gr 9+. + - B 83: Jul 1987. LJ 112: Jun 1 1987. This encyclopedia of over 400 events and people, arranged by dates, includes brief information, project suggestions, and bibliographies.

30. Wedgwood, C. V. Spoils of Time: A History from the Dawn of Civilization Through the Early Renaissance. Doubleday, 1985. 330 p. $20.

Gr 9+. B 81: Mar 15 1985. + - LJ 110: Mar 1 1985. This readable one-volume history of mankind from ancient times through the mid-16th century covers both cultural and political events.

31. Wetterau, Bruce. Macmillan Concise Dictionary of World History. Macmillan, 1983. 779 p. $40.

Gr 10+. B 80: Feb 1 1984. LJ 108: Oct 1 1983. This alphabetically arranged work includes chronologies and 10,000 concise entries covering historical, political, cultural, and social events, names, places, and terms from ancient to modern times.

32. What Citizens Need to Know About World Affairs. Rev. ed. (Social Issues Resources Series). U. S. News & World Report, 1983. 212 p. ill. $13.

Gr 9+. B 80: Feb 15 1984. BR 3: May/Jun 1984. VOYA 7: Jun 1984. Historical overviews by region are included in this global perspective of events in the 1980s on such topics as the balance of power, resources, population, religion, food distribution, technology, and trading patterns.

33. Wilcocks, Julie. Countries and Islands of the World. 2nd ed. Shoe String, 1985. 124 p. $17.

Gr 7+. + - B 81: Jul 1985. The names of countries and islands of the world are listed, with name changes, references to former names, alternate names, and transliterated names. Brief histories are included.

34. Worldmark Encyclopedia of the Nations. 6th ed. Worldmark Press; dist. by J. Wiley, 1984. 5 vol. ill. $200.

Gr 6+. B 81: Feb 15 1985. SLJ 31: May 1985. Volume 1 covers the United Nations. Volumes 2-5 cover 172 nations, providing information on 50 topics about each, arranged to facilitate comparisons.

0-1492

35. Billings, Malcolm. Cross and the Crescent: A History of the Crusades. Sterling, 1988. 239 p. ill. $20.

Gr 9+. B 85: Nov 1 1988. Billings' well-illustrated book covers 700 years of attempts by the Crusaders to gain control of the Holy Land, beginning in the 11th century. He introduces the leaders involved, their goals, tactics, successes, and failures.

36. Branigan, Keith. Prehistory. (History as Evidence). Warwick; dist. by Watts, 1984. 37 p. ill. $9.

Gr 4-10. B 81: Mar 1 1985. BR 4: Mar/Apr 1986. SLJ 31: Apr 1985. This illustrated introduction to ancient history includes a time chart to show how civilizations progressed in different areas of the world. Photos of archaeological finds highlight the text.

37. Carter, Ron. Early Civilizations. (World of Knowledge). Silver Burdett, 1980. 68 p. ill. Lib. ed. $8.

Gr 5-7. B 77: Mar 1 1981. This handy reference tool provides basic information on 13 early civilizations. It includes photos, drawings, diagrams, maps, and a time chart.

38. Caselli, Giovanni. First Civilizations, The. (History of Everyday Things). Peter Bedrick; dist. by Harper, 1985. 48 p. ill. $13.

Gr 5-10. B 82: Nov 15 1985. BR 4: Mar/Apr 1986. SLJ 32: Jan 1986. This British work includes hundreds of drawings of tools, weapons, clothing, lodging, and other artifacts, all briefly explained. Ice Age hunters, and ancient China, Crete, Greece, and the Etruscans are covered.

39. Chadefaud, Catherine. First Empires, The. (Human Story). Silver Burdett, 1988. 77 p. ill. $16.

Gr 5-8. B 85: Feb 15 1989. + - SLJ 35: Feb 1989. A chronology and an abundance of drawings and reproductions augment this oversized introduction to ancient Egypt, the Hittites, Assyrians, Persia, India, and China.

40. Coblence, Jean-Michel. Earliest Cities, The. (Human Story). Silver Burdett, 1987. 77 p. ill. $13.

Gr 4-10. BR 6: Jan 1988. SLJ 34: Feb 1988. Colorful illustrations and brief text introduce ancient cities and the customs of their inhabitants. Well organized.

41. Cotterell, Arthur. Encyclopedia of Ancient Civilizations, The. Mayflower, 1981. 367 p. ill. $30.

Gr 7+. B 77: Mar 15 1981. + - LJ 106: Jan 15 1981. Maps, photos, diagrams, and plans enrich essays by experts covering the essential features of early civilizations in America, China, Egypt, Europe, India, and West Asia.

42. Jenkins, Ian. Greek and Roman Life. Harvard University Press, 1986. 72 p. ill. Pb $8.

Gr 9+. SLJ 33: Mar 1987. Jenkins discusses the home life and culture of the ancient Greeks and Romans in this lavishly illustrated work.

43. Platt, Colin. Atlas of Medieval Man, The. St. Martin's, 1980. 256 p. ill. $23.

Gr 9+. B 76: Mar 1 1980. - LJ 105: Mar 1 1980. SLJ 26: Aug 1980. Global historical, political, and cultural events from 1000 to 1400 are covered in this profusely illustrated work.

44. Splendors of the Past: Lost Cities of the Ancient World. National Geographic Society, 1981. 295 p. ill. $17.

Gr 9+. B 78: Jun 15 1982. * SE 46: May 1982. SLJ 29: Sep 1982. Over 250 colorful photos, maps, and paintings enrich this oversized introduction to the history and culture of the ancient civilizations of Asia and Africa.

45. Whitehouse, Ruth. Making of Civilization: History Discovered Through Archeology. Knopf, 1986. 207 p. ill. Pb $16.

Gr 9+. B 83: Feb 1 1987. BR 5: Mar/Apr 1987. VOYA 10: Jun 1987. Ancient civilizations in China, India, Central and South America, and near the Mediterranean are examined, covering their towns and cities, economic systems, writing, and the role of the individual. Includes illustrations.

0-1492–Maps

46. Fagg, Christopher. Atlas of the Ancient World. Warwick; dist. by Watts, 1981. 59 p. ill. Lib. ed. $9.

Gr 5-8. + - B 77: May 1 1981. Colorful photos, chronologies, and helpful text augment maps that trace the growth of civilization from early man to 500 A.D.

0-1492–Social Life and Customs

47. Unstead, R. J. How They Lived in Cities Long Ago. Arco, 1981. 77 p. ill. $11.

Gr 5-7. B 78: Apr 1 1982. The layout and construction of 7 ancient cities and the way of life of their inhabitants are presented. These ancient civilizations were located in the Indus Valley, Egypt, Babylonia, China, Greece, Rome, and Mexico.

48. Veyne, Paul. History of Private Life; Vol. I: From Pagan Rome to Byzantium. Harvard University Press, 1987. 670 p. ill. $30.

Gr 10+. B 83: Apr 15 1987. LJ 112: Feb 15 1987. The everyday family life, social, sexual, and religious customs of ancient Rome, the Byzantine Empire, and the early Middle Ages are explored in this lavishly illustrated work.

1492-1899

49. Brosse, Jacques. Great Voyages of Discovery: Circumnavigators and Scientists, 1764-1843. Facts on File, 1985. 228 p. ill. $35.

Gr 9+. B 82: Nov 15 1985. BR 5: May/Jun 1986. This lavishly illustrated chronicle of the journeys of French, British, and American explorers of the 18th and 19th centuries includes biographical sketches and informative tables.

50.   Miquel, Pierre.   Age of Discovery, The.   (Silver Burdett Picture Histories).   Silver Burdett, 1981.   64 p. ill. $8.

Gr 5-8. B 77: Jul 15/Aug 1981. Miquel provides a broad perspective of European expansion along with unusual facts, key dates, a glossary, and numerous illustrations.

51.   Townson, W. D.   Atlas of the World in the Age of Discovery: 1453-1763.   Warwick; dist. by Watts, 1981. 61 p. ill. $10.

Gr 4-6. B 78: Sep 15 1981. SLJ 28: Mar 1982. Maps, charts, and illustrations highlight the navigations, explorations, scientific discoveries, rise of empires, and warfare of the age of discovery.

1900-1999

52.   Brett, Guy.   Through Our Own Eyes: Popular Art and Modern History.   New Society, 1987. 190 p. ill. $35. Pb $15.

Gr 9+. B 83: Mar 1 1987. Through their art ordinary people comment on the political realities of their lives. Included are works by laborers in Chile, Africa, England, and China.

53.   Cairns, Trevor.   Twentieth Century, The.   (Cambridge Introduction to History).   Lerner, 1984. 166 p. ill. $13.

Gr 7+. * SLJ 31: May 1985. International events since the turn of the century are traced and relationships among nations are explained in this comprehensive overview.   Helpful charts, photos, diagrams, maps, and posters are included.

54.   Evans, Harold.   Front Page History: Events of Our Century That Shook the World.   Salem House; dist. by Merrimack Publishers' Circle, 1984. 192 p. ill. $18.

Gr 9+. B 81: Nov 1 1984. Facsimiles of front pages for every year from 1900 to 1983 highlight notable events of the century.

55.   Eyewitness: 25 Years Through World Press Photos.   Morrow, 1981. 192 p. ill. $20.

Gr 9+. SLJ 28: Apr 1982. Captioned photos of major world events from 1956 to 1980 provide enjoyment for browsers or curriculum support.

56.   Ferrell, Robert H.   Twentieth Century, The.   World Almanac, 1984. 512 p. $25.

Gr 9+. + - B 81: Apr 1 1985. - VOYA 8: Aug 1985. This chronology covers world events from 1900 through 1983. Emphasis is on politics, but the sciences, arts, trends, and other topics are included.

57.   McWilliams, Wayne C.   World Since 1945: Politics, War, and Revolution in the Nuclear Age.   Lynne Reinner, 1988. 388 p. ill. $35. Pb $23.

Gr 10+. HT 22: May 1989. McWilliams' concise, objective overview of world political events since World War II examines the Cold War, rising nationalism, global power, and the Third World. Photos, maps, and graphs are included.

58.   Palmer, Alan.   Facts on File Dictionary of 20th Century History, The.   Facts on File, 1979. 402 p. $23.

Gr 10+. B 78: Nov 1 1981. This alphabetical guide covers concepts, events, persons, places, and terms of 20th-century world history to 1979.   The concise and informative entries cover a wide range of topics.

59.   Shirer, William L.   20th Century Journey: A Memoir of a Life and the Times. Vol. 2, The Nightmare Years: 1930-1940.   Little, Brown, 1984. 672 p. ill. $22.

Gr 9+. B 80: Mar 1 1984. As a noted journalist, Shirer was present at many of the primary events in world history since 1930, including Gandhi's efforts for India's independence and Hitler's rise to power.

60.   Taylor, A. J. P.   20th Century.   Rev. ed.   Purnell, 1979. 20 vol. ill. $300.

Gr 9+. B 77: Jan 15 1981. The turmoil, progress, and promise of the 20th century are examined in this profusely illustrated collection of essays that cover politics, religion, the women's movement, terrorism, sports, television, and other significant events, persons, and movements.

61.   Vadney, T. E.   World Since 1945: A Complete History of Global Change from 1945 to the Present.   Facts on File, 1987. 570 p. $30.

Gr 11+. BR 7: May/Jun 1988. The author presents his well-organized history of the world since 1945 in the context of a struggle between the United States and the U.S.S.R., and maintains that Third World conflicts are important because of the superpowers' involvement in them.

62.   Vermazen, Susan.   War Torn: Survivors and Victims in the Late Twentieth Century.   Pantheon, 1984. 139 p. ill. $30. Pb $15.

Gr 11+. BR 4: May/Jun 1985.   * VOYA 8: Apr 1985. Thirty-one photographers have contributed chilling and graphic photos of the effects of 20th-century wars on people around the world.   Biographical sketches on the photographers are included.

1900-1999–Biographies

63.   Dunn, Wendy.   Who's News!   Messner, 1985. 143 p. ill. $10.

Gr 6-9. BR 5: May/Jun 1986.   SLJ 32: Feb 1986. Photos accompany these alphabetically arranged two-page biographies of 49 contemporary persons from many different fields and many different nations.

64.   Harris, Nathaniel.   Great Depression, The.   (Living through History).   Batsford; dist. by David & Charles, 1988. 64 p. ill. $19.

Gr 7+. SLJ 35: Jan 1989. Quotations, photos, and other illustrations enrich these concise biographies of Europeans and Americans who were leaders during the Great Depression.

1900-1999–Military History

65.   Cook, Chris.   Atlas of Modern Warfare, The.   Putnam, 1978. 191 p. ill. $23.

Gr 9+. B 76: Jun 15 1980. This coverage of the history of worldwide military actions from 1945 to 1978 and the development of new weapons includes maps, photos, and an index to persons, places, and weapons.

66. Kidron, Michael. War Atlas: Armed Conflict—Armed Peace. Simon & Schuster, 1983. 128 p. ill. $20. Pb $10.

Gr 9+. B 80: Jan 15 1984. LJ 108: Jun 15 1983. Forty maps, with tables and notes, provide information about warfare since 1945, covering intelligence gathering, arms sales, and the damage caused by war.

1900-1999—Social Life and Customs

67. Rosenblatt, Roger. Children of War. Doubleday, 1983. 212 p. $14.

Gr 9+. B 79: Jul 1983. HB 60: Feb 1984. LJ 108: Aug 1983. * VOYA 7: APR 1984. Rosenblatt interviewed children in Israel, Lebanon, Northern Ireland, Palestine, and Thailand, all of whom have grown up in war-torn lands. Their moving stories present both tragedy and hope.

Airplanes and Pilots

68. Angelucci, Enzo. World Encyclopedia of Civil Aircraft: From Leonardo da Vinci to the Present. Crown, 1982. 414 p. ill. $50.

Gr 9+. B 79: Mar 1 1983. LJ 108: Feb 15 1983. LJ 108: May 15 1983. SLJ 30: May 1984. Basic data, color photos, drawings, and capsule histories are included in this work which covers aircraft from the earliest days to the space-shuttle orbiter.

69. Boyne, Walter J. Smithsonian Book of Flight for Young People, The. Atheneum; Aladdin, 1988. 128 p. ill. $17. Pb $10.

Gr 4+. B 85: Mar 15 1989. * BR 7: Mar/Apr 1989. HB 65: Mar/Apr 1989. * SE 53: Apr/May 1989. SLJ 35: Jan 1989. VOYA 12: Apr 1989. This profusely illustrated history of flight from gliders and balloons to rockets shows the effect of aviation on commerce, war, and everyday life.

America

70. Coe, Michael. Atlas of Ancient America. Facts on File, 1986. 240 p. ill. $35.

Gr 8+. B 83: Jan 1 1987. BR 6: Sep/Oct 1987. * LJ 112: Feb 1 1987. LJ 112: Apr 15 1987. SLJ 33: Mar 1987. The major Indian groups of North and South America are surveyed, including their geographic distribution, languages, environment, culture, and behavior. The text is enriched by illustrations, maps, charts, a chronology, and a gazetteer.

71. Galeano, Eduardo. Memory of Fire: Genesis, Part One of a Trilogy. Pantheon, 1985. 289 p. $19.

Gr 9+. B 82: Nov 15 1985. LJ 110: Oct 1 1985. Latin America is emphasized in this episodic history covering the origins of the Indian people, the arrival of European explorers, their conquest of the natives, and the experiences of early colonists.

72. Highwater, Jamake. Native Land: Sagas of the Indian Americas. Little, Brown, 1986. 256 p. ill. $25.

Gr 9+. B 83: Nov 1 1986. * LJ 111: Oct 15 1986. This overview of the history and culture of Indian tribes in North, Central, and South America before the coming of white men is based on the PBS television series "Native Land" and is highly illustrated.

73. Mysteries of the Ancient Americas. Reader's Digest, 1986. 320 p. ill. $26.

Gr 8+. BR 5: Nov/Dec 1986. SLJ 33: Oct 1986. VOYA 9: Feb 1987. This profusely illustrated topical examination of cultures in the Americas before 1492 covers religious practices, the first settlers, the pyramids, the Lost Cities, and agriculture.

Animals and Insects

74. Rahn, Joan Elma. Animals That Changed History. Atheneum, 1986. 114 p. ill. $12.

Gr 6+. B 83: Feb 1 1987. BC 40: Mar 1987. SLJ 33: Feb 1987. Horses, black rats, and beavers are an unlikely trio whose influence on human history is described in this lively account.

75. Ritchie, Carson I. Insects, the Creeping Conquerors and Human History. Elsevier/Nelson, 1979. 139 p. ill. $8.

Gr 9+. SE 44: Apr 1980. This account of the critical effect of insects on human history covers insects as friend and foe. The great plagues, the silk industry, and the role of insects in medicine and agriculture are included.

76. Ventura, Piero. Man and the Horse. Putnam, 1982. 80 p. ill. $12.

Gr K-8. BC 36: Jan 1983. + - SLJ 29: Jan 1983. This colorful book shows the influence of horses throughout history.

Antarctica

77. Soule, Gardner. Antarctica. (First Book). Watts, 1985. 72 p. ill. $10.

Gr 4-8. + - B 82: Feb 15 1986. BR 5: May/Jun 1986. SLJ 32: Mar 1986. This colorful history of Antarctica includes information on explorers, wildlife, climate, and geography.

Arab Countries

78. Archer, Jules. Legacy of the Desert: Understanding the Arabs. Little, Brown, 1976. 240 p. ill. $9.

Gr 7+. B 73: Nov 1 1976. B 86: Sep 1 1989. SLJ 23: Jan 1977. Archer's history of the Arab world is current to the mid-1970s. It explains the differences in culture and belief among the Arab nations and their conflict with Israel.

Arms and Armor

79. Berenstain, Michael. Armor Book, The. McKay, 1979. 32 p. ill. $7.

Gr 3-9. B 76: Feb 15 1980. SLJ 26: Apr 1980 Detailed drawings and concise text introduce armor that has been used throughout history.

80. Byam, Michele. Arms and Armor. (Eyewitness Books). Knopf, 1988. 64 p. ill. $13. Lib. ed. $14.

Gr 4-7. B 84: Aug 1988. Excellent photos and an interesting arrangement introduce arms from prehistoric times to the American Old West in a format suitable for study or browsing.

81. Diagram Group. Weapons: An International Encyclopedia from 5000 BC to 2000 AD. St. Martin's, 1981. 320 p. ill. $25.

Gr 9+. B 77: Mar 1 1981. LJ 106: Jan 15 1981. SLJ 27: Apr 1981. An abundance of illustrations show the worldwide development and use of weapons for hunting, self-defense, and warfare from the hand ax to nuclear weapons.

82.   Wilkinson, F. Arms and Armor. (Easy-Read Fact Book). Watts, 1984. 32 p. ill. $9.

Gr 2-6. B 81: Jan 1 1985. SLJ 31: May 1985. This well organized chronological introduction to all types of weaponry since ancient times includes an abundance of colorful illustrations.

Balloons

83.   Dean, Anabel. Up, Up, and Away! The Story of Ballooning. Westminster, 1980. 192 p. ill. $9.

Gr 4-8. B 76: Mar 1 1980. BC 34: Dec 1980. SLJ 26: Apr 1980. An abundance of illustrations highlights this history of balloons which shows their use in transportation, warfare, and research.

Battles

84.   Humble, Richard. Famous Land Battles: From Agincourt to the Six-Day War. Little, Brown, 1979. 184 p. ill. $18.

Gr 9+. B 76: Feb 1 1980. In discussing the causes, events, and results of 18 significant land battles since 1415, Humble reveals the development of modern techniques of warfare. Maps, photos, diagrams, and other illustrations are included.

Bibliographies

85.   Schon, Isabel. Hispanic Heritage, A. Scarecrow, 1980. 178 p. $ 19.

Gr K+. B 81: Jul 1985. This K-12 annotated bibliography of books about Central and South America and Spain indicates grade levels and notable books.

86.   Schon, Isabel. Hispanic Heritage, Series II. Scarecrow, 1985. 153 p. $14.

Gr K+. B 81: Jul 1985. Juvenile books, K-12, about the people and culture of Latin America and Spain are covered in this update to the author's 1980 volume.

Biographies

87.   Boughton, Simon. Great Lives. Doubleday, 1988. 279 p. ill. $18.

Gr 4+. B 85: Oct 1 1988. + - BC 42: Oct 1988. * BR 7: Nov/Dec 1988. + - SLJ 35: Sep 1988. Over 1000 people from ancient to modern times, involved in all occupations are represented in brief, illustrated sketches. A chronological table and a glossary are included.

88.   Corn, Kahane. Madcap Men and Wacky Women from History. Messner, 1987. 113 p. ill. $10.

Gr 5-9. B 83: Jul 1987. SLJ 34: Sep 1987. The eccentricities of noted figures worldwide, including Queen Christina of Sweden, Enrico Caruso, Victor Hugo, King Ludwig of Bavaria, and Henry Ford, provide entertaining reading.

89.   DeFord, Miriam Allen. Who Was When? A Dictionary of Contemporaries. 3rd ed. Wilson, 1976. 184 p. $38.

Gr 7+. B 81: May 15 1985. This chronological chart lists famous deceased persons according to their field of interest, allowing students to determine notable contemporaries in all disciplines.

90.   Donaldson, Norman. How Did They Die? St. Martin's, 1980. 416 p. ill. $13.

Gr 9+. B 76: Mar 15 1980. LJ 105: Mar 1 1980. In an alphabetical arrangement, Donaldson covers the illnesses, deaths, and burials of over 300 notable persons throughout history.

91.   Fraser, Antonia. Heroes and Heroines. A & W, 1980. 263 p. ill. $15.

Gr 9+. B 77: Jan 15 1981. LJ 105: Nov 1 1980. Heroic persons from ancient to modern times are highlighted, with myth separated from reality.

92.   Stetler, Susan L. Almanac of Famous People: Comprehensive Reference Guide to More than 25,000 Famous and Infamous Newsmakers from Biblical Times to the Present. 4th ed. Gale, 1989. 3 vol. $90.

Gr 9+. B 85: May 15 1989. Over 25,000 historic and contemporary persons are alphabetically listed, giving nicknames, nationalities, reasons for fame, and place and date of birth and death. Access is enhanced by geographic, chronologic, and occupation indexes.

93.   Weis, Frank W. Lifelines: Famous Contemporaries from 600 B.C. to 1975. Facts on File, 1982. 437 p. ill. $20.

Gr 9+. B 80: Oct 15 1983. VOYA 5: Dec 1982. Brief biographical entries, chronologically arranged in 25 segments, cover over 2000 of the most important figures from 600 B. C. to 1975.

94.   Wintle, Justin. Makers of Nineteenth Century Culture 1800-1914. Routledge & Kegan Paul, 1982. 709 p. $38.

Gr 9+. B 80: Nov 1 1983. Nearly 500 notable persons who made contributions in all fields during the 19th century are covered. Cross references by field and theme are included.

Biographies–Bibliographies

95.   Breen, Karen. Index to Collective Biographies for Young Readers. 4th ed. Bowker, 1988. 494 p. $35.

Gr 3+. B 85: Mar 1 1989. LJ 114: Mar 15 1989. This index to over 1000 collective biographies provides access to information on over 9000 persons.

Cities and Towns

96.   Hibbert, Christopher. Cities and Civilizations. Weidenfeld & Nicholson, 1986. 252 p. ill. $25.

Gr 9+. B 83: Dec 1 1986. Twenty-one major cities are presented as they were at the height of their prominence in world history, from ancient to modern times. Chronologically arranged and well illustrated.

Civil Rights

97. Frankel, Marvin E. Out of the Shadows of Night: The Struggle for International Human Rights. Delacorte, 1989. 248 p. $17. Pb $9.

Gr 7+. B 86: Oct 1 1989. BR 8: Nov/Dec 1989. SLJ 35: Dec 1989. Frankel describes worldwide human rights violations that have occurred since World War II.

98. Freeman, Charles. Human Rights. (Today's World). Batsford; dist. by David & Charles, 1988. 72 p. ill. $18.

Gr 6-10. B 84: Aug 1988. BR 7: Nov/Dec 1988. SLJ 35: Mar 1989. A list of human rights organizations and their addresses is included in Freeman's examination of historic and contemporary human rights concerns. Terminology is defined, and the relationship of individuals to the state throughout history is discussed.

99. Loescher, Gil. Human Rights: A Global Crisis. Dutton, 1979. 130 p. ill. $9.

Gr 7+. B 75: Apr 15 1979. BC 32: Jul 1979. HB 55: Jun 1979. * SE 44: Apr 1980. SLJ 25: May 1979. Loescher discusses what human rights are, gives examples of their violation in many nations, and describes the efforts of individuals and organizations to protect these rights.

100. MacDonald, Fiona. Working for Equality. (Women History Makers). Hampstead Press; dist. by Watts, 1988. 45 p. ill. $12.

Gr 5-9. B 85: Jan 1 1989. SLJ 35: Feb 1989. This profusely illustrated book explains the social background that led to the work of England's Millicent G. Fawcett (women's rights), Rosa Parks (United States, civil rights), and Winnie Mandela (South Africa, civil rights).

101. Totten, Samuel. Human Rights. Enslow, 1989. 256 p. ill. $17.

Gr 5+. + - B 85: Aug 1989. + - BC 42: May 1989. BR 8: Nov/Dec 1989. SLJ 35: Nov 1989. VOYA 12: Oct 1989. A history of efforts to protect human rights is followed by chapters on such topics as racism, genocide, political prisoners, torture, and hunger. A "Universal Declaration of Human Rights" is included.

Commerce

102. Barker, Albert. Spice Adventure, The. Messner, 1980. 96 p. ill. $8.

Gr 4-7. SLJ 27: Feb 1981. Before refrigeration, spices were highly valued. A discussion of their role in exploring expeditions and the struggle to control trade routes, and an explanation of the history and use of individual spices, are included.

Crime and Punishment

103. Rickard, Graham. Prisons and Punishment. Bookwright Press; dist. by Watts, 1987. 32 p. ill. $11.

Gr 3-6. BC 41: Dec 1987. SLJ 34: Dec 1987. This colorful introduction to the topic of crime and the various ways it has been punished throughout history is chronologically arranged from Anglo-Saxon times to the present.

104. Whiting, Roger. Crime & Punishment: A Study Across Time. Dufour, 1987. 220 p. Pb $13.

Gr 9+. BR 6: Mar/Apr 1988. Crime in Britain and the United States from Anglo-Saxon times is covered chronologically, along with the evolution of punishment and police techniques.

Developing Countries

105. Goldstein, Eleanor C. Third World, Volume I. (Social Issues Resources Series). Social Issues Resources Series, 1983. 1 vol. $65.

Gr 7+. * BR 2: Nov/Dec 1983. Reprints of 100 articles that describe daily life and political, military, and social conditions in the 97 nations of the Third World bloc are presented in a loose-leaf format.

106. Kurian, George Thomas. Encyclopedia of the Third World. 3rd ed. Facts on File, 1987. 3 vol. maps. $175.

Gr 10+. B 84: Sep 15 1987. Current to 1987, this work presents descriptive and statistical information on a wide variety of economic, social, and political topics for 126 developing countries.

107. Kurian, George Thomas. Atlas of the Third World. Facts on File, 1983. 381 p. ill. $85.

Gr 10+. B 80: Aug 1984. One hundred twenty-two developing nations are covered, including social, economic, and political topics. The arrangement allows for comparisons among nations. Current to 1983.

108. Kurian, George Thomas. Glossary of the Third World. Facts on File, 1989. 300 p. $35.

Gr 9+. BR 8: Nov/Dec 1989. + - LJ 114: Aug 1989. Over 10,000 words dealing with all aspects of the history, politics, and culture of Third World nations are briefly defined.

109. Worth, Richard. Third World Today, The. Watts, 1983. 88 p. ill. $9.

Gr 9+. + - BR 3: May/Jun 1984. SLJ 30: Jan 1984. VOYA 6: Feb 1984. + - VOYA 7: Apr 1984. Over 3 billion people on 4 continents live in underdeveloped nations. Worth provides a brief historic overview of the causes of their problems and the relations of these nations to the United States.

Disasters

110. Brown, Walter R. Historical Catastrophes: Floods. Addison Wesley, 1975. 175 p. ill. $6. Lib. ed. $5.

Gr 4-7. B 72: Sep 15 1975. SE 44: Oct 1980. SLJ 22: Sep 1975. Famous floods, such as the ones at Johnstown, Pa. (1889), Florence, Italy (1966), Buffalo Creek, West Va. (1972) and those in the southeastern U.S. that resulted from Hurricane Camille (1969) are discussed in this highly illustrated work.

111. Day, James. Hindenburg Tragedy, The. (Great Disasters). Bookwright Press; dist. by Watts, 1989. 32 p. ill. $11.

Gr 3-6. SLJ 35: May 1989. Excellent diagrams supplement this brief account of the Hindenburg disaster.

112. Great Disasters: Dramatic True Stories of Nature's Awesome Powers. Reader's Digest; dist. by Random, 1989. 320 p. ill. $29.

Gr 9+. B 86: Sep 15 1989. This colorfully illustrated work covers all types of past natural disasters and speculates on possible future disasters.

Economics

113. Kronenwetter, Michael. Capitalism vs. Socialism: Economic Policies of the USA and the USSR. (Economics Impact Book). Watts, 1986. 104 p. ill. $11.

Gr 9+. B 82: Jul 1986. BR 5: Nov/Dec 1986. + - SLJ 32: Aug 1986. Kronenwetter examines the basic tenets of capitalism and Soviet socialism and shows how each has been molded by practical considerations and the cultural traditions of the people.

114. Taylor, Peter. Smoke Ring: Tobacco, Money, and Multinational Politics. Pantheon, 1984. 328 p. $19.

Gr 9+. * B 80: Aug 1984. LJ 110: Jan 1985. The international economic and political power of the major tobacco companies is explored, showing the dependence of many Third World nations on tobacco and its role in United States and British politics.

Espionage and Spies

115. Buranelli, Vincent. Spy/Counterspy: An Encyclopedia of Espionage. McGraw-Hill, 1982. 361 p. $25.

Gr 9+. B 78: Jul 1982. B 80: Sep 15 1983. LJ 107: Aug 1982. This lively encyclopedia covers spies and their techniques since the mid-1500s.

116. Deacon, Richard. Spyclopedia: The Comprehensive Handbook of Espionage. Morrow, 1989. 416 p. ill. $21.

Gr 9+. B 85: Mar 1 1989. LJ 114: Mar 1 1989. Deacon's coverage of world espionage ranges from 510 B.C. to the present. Within each time period sketches on spies are alphabetically arranged. A glossary is included.

117. Healey, Tim. Spies. (Timespan). Silver Burdett, 1979. 61 p. ill. Lib. ed. $7.

Gr 6-8. B 76: Mar 15 1980. Healey's oversized, highly illustrated account of espionage covers from the days of ancient Greece to modern times.

118. Payne, Ronald. Who's Who in Espionage. St. Martin's, 1985. 234 p. $16.

Gr 9+. B 81: May 1 1985. LJ 110: Jun 1 1985. In addition to over 300 biographical sketches of persons involved in spying or intelligence work since World War II, Payne's work includes information on intelligence agencies and a glossary.

119. Silverstein, Herma. Spies among Us: The Truth about Modern Espionage. Watts, 1988. 144 p. ill. $13.

Gr 6+. + - B 85: Dec 1 1988. + - SLJ 35: Nov 1988. * VOYA 12: Apr 1989. A glossary of spy terminology and specific examples strengthen this account of modern espionage techniques and technology which exposes stereotypes and myths.

Exploration and Explorers

120. Beattie, Owen. Frozen in Time: Unlocking the Secrets of the Franklin Expedition. Dutton, 1988. 180 p. ill. $19.

Gr 9+. SLJ 35: Mar 1989. Beattie's engrossing book discusses the mystery of the fate of the HMS Erebus and HMS Terror, two British ships that disappeared as they explored the Arctic. The reasons for the failure of the well-prepared expedition and the death of its explorers are covered.

121. Berton, Pierre. Arctic Grail: Quest for the Northwest Passage and the North Pole, 1818-1909. Viking, 1988. 661 p. ill. $25.

Gr 9+. B 85: Oct 15 1988. Berton covers the exploration of the Arctic from 1818. He includes the exploits of such men as Sir John Ross, William Parry, Frederick Cook, and John Franklin. This readable book is illustrated.

122. Bitossi, Sergio. Ferdinand Magellan. (Why They Became Famous). Silver Burdett, 1985. 62 p. ill. Lib. ed. $10. Pb $7.

Gr 4-7. BR 4: Jan/Feb 1986. SLJ 32: Apr 1986. This introduction to the life of Magellan emphasizes his restless desire for recognition. Excerpts from his diary and notes on the completion of the voyage after his death are included.

123. Blackwood, Alan. Captain Cook. (Great Lives). Bookwright Press; dist. by Watts, 1987. 32 p. ill. $11.

Gr 3-7. B 83: Jun 1 1987. + - SLJ 34: Nov 1987. This brief, illustrated biography introduces James Cook, a poor farm boy who became a noted explorer.

124. Blackwood, Alan. Ferdinand Magellan. (Great Lives). Bookwright Press; dist. by Watts, 1986. 31 p. ill. $10.

Gr 4-7. SLJ 32: Aug 1986. Magellan's achievements are the focus of this brief, large-print biography.

125. Delpar, Helen. Discoverers: An Encyclopedia of Explorers and Exploration. McGraw-Hill, 1979. 471 p. ill. $30.

Gr 9+. B 76: Jan 15 1980. B 77: Oct 1 1980. LJ 105: Jan 1 1980. LJ 106: May 15 1981. SLJ 27: Dec 1980. Delpar includes biographies of explorers of many nationalities along with articles on topics such as cartography, the Northwest Passage, literature and exploration, space exploration, and women in travel and exploration.

126. Fradin, Dennis B. Explorers. (New True Book). Childrens Press, 1984. 44 p. ill. $8.

Gr 1-4. B 81: Mar 1 1985. SLJ 31: Apr 1985. Exploration from ancient times through the space program is introduced, and the motivations of the explorers are examined.

127. Goodnough, David. John Cabot & Son. (Adventures in the New World). Troll, 1979. 48 p. ill. $5. Pb $2.

Gr 5-8. + - SLJ 26: Jan 1980. This balanced account of Cabot's exploration provides information on the political and social climate of his time.

128. Grant, Neil. Discoverers, The. (Living Past). Arco, 1980. 61 p. ill. $7.

Gr 5+. B 76: Mar 1 1980. * SE 44: Oct 1980. SLJ 27: Sep 1980. This colorful introduction to the early explorers discusses the effects of their exploration on the cultures and economies of the old world and the new.

129. Gray, William R. Voyages to Paradise: Exploring in the Wake of Captain Cook. National Geographic Society, 1981. 215 p. ill. $9.

Gr 9+. SLJ 28: Sep 1981. Excellent photos enhance this readable account of Cook's extensive Pacific explorations, his scientific discoveries, and his humanistic philosophy.

130. Harley, Ruth. Captain James Cook. (Adventures in Discovery). Troll, 1979. 48 p. ill. $5. Pb $2.

Gr 5-8. SLJ 26: Jan 1980. Historical detail providing a sense of time and place is included in this accurate introduction to Cook and his explorations.

131. Harley, Ruth. Ferdinand Magellan. (Adventures in Discovery). Troll, 1979. 48 p. ill. $5. Pb $2.

Gr 5-8. SLJ 26: Jan 1980. This accurate introduction to Magellan and his explorations presents historic detail that provides a sense of time and place.

132. Hoobler, Dorothy. Voyages of Captain Cook, The. Putnam, 1983. 206 p. maps. $11.

Gr 6+. B 80: Apr 15 1984. HB 60: Apr 1984. SLJ 30: Apr 1984. VOYA 7: Jun 1984. From 1768 to 1779 Cook made three long sea voyages charting unknown areas. His concern for the health of his crew and for native cultures is made clear in this biography which provides a good sense of time and place.

133. Humble, Richard. Voyage of Magellan, The. Watts, 1989. 32 p. ill. $12.

Gr 4-8. B 85: Mar 15 1989. SLJ 35: May 1989. Colorful photos, a timeline, and a glossary augment this account of Magellan's voyage and the details of life aboard ship.

134. Knight, David. Vasco Da Gama. (Adventures in Discovery). Troll, 1979. 48 p. ill. $5. Pb $2.

Gr 5-8. + - SLJ 26: Jan 1980. Knight provides a factual background for Da Gama's life and work, and in documentary style presents an account of his explorations for Portugal around the tip of Africa to India.

135. Lomask, Milton. Great Lives: Exploration. Scribner, 1988. 249 p. ill. $23.

Gr 5-9. B 85: Mar 15 1989. BR 8: May/Jun 1989. HB 65: Mar/Apr 1989. SLJ 35: Jan 1989. Twenty-five explorers from the 4th to the 20th centuries are introduced in alphabetically arranged biographies about 9 pages in length. Illustrations and a chronology of important events of world exploration augment the text.

136. Pennington, Piers. Great Explorers, The. Facts on File, 1979. 336 p. ill. $18.

Gr 9+. B 76: Feb 15 1980. B 78: Jan 15 1982. + - LJ 105: Mar 1 1980. This chronologically arranged and profusely illustrated overview focuses on the achievements of over 50 explorers who have discovered and mapped unknown areas since ancient times.

137. Reid, Alan. Discovery and Exploration: A Concise History. Arco, 1982. 328 p. ill. $20.

Gr 9+. + - LJ 107: Apr 1 1982. SLJ 28: Aug 1982. Brief biographies of noted discoverers are included in this condensed history of exploration since 4000 B.C. A chronology by continent is also included.

138. Syme, Ronald. Magellan: First Around the World. Morrow, 1953. 71 p. ill. $10.

Gr 4-6. B 50: Sep 1 1953. B 82: Sep 15 1985. LJ 78: Oct 1 1953. This illustrated account of Magellan's voyages and discoveries is brief and simple.

139. Tames, Richard. Exploring Other Civilizations. (World of Change). Dufour, 1988. 52 p. ill. Pb $7.

Gr 6-8. + - BR 7: May/Jun 1988. This volume of a British series discusses such explorers as Captain John Smith, Leo Africanus, and Henry the Navigator.

140. Tinling, Marion. Women into the Unknown: A Sourcebook on Women Explorers and Travelers. Greenwood, 1989. 356 p. maps. $55.

Gr 9+. B 85: Jun 15 1989. LJ 114: May 1 1989. Forty-two 19th- and 20th-century women explorers are profiled. Quotations enrich the biographies.

141. Wilkie, Katherine. Ferdinand Magellan: Noble Captain. Houghton, 1963. 192 p. ill. Pb $3.

Gr 4-6. Metzner. Wilkie's detailed account of Magellan's life and accomplishments is illustrated.

Flags

142. Barrachlough, E. M. C. Flags of the World. New rev. ed. Frederick Warne, 1978. 250 p. ill. $25.

Gr 7+. B 76: Jun 15 1980. Good paper, type, and color enhance this work, which includes all national flags plus coats of arms, other military and official flags, and information on historic and current flag usage.

143. Inglefield, Eric. Flags. (Arco Fact Guides in Color). Arco, 1979. 123 p. ill. $7.

Gr 9+. B 77: May 15 1981. SLJ 26: Apr 1980. Inglefield's geographically arranged book discusses flag design, purpose, and history. In addition to national flags, military, regional, city, organizational, and historic flags are included.

144. Jefferis, David. Flags. (Easy-Read Fact Book). Watts, 1985. 32 p. ill. $10.

Gr K-5. B 82: Jan 15 1986. SLJ 32: Apr 1986. National and international flags, flags for heads of state and motor racing, a glossary, and a semaphore chart are included in this colorful book.

Food

145. Krensky, Stephen. Scoop After Scoop: A History of Ice Cream. Atheneum, 1986. 49 p. ill. $13.

Gr 4-8. B 83: Nov 15 1986. BC 40: Feb 1987. SLJ 33: Jan 1987. The history of ice cream and other frozen desserts is traced from the time of ancient Egypt to today, showing how culture and technology affect history. Illustrated by cartoons.

146. Ritchie, Carson I. Food in Civilization: How History Has Been Affected by Human Tastes. Beaufort; dist. by Scribners, 1981. 192 p. $11.

Gr 10+. LJ 106: Nov 15 1981. Ritchie's readable work shows how history has been influenced by the need for food, myths about food, and popular taste for certain types of food.

Genocide–Bibliographies

147. Charny, Israel W. Genocide: A Critical Bibliographic Review. Facts on File, 1988. 273 p. $40.

Gr 11+. B 85: Jan 1 1989. BR 8: Jan/Feb 1989. Genocide in general and specific genocides are covered in short essays by experts in such fields as psychology, history, sociology, literature, and political science. The bibliographies include print and nonprint material.

Gypsies

148. Hancock, Ian. Pariah Syndrome: An Account of Gypsy Slavery and Persecution. Karoma, 1987. 175 p. ill. $18.

Gr 9+. B 84: Oct 1 1987. Hancock documents the persecution of the Gypsies throughout history, including 500 years of slavery, restrictions on employment, and licensing based on ethnicity. His report covers Europe and the United States.

Islamic Countries

149. Barlow, Christopher. Islam. (Today's World). Batsford; dist. by David & Charles, 1983. 72 p. ill. $15.

Gr 6+. B 80: Oct 15 1983. BR 2: Mar/Apr 1984. This balanced and up-to-date introduction to Islamic history and the basic tenets of the faith also covers the culture and varying beliefs in many Islamic nations. Photos are included.

150. Robinson, Francis. Atlas of the Islamic World Since 1500. Facts on File, 1982. 238 p. ill. $35.

Gr 9+. B 79: Nov 1 1982. B 80: Oct 15 1983. LJ 107: Nov 15 1982. Muslim history, social, cultural, and religious life since 1500 are covered in this encyclopedic atlas that contains attractive photos and over 50 maps.

Jews

151. Alpher, Joseph. Encyclopedia of Jewish History: Events and Eras of the Jewish People. Facts on File, 1986. 287 p. ill. $35.

Gr 9+. B 82: Apr 15 1986. LJ 111: Apr 1 1986. Colorful photos, maps, diagrams, and numerous appendices augment this collection of essays on Jewish history from ancient times.

152. Arnold, Caroline. Anti-Semitism: A Modern Perspective. Messner, 1984. 223 p. ill. $10.

Gr 9+. B 81: Nov 1 1984. * BR 4: Mar/Apr 1986. + - SLJ 31: Apr 1985. This continent-by-continent account of the history and current conditions of anti-Semitism includes photos and a bibliography of fiction and nonfiction.

153. Ausubel, Nathan. Pictorial History of the Jewish People: From Bible Times to Our Own Day Throughout the World. 1st rev. ed. Crown, 1984. 456 p. ill. $20.

Gr 9+. B 81: Nov 1 1984. B 81: Feb 15 1985. SLJ 31: May 1985. VOYA 7: Feb 1985. Over 1000 photos highlight this extensive, worldwide history of the Jewish people from ancient to modern times, including information on contemporary issues.

154. Comay, Joan. Diaspora Story: The Epic of the Jewish People Among the Nations. Random, 1981. 288 p. ill. $20.

Gr 9+. B 78: Nov 15 1981. This overview of the history of the Jewish people since biblical times covers the Jews in all parts of the world and explains the ways that living among other people affect Jewish customs.

155. De Lange, Nicholas. Atlas of the Jewish World. Facts on File, 1984. 240 p. ill. $35.

Gr 7+. B 81: Mar 1 1985, Jun 1 1985. BR 4: Sep/Oct 1985. LJ 110: Feb 1 1985. SLJ 32: May 1986. Maps, photos, and commentary cover ancient and modern Jewish history, culture, religion, language, literature, and the impact of the Holocaust.

156. Dolan, Edward F. Anti-Semitism. Watts, 1985. 135 p. ill. $11.

Gr 6+. B 82: Feb 15 1986. BC 39: Mar 1986. * BR 5: May/Jun 1983. + - SLJ 32: Feb 1986. VOYA 9: Apr 1986. Dolan traces the origin and development of anti-Semitism and the treatment of the Jews wherever they have gone. Current anti-Semitism in the United States is also covered in this illustrated work.

157. Eban, Abba. Heritage: Civilization and the Jews. Summit, 1984. 308 p. ill. $30.

Gr 9+. B 81: Sep 1 1984. * LJ 109: Nov 1 1984. Five thousand years of Jewish history and culture are covered in this lavishly illustrated work that assesses the influence of Jewish people, and their beliefs on world civilization.

158. Patterson, Charles. Anti-Semitism: The Road to the Holocaust and Beyond. Walker, 1982. 150 p. $12.

Gr 7+. + - B 79: Nov 1 1982. + - HT 16: Aug 1983. + - SLJ 29: Feb 1983. VOYA 6: Feb 1983. * VOYA 6: Jun 1983. Patterson traces the history of anti-Semitism from ancient to modern times. A chronology provides clarification.

159. Shamir, Ilana. Young Reader's Encyclopedia of Jewish History, The. Viking, 1987. 128 p. ill. $16.

Gr 5-10. B 84: Mar 15 1988. BC 41: Feb 1988. BR 7: May/Jun 1988. * SE 52: Apr/May 1988. SLJ 34: Feb 1988. A timeline, maps, charts, and over 300 colorful photos enrich this informative chronological presentation of 7000 years of Jewish history.

160. Wiesenthal, Simon. Every Day Remembrance Day: A Chronicle of Jewish Martyrdom. Holt, 1987. 320 p. ill. $25.

Gr 10+. B 83: Aug 1987. + - BR 6: Jan/Feb 1988. LJ 112: Nov 1 1987. VOYA 11: Apr 1988. Wiesenthal records documented acts of anti-Semitism for each day of the year, covering events over the past 2000 years.

Jews–Biographies

161. Drucker, Malka. Eliezer Ben-Yehuda; The Father of Modern Hebrew. (Jewish Biography Series). Dutton, 1987. 96 p. ill. $12.

Gr 5-9. B 83: Jan 15 1987. BC 40: Jan 1987. * SE 52: Apr/May 1988. + - SLJ 33: Mar 1987. * VOYA 11: Apr 1988. Convinced that the nearly-dead Hebrew language should be revived, Ben-Yehuda moved to Palestine in 1881, established a Hebrew newspaper, and wrote a Hebrew dictionary. Today over 30 million people consider Hebrew their native language.

162. Gross, David C. Pride of Our People: The Stories of One Hundred Outstanding Jewish Men and Women. Doubleday, 1979. 424 p. ill. $15.

Gr 5-8. SLJ 26: Feb 1980. Essays from 1 to 3 pages in length provide biographical information on 100 Jewish contributors to science, literature, religion, and the governments of many nations.

Jews–Fiction

163. Halter, Marek. Book of Abraham, The. Holt, 1986. 722 p. $20.

Gr 10+. B 82: Feb 15 1986. + - BR 5: Sep/Oct 1986. LJ 111: Apr 1 1986. * VOYA 9: Jun 1986. This novel is a fictionalized account of the history of the author's family since 70 A.D. as they wandered from Jerusalem throughout Europe.

Kings, Queens, Rulers, etc.

164. Gurney, Gene. Kingdoms of Asia, the Middle East, and Africa: An Illustrated Encyclopedia of Ruling Monarchs from Ancient Times to the Present. Crown, 1986. 438 p. ill. $25.

Gr 9+. B 83: Oct 15 1986. Gurney discusses the history of each nation in Asia and Africa and highlights significant monarchs. A chronology of all monarchs is included in this well-illustrated work.

Labor Unions and Laborers

165. Sproule, Anna. Solidarity. (Women History Makers). Hampstead Press; dist. by Watts, 1988. 45 p. ill. $12.

Gr 5-9. B 85: Jan 1 1989. + - SLJ 35: Feb 1989. Sproule introduces labor leaders Annie Besant (Britain), Kageyama Hideko (Japan), and Mother Jones (United States) and the society of which each was a part.

Latin America

166. Aguilar, Luis E. Latin America. (World Today Series). Stryker-Post, 1983. 115 p. ill. Pb $5.

Gr 7+. B 80: Mar 1 1984. These brief profiles on the nations of Central and South America and the Caribbean include reviews of history and geography, current political and economic data, and ready-reference facts. Revised annually.

167. Bateman, Penny. Aztecs and Incas: AD 1300-1532. (Great Civilizations). Watts, 1988. 32 p. ill. $12.

Gr 3-7. B 85: Jan 1 1989. - SLJ Mar 1989. Colorful illustrations and chronologies augment this introduction to the histories and cultures of the Aztec and Inca nations.

168. Bethell, Leslie. Cambridge History of Latin America, Vols. 1 and 2: Colonial Latin America. Cambridge University Press, 1985. 2 vol. maps. $140.

Gr 7+. * LJ 110:May 15 1985. LJ 111: Apr 15 1986. The first 2 of 8 projected volumes, these present a lively and reliable examination of the region's history, politics, and economy during its colonial period.

169. Collier, Simon. Cambridge Encyclopedia of Latin America and the Caribbean, The. Cambridge University Press, 1985. 456 p. ill. $40.

Gr 7+. B 82: Oct 1 1985. B 82: Mar 15 1986. * BR 5: Sep/Oct 1986. HT 20: Feb 1987. * LJ 110: Sep 15 1985. LJ 111: Apr 15 1986. The text covers history, geography, social structure, culture, politics, economics, industry, and people of Central and South America, and is enhanced by photos, maps, charts, graphs, and timelines.

170. Hargreaves, Pat. Caribbean and Gulf of Mexico, The. (Seas and Oceans). Silver Burdett, 1981. 69 p. ill. $8.

Gr 4-8. B 77: Jul 15/Aug 1981. SLJ 28: Mar 1982. Graphs, maps, diagrams, photos, and a glossary augment this introduction to the people who have lived in the Caribbean area and along the shores of the Gulf. The region's history, exploration, and resources are also covered.

171. Karlowich, Robert A. Rise Up in Anger: Latin America Today. Messner, 1985. 176 p. ill. $10.

Gr 9+. B 81: Aug 1985. * BR 5: May 1986. - SLJ 32: Sep 1985. In separate sections common issues that concern Latin American nations are introduced, followed by specific comment about each nation. This well-organized work includes photos.

172. Nunez, Benjamin. Dictionary of Afro-Latin American Civilization. Greenwood, 1980. 525 p. ill. $45.

Gr 10+. B 78: Mar 1 1982. This dictionary covers significant events, persons, and terms concerning the culture of blacks in Latin American and Caribbean nations.

173. Pimlott, John. South and Central America. (Conflict in the 20th Century). Watts, 1988. 62 p. ill. $13.

Gr 6+. B 84: Jun 15 1988. * BR 7: Sep/Oct 1988. This balanced introduction to the 20th-century revolutions in Central and South America sets each in context and explains successes and failures. Photos are included.

Latin America–Biographies

174. Kellner, Douglas. Ernesto "Che" Guevara. (World Leaders Past & Present). Chelsea House, 1988. 112 p. ill. $17.

Gr 7+. B 85: Nov 15 1988. BR 8: May/Jun 1989, Sep/Oct 1989. SLJ 35: Jun 1989. VOYA 11: Feb 1989. Kellner's balanced biography explores the political and social events that surrounded Guevara's revolutionary activities in Cuba and several Latin American nations, the changes caused by his revolutionary activities, and his personal life.

175. Neimark, Anne. Che! Latin America's Legendary Guerilla Leader. Lippincott, 1989. 128 p. ill. $14. Lib. ed. $14.

Gr 6+. + - B 85: May 15 1989. SLJ 35: May 1989. - VOYA 12: Aug 1989. This somewhat fictionalized biography of Che Guevara shows the influence of his sickly childhood on his activities as a leader of violent revolutionaries in Latin America.

Latin America–Maps

176. Atlas of Central America and the Caribbean, The. Macmillan, 1985. 144 p. ill. $40.

Gr 9+. B 83: Oct 1 1986. This handy reference uses text, illustrations, maps, graphs, and tables to present a brief history and an overview of other basic information on the nations of Central America and the Caribbean.

177. Lombardi, Cathryn L. Latin American History: A Teaching Atlas. University of Wisconsin Press, 1984. 144 p. $23. Pb $7.

Gr 10+. HT 19: Nov 1985. This atlas has numerous maps on the colonial period in addition to maps showing current boundary disputes, debt, energy consumption, population, trade, gross national product, and urbanization.

Maps

178. Barraclough, Geoffrey. Times Atlas of World History. Rev. ed. Hammond, 1984. 360 p. maps. $75.

Gr 9+. B 81: Jun 15 1985. LJ 110: Jan 1985. SLJ 31: May 1985. This comprehensive atlas of world history includes over 600 full-color maps, a readable narrative concerning the achievements of all peoples in all times, a chronology, and a glossary.

179. Barraclough, Geoffrey. Times Concise Atlas of World History, The. Times Books; dist. by Hammond, 1982. 184 p. maps. $40.

Gr 9+. B 79: Jul 1983. LJ 108: Jan 1 1983. This abridged version of the Times Atlas of World History emphasizes the western world. Coverage begins in 6000 B.C. and is current through 1980.

180. Clapham, Frances M. Atlas of World History. Warwick; dist. by Watts, 1982. 93 p. ill. $12.

Gr 5-7. B 79: Oct 1 1982. Illustrations, lists of important dates, and brief commentary are included in this atlas that provides an overview of world development.

181. Historical Maps on File. Facts on File, 1984. 1 vol. maps. $145.

Gr 9+. B 81: Jan 1 1985. SLJ 31: May 1985. Arranged by continent and chronology are 300 clear maps that are intended to be reproduced. They cover world history from the Ice Age to 1980.

182. Moore, R. I. Rand McNally Atlas of World History. Rev. and updated ed. Rand McNally, 1987. 192 p. Pb $18.

Gr 9+. B 84: Jun 15 1988. These maps show political, economic, social, and cultural developments throughout the world since ancient times. There are 87 maps in the section on world history and 8 in the section on the United States.

183. Moore, R. I. Rand McNally Historical Atlas of the World. Rand McNally, 1981. 192 p. $30.

Gr 9+. B 79: Sep 1 1982. LJ 107: Feb 15 1982. World history from 40,000 B.C. to the late 1970s is presented through 92 full-color maps and a readable explanatory text.

184. Olliver, Jane. Warwick Atlas of World History, The. Warwick; dist. by Watts, 1988. 93 p. ill. $16.

Gr 3-8. B 85: Nov 15 1988. + - SLJ 35: Mar 1989. Maps, photos, and other illustrations accompany descriptions of important events, discoveries, and persons in this chronologically arranged historical atlas.

185. Rand McNally Children's Atlas of World History. Rand McNally, 1989. 93 p. ill. $13.

Gr 3-8. B 86: Dec 15 1989. Maps, illustrations, and a timeline provide an overview of world history from ancient to modern times.

186. Vidal-Naquet, Pierre. Harper Atlas of World History, The. Harper, 1987. 340 p. ill. $30.

Gr 9+. B 84: Feb 15 1988. LJ 113: Feb 1 1988. World cultural and political events are presented by means of maps and numerous photos, with brief descriptions. A continuous chronology that runs across the bottom of all pages is a convenient reference.

Medical Personnel

187. Cosner, Shaaron. War Nurses. Walker, 1988. 68 p. ill. $17. Lib. ed. $18.

Gr 5-9. B 85: Dec 1 1988. * BR 7: Mar/Apr 1989. SE 53: Apr/May 1989. SLJ 35: Dec 1988. Cosner surveys the wartime contributions of nurses, including the United States Civil War, the Crimean War, both World Wars, and the Korean and Vietnamese wars.

Military History

188. Chandler, David. Dictionary of Battles: The World's Key Battles from 405 B.C. to Today. 1st American ed. Holt, 1988. 255 p. ill. $25.

Gr 9+. B 84: Jun 15 1988. Informative essays cover battles from ancient to modern times. Arranged in 8 chapters, the book is well indexed and includes maps, portraits, and illustrations.

189. Dyer, Gwynne. War. Crown, 1985. 272 p. ill. $18.

Gr 9+. B 82: Dec 1 1985. Eight thousand years of warfare are covered in this illustrated work that shows the horrors of war, the failure of efforts to limit it, and the relationship of war to society.

190. Fralin, Frances. Indelible Image: Photographs of War–1846 to the Present. Abrams/Corcoran Gallery of Art, 1985. 254 p. ill. $35.

Gr 9+. B 82: Jan 1 1986. An essay on the nature of warfare enriches this collection of wartime photos that dates from the early days of photography. Captions clarify the situations depicted.

191. Giblin, James Cross. Walls: Defenses Throughout History. Little, Brown, 1984. 113 p. ill. $14.

Gr 9+. * B 81: Jan 15 1985. BC 38: Feb 1985. HB 61: Jan/Feb 1985. * SE 49: Apr 1985. SLJ 31: Jan 1985. The purpose and impact of such defensive structures as the wall of Jericho, the Great Wall of China, Hadrian's Wall, castles, forts, the Maginot Line, and the Berlin Wall are discussed. Photos, drawings, and a glossary are included.

192. Hartman, Tom. World Atlas of Military History, 1945-1984, A. Hippocrene, 1985. 108 p. $25.

Gr 10+. LJ 110: Jan 1985. Traditional wars and guerilla actions from 1945 to 1984 are covered by maps, chronologies, and balanced summaries.

193. Howard, Michael. Clausewitz. Oxford University Press, 1983. 79 p. $13.

Gr 10+. HT 19: May 1986. Clausewitz' ideas on the relation between war and politics have heavily influenced modern military thought. Howard's primer on the man and his ideas is suitable for high school and college students.

194. Justice, Jennifer L. War and Weapons. Rev. ed. (Modern Knowledge Library). Warwick; dist. by Watts, 1982. 48 p. ill. $9.

Gr 5-8. SLJ 28: Aug 1982. This brief, illustrated overview of the history of warfare since ancient times includes a glossary.

195. Keegan, John. Illustrated Face of Battle: A Study of Agincourt, Waterloo, and the Somme. Rev. ed. Viking, 1989. 303 p. ill. $30.

Gr 9+. B 85: May 1 1989. LJ 114: May 1 1989. The battles at Agincourt (1415), Waterloo (1815), and the Somme (1916), are analyzed in this revised illustrated edition of a classic work on military history.

196. Kohn, George C. Dictionary of Wars. Facts on File, 1986. 586 p. $30.

Gr 11+. B 83: Dec 1 1986. This list of major conflicts since 2000 B.C. provides their names, dates, causes, opposing sides, a summary of events, and the result. Wars and individual battles are included. Coverage is worldwide, in an alphabetical arrangement.

197. Land Power: A Modern Illustrated Military History. Phoebus, 1979. 352 p. ill. $15.

Gr 9+. + - B 77: Sep 1 1980. + - LJ 105: Jan 1 1980. This illustrated work deals with land fighting and land-based military vehicles from the days of foot soldiers through World War II.

198. Livesey, Anthony. Great Commanders and Their Battles. Macmillan, 1987. 200 p. ill. $40.

Gr 9+. B 84: Mar 15 1988. Livesey's highly illustrated account of the crucial battles of 20 great commanders includes Alexander the Great, Marlborough, Napoleon, Khan, Lee, and Yamashita.

199. MacDonald, John. Great Battlefields of the World. Macmillan, 1985. 200 p. ill. $35.

Gr 10+. B 81: Aug 1985. LJ 110: Aug 1985. Three-dimensional, computer-constructed maps show 30 major battlefields from 216 B.C. to the mid-1950s. Strategy, weapons, uniforms, and political issues are covered in a lively text.

200. Macksey, Kenneth. Guinness Book of Tank Facts and Feats: A Record of Armoured Fighting Vehicle Achievement. 3rd ed. (Guinness Superlatives Book). Sterling, 1980. 256 p. ill. $18.

Gr 9+. B 77: Mar 1 1981. This readable account of the history of tanks and armored vehicles is augmented by photos, maps, and appendices.

201. Mansfield, Sue. Some Reasons for War: How Families, Myths and Warfare Are Connected. Harper, 1988. 199 p. ill. $14.

Gr 6+. B 85: Oct 1 1988. * VOYA 11: Dec 1988. Mansfield's chronological examination of the various causes of warfare since ancient times is a synthesis of history, anthropology, folklore, and psychology intended to encourage critical thinking.

202. Perrett, Bryan. Desert Warfare: From Its Roman Origins to the Gulf Conflict. Sterling, 1989. 224 p. ill. $25.

Gr 9+. B 86: Sep 1 1989. Desert warfare in North Africa and the Middle East over the past 2000 years is presented in this profusely illustrated account that covers campaigns, battles, tactics, and weaponry.

203. Seymour, William. Yours to Reason Why: Decision in Battle. St. Martin's, 1982. 338 p. ill. $15.

Gr 9+. B 79: Sep 1 1982. LJ 107: Sep 1 1982. Ten major battles from 1066 to 1945 are analyzed and readers are invited to examine the various options open to commanders.

Military History–Aerial Operations/Aircraft

204. Angelucci, Enzo. Rand McNally Encyclopedia of Military Aircraft 1914-1980, The. Rand McNally, 1981. 546 p. ill. $100.

Gr 9+. B 78: Mar 1 1982. B 79: Oct 1 1982. LJ 107: Mar 1 1982. LJ 108: May 15 1983. SLJ 29: May 1983. Basic data, color photos, drawings, and capsule histories of worldwide military aircraft are included. Chapters cover World War I, between the wars, World War II, and from 1945 to the present.

205. Gunston, Bill. Air Power: A Modern Illustrated Military History. Phoebus, 1979. 392 p. ill. $15.

Gr 9+. B 77: Sep 1 1980. LJ 105: Jan 1 1980. Scale drawings and a profusion of photos of airplanes from many nations show the development and use of airplanes as tools of war.

206. Robinson, Anthony. Aerial Warfare: An Illustrated History. Galahad Books, 1982. 384 p. ill. $18.

Gr 9+. B 79: Dec 1 1982. LJ 107: Nov 15 1982. Heavily illustrated with photos and drawings, this history of aerial warfare covers activities from 1911 to 1973, but emphasizes World War II. In addition to coverage of campaigns and battles the role of aircraft in warfare is examined.

207. Taylor, Michael J. H. Encyclopedia of the World's Air Forces. Facts on File, 1988. 211 p. ill. $35.

Gr 9+. + - B 85: Apr 15 1989. BR 8: Sep/Oct 1989. LJ 114: Apr 15 1989. Photos and a brief text provide information on the world's 150 air forces.

Military History–Naval Operations/Ships

208. Batchelor, John. Sea Power: A Modern Illustrated Military History. Phoebus, 1979. 392 p. ill. $15.

Gr 9+. B 77: Sep 1 1980. LJ 105: Jan 1 1980. A profusion of photos and drawings illustrate this work on wartime ships from the middle of the 19th century to the end of World War II, with emphasis on the two world wars.

209. Howarth, David. Famous Sea Battles. Little, Brown, 1981. 185 p. ill. $23.

Gr 9+. B 78: Feb 15 1982. Maps, diagrams, and photos enhance this balanced and colorful account of sea battles from the days of Cleopatra through World War II. The battles, equipment, strategy, and techniques are all considered.

210. Natkiel, Richard. Atlas of Maritime History. Facts on File, 1986. 256 p. ill. $30.

Gr 9+. B 83: Sep 15 1986. B 83: Oct 15 1986. LJ 111: Aug 1986. Voyages of discovery, trade routes, and naval military action are presented in over 200 maps, charts, and graphs that cover from the ancient Phoenicians to the 1980s.

Military Personnel

211. Keegan, John. Soldiers. Viking, 1986. 288 p. $20.

Gr 9+. B 82: Dec 1 1986. BR 5: Nov 1986. LJ 111: Feb 1 1986. SLJ 33: Nov 1986. This readable and personal account of the effects of war on individuals includes many quotes from notable leaders. Coverage includes the historic role of the infantry, cavalry, tank corps, engineers, medical corps, and guerillas.

National Songs

212. Cartledge, T. M. National Anthems of the World. Blandford; dist. by Sterling, 1983. 511 p. $11.

Gr 7+. BR 2: Jan/Feb 1984. The music and words, in English, to 183 national anthems are included.

Occupations

213. Franck, Irene M. Builders. (Work Throughout History Series). Facts on File, 1986. 180 p. ill. $14.

Gr 5+. B 83: Sep 1 1986. BR 5: Nov/Dec 1986. SLJ 33: Oct 1986. The evolution of architecture as a profession and the development and historic role of such occupations as carpenter, plasterer, and construction laborer are covered in this illustrated work.

214. Franck, Irene M. Financiers and Traders. (Work Throughout History Series). Facts on File, 1986. 146 p. ill. $14.

Gr 5+. B 83: Sep 1 1986. * BR 5: Nov/Dec 1986. SLJ 33: Oct 1986. This volume examines, from a historical perspective, the social importance of bankers, merchants, money lenders, accountants, and insurance personnel.

215. Franck, Irene M. Leaders and Lawyers. (Work Throughout History Series). Facts on File, 1986. 188 p. ill. $14.

Gr 5+. B 83: Sep 1 1986. * BR 5: Nov/Dec 1986. SLJ 33: Oct 1986. Franck examines the historic role of persons who have made, enforced, and interpreted the law, including those in all types of police, legal, and judicial professions. She discusses political leadership and shows the importance of these professions to society.

216. Franck, Irene M. Manufacturers and Miners. (Work Throughout History Series). Facts on File, 1989. 117 p. ill. $18.

Gr 9+. + - B 85: Mar 15 1989. BR 8: Nov/Dec 1989. VOYA 12: Dec 1989. Occupations related to manufacturing and mining since ancient times are covered. Included are metalsmiths, quarriers, vehicle and weapon makers, factory workers, and miners.

217. Franck, Irene M. Performers and Players. (Work Throughout History Series). Facts on File, 1988. 196 p. ill. $18.

Gr 6+. + - B 85: Mar 15 1989. * BR 7: Mar/Apr 1989. SLJ 35: Jan 1989. The origin and development of their professions, and the historic influence of actors, acrobats, athletes, clowns, dancers, musicians, puppeteers, racers, and other entertainers, are covered in this illustrated work.

218. Franck, Irene M. Restaurateurs and Innkeepers. (Work Throughout History Series). Facts on File, 1988. 165 p. ill. $18.

Gr 9+. + - B 85: Mar 15 1989. BR 8: Sep/Oct 1989. This work covers aspects of occupations related to food and hospitality from ancient to modern times. Occupations covered include baker, miller, fishmonger, cook, butcher, waiter, and prostitute.

219. Franck, Irene M. Scholars and Priests. (Work Throughout History Series). Facts on File, 1988. 196 p. ill. $17.

Gr 6+. BR 7: Mar/Apr 1989. VOYA 12: Apr 1989. The social role of teachers, preachers, curators, monks, school administrators, scholars, and librarians from ancient to modern times are explored.

220. Franck, Irene M. Warriors and Adventurers. (Work Throughout History Series). Facts on File, 1988. 192 p. ill. $15.

Gr 5+. * BR 7: May/Jun 1988. + - SLJ 34: May 1988. + - VOYA 11: Jun 1988. The work of criminals, gamblers, flyers, sailors, and soldiers from ancient to modern times is explored, showing how these occupations have changed though the years.

Oceans, Seas, etc.

221. Hargreaves, Pat. Antarctic, The. (Seas and Oceans). Silver Burdett, 1981. 69 p. ill. $8.

Gr 4-8. B 77: Jul 15/Aug 1981. SLJ 28: Mar 1982. Diagrams, maps, and photos augment this account of the resources, history, and exploration of the waters surrounding Antarctica. These waters comprise southern portions of the Atlantic, Pacific, and Indian oceans, and are sometimes called the Antarctic Ocean.

222. Hargreaves, Pat. Arctic, The. (Seas and Oceans). Silver Burdett, 1981. 66 p. ill. $8.

Gr 4-8. B 77: Jul 15/Aug 1981. SLJ 28: Mar 1982. Hargreaves' account of the history, exploration, resources, and people of the Arctic Ocean includes graphs, maps, diagrams, photos, and a glossary.

223. Hargreaves, Pat. Atlantic, The. (Seas and Oceans). Silver Burdett, 1981. 68 p. ill. $8.

Gr 4-8. B 77: Jul 15/Aug 1981. SLJ 28: Mar 1982. Photos, diagrams, graphs, maps, and a glossary augment this account of the history, exploration, resources, and people of the area along the entire Atlantic shore.

224. Hargreaves, Pat. Mediterranean, The. (Seas and Oceans). Silver Burdett, 1981. 69 p. ill. $8.

Gr 4-8. B 77: Jul 15/Aug 1981. SLJ 28: Mar 1982. This account of the people who have lived along the shores of the Mediterranean, and the region's history, exploration, and resources includes maps, graphs, photos, diagrams, and a glossary.

225. Hargreaves, Pat. Pacific, The. (Seas and Oceans). Silver Burdett, 1981. 67 p. ill. $8.

Gr 4-8. B 77: Jul 15/Aug 1981. SLJ 28: Mar 1982. Maps, diagrams, photos, graphs, and a glossary augment this account of the history, exploration, resources, and people of the area along the entire Pacific shore.

Pacifists

226. Josephson, Harold. Biographical Dictionary of Modern Peace Leaders. Greenwood, 1985. 1133 p. $75.

Gr 9+. B 82: Feb 1 1986. * LJ 110: Aug 1985. These brief biographical essays cover 750 international peace leaders of the 19th and 20th centuries. An appendix shows the geographic areas represented.

227. Meyer, Peter. Peace Organizations Past & Present. McFarland, 1988. 280 p. $25.

Gr 9+. B 85: Feb 1 1989. + - BR 7: Jan/Feb 1989. LJ 113: Nov 1 1988. Meyer presents a survey of the history of peace movements and describes 92 organizations involved in the quest for peace.

Pirates

228. Earle, Peter. Sack of Panama, The. Viking, 1982. 304 p. ill. $17.

Gr 9+. B 78: Apr 1 1982. LJ 107: Mar 1 1982. SLJ 28: Aug 1982. English and Spanish archives were examined to compile an accurate account of the activities of Henry Morgan, a notorious pirate, who was really an English "irregular" acting for the crown. He raided Spanish colonies, attacked their ships, and in 1671 sacked Panama.

229. Marrin, Albert. Sea Rovers: Pirates, Privateers, and Buccaneers. Atheneum, 1984. 173 p. ill. $13.

Gr 5-9. B 81: Sep 1 1984. BC 37: May 1984. HB 60: Jun 1984. SLJ 30: Aug 1984. For 300 years pirates roamed the seas. Marrin presents lively biographies of major pirates and buccaneers, including women, and information on the way pirates lived.

230. McWilliams, Karen. Pirates. (First Book). Watts, 1989. 64 p. ill. $11.

Gr 3-6. BC 42: Apr 1989. + - SLJ 35: May 1989. The causes of piracy and the lives of pirates are introduced in this colorfully illustrated work.

231. Schoder, Judith. Brotherhood of Pirates. Messner, 1979. 96 p. ill. $8.

Gr 3-6. * SE 44: Apr 1980. SLJ 26: Jan 1980. Schoder's readable, illustrated introduction to 17th- and 18th-century pirates includes Mary Reed, Ann Bonney, Henry Morgan, William Kid, Blackbeard, and Jean Lafitte.

Politics

232. Archer, Jules. You Can't Do That To Me! Famous Fights for Human Rights. Macmillan, 1980. 232 p. $9.

Gr 7+. B 76: Jul 15 1980. BC 34: Dec 1980. SLJ 27: Nov 1980. Through the stories of such persons as Sun Yat-Sen, Indira Gandhi, and Spartacus, Archer discusses the struggle for human rights since the days of the Roman Empire.

233. Bialer, Seweryn. Global Rivals, The. Knopf, 1988. 211 p. $19.

Gr 9+. + - BR 7: Mar/Apr 1989. SLJ 35: May 1989. For students with background knowledge of Soviet and American history, an analysis of the causes and events of the 40-year struggle for supremacy between the two superpowers.

234. Daniels, Robert V. Year of the Heroic Guerrilla: World Revolution and Counterrevolution in 1968. Basic Books, 1989. 286 p. ill. $20.

Gr 10+. B 86: Sep 15 1989. LJ 114: Oct 1 1989. 1968 saw social, cultural, and political revolutions around the world. Daniels covers events in China, Czechoslovakia, France, Vietnam, the United States, and other nations.

235. Delury, George E. World Encyclopedia of Political Systems and Parties. 2nd ed. Facts on File, 1987. 1410 p. $175.

Gr 9+. B 84: Oct 1 1987. BR 6: Sep/Oct 1987. This examination of the political characteristics of nations covers the form of each nation's government, political parties, pressure groups, and the prospects for stability.

236. Green, Jonathon. Book of Political Quotes, The. McGraw-Hill, 1983. 246 p. ill. Pb $9.

Gr 9+. B 79: Jun 15 1983. Arranged by topic are approximately 3000 memorable quotes from world notables. Topics include politics, the press, revolution, war, and women.

237. Henning, Charles. Wit and Wisdom of Politics, The. Fulcrum, 1989. 305 p. Pb $13.

Gr 9+. BR 8: Nov/Dec 1989. + - LJ 114: May 1 1989. Words of humor and wisdom about politics from ancient to modern times are arranged by subject.

238. Leone, Bruno. Communism: Opposing Viewpoints. Rev. ed. (Isms, Modern Doctrines and Movements). Greenhaven Press, 1986. 216 p. ill. $12. Pb $7.

Gr 8+. B 82: Aug 1986. SLJ 33: Oct 1986. The Soviet application of the theories of communism is the focus of this work. It includes debates about communism, information on life in the Soviet Union, communism in the Third World, and United States foreign policy toward the U.S.S.R.

239. Leone, Bruno. Internationalism: Opposing Viewpoints. Rev. ed. (Isms, Modern Doctrines and Movements). Greenhaven Press, 1986. 175 p. ill. $12. Pb $7.

Gr 8+. B 82: Aug 1986. SLJ 33: Oct 1986. The feasibility of world government, and the successes and failures of the League of Nations, the United Nations, the World Bank, and other international organizations are discussed.

240. Leone, Bruno. Nationalism: Opposing Viewpoints. Rev. ed. (Isms, Modern Doctrines and Movements). Greenhaven Press, 1986. 145 p. ill. $12. Pb $7.

Gr 8+. B 82: Jul 1986. SLJ 33: Oct 1986. A wide range of views on the causes, growth, and effects of nationalism is represented. Coverage begins in the late 19th century with Italian and German unification, and includes Israel, South Africa, Japan, Czechoslovakia, and Hungary.

241. Leone, Bruno. Socialism: Opposing Viewpoints. Rev. ed. (Isms, Modern Doctrines and Movements). Greenhaven Press, 1986. 156 p. ill. $12. Pb $7.

Gr 8+. B 82: Aug 1986. SLJ 33: Oct 1986. Selections from articles from the 19th century through the 1980s present a wide range of views on the ideology of socialism and its applications.

Princes and Princesses

242. Levite, Christine. Princesses. Watts, 1989. 210 p. ill. $13.

Gr 5-9. B 86: Sep 15 1989. BC 43: Sep 1989. SLJ 35: Oct 1989. Numerous photos supplement this overview of the daily lives of modern princesses.

Prisoners of War

243. Reid, Pat. Prisoner of War. Beaufort, 1986. 192 p. ill. $18.

Gr 9+. B 82: Apr 1 1986. + - LJ 111: Apr 1 1986. The treatment of prisoners of war from ancient times through World War II is discussed by the author, who was a prisoner at the infamous Colditz Castle during World War II.

Refugees

244. Kismaric, Carole. Forced Out: The Agony of the Refugee in Our Time. Random, 1989. 191 p. ill. $20.

Gr 10+. BR 8: Nov/Dec 1989. VOYA 12: Dec 1989. A profusion of photos, maps, statistics, charts, and personal reminiscences augment this history of world refugees, which shows the economic and political reasons for leaving one's country.

Revolutions

245. Wheatcroft, Andrew. World Atlas of Revolutions, The. Simon & Schuster, 1983. 208 p. ill. $20. Pb $11.

Gr 9+. B 80: Jan 15 1984. LJ 109: Jan 1984. SLJ 30: May 1984. This overview of social and military revolutions around the world over the past 200 years includes information on their causes and consequences. Detailed maps, illustrations, and timetables are included.

Ships and Shipping

246. Hartman, Tom. Guinness Book of Ships and Shipping Facts and Feats. Guinness; dist. by Sterling, 1984. 265 p. ill. $20.

Gr 6+. B 80: Feb 1 1984. + - BR 3: Sep/Oct 1984. Topically arranged miscellany on ships and shipping for browsers, Hartman's book covers technological development, exploration, disasters, military and civilian ships, and records. Photos and glossaries are included.

247. Hudson, Kenneth. Tragedy on the High Seas: A History of Shipwrecks. A & W, 1979. 170 p. ill. $13.

Gr 9+. B 77: Dec 15 1980. This highly illustrated work includes brief entries on memorable sea disasters, information on the causes and prevention of shipwrecks, and on ships common throughout history.

248. Karmon, Yehuda. Ports Around the World. Crown, 1980. 310 p. ill. $16.

Gr 9+. B 76: Jun 15 1980. LJ 105: Aug 1980. The historic role of 75 major ports, their cities, and the surrounding regions are covered in this well-organized work that is enriched by colorful maps and photos.

249. Kemp, Peter. Encyclopedia of Ships and Seafaring. Crown, 1980. 256 p. ill. $16.

Gr 9+. B 77: Jan 1 1981. This account of the evolution of ships includes information on famous ships and great men in the history of seafaring. The text is enhanced by numerous photos, drawings, and maps.

250. Parry, J. H. Romance of the Sea. National Geographic Society, 1981. 312 p. ill. $20.

Gr 9+. B 78: Nov 1 1981. LJ 106: Dec 1 1981. Exploration of the sea since ancient times, naval wars, commercial sea ventures, and the use of the ocean's resources are included in this colorfully illustrated history of men, ships, and the sea.

251. Preston, Antony. Submarines. St. Martin's, 1983. 192 p. ill. $25.

Gr 9+. B 79: Apr 15 1983. + - LJ 108: Apr 15 1983. Over 200 photos and a concise text provide an introduction to the development and use of submarines.

Slavery

252. Meltzer, Milton. All Times, All Peoples: A World History of Slavery. Harper, 1980. 65 p. ill. $9. Lib. ed. $9.

Gr 4-9. B 77: Sep 15 1980. BC 34: Dec 1980. HB 56: Oct 1980. SLJ 27: Oct 1980. Since the days of ancient Mesopotamia some people have held others as slaves. Meltzer discusses the reasons for, and results of, this tragic fact.

Social Life and Customs

253. Giblin, James Cross. Chimney Sweeps: Yesterday and Today. Harper, 1982. 56 p. ill. $11. Lib. ed. $11.

Gr 4-8. B 79: Nov 15 1982. B 82: Jul 1985. BC 36: Dec 1982. HB 59: Feb 1983. SLJ 29: Jan 1983. Informative and readable, this history of chimney sweeps from the 12th century to today includes the folklore and superstition that have surrounded their work.

254. Greenleaf, Barbara Kaye. Children Through the Ages: A History of Childhood. McGraw-Hill, 1978. 165 p. ill. $9.

Gr 9+. B 74: Jul 15 1978. + - LJ 103: Jul 1978. + - SE 50: Apr/May 1986. This introduction to society's attitudes toward children and the ways they have been treated since ancient times includes photos.

Technology and Civilization

255. Boorstin, Daniel J. Discoverers, The. Random, 1983. 745 p. $25.

Gr 10+. HB 60: Jun 1984. LJ 108: Nov 15 1983. LJ 110: Mar 1 1985. SE 49: May 1985. Major discoveries since ancient times in such varied fields as geography, medicine, time, and science are covered in this readable work.

256. Bosetti, Noel. 1900, the Turn of the Century. (Events of Yesteryear). Silver Burdett, 1987. 69 p. ill. $15.

Gr 6+. * BR 6: Jan/Feb 1988. + - SLJ 34: Dec 1987. Photos and other illustrations enrich the text which introduces the lives of laborers and the middle class in 1900, and shows the impact of new inventions on cultures around the world.

257. Builders of the Ancient World: Marvels of Engineering. National Geographic Society, 1986. 199 p. ill. $10.

Gr 8+. + - SLJ 33: May 1987. Examples of ancient construction that combine engineering technology and beauty are presented in this colorfully illustrated work. Greece, Rome, Middle and South America, India, Southeast Asia, and China are represented in these selections.

258. Ceserani, Gian Paolo. Grand Constructions. Putnam, 1983. 103 p. ill. $13.

Gr 5-8. B 79: Jun 1 1983. * BC 36: Apr 1983. SLJ 29: Aug 1983. Oversized and highly illustrated, this attractive work traces the history of architecture from Stonehenge to skyscrapers, and shows how rulers and other persons influenced building styles.

259. Cosner, Shaaron. Paper Through the Ages. (Carolrhoda On My Own Books). Carolrhoda, 1984. 44 p. ill. $8.

Gr 1-5. B 81: Dec 15 1984. + - BC 38: Mar 1985. SLJ 31: Feb 1985. This illustrated and informative account of the invention of paper discusses its impact on civilization.

260. Fagg, Christopher. How They Built Long Ago. Warwick; dist. by Watts, 1981. 75 p. ill. $10.

Gr 5-8. B 78: Nov 15 1981. BC 35: Feb 1982. + - SLJ 29: Sep 1982. Fagg's account of worldwide building materials and methods from the Stone Age through the Renaissance includes a timeline and information on the natural resources available to the builders in various geographic regions, and the effects of culture on the builders.

261. Giblin, James Cross. Let There Be Light: A Book About Windows. Harper, 1988. 162 p. ill. $15. Lib. ed. $15.

Gr 5+. * B 85: Nov 1 1988. BC 42: Nov 1988. HB 65: Jan/Feb 1989. * SLJ 35: Nov 1988. Giblin's history of windows since ancient times is a well-illustrated account of how social, economic, religious, and climatic influences affect our everyday lives.

262. Gleasner, Diana C. Dynamite. (Inventions That Changed Our Lives). Walker, 1982. 64 p. ill. $8.

Gr 4-7. B 79: Mar 1 1983. + - BC 36: Feb 1983. SLJ 29: Jan 1983. The beneficial and destructive uses of dynamite are explained in this illustrated work, which also introduces Alfred Nobel and his family and shows how society treated him when the power of his invention became evident.

263. Lambert, David. Great Discoveries and Inventions. (World of Science). Facts on File, 1985. 64 p. ill. $10.

Gr 3-9. B 82: Sep 1 1985. BR 4: Jan/Feb 1986. SLJ 32: Oct 1985. A glossary and an abundance of illustrations supplement this introduction to discoveries and inventions from ancient times to space-age technology.

264. Logan, Robert. Alphabet Effect: Impact of the Phonetic Alphabet on the Development of Western Civilization. Morrow, 1986. 265 p. $17.

Gr 9+. * B 82: Aug 1986. - LJ 111: Oct 1986. Logan discusses the effects of the phonetic alphabet on the development of Western civilization, including law, logic, invention, and science.

265. Perry, Susan. How Did We Get Calendars & Clocks? (Creative's Little Question Books). Creative Education, 1981. 32 p. ill. $6.

Gr 2-4. SLJ 28: Aug 1982. Perry describes the history of calendars and the construction of clocks from the time of the ancient Sumerians.

266. Rahn, Joan Elma. More Plants That Changed History. Atheneum, 1985. 126 p. ill. $11.

Gr 6+. B 81: May 15 1985. + - SLJ 32: Oct 1985. VOYA 8: Oct 1985. This sequel to Plants That Changed History focuses on papyrus, paper, rubber, tea, and opium, showing how each has influenced human history.

267. Rahn, Joan Elma. Plants That Changed History. Atheneum, 1982. 144 p. ill. $10.

Gr 6+. B 79: Jun 15 1983. B 83: Oct 15 1986. BC 36: Oct 1982. * SE 47: Apr 1983. + - SLJ 29: Feb 1983. Rahn presents a lively account of the historic impact of cereals, coal forests, potatoes, spices, and sugar cane.

268. Smith, Elizabeth Simpson. Paper. (Inventions That Changed Our Lives). Walker, 1984. 64 p. ill. $11.

Gr 4-8. B 81: Feb 15 1985. SLJ 31: Mar 1985. The historical and modern uses of paper, and its social and economic impact, are introduced in this illustrated work.

269. Tunis, Edwin. Wheels: A Pictorial History. Harper, 1955; 1977. 96 p. ill. $20.

Gr 6+. Metzner. B 51: May 15 1955. HB 31: Aug 1955. * LJ 80: Jun 15 1955. This readable and profusely illustrated history covers wheeled vehicles from ancient to modern times.

270. Williams, Trevor I. History of Invention: From Stone Axes to Silicon Chips. Facts on File, 1987. 352 p. ill. $35.

Gr 7+. LJ 113: Mar 1 1988. VOYA 11: Oct 1988. Colorful photos, maps, timelines, and diagrams augment this chrono logical social history that shows how inventions and technology have changed civilization. Includes brief biographies of inventors.

Transportation

271. Hollingsworth, Brian. Atlas of the World's Railways. Everest, 1980. 350 p. ill. $25.

Gr 9+. B 77: Feb 15 1981. + - LJ 105: Sep 1 1980. The railroads of every nation are covered. Historic and technical information is included along with photos, maps, quotes, poems, songs, and statistics.

272. Marshall, John. Guinness Book of Rail Facts and Feats, The. 3rd ed. Guinness; dist. by Sterling, 1979. 252 p. ill. $16.

Gr 9+. B 77: Jan 15 1981. Worldwide facts about railroads, trains, tunnels, and bridges are included in this illustrated work that emphasizes British achievements.

273. Nock, O. S. World Atlas of Railways. Mayflower, 1978. 224 p. ill. $30.

Gr 9+. B 77: Sep 1 1980. This oversized pictorial encyclopedia includes railway development, systems and routes, a chronology, maps, and a section on notable persons involved in the development of railroads.

Trials

274. David, Andrew. Famous Political Trials. (On Trial). Lerner, 1980. 112 p. ill. Lib. ed. $7.

Gr 9+. B 77: Jan 15 1981. VOYA 3: Feb 1981. Famous trials of such persons as Joan of Arc, Sir Thomas More, Alfred Dreyfus, Anatoly Shcharansky, and Adolf Eichmann are covered.

United Nations

275. Carroll, Raymond. Future of the United Nations, The. (Impact Book). Watts, 1985. 122 p. ill. $11.

Gr 6+. B 82: Dec 15 1985. BR 4: Mar/Apr 1986. SLJ 32: Jan 1986. Carroll reviews the origin of the United Nations, its structure, the effectiveness of the Secretary General, and criticisms leveled at the United Nations.

276. Green, Carol. United Nations. (New True Book). Childrens Press, 1983. 45 p. ill. $8.

Gr 1-4. B 80: Feb 15 1984. SLJ 30: Mar 1984. This colorful introduction to the United Nations and its various agencies includes a glossary.

277. Osmancyzk, Edmund Jan. Encyclopedia of the United Nations and International Agreements, The. Taylor and Francis, 1985. 1059 p. $160.

Gr 9+. B 82: May 1 1986. + - LJ 111: Jan 1986. These alphabetically arranged entries on thousands of events, organizations, people, places, and documents that relate to the United Nations and its development cover a broad range of materials on economic, political, and social topics.

278. Parker, Nancy Winslow. United Nations from A to Z, The. Dodd, 1985. 80 p. ill. $13. Pb $5.

Gr 4-6 + - B 82: Feb 15 1986. BC 39: Mar 1986. + - BR 5: May/Jun 1986. + - SLJ 32: Mar 1986. United Nations history, agencies, and organizations are covered in an alphabetic arrangement. Maps, flags, lists of members, and cartoons are included.

279. Sheldon, Richard N. Dag Hammarskjold. (World Leaders Past & Present). Chelsea House, 1987. 112 p. ill. $17.

Gr 8+. B 84: Sep 1 1987. SLJ 34: Oct 1987. Hammarskjold spent 8 years as Secretary General of the United Nations. This biography emphasizes the years he spent as keeper of the peace in what he called "the most impossible job on earth."

280. Stein, R. Conrad. Story of the United Nations, The. (Cornerstones of Freedom). Childrens Press, 1986. 30 p. ill. $10.

Gr 3-6. B 82: Jul 1986. SLJ 33: Jan 1987. The creation of the United Nations, how it works, and its impact are covered in this illustrated introduction.

281. Urquhart, Brian. Life in Peace and War, A. Harper, 1987. 400 p. ill. $25.

Gr 10+. LJ 112: Sep 1 1987. The author worked for 40 years in the Secretariat of the United Nations. His memoir provides sketches on most of the major persons and events in United Nations history.

282. Woods, Harold. United Nations, The. (First Book). Watts, 1985. 65 p. ill. $10.

Gr 3-6. + - B 82: Dec 15 1985. BR 5: May/Jun 1986. + - SLJ 32: Jan 1986. The organization of the United Nations and the major issues surrounding its activities are introduced in this illustrated volume.

Violence

283. Coker, Chris. Terrorism and Civil Strife. (Conflict in the 20th Century). Watts, 1987. 62 p. ill. $13.

Gr 5-10. B 84: Feb 15 1988. * BR 6: Sep/Oct 1987. SLJ 34: Mar 1988. Global problems of terrorism and the role of television are discussed, as well as major personalities, and terrorist and anti-terrorist groups. Maps and photos enhance the text.

284. Dobson, Christopher. Never-Ending War: Terrorism in the 80's. Facts on File, 1989. 366 p. Pb $13.

Gr 9+. VOYA 12: Oct 1989. Worldwide terrorist activities 1968-1986 are examined chronologically. A who's who of terrorists, information about terrorist groups, and suggestions to control terrorism are included.

285. Edwards, Richard. International Terrorism. Rourke, 1988. 48 p. ill. $12.

Gr 5-8. B 85: Dec 15 1988. SLJ 35: May 1989. Edwards examines the activities of several terrorist groups and discusses the issues involved. Photos and a glossary are included.

286. Freeman, Charles. Terrorism. (Today's World). Batsford; dist. by David & Charles, 1981. 72 p. ill. $15.

Gr 7+. B 78: Jan 1 1982. Freeman uses graphic photos in showing examples of worldwide terrorism and argues that terrorism is an ineffective use of violence.

287. Raynor, Thomas. Terrorism: Past, Present, Future. Watts, 1982. 152 p. $11.

Gr 7+. B 79: Nov 15 1982. B 83: Apr 15 1987. BR 6: May/Jun 1987. SLJ 29: Jan 1983. SLJ 33: May 1987. VOYA 10: Aug 1987. Raynor traces terrorism and those who have supported it since the French Revolution, with emphasis on events since the 1960s. He shows the economic aspects of terrorism and quotes leaders who have opposed it.

288. Taylor, L. B. Hostage! Kidnapping and Terrorism in Our Time. Watts, 1989. 140 p. ill. $13.

Gr 7+. B 86: Dec 15 1989. BC 43: Sep 1989. Photos and accounts of personal experiences augment this examination of the uses of terrorism and kidnapping as a political tool.

289. Tucker, H. H. Combatting the Terrorists. Facts on File, 1988. 210 p. $25.

Gr 9+. + - BR 8: Jan/Feb 1989. Worldwide terrorist activities are explored in 7 essays written by authors, journalists, and experts.

Women

290. Duley, Margot. Cross Cultural Study of Women: A Comprehensive Guide. Feminist Press, 1986. 389 p. $30. Pb $13.

Gr 10+. LJ 111: Jul 1986. Historical and cultural surveys of women in developing nations are included, along with essays on such topics as male dominance, women and religion, and the effects of colonization and national development on women.

291. Edwards, Julia. Women of the World: The Great Foreign Correspondents. Houghton, 1988. 275 p. ill. $18.

Gr 9+. LJ 113: Aug 1988. SLJ 35: Jan 1989. As journalists, women have participated in wars around the world since the mid-19th century. Included in this lively account of their experiences are Mary Roberts Rinehart, Margaret Bourke-White, Margaret Fuller, and Georgie Ann Geyer.

292. Fisher, Maxine P. Women in the Third World. Watts, 1989. 176 p. ill. $14.

Gr 7+. B 85: Jul 1989. BC 42: Jun 1989. BR 8: Nov/Dec 1989. * SLJ 35: Jul 1989. VOYA 12: Oct 1989. Brief histori-

cal information is included in this balanced and readable account of the daily lives of ordinary women in Third World nations.

293. Fraser, Antonia. Warrior Queens, The. Knopf, 1989. 400 p. ill. $23.

Gr 9+. B 85: Jan 15 1989. Queens Isabella of Spain, Boadacia of England, Tamara of Georgia, and British Prime Minister Margaret Thatcher are the focus of this examination of women rulers who successfully waged war.

294. O'Neill, Lois Decker. Women's Book of World Records and Achievements, The. Doubleday, 1979. 798 p. ill. $20. Pb $10.

Gr 9+. B 76: Feb 1 1980. LJ 105: Apr 15 1980. Arranged chronologically under many fields are brief entries on the lives and achievements of 5000 notable women of the late 19th century and the 20th century, indexed by subject and personal name.

295. Stott, Carole. Into the Unknown. (Women History Makers). Hampstead Press; dist. by Watts, 1989. 48 p. ill. $12.

Gr 5-8. B 85: Mar 15 1989. SLJ 35: Sep 1989. This introduction to three women who pioneered in male-dominated professions includes Caroline Herschel, an astronomer, Amy Johnson, a pilot, and Sally Ride, an astronaut.

296. Uglow, Jennifer S. International Dictionary of Women's Biography, The. Continuum, 1982. 534 p. ill. $28.

Gr 9+. B 80: Dec 15 1983. B 80: Jun 15 1984. LJ 108: Mar 1 1983. A subject index and illustrations enrich these brief biographies of 1500 influential women of all occupations, from ancient to modern times.

297. Women: A World Report. Oxford University Press, 1986. 376 p. ill. $19.

Gr 9+. B 82: Jan 15 1986. LJ 111: Jan 1986. At the end of the United Nations Decade for Women, 1975-1985, this report was compiled, recording the worldwide status of women and work, the family, politics, and sex. Statistical data and analytical essays are included.

Women–Bibliographies

298. Reese, Lyn. Women in the World: Annotated History Resources for the Secondary Student. Scarecrow, 1987. 220 p. ill. $20.

Gr 9+. B 84: Apr 1 1988. BR 7: May/Jun 1988. VOYA 11: Apr 1988. Arranged topically, these annotated bibliographies of print and nonprint materials cover women from all times and all regions of the world.

World War I

General

299. Brook-Shepherd, Gordon. Royal Sunset: The Dynasties and the Great War. Doubleday, 1987. 341 p. ill. $18.

Gr 10+. B 83: Apr 1 1987. LJ 112: Apr 1 1987. The royal families of pre-World War I Europe are introduced and their role in causing the war is examined.

300. Tuchman, Barbara. Guns of August, The. Macmillan; Bantam, 1962. 511 p. maps. $20. Pb $5.

Gr 9+. B 58: Mar 1 1962. B 82: Jan 1986. LJ 87: Jan 15 1962. This detailed reconstruction of the events of the first month of World War I includes profiles of the leading military and political figures.

301. Vansittart, Peter. Voices 1870-1914. Watts, 1985. 304 p. ill. $5.

Gr 9+. BR 4: Mar 1986. SLJ 32: Oct 1985. Poetry and prose have been selected from the writings of rulers, politicians, novelists, and poets, all looking for the causes of the war.

302. Vansittart, Peter. Voices from the Great War. Watts, 1984. 303 p. ill. $15.

Gr 9+. SLJ 31: Jan 1985. * VOYA 7: Dec 1984. These selections from the writings of rulers, novelists, and politicians who were eyewitnesses to the war represent all points of view.

303. Winter, J. M. Experience of World War I, The. Oxford University Press, 1989. 256 p. ill. $30.

Gr 9+. B 85: May 1 1989. A profusion of photos and a brief text cover the economic, military, political, social, and technological issues of the war.

Aerial Operations and Aircraft

304. Campbell, Christopher. Aces and Aircraft of World War I. Blandford; dist. by Sterling, 1981. 144 p. ill. $25. Lib. ed. $20.

Gr 9+. B 77: May 15 1981. LJ 106: Jun 1 1981. Campbell's chronological overview presents an account of each flier, with numerous photos and illustrations of their airplanes, uniforms, and armament.

Aerial Operations and Aircraft–Fiction

305. Cameron, Ian. Young Eagles: A Novel. St. Martin's, 1980. 249 p. $11.

Gr 9+. B 76: May 15 1980. LJ 105: Mar 1 1980. Two friends, one English, one German, find themselves mortal enemies because of the war. Exciting aerial battle scenes add to the story.

306. Dank, Milton. Khaki Wings: A Novel. Delacorte, 1980. 170 p. $9.

Gr 7+. B 77: Oct 15 1980. HB 56: Dec 1980. + - SLJ 27: Jan 1981. VOYA 4: Apr 1981. Sixteen-year-old Edward, who could already fly a plane, joins the Royal Air Force. His observations of the war and the battle sequences evoke the flavor of the war.

307. Hough, Richard. Flight to Victory. Dutton, 1985. 175 p. $13.

Gr 7-10. B 81: Apr 1 1985. + - SLJ 31: Aug 1985. This story of a boy who runs away to join the air force in order to prove himself presents an authentic account of how pilots learned to fly and their World War I aerial combat experiences.

308. Nordhoff, Charles Bernard. Falcons of France: A Tale of Youth and the Air. Little, Brown; Ayer, 1929; 1979. 332 p. ill. $31.

Gr 7+. Metzner. B 26: Nov 1929. This exciting adventure gives an accurate picture of the life of the airmen on the western front.

Battles

309. Livesey, Anthony. Great Battles of World War I. Macmillan, 1989. 200 p. ill. $40.

Gr 9+. B 86: Sep 1 1989. LJ 114: Sep 1 1989. This balanced and profusely illustrated book examines the battles of World War I, with additional information on noted persons, battle tactics, weapons, and uniforms.

Espionage and Spies

310. Cowen, Ida. Spy for Freedom: The Story of Sarah Aaronsohn. (Jewish Biography Series). Dutton, 1984. 156 p. ill. $15.

Gr 5+. B 81: Mar 1 1985. + - BC 38: May 1985. BR 4: Sep/Oct 1985. + - SLJ 31: Feb 1985. VOYA 8: Aug 1985. This exciting, fictionalized biography of Sarah Aaronsohn, a young Jewish Zionist who provided Turkish military information to the British in 1916-1917, is based on primary sources.

311. Howe, Russell Warren. Mata Hari: The True Story. Dodd, 1986. 320 p. ill. $18.

Adult. B 82: May 1 1986. LJ 111: May 1 1986. The myths surrounding Mata Hari are explored in this lively biography, which argues that she was not a spy at all.

Fiction

312. Darrell, Elizabeth. At the Going Down of the Sun. St. Martin's, 1985. 503 p. $15.

Gr 10+. B 81: Feb 15 1985. LJ 110: Jan 1985. English country gentlemen Rex, Chris, and Roland Sheridan find themselves caught in the horrors of a war that is destroying their way of life. A moving novel that combines romance and gripping action.

313. Frank, Rudolf. No Hero for the Kaiser. Lothrop, 1986. 222 p. ill. $13.

Gr 6-10. B 83: Sep 1 1986. BC 40: Oct 1986. BR 5: Nov/Dec 1986. * SE 51: Apr/May 1987. + - SLJ 33: Oct 1986. This understated anti-war novel centers around Jan, a 14-year-old Polish boy who became a mascot to a German unit. First published in Germany in 1931, the book was burned by Hitler.

314. Hennessy, Max. Bright Blue Sky, The. Atheneum, 1983. 250 p. $11.

Gr 10+. B 79: Jun 1 1983. LJ 108: Mar 15 1983. As a civilian-soldier Dicken Quinney was enamored of flying, and soon found himself flying combat missions in spite of equipment failures, exhaustion, and the constant threat of death.

315. Hill, Reginald. No Man's Land. St. Martin's, 1986. 352 p. $16.

Gr 9+. B 82: Feb 1 1986. LJ 111: Jan 1986. Between the English and German lines was a no-man's land where three deserters struggled to evade capture. Their vivid recollections of battles and military life are based on actual experiences.

316. McCutcheon, Elsie. Summer of the Zeppelin. Farrar, 1985. 168 p. $11.

Gr 5-8. B 81: Mar 15 1985. BC 38: Mar 1985. HB 61: May/Jun 1985. SLJ 31: May 1985. * VOYA 8: Jun 1985.

Elvira's father is missing in action. Feeling isolated from her stepmother, she seeks refuge in a run-down house where she discovers and befriends an escaped German prisoner. Set in rural Britain.

317. Morpurgo, Michael. War Horse. Greenwillow, 1983. 148 p. $9.

Gr 5-8. B 80: Feb 1 1984. BR 2: Mar/Apr 1984. HB 59: Dec 1983. - SLJ 30: Oct 1983. + - VOYA 7: Apr 1984. This story of a horse who served both the British and the German armies during the war illustrates courage, devotion, and pain.

318. Remarque, Erich Maria. All Quiet on the Western Front. Little, Brown; Fawcett Crest, 1929. 291 p. $15. Pb $3.

Gr 8+. B 25: Jul 1929. B 82: May 15 1986. This anti-war novel transcends nationality. It concerns a group of German boys who were taken from school and sent to fight for a cause which meant nothing to them.

319. Smith, Helen Zenna. Not So Quiet: Stepdaughters of War. Feminist Press; dist. by Talman, 1989. 300 p. $27. Pb $10.

Gr 10+. B 85: May 1 1989. The author bases her novel on her experiences as an ambulance driver during World War I.

320. Treadgold, Mary. Journey from the Heron. Jonathan Cape; dist. by Merrimack Publishers' Circle, 1983. 160 p. $10.

Gr 5-9. + - B 79: Aug 1983. + - BC 36: Jun 1983. HB 59: Aug 1983. + - SLJ 30: Oct 1983. Period details are the strength of this story of Betsy, who spends four dramatic days in London during the war.

Military Personnel

321. Berman, Russell A. Paul von Hindenburg. (World Leaders Past & Present). Chelsea House, 1987. 112 p. ill. $17.

Gr 6-10. + - B 83: Aug 1987. SLJ 34: Nov 1987. This introduction to Germany's World War I hero, von Hindenburg, shows how a strong military leader may be a weak political leader, and introduces students to the problems of Germany between the world wars.

322. Masefield, John. John Masefield's Letters from the Front, 1915-1917. Watts, 1985. 307 p. $19.

Gr 9+. B 81: Apr 1 1985. * BR 4: Sep/Oct 1985. LJ 110: Apr 1 1985. SLJ 31: Aug 1985. Masefield served as a medical orderly during World War I. His letters report the horrors and carnage he witnessed.

323. Windrow, Martin. World War I Tommy, The. (Soldier Through the Ages). Watts, 1986. 32 p. ill. $11.

Gr 4-7. * SE 51: Apr/May 1987. SLJ 33: Dec 1986. The daily lives of soldiers, their uniforms, and equipment are presented in this colorfully illustrated work.

Personal Narratives

324. Vaughan, Edwin Campion. Some Desperate Glory. Holt, 1981; 1988. 232 p. $20.

Gr 11+. BR 7: Nov/Dec 1988. Vaughan's diary is a detailed and graphic record of his experiences during 8 months of trench warfare.

Ships and Shipping

325. Howarth, David. Dreadnoughts, The. (Seafarers). Time-Life; dist. by Silver Burdett, 1980, 176 p. ill. $11.

Gr 10+. LJ 105: Jan 15 1980. Howarth's well written and illustrated history of the development of the modern battleship includes personal anecdotes.

World War II

General

326. Baudot, Marcel. Historical Encyclopedia of World War II, The. Facts on File, 1980. 548 p. ill. $25.

Gr 9+. B 78: Sep 15 1981. + - LJ 106: Feb 15 1981. This one-volume encyclopedia of the war covers social and political issues, personalities, and military topics. Photos and maps are included.

327. Dolan, Edward F. Victory in Europe: The Fall of Hitler's Germany. Watts, 1988. 159 p. ill. $13.

Gr 6+. B 85: Sep 1 1988. + - BR 7: Sep/Oct 1988. SLJ 34: Jun/Jul 1988. + - VOYA 11: Aug 1988. The last battles of the war, the Yalta Conference, the last days of the Third Reich, and the liberation of the death camps are all covered in this illustrated account.

328. Gordon, Sheila. 3rd September 1939 (Day That Made History). Batsford; dist. by David & Charles, 1988. 64 p. ill. $17.

Gr 7+. SLJ 35: Jan 1989. Gordon presents a clear account of the events that led up to Hitler's invasion of Poland, which finally pushed Great Britain to declare war on Germany.

329. Hoyt, Edwin P. Japan's War: The Great Pacific Conflict, 1853 to 1952. McGraw-Hill, 1986. 624 p. ill. $20.

Gr 9+. B 82: Jan 15 1986. * LJ 111: Mar 15 1986. The causes and events of the war in the Pacific theater are seen from the Japanese point of view in Hoyt's account, based on Japanese documents.

330. Klingaman, William A. 1941: Our Lives in a World on the Edge. Harper, 1988. 528 p. ill. $23.

Gr 9+. B 85: Sep 1 1988. LJ 113: Oct 1 1988. Excerpts from journals, diaries, and letters reveal social, cultural, and wartime events of the year the United States entered the war.

331. Krasilishchik, S. World War II: Dispatches from the Soviet Front. International Universities Press, 1985. 372 p. $20.

Gr 11+. BR 5: Sep/Oct 1986. These documents provide insight into World War II from the Soviet point of view.

332. Lawson, Don. Album of World War II Home Fronts, An. (Picture Album). Watts, 1980. 90 p. ill. Lib. ed. $8.

Gr 6+. B 76: Jun 1 1980. SLJ 27: Mar 1981. A simple text and a profusion of photos show the everyday wartime experiences of civilians in Europe, Asia, and the United States. These ranged from rationing and black market activities to resistance fighting and daily bombing raids.

333. Lidz, Richard. Many Kinds of Courage: An Oral History of World War II. Putnam, 1980. 266 p. $10.

Gr 9+. * B 76: Jun 15 1980. LJ 105: Jun 15 1980. SLJ 26: May 1980. Eighteen moving personal narratives, set in context, provide a good view of the war. Interviewees include a British ambulance driver, prisoners from German and Japanese camps, soldiers from battles in North Africa and on Omaha Beach, and a survivor of Hiroshima.

334. Macmillan, Harold. War Diaries: Politics and War in the Mediterranean 1943-1945. St. Martin's, 1984. 804 p. ill. $30.

Gr 9+. SLJ 31: May 1985. The former British prime minister presents the candid daily journal that he wrote during the war. He was responsible for British policy throughout the Mediterranean.

335. Rossel, Seymour. Holocaust: The Fire That Raged. Watts, 1989. 96 p. ill. $12.

Gr 4-9. B 85: Jun 1 1989. BR 8: Nov/Dec 1989. SLJ 35: Aug 1989. Photos, maps, and a chronology augment this brief history of Nazism and its efforts to eliminate the Jewish people.

336. Shirer, William L. Rise and Fall of the Third Reich: A History of Nazi Germany. Ballantine/Fawcett, 1960. 1599 p. Pb $4.

Gr 10+. * B 57: Nov 1 1960. B 82: Jan 1 1986. * LJ 85: Oct 1 1960. This extensive history covers Germany from the end of World War I through the rise of the Nazi party, the events of World War II, and the fall of Hitler and the Third Reich.

337. Smith, Gene. Dark Summer: An Intimate History of Events that Led to World War II. Macmillan, 1987. 320 p. ill. $23.

Gr 9+. B 84: Nov 1 1987. LJ 112: Nov 15 1987. Focusing on the summer and fall of 1939, Smith profiles the key players, including Chamberlain, King George VI, Hitler, and Stalin. He also highlights the main events and records the reactions of ordinary people.

338. Taylor, James. Third Reich Almanac, The. World Almanac; dist. by St. Martin's, 1988. 392 p. ill. $25.

Gr 9+. B 85: Apr 1 1989. Alphabetically arranged entries cover the people, places, and events of the war. Chronologies of major events and major campaigns, quotations, and photos augment the text.

339. Zeman, Zbynek. Heckling Hitler: Caricatures of the Third Reich. University Press of New England, 1987. 129 p. ill. $25. Pb $15.

Gr 9+. B 83: Apr 15 1987. LJ 112: Jul 1987. International political cartoonists responded to the growth of Hitler's power in these captioned cartoons which are placed in context.

Aerial Operations and Aircraft

340. Blanco, Richard L. Luftwaffe in World War II: The Rise and Decline of the German Air Force. Messner, 1987. 214 p. ill. $11.

Gr 7+. B 83: Jun 15 1987. SLJ 33: Aug 1987. Photos, diagrams, maps, and statistics augment this examination of the involvement of the Luftwaffe in all sectors of the European war.

341. Dahl, Roald. Going Solo. Farrar, 1986. 208 p. ill. $15.

Gr 7+. * B 83: Sep 1 1986. HB 63: Jan 1987. LJ 111: Oct 15 1986. VOYA 9: Feb 1987. Dahl's experiences as a young and inexperienced Royal Air Force pilot in Africa and Greece (1938-1941) provide lively reading. His account is filled with eccentric characters and authentic excitement.

342. Gunston, Bill. Illustrated Dictionary of Fighting Aircraft of World War II, The. Arco/Prentice-Hall, 1988. 479 p. ill. $16.

Gr 4+. BR 7: Jan/Feb 1989. The aircraft of the Allies and the Axis powers are covered in this highly illustrated work which includes a history of the major planes, statistical data, and their strengths and weaknesses. Suitable for elementary and high school students.

343. Hoyt, Edwin P. Kamikazes, The. Arbor House, 1983. 277 p. ill. $17.

Gr 10+. LJ 108: Sep 15 1983. Administrative and technical details augment this anecdotal account of the wartime role of Japanese aviators, told from the Japanese point of view.

344. Jackson, Robert. Fighter! The Story of Air Combat, 1936-45. St. Martin's, 1980. 168 p. $9.

Gr 9+. B 76: Mar 1 1980. - LJ 105: Jan 1 1980. These dramatic true stories of air combat in both the European and Pacific theaters clarify the strategic role of fighter planes during the course of the war.

345. Taylor, Theodore. Rocket Island. Avon, 1985. 160 p. Pb $3.

Gr 7+. B 82: Oct 1 1985. VOYA 8: Dec 1985. In this dramatic account of the secret rocket experiments of the Germans before and during World War II, Taylor discusses the work of the leading rocket scientist, Wernher von Braun, and the head of the program, Walter Dornberger.

Aerial Operations and Aircraft–Fiction

346. Crisp, N. J. Yesterday's Gone. Viking, 1983. 318 p. $17.

Gr 9+. B 80: Sep 1 1983. LJ 108: Sep 1 1983. Based on the log book of an RAF squadron leader, this is the story of a young bomber flying over Berlin before D-Day. Technical details and believable characters add to the exciting story.

347. Dank, Milton. Red Flight Two. Delacorte, 1981. 184 p. $10.

Gr 6-10. B 78: Oct 1 1981. HB 57: Dec 1981. SLJ 28: Sep 1981. The battles of the Royal Air Force, and the experiences of the men who fought them, provide the background for this story about a pilot who became a flight instructor and a commander. Sequel to Khaki Wings.

348. Hough, Richard. Wings Against the Sky. Morrow, 1979. 297 p. $10.

Gr 9+. B 76: Mar 1 1980. + - LJ 105: Mar 15 1980. An accurate account of the war in the air before the Battle of Britain is presented in this fast-moving adventure story.

Atrocities

349. Ashman, Chuck. Nazi Hunters: Behind the Worldwide Search for Nazi War Criminals. Pharos; dist. by Ballantine, 1988. 320 p. $19.

Gr 9+. B 85: Oct 15 1988. Evidence is presented that many Nazi war criminals are still in hiding, and the work of Nazi-hunters is explored.

350. Infield, Glenn B. Secrets of the SS. Stein & Day, 1982. 225 p. ill. $15.

Gr 9+. B 78: Mar 15 1982. Citing incidents, policies, and programs, Infield provides a graphic account of SS brutality against the Jews, prisoners of war, and civilians in occupied territories.

351. Lyttle, Richard B. Nazi Hunting. (Triumph Book). Watts, 1982. 101 p. ill. $9.

Gr 5-9. SLJ 29: Oct 1982. SLJ 34: Feb 1988. This account of the search for six Nazi war criminals is simply written and includes photos.

352. MacPherson, Malcolm C. Blood of His Servants, The. Times Books, 1984. 312 p. $16.

Gr 10+. B 80: Feb 15 1984. LJ 109: Feb 15 1984. Pieter Menten, a Nazi art dealer, gunned down all the Jewish citizens of a Polish village in 1941. This is the account of the events that led to the tragedy, Menten's rise to power, and his eventual capture.

Battles

353. Bliven, Bruce. Story of D-Day. (Landmark Book). Random, 1956; 1987. 160 p. ill. $8. Pb $3.

Gr 5-9. Metzner. B 53: Jan 1 1957. Bliven's profusely illustrated work provides an hour-by-hour account of operations on D-Day.

354. Breuer, William B. Death of a Nazi Army: The Falaise Pocket. Stein & Day, 1985. 328 p. $20.

Gr 9+. B 82: Sep 15 1985. The battle at Falaise Gap, 1944, which resulted in the destruction of most of the German armed forces in the west, is detailed in this portrayal, which includes personal experiences of combatants.

355. Deighton, Len. Battle of Britain. Coward, McCann, 1980. 224 p. ill. $20.

Gr 9+. B 77: Nov 15 1980. Deighton examines both sides of the Battle of Britain in the context of history, and recounts the impact of air technology. Quotes, photos, maps, diagrams, and other illustrations augment the text.

356. Harman, Nicholas. Dunkirk: The Patriotic Myth. Simon & Schuster, 1980. 288 p. $13.

Gr 9+. B 76: May 15 1980. + - LJ 105: Jun 1 1980. Harman examined the records concerning the British Expeditionary Force and the evacuation at Dunkirk and presents a day-to-day account that differs from popular belief.

357. Hastings, Max. Victory in Europe: D-Day to V-E Day. Little, Brown, 1985. 192 p. ill. $25.

Gr 9+. B 81: Jun 15 1985. LJ 110: Jul 1985. From the only color documentary film of the war 200 photos never before published were selected for this work. They are accompanied by a lively and informative text covering allied activities from June 1944 to April 1945.

358. Hough, Richard. Battle of Britain: The Greatest Air Battle of World War II. Norton, 1989. 397 p. $30.

Gr 10+. B 86: Nov 1 1989. Events leading up to the Battle of Britain and details of the battle are presented in this account, based on over 300 interviews with survivors.

359. Lord, Walter. Miracle of Dunkirk, The. Viking, 1982. 323 p. ill. $18.

Gr 9+. B 79: Sep 1 1982. LJ 107: Oct 1 1982. SLJ 29: Apr 1983. Lord's hour-by-hour chronicle of the rescue of thousands of Allied troops by British civilians is filled with rich detail.

360. Markl, Julia. Battle of Britain. (Turning Points of World War II). Watts, 1984. 106 p. ill. $10.

Gr 6+. B 81: Dec 15 1984. BR 4: Sep/Oct 1985. SLJ 31: Dec 1984. VOYA 7: Feb 1985. Markl presents a balanced account of the Battle of Britain, covering the causes, preparations, goals, events, and results from both the Allied and Axis perspectives.

361. Saunders, Alan. Invasion of Poland, The. (Turning Points of World War II). Watts, 1984. 104 p. ill. $10.

Gr 6-10. B 81: Dec 15 1984. + - BR 4: Sep/Oct 1985. SLJ 31: Dec 1984. This concise, illustrated account of the causes, events, and results of the Nazi invasion of Poland discusses the impact of this invasion on the course of the war.

362. Skipper, G. C. Battle of Britain. (World at War). Childrens Press, 1980. 44 p. ill. Lib. ed. $6.

Gr 4-7. B 77: Feb 1 1981. - SLJ 27: Mar 1981. Skipper's brief, illustrated introductory overview of the Battle of Britain includes some fictionalized dialogue.

363. Skipper, G. C. Battle of Stalingrad. (World at War). Childrens Press, 1981. 44 p. ill. $7.

Gr 4-7. B 78: Jan 15 1982. This brief, introductory overview of the Battle of Stalingrad includes some fictionalized dialogue.

364. Skipper, G. C. Invasion of Poland. (World at War). Childrens Press, 1983. 48 p. ill. $7.

Gr 4-7. B 80: Feb 15 1984. + - SLJ 30: Apr 1984. The causes and events of the Nazi invasion of Poland are explained in this brief, illustrated overview.

365. Stein, R. Conrad. Dunkirk. (World at War). Childrens Press, 1982. 46 p. ill. $7.

Gr 4-6. B 79: Feb 15 1983. SLJ 29: Apr 1983. The remarkable accomplishments of British civilians who rescued their army from the beaches at Normandy in 1940 are introduced in Stein's illustrated account.

366. Stein, R. Conrad. Fall of Singapore. (World at War). Childrens Press, 1982. 45 p. ill. $7.

Gr 4-6, B 79: Feb 15 1983. Stein's concise, illustrated, and simply written account is an introduction to the battle of Singapore, a city that was thought to be safe, but which fell to the Japanese in three months.

367. Stein, R. Conrad. Invasion of Russia. (World at War). Childrens Press, 1985. 47 p. ill. $8.

Gr 4-7. B 82: Oct 15 1985. SLJ 32: Feb 1986. In a brief, highly illustrated introduction to the battles on the Russian front, Stein shows how Russian tenacity and German misman-agement turned the tide.

368. Stein, R. Conrad. Siege of Leningrad. (World at War). Childrens Press, 1983. 47 p. ill. $7.

Gr 3-6. B 79: Aug 1983. - SLJ 30: Nov 1983. The 900-day siege at Leningrad is concisely and simply introduced in Stein's illustrated work.

Biographies

369. Astor, Gerald. Last Nazi, The. Paperjacks, 1986. 305 p. Pb $4.

Gr 10+. BR 5: Mar/Apr 1987. In exploring Mengele's activities during and after World War II, Astor examines anti-Semit-ism in Europe at that time and in the 1980s.

370. Bierman, John. Righteous Gentile: The Story of Raoul Wallenberg, Missing Hero of the Holocaust. Vi-king, 1981. 209 p. $13.

Gr 9+. B 77: May 1981. LJ 106: Aug 1981. Wallenberg, a Swedish diplomat, is credited with saving nearly 100,000 Hungarian Jews from Nazi death camps. When the Russians occupied Budapest he disappeared. The Soviets insist that he is dead, but Bierman provides evidence that he was alive in Russia in the 1970s.

371. Blanco, Richard L. Rommel the Desert Warrior: The Afrika Korps in World War II. Messner, 1982. 191 p. ill. $10.

Gr 7+. * B 78: Jun 1 1982. SLJ 29: Dec 1982. This biogra-phy of the brilliant German general who led the fighting in Libya and Egypt presents a clear picture of the African cam-paigns and their importance in the war.

372. Butterworth, Emma Macalik. As the Waltz Was Ending. Scholastic, 1982. 187 p. $10.

Gr 7+. B 79: Jan 1 1983. B 85: Jun 15 1989. BC 36: Jun 1983. SLJ 29: Apr 1983. * VOYA 6: Apr 1983. Emma But-terworth's graphic account of her wartime experiences shows the horrors of war in Vienna, first under Nazi domination and then under the Russians. She began the war as a serious stu-dent of ballet but soon was struggling just to survive.

373. Calic, Edouard. Reinhard Heydrich: Key to the Third Reich. Morrow, 1984. 263 p. ill. $16.

Gr 9+. B 81: Dec 1 1984. LJ 110: Jan 1985. Calic shows the development of Heydrich's nationalistic and racist beliefs which led him to become the head of Hitler's SS and Gestapo and to organize the concentration camps.

374. Casey, William. Secret War Against Hitler, The. Regnery Gateway; dist. by Kampmann, 1988. 250 p. $20.

Gr 9+. B 84: May 15 1988. LJ 113: Apr 15 1988. The former head of the CIA discusses the intelligence activities that he managed during World War II.

375. Dolan, Edward F. Adolf Hitler: A Portrait in Tyr-anny. Dodd, 1981. 240 p. ill. $9.

Gr 7+. * B 78: Sep 1 1981. HB 58: Feb 1982. + - SLJ 28: Oct 1981. Dolan relates the significant events in Hitler's life in the context of German history, showing his shrewdness and the horrors of the Third Reich.

376. Gray, Ronald. Hitler and the Germans. (Cam-bridge Topic Book). Lerner, 1983. 35 p. ill. $7.

Gr 6-9. B 80: Oct 1 1983. SLJ 28: Aug 1982. Photos, car-toons, and posters augment this concise introduction to Hitler, his cronies, and the results of his policies.

377. Hecht, Ingeborg. Invisible Walls: A German Fam-ily Under Nuremberg Laws. Harcourt, 1985. 113 p. $14.

Gr 9+. B 82: Oct 1 1985. LJ 110: Oct 1 1985. Hecht tells of the experiences of her family and others who were half-Jewish and half-Aryan and regulated by the brutal Nuremberg Laws.

378. Huneke, Douglas K. Moses of Rovno: The Stir-ring Story of Fritz Graebe, a German Christian Who Risked His Life to Lead Hundreds of Jews to Safety During the Holocaust. Dodd, 1985. 222 p. $18.

Gr 9+. B 82: Nov 1 1985. LJ 110: Nov 1 1985. By providing them with false papers Graebe was able to rescue over a thou-sand Jews from the Nazis. After he served as a witness at Nuremberg his family was ostracized and moved to the United States.

379. Hunt, Antonia. Little Resistance: A Teenage Eng-lish Girl's Adventures in Occupied France. St. Martin's, 1982. 149 p. ill. $10.

Gr 9+. B 79: Jan 15 1983. LJ 107: Dec 1 1982. Antonia Hunt was a naive British teenager trapped in France by the outbreak of the war. Thought to be a part of the Resistance she was imprisoned.

380. Irving, David. Goering: A Biography. Morrow, 1989. 512 p. ill. $23.

Gr 9+. B 85: Jan 15 1989. The details of Goering's personal and political life are presented in this balanced biography.

381. Koehn, Ilse. Mischling, Second Degree: My Childhood in Nazi Germany. Greenwillow, 1977. 240 p. $13.

Gr 7+. B 74: Dec 1 1977. B 85: Jun 15 1989. * BC 31: Jan 1978. HB 53: Dec 1977. * SLJ 24: Nov 1977. Although Koehn's family was strongly anti-Nazi, and she is part Jewish, her survival required that she be a member of the Hitler Youth groups. Her account of the confusion and fear of the war years covers political and military events and personal experi-ences.

382. Lampton, Christopher. Wernher Von Braun. Watts, 1988. 160 p. ill. $12.

Gr 5+. B 85: Nov 1 1988. * BR 7: Jan 1989. SLJ 35: Feb 1989. VOYA 12: Apr 1989. This biography of Von Braun emphasizes his work as a German rocket scientist responsible for the V-2 that blitzed London, but also covers his role in the United States space program in the 1960s.

383. Laquer, Walter. Breaking the Silence. Simon & Schuster, 1987. 320 p. Pb $9.

Gr 9+. SLJ 34: Feb 1988. Edward Schulte was a German industrialist who exposed Nazi treatment of the Jews.

384. Lester, Eleanore. Wallenberg: The Man in the Iron Web. Prentice-Hall, 1982. 183 p. ill. $13.

Gr 10+. SLJ 34: Feb 1988. Wallenberg was a noted Swede who risked his life to rescue thousands of Jews, only to disappear into the Soviet prison system at the end of the war. Lester speculates on his fate and whether he was involved in espionage.

385. Luck, Hans von. Panzer Commander. Praeger, 1989. 282 p. ill. $25.

Gr 10+. B 86: Oct 15 1989. LJ 114: Oct 15 1989. Von Luck was a commander of the elite Panzer Division. His memoirs discuss military events of the war, the leadership of Rommel, and German attitudes toward Hitler.

386. Lyttle, Richard B. Duce: The Rise & Fall of Benito Mussolini. Atheneum, 1987. 213 p. $14.

Gr 7+. B 84: Oct 1 1987. * BC 41: Sep 1987. HB 64: Jan/Feb 1988. SLJ 34: Jan 1988. This balanced chronological account of Mussolini's life shows the growth of Fascism in Italy.

387. Marrin, Albert. Hitler. Viking, 1987. 249 p. ill. $14.

Gr 8+. B 83: Jul 1987. * BR 6: Jan/Feb 1988. HB 63: Sep/Oct 1987. * SLJ 33: Jun/Jul 1987. Marrin provides insight into the development of Hitler's charismatic personality, the reasons for his political success, and the results of his fanatic hatreds.

388. Marton, Kati. Wallenberg. Random, 1982. 243 p. $15.

Gr 10+. B 78: Apr 15 1982. LJ 107: May 15 1982. VOYA 5: Dec 1982. Merton's vivid account of the life and work of the Swedish diplomat who saved thousands of Hungarian Jews from the Nazis includes information from numerous interviews with persons who worked with him.

389. Nicholson, Michael. Raoul Wallenberg. (People Who Have Helped the World). Gareth Stevens, 1989. 68 p. ill. Lib. ed. $13.

Gr 5-9. B 85: Aug 1989. SLJ 35: Nov 1989. A chronology, glossary, quotations, and photos enrich this introduction to the life of a Swedish diplomat who saved 100,000 Jews from the Nazis.

390. Rubenstein, Joshua. Adolf Hitler. (Impact Biography). Watts, 1982. 120 p. ill. $9.

Gr 6+. B 79: Feb 1 1983. SLJ 29: Nov 1982. Excerpts from the writings of Hitler and his supporters clarify his beliefs and personality. Rubenstein also describes Hitler's youth and his abilities as an organizer and politician.

391. Skipper, G. C. Death of Hitler. (World at War). Childrens Press, 1980. 44 p. ill. Lib. ed. $6.

Gr 4-7. B 77: Feb 1 1981. + - SLJ 27: Mar 1981. This brief, introductory overview of the events surrounding the death of Hitler includes some fictionalized dialogue.

392. Skipper, G. C. Fall of the Fox: Rommel. (World at War). Childrens Press, 1980. 46 p. ill. Lib. ed. $6.

Gr 4-7. B 77: Feb 1 1981. + - SLJ 27: Mar 1981. This brief, introductory overview of Rommel's military career includes some fictionalized dialogue.

393. Skipper, G. C. Goering and the Luftwaffe. (World at War). Childrens Press, 1980. 44 p. ill. Lib. ed. $6.

Gr 4-7. B 77: Feb 1 1981. + - SLJ 27: Mar 1981. This brief, introductory overview of Goering's military leadership includes some fictionalized dialogue.

394. Skipper, G. C. Mussolini: A Dictator Dies. (World at War). Childrens Press, 1981. 44 p. ill. $6.

Gr 3-6. B 77: Jul 1981. SLJ 28: Sep 1981. This brief, illustrated overview of Mussolini's life and the events surrounding his death includes some fictionalized dialogue.

395. Smith, Danny. Wallenberg: Lost Hero. Templegate, 1987. 192 p. Pb $9.

Gr 9+. B 83: Apr 1 1987. This chronological account tells of the heroic rescue of Hungarian Jews by Wallenberg, a Swedish Protestant, from 1942 until he was captured by the Russians in 1945.

396. Stone, Norman. Hitler. Little, Brown, 1980. 195 p. ill. $13.

Gr 9+. B 77: Sep 1 1980. LJ 105: Jun 1 1980. Stone's concise work analyzes Hitler's career and the policies of the Nazi party.

397. Swearingen, Ben E. Mystery of Hermann Goering's Suicide, The. Harcourt, 1985. 223 p. $23.

Gr 9+. B 82: Oct 1 1985. Swearingen speculates that an American guard assisted Goering in committing suicide so he could avoid hanging following his trial at Nuremberg.

398. Tames, Richard. Nazi Germany. (Living Through History). Batsford; dist. by David & Charles, 1986. 72 p. ill. $15.

Gr 9+. SLJ 32: Apr 1986. Profiles of persons who supported and opposed Hitler present a balanced view of life in Germany during the Nazi era.

399. Thomas, Walter Hugh. Murder of Rudolf Hess, The. Harper, 1979. 214 p. ill. $10.

Gr 9+. B 76: Nov 1 1979. Thomas, a British army surgeon who examined the prisoner in Spandau, argues that the person imprisoned there was not Hess but a double arranged by Himmler.

400. Toland, John. Adolf Hitler. Doubleday; Ballantine, 1976. 1035 p. ill. $20. Pb $10.

Gr 10+. B 82: Jan 1 1986. LJ 101: Aug 1976. Toland based his biography on interviews, documents, reports, correspondence, speeches, and memoirs. The result is a lengthy but readable and enlightening account of Hitler's personality, political beliefs, and actions.

401. Von der Grun, Max. Howl Like the Wolves: Growing Up in Nazi Germany. Morrow, 1980. 285 p. ill. $10. Lib. ed. $10.

Gr 8+. BC 34: Feb 1981. * SE 45: Apr 1981. + - SLJ 27: Dec 1980. In telling the story of his youth Von der Grun incorporates excerpts from speeches, documents, and letters that record the violence of the Third Reich.

402. Von Hassell, Fey. Hostage of the Third Reich: Story of My Imprisonment and Rescue from the SS. Scribner, 1989. 288 p. ill. $23.

Gr 9+. B 86: Oct 1 1989. The author's father was one of the persons executed as a result of the aborted effort to assassinate Hitler. She tells of the months she spent in concentration camps and of her rescue.

403. Willmott, Phyllis. Coming of Age in Wartime. Peter Owen; dist. by Dufour Editions, 1988. 154 p. $28.

Gr 9+. B 85: Sep 15 1988. The Blitz and the difficulties of life in wartime England are told in Phyllis Willmott's autobiography. This is a sequel to A Green Girl.

404. Zamoyska-Panek, Christine. Have You Forgotten? A Memoir of Poland, 1939-1945. Doubleday, 1989. 336 p. ill. $20.

Gr 9+. B 86: Sep 1 1989. Christine Zamoyska-Panek, who was a 16-year-old Polish countess when the war began, presents a moving memoir of her experiences under the Nazi and Soviet occupations of Poland.

405. Zeller, Frederic. When Time Ran Out: Coming of Age in the Third Reich. Permanent Press, 1989. 205 p. $20.

Gr 9+. B 85: Mar 1 1989. LJ 114: Apr 15 1989. Zeller was an adolescent boy growing up in Berlin as Hitler came to power. His account of the growing threat to the Jews, his escape, and the deaths of family members is based on his notes and diaries.

Children

406. David, Kati. Child's War: Fifteen Children Tell Their Story. Four Walls Eight Windows, 1989. 204 p. $18.

Gr 9+. B 85: May 1 1989. LJ 114: May 1 1989. David presents the wartime experiences of many types of children–Jews, Gypsies, Germans, Hungarians, and English, as well as the children of resistance fighters and Nazi collaborators.

407. Duboscq, Genevieve. My Longest Night. Seaver Books; dist. by Grove Press, 1981. 284 p. ill. $14.

Gr 9+. B 77: Jun 15 1981. + - LJ 106: Apr 1 1981. During the D-Day invasions many American soldiers and their supplies landed in the marshes surrounding the farm home of the author's family. This grim and dramatic story tells of a little girl's experiences during this dangerous time.

408. Westall, Robert. Children of the Blitz: Memories of a Wartime Childhood. Viking, 1986. 237 p. $17.

Gr 7+. B 82: Feb 15 1986. LJ 111: Mar 1 1986. Adults describe their childhood experiences in Britain during the war, including forced separation from families, food shortages, spies, blackouts, fun, excitement, and tedium.

409. Wicks, Ben. No Time to Wave Goodbye. St. Martin's, 1989. 240 p. ill. $16.

Gr 10+. B 86: Sep 1 1989. LJ 114: Sep 1 1989. Excerpts from thousands of interviews with persons who were, as children, evacuated from London, show both the beneficial and the tragic results of this policy.

Concentration Camps

410. Chamberlin, Brewster. Liberation of the Nazi Concentration Camps 1945: Eyewitness Accounts of the Liberators. U. S. Government Printing Office, 1987. 214 p. ill. $12.

Gr 10+. BR 6: Jan/Feb 1988. SLJ 34: Feb 1988. Testimony of survivors of concentration camps and their liberators reveals what they saw and how it affected their lives.

411. Kulka, Erich. Escape from Auschwitz. Bergin & Garvey, 1986. 150 p. ill. $28. Pb $13.

Gr 9+. B 82: Apr 1 1986. This true story that reads like fiction presents a dramatic account of how Pestek, an SS guard at Auschwitz, helped a prisoner escape.

Espionage and Spies

412. Bar-Zohar, Michael. Arrows of the Almighty: The Most Extraordinary True Spy Story of World War II. Macmillan, 1985. 224 p. $16.

Gr 9+. B 82: Sep 1 1985. + - LJ 110: Sep 1 1985. Improbable but true is this story of a Jew who was released from a concentration camp by the Nazis and sent to spy on the British in Palestine.

413. Bloch, Michael. Operation Willi: The Plot to Kidnap the Duke of Windsor, July 1940. Weidenfeld & Nicholson, 1986. 266 p. ill. $18.

Gr 9+. B 83: Sep 1 1986. + - LJ 111: Nov 15 1986. In 1940 the Germans plotted to convince the Duke of Windsor to support their cause, with the promise of returning him to his throne.

414. Breuer, William B. Secret War with Germany: Deception, Espionage, and Dirty Tricks. Presidio, 1988. 278 p. ill. $18.

Gr 9+. B 84: Nov 15 1987. LJ 113: Mar 1 1988. Accounts of dummy airfields, double agents, and electronic espionage are included in this broad coverage of covert operations in the European theater.

415. Goldston, Robert C. Sinister Touches: The Secret War Against Hitler. Dial, 1982. 192 p. $12.

Gr 7+. B 78: May 1 1982. * BC 35: Jul/Aug 1982. HB 58: Jun 1982. * SLJ 28: Apr 1982. * VOYA 5: Dec 1982. This lively history of World War II focuses on espionage activities, telling the reasons, events, and results of each, as well as providing information on persons involved in espionage on both sides.

416. Mosley, Leonard. Druid, The. Atheneum, 1981. 256 p. $13.

Gr 9+. B 77: Mar 15 1981. + - LJ 106: Feb 15 1981. SLJ 28: Sep 1981. Convinced that a German victory would mean freedom for his native Wales, "The Druid" spied in Great Britain for the Nazis throughout the war and was never caught.

Espionage and Spies–Fiction

417. Westall, Robert. Fathom Five. Greenwillow, 1980. 256 p. $8. Lib. ed. $8.

Gr 7+. B 77: Nov 1 1980. BC 34: Oct 1980. + - HB 56: Oct 1980. SLJ 27: Oct 1980. VOYA 3: Feb 1981. In a dramatic and fast-moving adventure, 16-year-old Chas' efforts to track down a German spy become deadly dangerous. Set in England in 1943, this is a sequel to the Machine Gunners.

Fiction

418. Allan, Mabel Esther. Lovely Tomorrow, A. Dodd, 1980. 186 p. $7.

Gr 7+. + - B 76: Apr 1 1980. + - BC 33: Jul/Aug 1980. - SLJ 26: Apr 1980. VOYA 3: Aug 1980. After her parents are killed in a bombing raid on London in 1944, Frue has to live with her domineering aunt.

419. Allan, Mabel Esther. Strange Enchantment, A. Dodd, 1982. 191 p. $9.

Gr 7+. B 78: Jul 1982. + - BC 36: Nov 1982. + - SLJ 29: Sep 1982. * VOYA 6: Feb 1983. An English girl decided to do her bit for the war effort by working on a farm, but it turned out to be harder work than she expected.

420. Baer, Frank. Max's Gang. Little, Brown, 1983. 281 p. $17.

Gr 6+. B 79: Jun 1 1983. BC 37: Oct 1983. HB 59: Jun 1983. + - SLJ 30: Sep 1983. SLJ 31: Oct 1984. + - VOYA 6: Oct 1983. In the chaos during the last days of the war a group of children became separated from responsible adults and had to survive enemy troops, illness, and starvation. Based on the experiences of survivors.

421. Baklanov, Grigory. Forever Nineteen. Harper, 1989. 176 p. ill. $14. Lib. ed. $14.

Gr 7+. B 85: May 1 1989. HB 65: Sep/Oct 1989. + - SLJ 35: May 1989. Baklanov's powerful novel about a young Russian soldier is based on his own experiences. It shows authentically the confusion of war and the tragedy of lost youth.

422. Ballard, J. G. Empire of the Sun. Simon & Schuster; Pocket/Washington Square Press, 1984. 302 p. $17. Pb $5.

Gr 7+. B 82: Apr 15 1986. B 85: Nov 1 1988. LJ 109: Nov 1 1984. When the Japanese captured Shanghai, 11 year-old Jim was separated from his parents and had to rely on himself during 3 years in a prison camp.

423. Bawden, Nina. Henry. Lothrop, 1988. 99 p. ill. $13.

Gr 3-6. * B 84: Apr 15 1988. BC 41: Mar 1988. HB 64: May/Jun 1988. * SLJ 34: Apr 1988. Adjustment to change and loss is the theme of this story about a British family who befriended an injured squirrel while their father was gone to war.

424. Benchley, Nathaniel. Bright Candles, The. Harper, 1974. 256 p. $14.

Gr 7-10. * B 70: Mar 1 1974. B 84: Jul 1988. B 85: Jun 15 1989. BC 27: Jul 1974. HB 50: Jun 1974. * LJ 99: May 15 1974. SLJ 29: Apr 1983. Through the story of 16-year-old Jens and his involvement with the Resistance, the reader sees how the war affected life in Denmark.

425. Bishop, Claire. Twenty and Ten. Peter Smith; Penguin, 1952; 1984. 73 p. ill. $14. Pb $4.

Gr 5-9. Metzner. B 49: Oct 15 1952. * HB 28: Oct 1952. * LJ 77: Oct 1 1952. A compelling story about the courage and compassion of 20 children in a French convent school who protected 10 Jewish children when the Nazis came.

426. Boulle, Pierre. Bridge over the River Kwai, The. Bantam, 1954. 224 p. Pb $3.

Gr 9+. B 51: Oct 15 1954. B 84: Jul 1988. LJ 79: Oct 1 1954. The Japanese have instructed their prisoner, Colonel Nicholson, to supervise other British prisoners in the construction of a critical railway bridge. In his determination to prove the quality of his men, the Colonel loses sight of the objectives of the war.

427. Buchan, Stuart. All Our Yesterdays. Crosswinds, 1987. 154 p. $3.

Gr 7-8. + - VOYA 10: Dec 1987. Julie, who spent the war years safely in England, returned to Malaya to her family, who spent those years in prison camps. This is the story of their adjustment to the changes in their lives.

428. Burnford, Sheila Every. Bel Ria. Atlantic; dist. by Little, Brown, 1978. 215 p. $13.

Gr 9+. B 74: Jan 15 1978. B 84: Jul 1988. SLJ 26: Aug 1980. Vivid descriptions of wartime strengthen this warm novel about a carnival dog who is left homeless by the war, and the people whom he befriends.

429. Bykov, Vasil. Pack of Wolves. Crowell, 1981. 181 p. $11. Lib. ed. $10.

Gr 7+. B 78: Jan 1 1982. BC 35: Jan 1982. SLJ 28: Oct 1981. SLJ 31: Oct 1984. The elderly Levchuk reminisces about the early days of World War II when he, three other soldiers, and a pregnant radio operator hid in the swamp to escape the Germans and their dogs.

430. Cooper, Susan. Dawn of Fear, The. Harcourt, 1970. 157 p. ill. $6.

Gr 5-7. B 83: Apr 15 1987. HB 46: Oct 1970. HB 58: Aug 1982. LJ 95: Nov 15 1970. A group of English children grow up doing all the normal things while around them men leave for war and air raids bring destruction and death.

431. Coulonges, Henri. Farewell, Dresden. Summit, 1989. 266 p. $19.

Gr 9+. B 85: Dec 15 1988. The terror of wartime is clearly represented in this story of a girl who was caught in the firebombing of Dresden.

432. Degens, T. Transport 7-41-R. Viking, 1974. 171 p. $12.

Gr 6-9. * B 71: Sep 1 1974. B 71: Mar 15 1975. B 85: Jun 15 1989. BC 28: Mar 1975. HB 50: Oct 1974. LJ 99: Dec 15 1974. An independent 13-year-old girl is one of a group of evacuees traveling on a freight train out of the Russian zone to Cologne in 1946. The details of her friendship with an elderly couple and the trials of their trip are merged in a powerful rite-of-passage story.

433. Degens, T. Visit, The. Viking, 1982. 150 p. $11.

Gr 6-10. + - B 79: Nov 1 1982. BC 36: Nov 1982. * BR 1: Nov/Dec 1982. HB 59: Feb 1983. + - SLJ 29: Oct 1982. * VOYA 6: Apr 1983. This account of two sisters' experiences at a Hitler youth camp in 1943 shows how the selfish ambitions of the elder led to the death of her more perceptive younger sister.

434. Deighton, Len. Goodbye, Mickey Mouse. Knopf, 1982. 355 p. $14.

Gr 9+. B 79: Sep 1 1982. LJ 107: Sep 1 1982. The friendship and adventures of two fighter pilots who escort bombers over Germany are detailed in a gripping story.

435. Dial, Joan. Echoes of War. St. Martin's, 1984. 352 p. $14.

Gr 9+. B 81: Nov 15 1984. LJ 110: Jan 1985. Tony is in the Royal Air Force and Kate works in the French underground. The story of their wartime romance is filled with excitement.

436. Fife, Dale. Destination Unknown. Dutton, 1981. 96 p. $10.

Gr 4-8. B 78: Feb 1 1982. HB 58: Feb 1982. SLJ 28: Nov 1981. Twelve-year-old Jon smuggles aboard a Norwegian fishing vessel, thinking it will take him to his parents. When the war interferes he and the crew risk U-boats, icebergs, and the stormy Atlantic to reach safety in the United States.

437. Finlay, Lilian Roberts. Always in My Mind. St. Martin's, 1989. 352 p. $19.

Gr 9+. B 85: Jan 15 1989. + - LJ 114: Jan 1989. The unwavering love of an Irish woman and a Jewish man is tested when they are separated by the war and he is captured and sent to Auschwitz.

438. Gardam, Jane. Long Way from Verona, A. Macmillan, 1972. 190 p. $5.

Gr 6+. B 68: Jun 1 1972. BC 26: Sep 1972. HB 48: Aug 1972. LJ 97: Jun 15 1972. * VOYA 11: Feb 1989. Jessica, age 13, is an aspiring writer who lives in the English countryside during World War II. Her humorous and perceptive story was an award winner when it was first published in 1971.

439. Gehrts, Barbara. Don't Say a Word. Macmillan, 1986. 169 p. $12.

Gr 7+. B 83: Oct 1 1986. B 85: Jun 15 1989. BC 40: Nov 1986. HB 63: Mar/Apr 1987. + - SLJ 33: Dec 1986. VOYA 9: Feb 1987. In fictional form the author records her family's experiences. Her father was a Luftwaffe officer who opposed Hitler and was executed. Her brother and first love both died, and their home was totally destroyed, leaving her and her mother in a war-torn land.

440. Gessner, Lynne. Edge of Darkness. Walker, 1979. 181 p. $9.

Gr 6+. BC 33: Jan 1980. HB 56: Feb 1980. - SLJ 26: Nov 1979. + - VOYA 2: Feb 1980. A 13-year-old Latvian peasant boy and his family are the focus of this dramatic story that shows the destruction of the land by the occupying Russians and Germans, and the struggle of the people to endure.

441. Gillham, Bill. Home Before Long. Andre Deutsch; dist. by Dutton, 1984. 102 p. ill. $11.

Gr 3-5. B 80: Aug 1984. HB 60: Jun 1984. + - SLJ 31: Sep 1984. Dorothy and Billy are evacuated from their London home to live in the country. Their host family is unfriendly and the children save their money so they can run away to London to find their mother.

442. Hartling, Peter. Crutches. Lothrop, 1988. 163 p. $12.

Gr 5-9. B 85: Feb 1 1989, Apr 1 1989, Jun 15 1989. BC 42: Nov 1988. HB 64: Nov/Dec 1988. + - SLJ 35: Nov 1988. VOYA 12: Feb 1989. When Thomas is separated from his mother immediately after the war he is helped by a one-legged veteran. His story shows the chaos and drudgery of life in war-torn Europe.

443. Hartman, Evert. War Without Friends. Crown, 1982. 218 p. $11.

Gr 7+. B 79: Sep 1 1982. BC 36: Dec 1982. HB 58: Dec 1982. * SE 47: Apr 1983. SLJ 29: Oct 1982. VOYA 5: Dec 1982. VOYA 6: Jun 1983. Arnold has accepted the beliefs of his father, a fervent Nazi. They live in occupied Holland where Nazis are few, and lonely Arnold gradually examines his beliefs.

444. Haugaard, Erik Christian. Chase Me, Catch Nobody! Houghton, 1980. 192 p. $8.

Gr 5-9. B 76: May 1 1980. BC 33: Jun 1980. HB 56: Jun 1980. + - SLJ 26: Apr 1980. VOYA 3: Aug 1980. While on a school trip from Denmark to Germany in 1937, 14-year-old Erik inadvertently became a target of the Gestapo and helped a Jewish girl escape to freedom.

445. Hennessy, Max. Once More the Hawks. Atheneum, 1984. 216 p. $12.

Gr 9+. + - B 80: Mar 1 1984. + - LJ 109: Feb 15 1984. The continuing adventures of Dicken Quinney, pilot, take him to all the hot spots of the war.

446. Heuck, Sigrid. Hideout, The. Dutton, 1988. 183 p. $14.

Gr 4-9. + - B 84: Aug 1988. BC 41: Jun 1988. + - HB 64: Jul/Aug 1988. + - SLJ 35: Jun/Jul 1988. An orphaned girl finds security in an orphanage and a friendship until the war comes closer and her world crumbles.

447. Horgan, Dorothy. Edge of War, The. Oxford University Press, 1988. 112 p. $14.

Gr 5-8. + - B 84: Jul 1988. B 85: Jun 15 1989. - BC 41: Jul 1988. - SLJ 35: Jun/Jul 1988. Anna's German Catholic family were not Nazis and so received second-class citizen treatment. A series of vignettes tells of their experiences.

448. Hough, Richard. Razor Eyes. Dutton, 1983. 117 p. $11.

Gr 7+. B 80: Oct 1 1983. BC 37: Apr 1984. BR 5: May/Jun 1986. HB 60: Feb 1984. SLJ 30: Jan 1984. VOYA 7: Jun 1984. Based on his own experience, Hough tells the story of a young pilot who overcame his fears and became a hero because of his extremely sharp eyesight.

449. Innocenti, Roberto. Rose Blanche. Creative Education, 1985. 32 p. ill. $15.

Gr 5-7. B 82: Nov 1 1985. B 83: Sep 15 1986. B 83: Mar 1 1987. + - SLJ 32: Oct 1985. SLJ 34: Jan 1988. For students with background on the war, an emotion-packed picture book account of Rose, a little German girl who takes food daily to a nearby concentration camp and is killed in the crossfire at the end of the war.

450. Kennedy, Lena. Kitty. Pocket Books, 1981. 309 p. $3.

Gr 8+. BR 1: May/Jun 1982. This easy-to-read romance tells the story of Kitty, who lived in London during the war.

451. Kerr, M. E. Gentlehands. Harper; Bantam, 1978. 192 p. $13. Pb $3.

Gr 7+. B 74: Mar 15 1978. B 85: Jun 15 1989. BC 31: Apr 1978. HB 54: Jun 1978. SLJ 24: Mar 1978. SLJ 24: May 1978. Buddy discovers that his grandfather is not the cultured gentleman that he appears to be, but is a wanted Nazi war criminal.

452. Koehn, Ilse. Tilla. Greenwillow, 1981. 240 p. $9.

Gr 10+. + - B 78: Oct 1 1981. + - BC 35: Nov 1981. SLJ 28: Oct 1981. + - VOYA 4: Feb 1982. In this realistic and complex autobiographical story set at the end of the war, a teenage girl and boy, whose families are dead, meet as they travel through the devastated countryside toward Berlin.

453. Korschunow, Irina. Night in Distant Motion, A. Godine, 1983. 151 p. $11.

Gr 7+. B 80: Oct 15 1983. B 85: Jun 15 1989. BC 37: Jan 1984. HB 59: Dec 1983. + - VOYA 6: Feb 1984. In a series of flashbacks Regine remembers her youth in Germany. During the early days of the war she accepted Nazi doctrine, but after she met a Polish Jew her changing attitudes put her in danger.

454. Lingard, Joan. File on Fraulein Berg, The. Elsevier/Nelson, 1980. 153 p. $8.

Gr 6-9. B 76: Apr 15 1980. BC 34: Jan 1981. HB 56: Aug 1980. + - SLJ 26: May 1980. Three friends decide that the German woman who has come to teach at their Dublin school is a spy, and they determine to prove it. Because of their persecutions she eventually leaves, but years later they learn that she was a Jewish refugee.

455. Lowry, Lois. Number the Stars. Houghton, 1989. 160 p. $13.

Gr 3-7. * B 85: Mar 1 1989. BC 42: Mar 1989. HB 65: May/Jun 1989. * SLJ 35: Mar 1989. An appended author's note describes the real events on which this story is based. It concerns the courage of a Danish family in protecting their daughter's Jewish friend and in smuggling other Jews out of the country.

456. MacBeth, George. Katana, The. Simon & Schuster, 1982. 239 p. $15.

Gr 9+. B 78: Feb 15 1982. LJ 107: Jan 1 1982. SLJ 28: Mar 1982. This novel of espionage and high adventure is set in the China-Burma-India area. It involves double agents and an attempt to assassinate Lord Mountbatten in India in 1944.

457. Mace, Elisabeth. Brother Enemy. Beaufort, 1981. 175 p. $11.

Gr 6-10. HB 57: Oct 1981. + - SLJ 27: Apr 1981. Seven-year-old Andreas is sent from his home in Hamburg to England because he is half Jewish. He endures the war years feeling an alien, only to return to Germany in 1947 and find that the culture he remembers has been destroyed.

458. MacLean, Alistair. Guns of Navarone, The. Fawcett, 1957. 320 p. Pb $3.

Gr 9+. B 53: Feb 1 1957. B 84: Jul 1988. HB 33: Jun 1957. LJ 82: Mar 15 1957. This realistic story, filled with tension and suspense, concerns a group of British commandoes attempting to destroy German guns that endangered the lives of 1200 British soldiers.

459. Magorian, Michelle. Good Night, Mr. Tom. Harper, 1982. 318 p. $12. Lib. ed. $11.

Gr 7+. * B 78: Apr 15 1982. BC 35: Mar 1982. HB 58: Jun 1982. * SE 47: Apr 1983. + - SLJ 28: Apr 1982. VOYA 5: Jun 1982. Willie, an abused evacuee from London, is sent to the country to stay with a crusty recluse. This warm story shows the growth of their affection and details of life in wartime England.

460. Maspero, Francois. Cat's Grin. Knopf, 1986. 308 p. $17.

Gr 9+. B 82: Apr 15 1986. LJ 111: May 1 1986. The war in occupied France is seen in this autobiographical novel of a boy whose family is destroyed by the war.

461. Mattingley, Christobel. Angel with a Mouth Organ, The. Holiday, 1986. 185 p. ill. $13.

Gr 3-5. B 83: Mar 1 1987. * BC 39: Mar 1986. * SE 51: Apr/May 1987. + - SLJ 33: Oct 1986. A mother shares her childhood memories of a Christmas in war-torn Europe when her refugee family was driven from place to place, hungry, cold, and fearful.

462. McSwigen, Marie. Snow Treasure. Scholastic, 1942; 1986. 178 p. Pb $3.

Gr 4-9. Metzner. B 38: Mar 15 1942. * HB 18: May 1942. LJ 67: Mar 14 1942. Based on fact, this is the story of a 12-year-old Norwegian boy who, with his friends, brought gold down the mountain on sleds and hid it under snowmen until grownups could smuggle it out of the country so that the Nazi conquerors could not get it.

463. Mulisch, Harry. Assault, The. Pantheon, 1985. 162 p. $13.

Gr 9+. B 81: Jun 15 1985. LJ 110: Jun 1 1985. Anton was a boy when his Dutch family was imprisoned for resistance activities. This powerful novel tells of his search for the truth about the complex events that resulted in the deaths of his mother, father, and brother.

464. Noonan, Michael. McKenzie's Boots. Orchard, 1988. 249 p. $14. Lib. ed. $14.

Gr 7+. B 84: Apr 1 1988. BC 41: Apr 1988. BR 7: Nov/Dec 1988. - SLJ 34: Apr 1988. VOYA 11: Aug 1988. At age 15 Rod McKenzie is 6 feet tall, so he is able to bluff his way into the Australian army, which sends the naive and still growing boy to fight in the New Guinea jungle.

465. Panger, Daniel. Search in Gomorrah. Dembner Books; dist. by Norton, 1982. 243 p. $14.

Gr 10+. - LJ 107: Jul 1982. VOYA 6: Feb 1983. An American soldier who has killed 5 unarmed members of the German SS tries to discover what kind of men they were in this graphic and explicit war novel.

466. Paretti, Sandra. Maria Canossa. St. Martin's, 1981. 294 p. $12.

Gr 10+. B Jul 1 1981. LJ 106: Jun 1 1981. SLJ 28: Sep 1981. Occupied Rome in 1943 is the setting for this novel of intrigue, suspense, and romance.

467. Phillips, Michael. Shadows Over Stonewycke. Bethany House, 1988. 400 p. Pb $7.

Gr 6+. + - VOYA 12: Apr 1989. Logan is a member of the French underground. Allison, his wife, remains in England. The realities of war strain their marriage and their religious beliefs.

468. Pople, Maureen. Other Side of the Family, The. Holt, 1988. 166 p. $14.

Gr 6-10. B 84: Jun 15 1988. BC 42: Oct 1988. Sent for safety to the interior of Australia where an unknown grandmother lives, Kate gains new insights into human relations. Her story provides a sense of time and place.

469. Prince, Alison. How's Business. Four Winds, 1988. 139 p. $13.

Gr 4-7. B 85: Nov 15 1988. BC 42: Oct 1988. + - SLJ 35: Sep 1988. + - VOYA 11: Dec 1988. The war forces Howard's mother to send him to stay with relatives in the countryside, but he is lonely and tormented by bullies, so when letters stop coming from his mother he runs away to London.

470. Ramati, Alexander. And the Violins Stopped Playing: A Story of the Gypsy Holocaust. Watts, 1986. 236 p. $16.

Gr 9+. B 83: Sep 1 1986. B 85: Jun 15 1989. * BR 5: Nov 1986. LJ 111: Oct 15 1986. SLJ 33: Jan 1987. VOYA 9: Feb 1987. Ramati based his story on notes kept by a Gypsy whose family was sent to Birkenau, where most of them died along with half a million other Gypsies.

471. Rees, David. Exeter Blitz, The. Elsevier/Nelson, 1980. 128 p. $7.

Gr 5-10. B 77: Sep 1 1980. HB 56: Oct 1980. + - SLJ 27: Sep 1980. This vivid account of the experiences of one family during the devastating bombing of Exeter, England, in 1942 shows how warfare affects civilians.

472. Richmond, Donald. Dunkirk Directive, The. Stein & Day, 1980. 375 p. $11.

Gr 9+. B 76: Jul 15 1980. + - LJ 105: Jun 15 1980. During the confusion of the retreat at Dunkirk 12 German soldiers in British uniforms gain entry to England in order to destroy a strategic bomber factory.

473. Richter, Hans Peter. Friedrich. Penguin, 1970. 149 p. Pb $5.

Gr 5-9. B 67: Apr 1 1971. B 85: Jun 15 1989. BC 24: Feb 1971. HB 47: Apr 1971. LJ 96: May 15 1971. The narrator is a German boy from a poor family. His best friend is Friedrich, a Jewish boy who lives upstairs. As events of the war sweep both families along, the simply told story shows the victimization of ordinary people.

474. Royce, Kenneth. Channel Assault. McGraw-Hill, 1983. 252 p. $14.

Gr 10+. B 79: Mar 15 1983. LJ 108: Mar 15 1983. A British doctor, a captive on the German-held island of Alderny, seeks to stop a plan to assassinate Churchill.

475. Shute, Nevil. Town Like Alice, A. Heinemann; dist. by David & Charles/Ballantine, 1950. 310 p. $24. Pb $3.

Gr 10+. B 82: May 15 1986. B 84: Jul 1988. The people of Malaya and an Australian soldier helped Jean when she was a Japanese prisoner. Following the war she returned to Malaya to pay her debt of honor and then searched for the soldier who helped her.

476. Smith, Henry T. Last Campaign, The. Walker, 1985. 191 p. $14.

Gr 9+. B 82: Nov 15 1985. This semicomic novel follows a group of German soldiers as they return home from the eastern front at the close of the war.

477. Stachow, Hasso G. If This Be Glory. Doubleday, 1982. 257 p. $15.

Gr 9+. B 78: Apr 15 1982. LJ 107: Mar 1 1982. SLJ 29: Sep 1982. Stachow's fictionalized memoir shows the experiences of a young German soldier on the eastern front, his early training, and his determination to survive to help his nation.

478. Szambelan-Strevinsky, Christine. Dark Hour of Noon. Lippincott, 1982. 215 p. $11. Lib. ed. $11.

Gr 6-9. BC 36: Jan 1983. HB 58: Oct 1982. * SE 47: Apr 1983. - SLJ 29: Oct 1982. VOYA 5: Oct 1982. This dramatic and grim story is about a Polish girl whose innocence is destroyed by the vicious things she sees. She becomes a part of the Polish children's underground and seeks revenge in sabotage and murder.

479. Temperley, Alan. Murdo's War. Cannongate; dist. by David & Charles, 1989. 264 p. $17.

Gr 6-10. SLJ 35: Dec 1989. A harsh Scottish winter plays a role in this espionage adventure in which 12-year-old Murdo and his friend, an elderly fisherman, become involved in a Nazi plan to invade Britain.

480. Tsuchiya, Yukio. Faithful Elephants: A True Story of Animals, People and War. Houghton, 1988. 29 p. ill. $14.

Gr 3-8. BC 42: Nov 1988. HB 65: Jan/Feb 1989. - SLJ 35: Nov 1988. This sad story tells of the decision that the animals in the Tokyo Zoo must die because the bombing of the city might allow them to escape and harm the people.

481. Uhlman, Fred. Reunion. Farrar; Penguin, 1977. 112 p. $7. Pb $4.

Gr 8+. B 73: Mar 15 1977. B 82: May 15 1986. B 84: Jul 1988. LJ 102: Mar 1 1977. The friendship of an aristocratic German youth and a Jewish boy is destroyed by the implementation of Hitler's policies.

482. Vander Els, Betty. Bomber's Moon, The. Farrar, 1985. 167 p. map. $12.

Gr 5-9. B 82: Nov 1 1985. BC 39: Sep 1985. HB 61: Sep/Oct 1985. + - SLJ 31: Aug 1985. VOYA 9: Apr 1986. As the danger of Japanese invasion comes near, Ruth and Simon and other children of missionaries in China are moved from place to place in the Himalayas and India in an effort to keep them safe. This is Ruth's account of their daily experiences.

483. Walsh, Jill Paton. Fireweed. Avon, 1970. 133 p. Pb $2.

Gr 6-9. B 84: Jul 1988. HB 46: Jun 1970. LJ 95: May 15 1970. Bill and Julie were supposed to be among the teenagers evacuated from London during the war, but they refused to leave. Their chance meeting led to their helping each other through the fear and misery of the Blitz.

484. Watkins, Paul. Night over Day over Night. Knopf, 1988. 293 p. $18.

Gr 9+. B 84: Mar 15 1988. + - LJ 113: Apr 1 1988. Although he knows the war is nearly lost, 17-year-old Sebastian enlists in the SS. His increasing loss of innocence and growing bitterness are seen through the vivid accounts of his training and the horrors of battle.

485. Watkins, Yoko Kawashima. So Far from the Bamboo Grove. Lothrop, 1986. 183 p. $11.

Gr 7+. + - B 82: Aug 1986. BC 39: Jun 1986. BR 5: Sep/Oct 1986. HB 62: Jul/Aug 1986. * SE 51: Apr/May 1987. * SLJ 33: Sep 1986. VOYA 9: Aug/Oct 1986. This autobiographical novel is an account of the harrowing flight of a Japanese family from North Korea to Seoul, and finally to Japan at the end of the war, only to find themselves unwelcome there too.

486. Westall, Robert. Blitzcat. Scholastic, 1989. 230 p. $13.

Gr 7+. B 86: Dec 15 1989. + - BC 43: Nov 1989. SLJ 35: Nov 1989. Lord Gort, a cat, searches war-torn Britain and Europe for the pilot who is her owner. A realistic picture of the war is presented through her involvement with humans along the way.

487. Westall, Robert. Machine Gunners, The. Greenwillow, 1976. 186 p. $7. Lib. ed. $6.

Gr 5-9. * B 73: Nov 1 1976. B 83: Apr 15 1987. BC 30: Nov 1976. HB 53: Feb 1977. * SLJ 23: Dec 1976. British Chas and his friends salvage a gun from a crashed German plane to try to fight back against the daily strafing. This taut story is enriched by strong characterizations.

488. Westheimer, David. Von Ryan's Express. New American Library, 1964. 327 p. Pb $4.

Gr 9+. B 84: Jul 1988. LJ 89: Jan 15 1964. In this taut adventure Colonel Ryan leads a group of Allied prisoners of war in a daring escape from a German prison.

489. Williams, Eric. Wooden Horse. Penguin, 1950; 1958. 240 p. Pb $5.

Gr 7+. Metzner. B 46: Jan 15 1950. HB 26: May 1950. * LJ 75: Jan 15 1950. * Feb 15 1950. Williams' suspenseful and accurate novel describes life in a prisoner of war camp and a successful escape.

490. Ziefert, Harriet. New Coat for Anna, A. Knopf, 1986. 32 p. ill. $11. Lib. ed. $11.

Gr K-3. B 83: Mar 1 1987. BC 40: Mar 1987. HB 63: Mar/Apr 1987. * SE 51: Apr/May 1987. SLJ 33: Dec 1986. Anna has outgrown her old coat, but World War II has just ended and there are no coats to buy, so Anna and her mother trade family heirlooms for wool to make the yarn that will be woven into a new red coat. This richly illustrated story is based on a true event.

Germany

491. Allen, William Sheridan. Nazi Seizure of Power: The Experience of a Single German Town, 1922-1945. Rev. ed. Watts, 1984. 388 p. $19. Pb $10.

Gr 9+. B 80: Apr 15 1984. BR 3: Nov/Dec 1984. SE 47: Oct 1983. The years 1922 to 1945 are seen from the perspective of the citizens of Northeim, a middle-class German town that gradually came under the control of the Nazis.

492. Beck, Earl R. Under the Bombs: The German Home Front, 1942-1945. University Press of Kentucky, 1986. 240 p. $21.

Gr 9+. B 82: Mar 1 1986. LJ 111: May 1 1986. Daily life in German cities that suffered 3 years of aerial bombardment is described in this balanced account that is based on personal and official documents.

493. Freeman, Michael. Atlas of Nazi Germany. Macmillan, 1987. 205 p. ill. $55.

Gr 10+. B 84: Dec 15 1987. Charts, graphs, tables, photos, and maps encompass over half of this broad overview of the political, economic, and military history of Nazi Germany.

494. Reichel, Sabine. What Did You Do in the War, Daddy? Growing Up German. Hill & Wang, 1989. 186 p. $20.

Gr 9+. B 85: Feb 15 1989. LJ 114: Apr 1 1989. Reichel, who was born in 1946, interviewed her middle-class parents and other Germans who survived the war, including Nazis, soldiers, civilians, and concentration camp victims in an effort to understand the veil of silence that her elders drew over the war years.

495. Stein, R. Conrad. Hitler Youth. (World at War). Childrens Press, 1985. 47 p. ill. $11.

Gr 4-6. B 82: Mar 1 1986. This brief, highly illustrated work shows how German youth were trained to further the Nazi cause.

496. Steinhoff, Johannes. Voices from the Third Reich: An Oral History. Regnery Gateway; dist. by Kampmann, 1989. 512 p. $25.

Gr 10+. B 85: Jun 1 1989. LJ 114: Apr 15 1989. Excerpts from hundreds of interviews with Germans are arranged by topic to provide an account of the war as these people remember it.

Japan

497. Children of Hiroshima. Pub. Committee of Children of Hiroshima; dist. by Oelgeschlager Gunn, 1981. 335 p. $23. Pb $10.

Gr 7+. B 78: Jan 15 1982. B 80: Mar 15 1984. + - LJ 107: Feb 15 1982. SE 47: Nov/Dec 1983. This collection of short, graphic essays documents the reminiscences of children who survived Hiroshima.

498. Chisholm, Anne. Faces of Hiroshima: A Report. Jonathan Cape; dist. by Merrimack Publishers' Circle, 1986. 182 p. Pb $10.

Gr 9+. * B 82: Feb 15 1986. Chisholm's account of the Hiroshima Maidens, 25 young women who were burn victims of the atomic bombs and later came to the United States for plastic surgery, is based on interviews with these women and their sponsors.

499. Hersey, John. Hiroshima. Knopf, 1985. 144 p. $14.

Gr 9+. LJ 110: Sep 15 1985. SE 47: Nov/Dec 1983. SLJ 31: Apr 1985. Hersey's work tells, through the experiences of 6 persons, what it was like in Hiroshima before, during, and after the bombing. First published in 1945, this 1985 edition includes a chapter bringing the reader up-to-date on the lives of these survivors.

500. Hoare, Stephen. Hiroshima. (Day That Made History). Batsford; dist. by David & Charles, 1987. 64 p. ill. $17.

Gr 4-10. * BR 6: Nov/Dec 1987. SLJ 34: Dec 1987. The causes for the development and use of the atomic bomb, its impact on the Japanese people, and the subsequent arms race are introduced in this illustrated work.

501. Kanda, Mikio. Widows of Hiroshima: The Life Stories of Nineteen Peasant Wives. St. Martin's, 1989. 200 p. $22.

Gr 9+. B 85: Feb 1 1989. The husbands of these peasant women had gone into Hiroshima the day the atomic bomb was dropped. Interviews reveal the horror of the women's experiences.

502. Lifton, Betty Jean. Place Called Hiroshima, A. Kodansha; dist. by Harper, 1985. 151 p. ill. $18.

Gr 6+. B 82: Oct 1 1985. B 82: Jan 15 1986. LJ 110: Jul 1985. SLJ 32: Nov 1985. Lifton records in moving photos and text the ongoing trauma of the city of Hiroshima and the individuals who were victims of the A-bomb.

503. Maruki, Toshi. Hiroshima No Pika. Lothrop, 1982. 48 p. ill. $12.

Gr 2-7. * B 79: Oct 1 1982. B 79: Jun 1 1983. B 83: Mar 1 1987. BC 36: Oct 1982. HB 58: Oct 1982. * SE 47: Apr 1983. * SLJ 28: Aug 1982. SLJ 29: May 1983. Vivid paintings and a sparse text tell the story of 7-year-old Mii and her family on August 6, 1945. They were peacefully eating breakfast when the atomic bomb fell on their city.

504. Miner, Jane Claypool. Hiroshima and Nagasaki. (Turning Points of World War II). Watts, 1984. 106 p. ill. $10.

Gr 6+. B 81: Dec 15 1984. BR 4: Sep/Oct 1985. SLJ 31: Dec 1984. Quotations, anecdotes, and photos supplement the clearly written text that discusses the bombing of Hiroshima and Nagasaki and closes with a discussion of the nuclear arms race that followed World War II.

505. Nakazawa, Keija. Barefoot Gen: The Day After (A Cartoon Story of Hiroshima). New Society, 1988. 192 p. $30. Pb $9.

Gr 7+. BR 7: May/Jun 1988. * VOYA 11: Aug 1988. The horrors of the atomic blast at Hiroshima are graphically portrayed in this autobiographical pictorial account.

506. Unforgettable Fire: Pictures Drawn by Atomic Bomb Survivors. Pantheon; dist. by Random, 1981. 109 p. ill. $16. Pb $8.

Gr 9+. B 77: Mar 15 1981. LJ 106: Mar 15 1981. SLJ 28: Sep 1981. Survivors of the atomic explosion at Hiroshima were asked to share their experiences through drawings, paintings, and words. The powerful result of this project is presented with a minimum of explanatory text.

Japanese Canadians–Fiction

507. Kogawa, Joy. Obasan. Godine, 1984. 250 p. Pb $9.

Gr 7+. BR 3: Sep/Oct 1984. Just as the Japanese-Americans suffered internment and prejudice during the war, so did the Japanese in Canada. Kogawa based her story on her memories.

Jews

508. Abells, Chana Byers. Children We Remember, The. Greenwillow, 1986. 48 p. ill. $10. Lib. ed. $11.

Gr 2+. * B 83: Oct 1 1986. BC 40: Oct 1986. BR 5: Jan/Feb 1987. * HB 62: Nov/Dec 1986. * SE 51: Apr/May 1987. SLJ 30: Sep 1983. SLJ 34: Feb 1988. Abell's moving photo-documentary of Jewish children before, during, and after the Nazi regime is suitable for all ages.

509. Adler, David A. Number on My Grandfather's Arm, The. Union of American Hebrew Congregations, 1987. 28 p. ill. $8.

Gr 1-4. SLJ 34: Feb 1988. SLJ 34: Apr 1988. A beloved grandfather explains the number on his arm in a simple but informative account of his experiences at Auschwitz.

510. Asscher-Pinkhof, Clara. Star Children. Wayne State University Press, 1986. 259 p. ill. $18.

Gr 10+. LJ 111: Dec 1986. The experiences of Jewish children in detention and concentration camps during World War II are examined in these moving vignettes.

511. Bernbaum, Israel. My Brother's Keeper. Putnam, 1985. 63 p. ill. $17.

Gr 5+. B 82: Sep 1 1985. B 82: Oct 1 1985. + - BC 39: Sep 1985. * SE 50: Apr/May 1986. * SLJ 31: Aug 1985. SLJ 34: Jan 1988. * VOYA 8: Dec 1985. The artist/author portrays the story of the Warsaw ghetto with vivid paintings and moving personal accounts.

512. Bierman, John. Odyssey. Simon & Schuster, 1984. 255 p. ill. $17.

Gr 9+. B 81: Nov 1 1984. LJ 109: Nov 15 1984. From 1940 to 1944 514 Jews survived disease, hunger, imprisonment, delay, and a sunken ship in their amazing trip from Czechoslovakia to freedom in Palestine.

513. Chaikin, Miriam. Nightmare in History: The Holocaust 1933-1945. Clarion, 1987. 150 p. ill. $15.

Gr 5-10. * B 84: Dec 15 1987. B 85: Jun 15 1989. BC 41: Jan 1988. * BR 7: May 1988. HB 64: Mar 1988. * SE 52: Apr 1988. SLJ 34: Jan 1988. + - VOYA 11: Apr 1988. In a simple style Chaikin briefly reviews anti-Semitism throughout history and then explains clearly what happened to the Jews under Naziism. Quotes and photos supplement the text.

514. Czarnecki, Joseph P. Last Traces: The Lost Art of Auschwitz. Atheneum, 1989. 175 p. ill. $30.

Gr 10+. B 86: Sep 1 1989. LJ 114: Sep 15 1989. Czarnecki, a Polish photo journalist, presents the drawings, paintings, decorations, and poems that he found on walls of buildings in Auschwitz, and tells of the lives of the inmate-artists.

515. Eisenberg, Azriel. Lost Generation: Children in the Holocaust. Pilgrim, 1982. 384 p. $18.

Gr 9+. B 78: Apr 15 1982. B 81: Oct 1 1984. LJ 107: May 15 1982. This graphic account of the cruelties suffered by Jewish children, ages 4 to 14, from the 1920s through World War II shows their will to live, learn, and love.

516. Finkelstein, Norman H. Remember Not To Forget: A Memory of the Holocaust. Watts, 1985. 31 p. ill. $9.

Gr 3-5. B 82: Sep 15 1985. B 85: Jun 15 1989. + - BC 38: May 1985. SLJ 32: Sep 1985. SLJ 34: Feb 1988. Beginning with the expulsion of the Jews from Jerusalem in 70 A.D., anti-Semitism through World War II is examined in a straightforward illustrated text.

517. Gilbert, Martin. Holocaust: A History of the Jews of Europe during the Second World War. Holt, 1986. 959 p. ill. $20.

Gr 9+. LJ 111: Feb 1 1986. SLJ 32: Aug 1986. This detailed chronological account of the treatment of the Jews by the Nazis from 1933 to 1945 is based on hundreds of documents and quotes.

518. Gross, Leonard. Last Jews in Berlin, The. Simon & Schuster, 1982. 349 p. $16.

Gr 9+. B 78: May 15 1982. LJ 107: Apr 15 1982. SLJ 29: Nov 1982. Gross interviewed Jews who went underground in Berlin and, with the help of German gentiles, survived the war.

519. Hellman, Peter. Auschwitz Album: A Book Based on an Album Discovered by a Concentration Camp Survivor, Lilly Meier. Random, 1982. 200 p. ill. $24.

Gr 9+. B 78: Nov 15 1981. LJ 106: Dec 15 1981. SLJ 29: Oct 1982. Photos of concentration camps were forbidden, but Meier discovered an album, kept by an unknown German soldier, that records the arrival and processing of prisoners of Auschwitz.

520. Josephs, Jeremy. Swastika Over Paris. Little, Brown, 1989. 256 p. ill. $20.

Gr 10+. B 86: Oct 1 1989. * LJ 114: Sep 15 1989. The experiences of Jews in Paris during the war are revealed in this account of a Jewish businessman who remained in Paris and a teenage girl who joined the Resistance.

521. Lanzmann, Claude. Shoah: An Oral History of the Holocaust. Pantheon, 1985. 200 p. ill. $12.

Gr 9+. B 82: Jan 1 1986. BR 5: May/Jun 1986. * VOYA 9: Apr 1986. This oral history of eyewitnesses to the Holocaust includes interviews with Jewish survivors, employees of concentration camps, persons who lived nearby, and SS officers. This is the text of a French film by the same name.

522. Levi, Primo. Moments of Reprieve. Summit, 1986. 147 p. $15.

Gr 9+. B 82: Feb 1 1986. An Italian Jew who survived Auschwitz records 15 episodes that happened there.

523. Lewin, Rhoda G. Witnesses to the Holocaust: An Oral History. Twayne, 1989. 248 p. $20.

Gr 10+. B 86: Sep 15 1989. Interviews with survivors of the Holocaust and those who worked to help them relate the experiences of 60 persons.

524. Meltzer, Milton. Never to Forget: The Jews of the Holocaust. Harper, 1976. 217 p. $11.

Gr 9+. B 80: Oct 15 1983. B 85: Jun 15 1989. HB 52: Jun 1976. LJ 101: Sep 1 1976. SLJ 22: Apr 1976. Meltzer shows the development of anti-Semitism in Germany and uses excerpts from memoirs, letters, and diaries to reveal everyday life in ghettos and labor and death camps.

525. Read, Anthony. Kristallnacht: The Tragedy of the Nazi Night of Terror. Times Books, 1990. 320 p. ill. $20.

Gr 10+. B 86: Nov 1 1989. Read clearly explains the causes and events of Kristallnacht, when Nazi mobs shattered the windows of Jewish-owned shops and ransacked them, and shows how the lack of international response encouraged further action against the Jews.

526. Rogasky, Barbara. Smoke and Ashes: The Story of the Holocaust. Holiday, 1988. 187 p. ill. $17.

Gr 6+. * B 84: Jun 15 1988. * BC 41: Jun 1988. HB 64: Sep/Oct 1988. HB 65: Jan/Feb 1989. * SLJ 34: Jun/Jul 1988. * VOYA 11: Dec 1988. Rogasky's illustrated account of the Holocaust explores its causes, reactions by Britain and the United States, and details of life and death in concentration camps.

527. Rossel, Seymour. Holocaust, The. Watts, 1981. 148 p. maps. $9.

Gr 6+. B 78: Nov 1 1981. B 85: Jun 15 1989. HB 58: Feb 1982. SLJ 28: Apr 1982. SLJ 34: Feb 1988. Rossel presents a picture of Germany in the 1930s and shows how Hitler's rise to power came about. He clearly shows the horrors of the death camps, and examines the results of the Holocaust.

528. Spiegelman, Art. Maus: A Survivor's Tale. Pantheon, 1986. 159 p. ill. Pb $9.

Gr 9+. B 83: Sep 1 1986. SLJ 33: May 1987. In a unique comic book format, showing the Jews with the heads of mice and the Nazis with the heads of cats, the author tells the story of his father's terrifying experiences during the Holocaust.

529. Stein, R. Conrad. Warsaw Ghetto. (World at War). Childrens Press, 1985. 47 p. ill. $8.

Gr 4-7. B 81: Oct 15 1985. SLJ 32: Feb 1986. SLJ 34: Feb 1988. The horrors endured by the Jews in the Warsaw ghetto are briefly introduced in this highly illustrated work.

530. Tokayer, Marvin. Fugu Plan: Untold Story of the Japanese and the Jews During World War II. Paddington Press; Dell, 1979. 287 p. $11. Pb $3.

Gr 11+. SE 45: May 1981. Twenty thousand Jews spent World War II in safety in Japan. This incredible account tells why the Japanese welcomed the Jews while their German allies were trying to exterminate them.

531. Vegh, Claudine. I Didn't Say Good-bye: Interviews with Children of the Holocaust. Dutton, 1985. 179 p. map. $15.

Gr 9+. SLJ 33: Sep 1986. VOYA 8: Oct 1985. Based on interviews with survivors of the Holocaust who, as children, were hidden away and able to live while the rest of their families went to death camps.

532. Volavkov, Hana. I Never Saw Another Butterfly: Children's Drawings and Poems from Terezin Concentration Camp, 1942-1944. Schocken, 1978. 80 p. ill. $7.

Gr 4-9. B 85: Jun 15 1989. The fear and confusion experienced by children at the camp at Terezin is reflected in this selection of their poems and drawings.

533. Wiesenthal, Simon. Max and Helen. Morrow, 1982. 163 p. $10.

Gr 9+. B 78: Apr 15 1982. LJ 107: Apr 15 1982. In the story of Max and Helen, Wiesenthal, a noted Nazi hunter, tells why there was one Nazi he chose not to prosecute.

Jews–Bibliographies

534. Szonyi, David M. Holocaust, The. KTAV, 1985. 395 p. $30. Pb $17.

Gr 9+. + - B 81: Aug 1985. LJ 110: Apr 1 1985. Annotated bibliographies of fiction, nonfiction, art, all types of audiovisual materials, and journal articles about the Holocaust are included.

Jews–Biographies

535. Appleman-Jurman, Alicia. Alicia: My Story. Bantam, 1988. 356 p. $19.

Gr 8+. * BR 8: May/Jun 1989. + - LJ 113: Nov 15 1988. Jurman, a Polish Jew, was a child during the war years. She tells of her struggle to survive the Russian and German invasions as her family, one-by-one, were killed.

536. Auerbacher, Inge. I Am a Star: Child of the Holocaust. Prentice-Hall; dist. by Simon & Schuster, 1987. 87 p. ill. $10. Pb $5.

Gr 4-7. B 83: Jun 1 1987. + - BC 40: Jul/Aug 1987. * SE 52: Apr/May 1988. + - SLJ 33: Apr 1987. SLJ 34: Feb 1988. The author tells of her experiences in Terezin, a concentration

camp in Czechoslovakia. Of 15,000 imprisoned children, only 100 survived.

537. Baldwin, Margaret. Boys Who Saved the Children, The. Messner, 1981. 62 p. ill. $9.

Gr 5+. B 78: Feb 15 1982. SLJ 34: Feb 1988. VOYA 5: Aug 1982. Forced by the Nazis to work in a coat factory, young Ben Edelman and his friends saved scraps of fur to make a coat for the commandant's wife in the hope that she would keep them from the death camps. Based on memoirs.

538. Bauman, Janina. Winter in the Morning: A Young Girl's Life in the Warsaw Ghetto and Beyond, 1939-1945. Free Press, 1986. 195 p. ill. $17.

Gr 9+. B 82: Jun 1 1986. LJ 111: Mar 1 1986. Thirteen-year-old Bauman lived with hunger and constant fear as she hid from the Nazis in Warsaw. This account is based on her diaries.

539. Bernheim, Mark. Father of the Orphans: The Life of Janusz Korczak. (Jewish Biography Series). Dutton, 1988. 139 p. ill. $15.

Gr 6-9. B 85: Feb 1 1989. SLJ 35: May 1989. Janusz Korczak was a Polish physician who ran a home for orphaned children in Poland. He refused to leave, and remained to care for the children until he and the children were all killed at Treblinka.

540. Bull, Angela. Anne Frank. (Profiles). Hamilton; dist. by David & Charles, 1984. 60 p. ill. $8.

Gr 5-8. SLJ 31: Mar 1985. Based on Anne Frank's diary and other research, Bull tells the story of the Frank family, their efforts to survive, the causes and effects of anti-Semitism, and the fate of the family.

541. Fenelon, Fania. Playing for Time. Berkley, 1977. 262 p. Pb $4.

Gr 9+. B 74: Oct 1 1977. B 81: Oct 1 1984. B 82: Jan 1 1986. A talented musician, Fenelon was one of a group of Jewish musicians in Birkenau whose survival depended on their nightly performances to entertain the SS.

542. Frank, Anne. Anne Frank: The Diary of a Young Girl. Doubleday; Pocket/Washington Square Press, 1952; 1967. 308 p. $18. Pb $4.

Gr 9+. B 82: Jan 1 1986. B 84: Oct 15 1987. B 85: Jun 15 1989. SLJ 33: Nov 1986. SLJ 34: Apr 1988. Anne Frank kept a diary that recounted her experiences during the 2 years that her family hid from the Nazis before they were discovered and taken to a concentration camp.

543. Frank, Anne. Diary of Anne Frank: The Critical Edition. Doubleday, 1989. 720 p. ill. $30.

Gr 9+. B 85: May 15 1989. LJ 114: Jun 1 1989. Three versions of Anne Frank's diary, accounts of how the work was handed down and published, and information on the Frank family are included in this detailed work.

544. Friedman, Ina R. Escape or Die: True Stories of Young People Who Survived the Holocaust. Addison-Wesley, 1982. 146 p. ill. $10.

Gr 5+. + - B 78: Jul 1982. B 85: Jun 15 1989. HB 58: Oct 1982. + - SLJ 29: Oct 1982. SLJ 34: Feb 1988. VOYA 5: Oct 1982. Twelve persons who, as children, survived the

Holocaust tell of their experiences. They represent 10 countries.

545. Gelman, Charles. Do Not Go Gentle: A Memoir of Jewish Resistance in Poland, 1941-1945. Archon, 1989. 223 p. $25.

Gr 10+. B 85: Aug 1989. LJ 114: Jul 1989. Gelman tells of his experiences as a Jewish member of the Polish Resistance. He was involved in sabotage for 4 years.

546. Gies, Miep. Anne Frank Remembered: The Story of Miep Gies, Who Helped to Hide the Frank Family. Simon & Schuster, 1987. 252 p. ill. $18.

Gr 9+. B 83: Apr 1 1987. LJ 112: May 15 1987. SLJ 34: Nov 1987. SLJ 34: Feb 1988. * VOYA 10: Dec 1987. Miep Gies was the trusted employee to whom Otto Frank turned for help. She hid the Frank family and others for 2 years and was responsible for saving Anne Frank's diary.

547. Gissing, Vera. Pearls of Childhood. St. Martin's, 1989. 256 p. ill. $17.

Gr 10+. B 85: May 15 1989. LJ 114: Jun 1 1989. Gissing tells about her experiences as a refugee child. Her Jewish parents sent her from Czechoslovakia to safety in Britain, but they remained behind and died in concentration camps.

548. Greene, Carol. Elie Wiesel: Messenger from the Holocaust. (Picture-Story Biographies). Childrens Press, 1987. 31 p. ill. $8.

Gr 2-4. SLJ 34: Feb 1988. Simply written, featuring photos and large type, this biography introduces Elie Wiesel, winner of the 1986 Nobel Peace Prize. After Wiesel survived the Holocaust he devoted his life to speaking and writing about it so it would not be forgotten.

549. Haas, Gerda. These I Do Remember: Fragments from the Holocaust. Cumberland/Bond Wheelright, 1982. 256 p. ill. $17.

Gr 9+. B 79: Sep 15 1982. B 81: Oct 1 1984. B 85: Jun 15 1989. LJ 107: Sep 1 1982. The author tells her story and that of 8 other persons from several European countries, all of whom suffered during the Holocaust.

550. Hart, Kitty. Return to Auschwitz: The Remarkable Story of a Girl Who Survived the Holocaust. Atheneum, 1982. 178 p. ill. $13.

Gr 9+. B 78: Apr 1 1982. LJ 107: Mar 15 1982. Hart presents a personal account of her experiences as a teenager in the concentration camp at Auschwitz and recounts the influence of these experiences on her later life.

551. Hillesum, Etty. Letters from Westerbork. Pantheon, 1986. 129 p. ill. $14.

Gr 9+. B 83: Nov 15 1986. LJ 111: Nov 1 1986. At a Dutch concentration camp Hillesum, age 27, worked to make conditions bearable for others. Until her death she wrote these letters about their experiences.

552. Hurwitz, Johanna. Anne Frank: Life in Hiding. Jewish Publication Society, 1988. 62 p. ill. $13.

Gr 3-8. B 85: Apr 15 1989. B 85: Jun 15 1989. * SE 53: Apr/May 1989. + - SLJ 35: Aug 1989. Pencil sketches supplement this introduction to Anne Frank, the months when she and her family were in hiding, and the events at Bergen-Belsen that led to her death.

553. Isaacman, Clara. Clara's Story. Jewish Publication Society, 1984. 119 p. $12.

Gr 5-9. B 81: Mar 15 1985. B 85: Jun 15 1989. SLJ 34: Feb 1988. In this episodic and fast-paced account the author tells of her family's experiences in hiding from the Nazis in Belgium.

554. Jackson, Livia E. Bitton. Elli: Coming of Age in the Holocaust. Times Books, 1980. 248 p. $11.

Gr 9+. B 76: Jul 1 1980. B 81: Oct 1 1984. LJ 105: May 15 1980. VOYA 3: Feb 1981. In a searing personal account Jackson tells of her concentration camp experiences, which were so traumatic that her liberators thought the 14-year-old girl was a 60-year-old man.

555. Korenblit, Michael. Until We Meet Again: A True Story of Love and War, Separation and Reunion. Putnam, 1983. 304 p. $15.

Gr 10+. B 79: Aug 1983. LJ 108: Jul 1983. The author's parents were teenagers in love, living in a Polish village, when the war separated them. Surviving concentration camps, they eventually came to the United States.

556. Krall, Hanna. Shielding the Flame: An Intimate Conversation with Dr. Marek Edelman, the Last Surviving Leader of the Warsaw Ghetto Uprising. Holt, 1986. 124 p. $14.

Gr 9+. B 82: Aug 1986. LJ 111: Aug 1986. Edelman, a cardiologist, was the last survivor of the leaders of the Warsaw ghetto uprising in 1943. In this conversation he reflects on those events and their meaning.

557. Kuchler-Silberman, Lena. My Hundred Children. Dell, 1987. 253 p. Pb $4.

Gr 7+. + - B 83: Apr 1 1987. BR 6: Jun 1987. + - VOYA 10: Jun 1987. Disguised as a gentile, the author survived the war. When it was over she established a home for 100 Jewish children, eventually taking them to Israel.

558. Leigh, Vanora. Anne Frank. Bookwright Press; dist. by Watts, 1985. 30 p. $10.

Gr 3-6. BC 39: Feb 1986. SLJ 32: Feb 1986. In a concise text with short chapters, Leigh provides background on conditions in Europe and the Frank family's struggle to find safety, as an introduction to the Diary of Anne Frank.

559. Leitner, Isabella. Fragments of Isabella: A Memoir of Auschwitz. Crowell, 1978. 112 p. $9.

Gr 9+. B 80: Oct 15 1983. HB 55: Aug 1979. LJ 103: Sep 15 1978. In a moving account the author describes the 9 months she spent at Auschwitz.

560. Leitner, Isabella. Saving the Fragments: From Auschwitz to New York. New American Library, 1985. 131 p. $13.

Gr 9+. B 82: Oct 15 1985. LJ 110: Oct 1 1985. SLJ 32: Aug 1986. These memoirs of a survivor of Auschwitz cover the early days of her freedom as she struggled to return to the normal world.

561. Lewin, Abraham. Cup of Tears: A Diary of the Warsaw Ghetto. Basil Blackwell/Institute of Polish-Jewish Studies, 1989. 299 p. ill. $20.

Gr 9+. B 85: Feb 1 1989. LJ 114: Feb 1 1989. Lewin and his daughter perished in the Warsaw ghetto. His powerful diary records the events of daily life and the growing terror. Photos and an introduction that provides historic perspective augment the text.

562. Lichter, Uri. In the Eye of the Storm: Surviving Against All Odds, 1939-1945. Holocaust Library; dist. by Schocken, 1987. 272 p. ill. $19.

Gr 9+. LJ 112: Sep 15 1987. SLJ 34: Nov 1987. Lichter was 19 when the Holocaust threatened to engulf his orthodox Jewish family. With the help of forged documents and Polish Christians 5 of the family members were saved. Their story is a spell-binding account of courage and faith.

563. Mann, Peggy. Giselle Save the Children! Everest, 1980. 302 p. $13.

Gr 9+. B 77: Dec 15 1980. LJ 105: Nov 15 1980. Mann collaborated with Giselle Hersh in telling Hersh's experiences after the Nazis sent her family from their home in Hungary to a concentration camp.

564. Mishell, William. Kaddish for Kovno: Life and Death in a Lithuanian Ghetto, 1941-45. Chicago Review Press, 1988. 384 p. ill. $19.

Gr 9+. B 84: May 15 1988. LJ 113: Jul 1988. Mishell presents a detailed account of his experiences in the Jewish ghetto in Kovno, Lithuania.

565. Niemark, Anne E. One Man's Valor: Leo Baeck and the Holocaust. (Jewish Biography Series). Dutton, 1986. 113 p. $15.

Gr 5-9. B 82: Aug 1986. + - BC 39: Apr 1986. HB 62: Sep/Oct 1986. * SE 51: Apr/May 1987. + - SLJ 33: Oct 1986. SLJ 34: Feb 1988. VOYA 9: Dec 1986. Baeck was a rabbi who sacrificed his safety to help German Jews. His ideas and the persecution he suffered are clearly presented.

566. Nir, Yehuda. Lost Childhood, The. Harcourt, 1989. 212 p. $20.

Gr 10+. B 86: Sep 1 1989. LJ 114: Sep 1 1989. The author, a Polish Jew, tells of the World War II experiences of his sister, his mother, and himself. They survived the war by changing identities and living by their wits.

567. Noble, Iris. Nazi Hunter, Simon Wiesenthal. Messner, 1979. 160 p. Lib. ed. $8.

Gr 9+. B 76: Nov 1 1979. BC 33: Feb 1980. * SE 44: Apr 1980. SLJ 26: Feb 1980. Wiesenthal was in a concentration camp during the war. Since then he has searched for Nazi war criminals and has brought many to justice. Noble explores his personality and the frustrations of his work.

568. Oberski, Jona. Childhood: A Remembrance. Doubleday, 1983. 119 p. $12.

Gr 9+. LJ 108: Apr 1 1983. SLJ 30: Sep 1983. SLJ 34: Feb 1988. This memoir of the Holocaust tells how the author experienced it as a child, gradually becoming aware of the horrors around him.

569. Orenstein, Henry. I Shall Live: The Story of a Survivor of 1939-1945. Beaufort, 1987. 286 p. ill. $17.

Gr 9+. B 83: Aug 1987. LJ 112: Sep 15 1987. Orenstein tells of daily life of Polish Jews early in the war and his own experiences in five concentration camps over a 30-month period.

570. Poltawska, Wanda. And I Am Afraid of My Dreams. Hodder and Stoughton; dist. by Hippocrene, 1989. 191 p. maps. $15.

Gr 9+. SLJ 35: Sep 1989. The author tells of her experiences as one of the Jews who served as human "guinea pigs" in Nazi medical experiments.

571. Rothchild, Sylvia. Voices from the Holocaust. New American Library, 1981. 464 p. $15.

Gr 9+. B 77: Apr 1 1981. LJ 106: Apr 1 1981. Survivors of the Holocaust tell their stories of their lives before, during, and after the war. These accounts represent the experiences of many different types of Jews and indicate reasons why these persons survived.

572. Schloss, Eva. Eva's Story: A Survivor's Tale by the Step-Sister of Anne Frank. St. Martin's, 1989. 224 p. ill. $17.

Gr 9+. B 85: May 15 1989. LJ 114: Apr 15 1989. Anne Frank's step-sister tells the story of her family's experiences hiding from the Nazis and in a concentration camp.

573. Sender, Ruth Minsky. Cage, The. Macmillan, 1986. 245 p. $14.

Gr 7+. B 83: Sep 15 1986. + - BC 40: Nov 1986. + - BR 6: May/Jun 1987. HB 63: Jan/Feb 1987. * SE 51: Apr/May 1987. + - SLJ 33: Nov 1986. SLJ 34: Feb 1988. In a detailed personal account the author tells of her experiences in the ghetto at Lodz, at Auschwitz, and in a slave labor camp.

574. Sender, Ruth Minsky. To Life. Macmillan, 1988. 234 p. $14.

Gr 6+. B 85: Oct 15 1988. + - BR 7: Jan/Feb 1989. HB 65: Mar/Apr 1989. * SE 53: Apr/May 1989. SLJ 35: Nov 1988. VOYA 11: Dec 1988. In her sequel to The Cage, Sender tells of the difficulties of life in war-torn Europe after her release from a concentration camp.

575. Sevela, Ephraim. We Were Not Like Other People. Harper, 1989. 224 p. $13.

Gr 6+. * B 86: Sep 1 1989. BC 43: Oct 1989. VOYA 12: Dec 1989. For 8 years the author, a Russian Jewish boy, lived as a refugee. His episodic memoirs tell of hunger, mistreatment, fear, and survival.

576. Stern, Ellen Norman. Elie Wiesel: Witness for Life. KTAV, 1982. 224 p. ill. $13. Pb $7.

Gr 7+. B 78: May 1 1982. SLJ 34: Feb 1988. Stern used an extensive interview with the noted French author, plus other sources, to tell the story of Wiesel's Holocaust experiences and his post-war efforts to tell what he saw.

577. Stiffel, Frank. Tale of the Ring: A Kaddish. Pushcart Press, 1984. 348 p. ill. $22.

Gr 9+. B 80: Feb 15 1984. LJ 109: Feb 15 1984. The author was a medical student in Poland at the time of the Nazi invasion. This account of his experiences in Treblinka and Auschwitz is based on his diaries.

578. Tridenti, Lina. Anne Frank. (Why They Became Famous). Silver Burdett, 1985. 62 p. Lib. ed. $10. Pb $7.

Gr 4-7. BR 4: Jan/Feb 1986. SLJ 32: Apr 1986. Quotations from her diary enhance this introduction to the story of Anne Frank.

579. Waterford, Helen. Commitment to the Dead: One Woman's Journey Toward Understanding. Renaissance House, 1987. 180 p. ill. $19. Pb $10.

Gr 9+. B 84: Oct 1 1987. As an adult Waterford has lectured on her childhood experiences at Auschwitz. In this work she tells her story, interspersed with questions and answers from the lectures.

580. Weinstein, Frida Scheps. Hidden Childhood: A Jewish Girl's Sanctuary in a French Convent, 1942-1945. Hill & Wang, 1985. 151 p. $14.

Gr 7+. B 81: May 1 1985. LJ 110: May 15 1985. VOYA 8: Oct 1985. The author was hidden in a convent school from 1942 to 1945. Confused by the war and her parents' apparent abandonment, and attracted by the religious beliefs of those around her, the 7-year-old struggled to come to terms with her own heritage.

581. Wurman, Nachemia. Nachemia: German and Jew in the Holocaust. New Horizon; dist. by Macmillan, 1989. 300 p. $22.

Gr 9+. + - B 85: Mar 1 1989. Wurman tells of his experiences as a Jew in the Polish underground.

582. Zar, Rose. In the Mouth of the Wolf. Jewish Publication Society, 1983. 225 p. $11.

Gr 9+. B 80: Apr 15 1984. B 85: Jun 15 1989. HB 60: Jun 1984. SLJ 34: Feb 1988. Familiar with the Catholic faith, able to speak Polish without an accent, and using forged papers, Ruszka escaped from a Jewish ghetto and survived the war by working for a German officer, in danger of exposure every day.

583. Zuker-Bujanowska, Liliana. Liliana's Journal: Warsaw, 1939-1945. Dial, 1980. 162 p. ill. $9.

Gr 9+. LJ 105: Aug 1980. SLJ 27: Oct 1980. The author recounts her experiences as an orphaned Jewish teenager struggling to find food and shelter during the war.

584. Zyskind, Sara. Stolen Years. Lerner, 1981. 288 p. $12.

Gr 9+. * SE 46: Apr 1982. Zyskind's detailed account of her experiences in a Polish ghetto and a concentration camp reveals both suffering and a determination to survive.

585. Zyskind, Sara. Struggle. Lerner, 1989. 325 p. $15.

Gr 8+. B 85: Jun 15 1989. B 85: Jul 1989. Zyskind records her husband's experiences as a young Polish Jew during the Nazi occupation.

Jews—Fiction

586. Aaron, Chester. Gideon. Lippincott; dist. by Harper, 1981. 181 p. $11. Lib. ed. $10.

Gr 7+. + - B 78: Apr 1 1982. BC 35: Jun 1982. + - BR 1: Sep/Oct 1982. + - SLJ 28: Apr 1982. A street-wise 14-year-old Jew from Warsaw tells the story of his experiences in the ghetto and at Treblinka, where he participated in the 1943 revolt.

587. Appelfeld, Aharon. For Every Sin. Weidenfeld & Nicholson, 1989. 169 p. $16.

Gr 10+. B 85: May 1 1989. * LJ 114: Apr 15 1989. A young man who has been released from a concentration camp at the end of the war remembers his experiences and plans his future as he walks across war-torn Europe toward his home.

588. Baer, Edith. Frost in the Night, A. Schocken, 1988. 208 p. $8.

Gr 6+. BR 7: Jan/Feb 1989. Eva's comfortable life in a German town in the early 1930s changed gradually as Hitler came to power, but it was difficult for her family to recognize the danger they were in.

589. Dagan, Avigdor. Court Jesters, The. Jewish Publication Society, 1989. 180 p. $16.

Gr 10+. B 86: Nov 1 1989. LJ 114: Oct 1 1989. This powerful novel concerns a dwarf, an astrologer, a humpback, and a juggler who were able to survive the war because of their ability to amuse the commandant of the concentration camp.

590. Demetz, Hana. House on Prague Street, The. St. Martin's, 1980. 186 p. $9.

Gr 9+. B 76: Jul 1 1980. LJ 105: Aug 1980. SLJ 27: Oct 1980. In a simple first-person narrative, Helena tells of her coming of age during the Holocaust, a time of confusion, torn loyalties, and the desire to live.

591. Fink, Ida. Scrap of Time: And Other Stories. Pantheon, 1987. 153 p. $15.

Gr 9+. * B 83: Jun 1 1987. LJ 112: Aug 1987. Many of the 23 stories in this gripping anthology about the Holocaust are autobiographical.

592. Forman, James. Survivor, The. Farrar, 1976. 256 p. $9.

Gr 7+. * B 72: May 1 1976. B 85: Jun 15 1989. BC 30: Sep 1976. SE 41: Apr 1977. SLJ 22: Apr 1976. The experiences of many European Jews is revealed in the story of David, whose family considered themselves more Dutch than Jewish and failed to flee in time to avoid the horror of the Holocaust.

593. Gershon, Karen. Bread of Exile, The. Victor Gollancz; dist. by David & Charles, 1986. 184 p. $19.

Gr 9+. B 82: Feb 1 1986. LJ 111: Jan 1986. At age 13 Inge was one of the Jewish children sent to Great Britain for safety just before the war began. Alone in an alien culture she befriended other outcasts. This semi-autobiographical novel has good characterizations.

594. Hersey, John. Wall, The. 1st ed. Knopf, 1950. 632 p. $13.

Gr 10+. B 46: Feb 15 1950. B 81: Jul 1985. * HD 26: May 1950. * LJ 75: Mar 1 1950. Hersey's triumphant novel shows the harrowing experiences of Jews facing annihilation in the Warsaw ghetto.

595. Holm, Anne. North to Freedom. Peter Smith, 1965; 1984. 190 p. $16.

Gr 5-9. Metzner. LJ 90: May 15 1965. This story of David, a 12-year-old who had been imprisoned for most of his life, follows his escape as he made his way back to Denmark and learned how to live in freedom.

596. Kerr, Judith. When Hitler Stole Pink Rabbit. Putnam, 1972. 191 p. ill. $9.

Gr 4-7. B 68: Apr 15 1972. B 85: Jun 15 1989. BC 25: Jun 1972. HB 48: Aug 1972. * LJ 97: May 15 1972. SLJ May 1972. Because her family fled their Berlin home as Hitler was coming to power they avoided the Holocaust, but little Anna learned what it meant to be a refugee. An autobiographical story.

597. Leahy, Syrell Rogovin. Circle of Love. Putnam, 1980. 273 p. $11.

Gr 10+. LJ 105: Aug 1980. SLJ 27: Oct 1980. The sense of loneliness, isolation, and loss of Holocaust survivors, and their desire to find comfort and love, is seen in this mature novel about Anna and Anton.

598. Levoy, Myron. Alan and Naomi. Harper, 1977. 192 p. $13. Pb $3.

Gr 5-10. * B 74: Feb 15 1978. B 85: Jun 15 1989. BC 31: Jun 1978. HB 53: Dec 1977. SLJ 24: Nov 1977. Naomi, who saw her father murdered by the Gestapo, is in a delicate mental state. Alan's natural humor helps her on the road to recovery until they endure an anti-Semitic incident.

599. Matas, Carol. Lisa's War. Scribner, 1989. 128 p. $13.

Gr 6-10. B 85: Apr 1 1989. B 85: Jun 15 1989. BC 43: Sep 1989. + - BR 8: Sep 1989. HB 65: May/Jun 1989. + - SLJ 35: May 1989. VOYA 12: Jun 1989. Lisa was 12 when the Nazis invaded Denmark. She soon was involved in underground activities in spite of her fear, and eventually helped a group of over 6000 fellow Jews escape to Sweden. Based on interviews with survivors.

600. Mautner, Gabriella. Lovers and Fugitives. Mercury House; dist. by Kampmann, 1986. 352 p. maps. $17.

Gr 9+. SLJ 33: Sep 1986. Suspense, terror, and romance are found in this story about David and Saskia, young German Jews in love who are trying to avoid the Nazis and find freedom just over the Swiss border.

601. Meras, Icchokas. Stalemate. Lyle Stuart, 1980. 173 p. $9.

Gr 9+. * B 76: Jun 1 1980. The outcome of a chess game between a Nazi commandant and a young Lithuanian Jew will determine the fate of the boy and a group of children. A gripping novel filled with hope.

602. Moskin, Marietta D. I Am Rosemarie. Dell, 1972. 190 p. Pb $3.

Gr 7+. B 69: Nov 15 1972. B 85: Jun 15 1989. BC 26: Nov 1972. HB 49: Feb 1973. LJ 97: Nov 15 1972. This simply told story provides a detailed account of typical experiences of young Jewish girls in concentration camps.

603. Orgel, Doris. Devil in Vienna, The. Dial; Penguin/Puffin, 1978. 246 p. $9. Pb $4.

Gr 4-8. * B 75: Oct 15 1978. B 85: Jun 15 1989. BC 32: Dec 1978. HB 55: Feb 1979. SLJ 25: Nov 1978. This fictionalized autobiography tells the story of two girls, one Jewish and one Catholic, who lived in Austria at the time of the Nazi occupation.

604. Orlev, Uri. Island on Bird Street, The. Houghton, 1984. 162 p. $11.

Gr 4-7. B 80: Mar 15 1984. B 85: Nov 1 1988, Jun 15 1989. BC 37: Jun 1984. HB 60: Apr 1984. * SE 49: Apr 1985. * SLJ 30: Aug 1984. During the Nazi occupation of Poland Alex hid in an abandoned building, scrounging for food and caring for himself, awaiting the promised return of his father.

605. Ossowski, Leonie. Star Without a Sky. Lerner, 1985. 214 p. $13.

Gr 7-10. + - B 81: Jul 1985. B 85: Jun 15 1989. + - SLJ 32: Oct 1985. In the last days of the war a young Jewish boy is found hiding in a bombed out building by 5 boys who must decide his fate as Russian troops move closer daily. Based on a true story.

606. Ozick, Cynthia. Shawl, The. Knopf, 1989. 80 p. $13.

Gr 10+. B 86: Sep 1 1989. LJ 114: Aug 1989. Two stories tell of the death of a baby in a concentration camp and of the experiences of the child's mother after the war.

607. Provost, Gary. David And Max. Jewish Publication Society, 1988. 180 p. $13.

Gr 5-8. B 85: Jan 1 1989, * Jun 15 1989. BC 42: Jan 1989. * SE 53: Apr/May 1989. When Max sees a man he believes may be the friend he thought had died in a concentration camp, he and his grandson, David, try to find the friend and in the process David learns about the Holocaust.

608. Ramati, Alexander. Barbed Wire on the Isle of Man. Harcourt, 1980. 160 p. $8.

Gr 9+. B 76: Jul 1 1980. LJ 105: Sep 1 1980. Fear of infiltrators caused the British to intern many Jews who fled the Nazis. This story of 8-year-old Gerda Marie and her parents is based on experiences of the author's family.

609. Reiss, Johanna. Upstairs Room, The. Crowell, 1972. 196 p. $13.

Gr 5-9. B 84: Mar 1 1988. B 85: Jun 15 1989. HB 49: Feb 1973. LJ 97: Dec 15 1972. Reiss writes a story based on her own experiences as a Jewish child who was kept hidden all through the war by a Dutch farm family.

610. Romano, Elio. Generation of Wrath: A Story of Embattlement, Survival, and Deliverance During the Holocaust of World War II. Salem House; dist. by Merrimack Publishers' Circle, 1986. 288 p. $15.

Gr 9+. B 82: Mar 1 1986. This autobiographical novel is about a 15-year-old boy who spent the war years in a series of concentration camps.

611. Roth-Hano, Renee. Touch Wood: A Girlhood in Occupied France. Macmillan, 1988. 274 p. $14.

Gr 5+. B 84: Aug 1988. BC 41: May 1988. BR 7: Jan/Feb 1989. HB 65: Jan/Feb 1989. SLJ 34: Jun/Jul 1988. VOYA

11: Aug 1988. Roth-Hano uses a diary format in her novel, based on her own experiences. It is the story of a 9-year-old Jewish girl whose family placed her in a French convent to protect her during the Nazi invasion of France.

612. Siegal, Aranka. Grace in the Wilderness: After the Liberation, 1945-1948. Farrar, 1985. 220 p. $13.

Gr 7+. B 82: Nov 15 1985. B 85: Jun 15 1989. BC 39: Dec 1985. BR 5: Sep 1986. HB 62: Mar/Apr 1986. * SE 50: Apr/May 1986. * SLJ 32: Dec 1985. This fictionalized autobiography begins with Piri's release from the concentration camp at Bergen-Belsen. As she tries to regain her health and adjust to freedom and the death of her family, she is tormented by memories. Sequel to Upon the Head of the Goat.

613. Siegal, Aranka. Upon the Head of the Goat: A Childhood in Hungary 1939-1944. Farrar, 1981. 213 p. $10.

Gr 7+. * B 78: Feb 1 1982. B 85: Jun 15 1989. BC 35: Feb 1982. HB 58: Apr 1982. * SLJ 28: Dec 1981. SLJ 34: Feb 1988. VOYA 5: Jun 1982. This fictionalized autobiography recounts the persecution of the Hungarian Jews that culminated at Auschwitz, and the heroic efforts of a mother to preserve her family's human dignity. This is a prequel to Grace in the Wilderness.

614. Yolen, Jane. Devil's Arithmetic, The. Viking, 1988. 143 p. $12.

Gr 7+. B 85: Sep 1 1988. + - BC 42: Oct 1988. * BR 7: Jan/Feb 1989. * SE 53: Apr/May 1989. * SLJ 35: Nov 1988. Modern day Hannah travels through time and finds herself in a Polish village in 1942. The brutal experiences she endures in a concentration camp are vividly portrayed.

Jews—Rescue

615. Meltzer, Milton. Rescue: The Story of How Gentiles Saved Jews in the Holocaust. Harper, 1988. 167 p. $13. Lib. ed. $13.

Gr 5-10. * B 85: Oct 1 1988. BC 41: Jun 1988. * BR 7: Jan/Feb 1989. HB 65: Mar/Apr 1989. * SLJ 34: Aug 1988. * VOYA 11: Aug 1988. Eyewitness reports enhance Meltzer's account of the efforts of the "righteous Gentiles" who risked their own lives to help Jews escape the Holocaust.

Maps

616. Messenger, Charles. Chronological Atlas of World War II, The. Macmillan, 1989. 255 p. ill. $33.

Gr 10+. B 86: Nov 1 1989. This extensive collection of 2-color maps covers every theater of the war and every major battle and campaign. The informative text also covers planning, resistance movements, costs, and other topics.

Military History

617. Davis, Brian L. Waffen-SS. (Blandford War Photo-Files). Blandford, dist. by Sterling, 1986. 125 p. ill. $18. Pb $8.

Gr 9+. B 82: Jun 1 1986. The history of Germany's elite fighting force is shown in nearly 200 captioned photos from archives and private collections.

618. Dear, Ian. Ten Commando, 1942-1945. St. Martin's, 1989. 208 p. ill. $17.

Gr 9+. B 86: Oct 1 1989. Ten Commando was a fighting unit composed of soldiers from Nazi-occupied nations. They were involved in secret missions, raids, and battles to free their homelands.

619. Goodenough, Simon. War Maps: World War II from September 1939 to August 1945, Air, Sea, and Land, Battle by Battle. St. Martin's, 1983. 192 p. ill. $19.

Gr 9+. + - B 79: Jan 15 1983. LJ 107: Dec 1 1982. Photos and a brief and clear text enhance this collection of World War II theater charts, battle plans, and campaign maps.

620. Harris, Sarah. Fighting in World War II. (Finding Out About Series). Batsford; dist. by David & Charles, 1984. 48 p. ill. $13.

Gr 7+. + - SLJ 30: Apr 1984. This British publication explores British involvement in World War II. Many photos, illustrations, maps, quotes, and excerpts from newspapers are included.

621. Lucas, James. Kommando: German Special Forces of World War II. St. Martin's, 1985. 256 p. ill. $17.

Gr 9+. LJ 110: Sep 1 1985. SLJ 33: Oct 1986. Lucas examines the effectiveness of the German land, sea, and air special forces, explains their early successes, and the reasons for their lack of success in the last months of the war.

622. Reader's Digest Illustrated History of World War II: The World at Arms. Reader's Digest; dist. by Random, 1989. 480 p. ill. $28.

Gr 9+. * B 86: Sep 1 1989. Photos, drawings, maps, and a glossary enrich this well-written history of World War II.

623. Westwood, J. N. Eastern Front: The Soviet-German War, 1941-45. Military Press; dist. by Crown, 1984. 190 p. ill. $13.

Gr 9+. B 81: Dec 15 1984. The Soviet-German war on land, sea, and in the air is covered in this generously illustrated volume.

624. Wheeler, Keith. Road to Tokyo, The. (World War II). Time-Life; dist. by Silver Burdett, 1980. 208 p. ill. $11.

Gr 9+. LJ 105: Jun 15 1980. Photos from Life magazine are the focus of this account of the Pacific war. Volume 19 of the series.

Military Personnel

625. Carter, Hodding. Commandos of World War II, The. (World Landmark Books). Random, 1966. 160 p. ill. $3.

Gr 5-9. Metzner. LJ 91: Jul 1966. A straightforward and dramatic account of the heroism of volunteer commandoes who specialized in speed and surprise in their guerilla warfare against Germany.

626. Mitcham, Samuel W. Hitler's Field Marshals and Their Battles. Stein & Day, 1987. 421 p. maps. $23.

Gr 9+. B 83: May 1 1987. Mitcham presents balanced and clearly written biographies on all the Wehrmacht's marshals, including Rommel, von Rundstedt, von Reichenau, Paulus, and von Witzleben.

627. Mowat, Farley. And No Birds Sang. Atlantic; dist. by Little, Brown, 1980. 219 p. $11.

Gr 9+. B 76: Jan 15 1980. HB 56: Aug 1980. LJ 105: Jan 15 1980. A noted writer on conservation, Farley writes of his experiences as a young Canadian officer serving in Europe during the war.

628. Windrow, Martin. World War II GI, The. (Soldier Through the Ages). Watts, 1986. 32 p. ill. $11.

Gr 4-7. SLJ 33: Dec 1986. This colorfully illustrated work introduces the uniforms and equipment used by soldiers and presents a picture of their daily activities.

Naval Operations and Ships

629. Forester, Cecil Scott. Last Nine Days of the Bismarck. Little, Brown, 1959. 138 p. maps. $14.

Gr 7+. Metzner. * B 55: Apr 15 1959. * HB 35: Jun 1959. * LJ 84: Mar 1 1959. Forester's reconstruction of the sinking of the German Bismarck includes fictionalized dialogue.

630. Hoyt, Edwin P. U-Boats: A Pictorial History. McGraw-Hill, 1986. 289 p. ill. $20.

Gr 9+. + - B 83: Dec 15 1986. SLJ 33: Apr 1987. This highly illustrated overview of the history of German U-boats and the war they fought includes many anecdotes.

631. Hoyt, Edwin P. Sunk by the Bismarck: The Life and Death of the Battleship HMS Hood. Stein & Day, 1980. 160 p. ill. $10.

Gr 9+. B 77: Nov 15 1980. LJ 105: Sep 15 1980. The pride of the British navy following World War I, the HMS Hood was sunk in its first encounter with the Germans in World War II. Hoyt presents a history of the Hood and details of life aboard.

632. MacIntyre, Donald G. Fighting Ships and Seamen. St. Martin's; 1963; 1978. 195 p. ill. $35.

Gr 7+. Metzner. B 60: Apr 15 1964. This illustrated work emphasizes the accomplishments of the British navy in World War II. Background material on earlier British naval battles is included.

633. Skipper, G. C. Battle of the Atlantic. (World at War). Childrens Press, 1981. 44 p. ill. $7.

Gr 4-6. B 78: Jan 15 1982. This illustrated introduction to the battles in the Atlantic features large type and a simple text.

634. Taylor, Theodore. Battle in the English Channel. (Great Sea Battles of World War II). Avon, 1983. 141 p. ill. Pb $3.

Gr 7+. B 80: Oct 1 1983. HB 60: Feb 1984. SLJ 30: Apr 1984. * VOYA 7: Jun 1984. Taylor's fast-moving account examines the successful German mission in 1942 to move three major ships through the English Channel in spite of the efforts of British naval and air forces.

635. Taylor, Theodore. H.M.S. Hood vs. Bismarck: The Battleship Battle. (Great Sea Battles of World War II). Avon, 1982. 135 p. Pb $3.

Gr 7+. B 79: Oct 1 1982. BR 2: Sep/Oct 1983. This fast-moving account of the last days of the Bismarck includes background on the war and the naval objectives of Britain and Germany.

Naval Operations and Ships–Fiction

636. MacLean, Alistair. San Andreas. Doubleday, 1985. 326 p. $16.

Gr 9+. B 82: Sep 1 1985. LJ 110: Nov 1 1985. Nearby U-boats add to the tension in this exciting story about a British hospital ship that has a saboteur aboard.

637. Monsarrat, Nicholas. Cruel Sea, The. Knopf, 1951. 509 p. $20.

Gr 10+. B 48: Sep 1 1951. B 84: Jul 1988. * LJ 76: Apr 15 1951. This powerful story is about British sailors seeking to keep supply lines open in spite of storms and German U-boats.

Prisoners of War

638. Baybutt, Ron. Colditz: The Great Escapes. Little, Brown, 1983. 127 p. ill. $15.

Gr 9+. B 80: Nov 1 1983. The Nazis kept photographic records of escape attempts from Colditz Castle, where they kept the prisoners most likely to attempt to escape. The ingenuity and courage of the prisoners is seen in the well-captioned photos.

639. Rieul, Roland. Escape into Espionage: The True Story of a French Patriot in World War Two. Walker, 1987. 221 p. ill. $16.

Gr 9+. B 83: May 1 1987. LJ 112: May 1 1987. As a prisoner of war Rieul made several attempts at escape, receiving more severe treatment after each attempt. When he did succeed in escaping he was trained as a spy and returned to France, where he obtained valuable information.

Underground Movements

640. Atkinson, Linda. In Kindling Flame: The Story of Hannah Senesh, 1921-1944. Lothrop, 1984. 214 p. ill. $11.

Gr 9+. B 81: Sep 1 1984. BC 38: Mar 1985. * BR 3: Mar 1985. * HB 61: May 1985. * SE 50: Apr 1986. * SLJ 31: May 1985. * VOYA 8: Oct 1985. Senesh was a Jewish poet who worked with the Resistance to rescue Jews and British soldiers. At age 23 she was captured and executed by the Nazis.

641. Bartoszewski, Wladyslaw. Warsaw Ghetto: A Christian's Testimony. Beacon; dist. by Harper, 1988. 160 p. $15.

Gr 9+. B 84: Feb 1 1988. The author recounts his experiences as a Catholic member of the Polish Resistance. He was active in forging documents, hiding Jews, and getting Jews from the ghetto to the underground.

642. Haas, Albert. Doctor and the Damned, The. St. Martin's, 1984. 333 p. $16.

Gr 9+. B 80: May 1 1984. LJ 109: Apr 1 1984. Haas' graphic account of his experiences in the Resistance and as a physician in a concentration camp shows the dignity and courage of the prisoners he knew.

643. Hay, Peter. Ordinary Heroes: Chana Szenes and the Dream of Zion. Putnam, 1986. 336 p. ill. $23.

Gr 9+. B 83: Sep 15 1986. LJ 111: Nov 1 1986. Hannah Senesh (Chana Szenes) was a young gifted Hungarian woman. Her Zionist beliefs led her to attempt a rescue mission of Hungarian Jews who were in concentration camps, resulting in her capture and execution. Hay's lively account of her courageous life includes photos.

644. Healey, Tim. Secret Armies: Resistance Groups in World War Two. MacDonald; dist. by Silver Burdett, 1982. 48 p. ill. $12.

Gr 5-9. B 78: Jun 1 1982. + - BC 36: Sep 1982. SLJ 29: Nov 1982. The secret war against Hitler involved spies, sabotage, and propaganda. This well-illustrated account includes a list of resistance organizations and industries.

645. Lawson, Don. French Resistance, The. (Spy Shelf). Messner, 1984. 192 p. $9. Pb $4.

Gr 5+. B 80: Mar 1 1984. * VOYA 7: Feb 1985. Lawson's stirring account of how ordinary French citizens worked in secret against the Nazis shows how separate underground units cooperated with each other.

646. Mayer, Allan J. Gaston's War: A True Story of a Hero of the Resistance in World War II. Presidio, 1988. 206 p. ill. $18.

Gr 9+. B 84: Jan 1 1988. LJ 112: Dec 1987. SLJ 35: Feb 1989. Gaston Vandermeersche was still in his teens when he became a successful Resistance organizer. He formed a network of over 1500 agents who worked against the Nazis. Mayer's biography shows the importance of the Resistance work of ordinary people.

647. Richardson, Nigel. July Plot, The. (Day That Made History). Dryad; dist. by David & Charles, 1987. 64 p. ill. $16.

Gr 6-9. B 83: Aug 1987. * BR 6: Sep/Oct 1987. The attempted assassination of Hitler in July 1944 is chronicled, and the effect of this event on subsequent happenings is explored. Photos are included.

648. Schoenbrun, David. Soldiers of the Night: The Story of the French Resistance. Dutton, 1980. 512 p. $18.

Gr 9+. B 76: Jun 15 1980. LJ 105: Jun 1 1980. In this account of the French Resistance, Schoenbrun emphasizes the deeds of individuals and shows how diverse the underground was.

649. Schur, Maxine. Hannah Szenes–A Song of Light. Jewish Publication Society, 1986. 106 p. ill. $11.

Gr 5-9. + - BC 40: Oct 1986. * SE 51: Apr/May 1987. + - SLJ 33: Oct 1986. SLJ 34: Feb 1988. Numerous quotes from her poems are used in telling the story of a young Jewish woman who gave her life to rescue other Jews from Yugoslavia.

650. Stein, R. Conrad. Resistance Movements. (World at War). Childrens Press, 1982. 47 p. ill. $7.

Gr 3-6. B 79: Feb 15 1983. SLJ 29: Apr 1983. Stein's overview of resistance to the Nazis in France, Greece, Yugoslavia, and other regions is highly illustrated.

651. Vinke, Herman. Short Life of Sophie Scholl, The. Harper, 1984. 192 p. ill. $11. Lib. ed. $11.

Gr 8+. B 85: Apr 1 1989. BC 37: May 1984. * BR 3: Nov 1984. HB 60: Aug 1984. SLJ 31: Sep 1984, + - Oct 1984. SLJ 34: Feb 1988. VOYA 7: Aug 1984. Sophie Scholl was executed at the age of 21 for her participation in the White Rose, an underground movement opposing the Nazi government.

Women

652. Saywell, Shelley. Women in War. Viking, 1985. 324 p. ill. $18.

Gr 9+. B 82: Oct 15 1985. LJ 110: Dec 1985. During the war women from around the world worked as reporters, pilots, guerilla soldiers, marines, medical personnel, and in a variety of other jobs. Saywell relates their experiences through illustrated biographical sketches.

Africa

General

654. Africa South of the Sahara 1978-79. Gale, 1978. 1256 p. ill. $69.

Gr 10+. + - B 76: Apr 15 1980. Part 1 includes background on the history, economy, and culture of southern Africa. Part 2 lists regional organizations. Part 3 includes essays on recent political and economic developments.

655. Ajayi, J. F. Ade. Historical Atlas of Africa. Cambridge University Press, 1985. 72 p. maps. $75.

Gr 9+. B 82: Mar 1 1986. B 83: Sep 1 1986. * BR 5: Nov/Dec 1986. * LJ 110: Oct 1 1985. SLJ 32: May 1986. Colorful event maps, process maps, and quantitative maps; photos; drawings; and text, all carefully indexed, trace African history from ancient times to 1980.

656. Anderson, Lydia. Nigeria, Cameroon, and the Central African Republic. (First Book). Watts, 1981. 66 p. $7.

Gr 6-8. B 77: Jul 15/Aug 1981. SLJ 27: Aug 1981. The history, geography, culture, government, and people of 3 nations in west central Africa are introduced.

657. Atmore, Anthony. Black Kingdoms, Black Peoples: The West African Heritage. Putnam, 1980. 128 p. ill. $15.

Gr 9+. B 76: Apr 15 1980. Atmore's highly illustrated introduction covers the history, culture, and legends of the nations in west Africa before European colonization.

658. Baynham, Simon. Africa from 1945. (Conflict in the 20th Century). Watts, 1987. 62 p. ill. $13.

Gr 6+. B 84: Jan 15 1988. BR 6: Jan/Feb 1988. SLJ 34: Jan 1988. This well-organized book may be used to study the history of Africa as a whole or by regions or by nations. The reasons for events are explained, and brief biographies, photos, and maps are included.

659. Blumberg, Rhoda. Southern Africa: South Africa, Namibia, Swaziland, Lesotho, and Botswana. (First Book). Watts, 1981. 62 p. ill. $7.

Gr 6-8. B 77: Jul 15/Aug 1981. SLJ 27: Aug 1981. The history, government, culture, and people of the region of southern Africa and of individual nations are introduced in this illustrated work.

660. Boyd, Herb. Former Portuguese Colonies: Angola, Mozambique, Guinea-Bissau, Cape Verde, Sao Tome, and Principe. (First Book). Watts, 1981. 62 p. ill. $7.

Gr 6-8. B 77: Jul 15/Aug 1981. SLJ 27: Aug 1981. The former Portuguese colonies in Africa are presented in this illustrated introduction that provides information on their history, culture, people, and government.

661. Brooks, George, E. Themes in African and World History. Indiana University Press, 1982. 59 p. Pb $4.

Gr 10+. HT 18: Feb 1985. The 3 essays in Brooks' work are entitled "The African Heritage and the Slave Trade"; "Tropical Africa; a Colonial Heritage"; and "A Scheme for Integrating Africa into World History."

662. Chiasson, John. African Journey. Macmillan, 1987. 55 p. ill. $17.

Gr 4-9. * B 84: Dec 1 1987. + - BC 41: Jan 1988. HB 64: Jan 1988. * SE 52: Apr 1988. SLJ 34: Jan 1988. VOYA 10: Feb 1988. Chiasson's colorful photo-essay shows how the juxtaposition of traditional customs, environment, and contemporary problems influence daily life in Africa.

663. Cohen, Daniel. Henry Stanley and the Quest for the Source of the Nile. (Great Adventurers Series). Evans; dist. by Dutton, 1985. 175 p. ill. $12.

Gr 6+. B 81: Feb 15 1985. SLJ 32: May 1985. Cohen uses excerpts from Stanley's writings to show effectively his childhood sufferings and the development of the character and personality that led him to become a noted explorer of Africa. Photos and maps are included.

664. Cook, Chris. African Political Facts Since 1945. Facts on File, 1983. 263 p. $20.

Gr 7+. B 81: Nov 1 1984. LJ 108: May 15 1983. This reference tool covers all aspects of African political and economic history since 1945. Statistical and biographical information is included.

665. Davidson, Basil. Africa in History: Themes and Outlines. Rev. & enl. ed. Macmillan, 1969; 1974. 318 p. ill. Pb $10.

Gr 7+. Metzner. Davidson clarifies the historical development of Africa from ancient to modern times.

666. Dostert, Pierre Etienne. Africa 1983. (World Today Series). Stryker-Post, 1983. 138 p. ill. Pb $5.

Gr 7+. B 80: Mar 1 1984. The history of Africa is examined by regional area. Maps of 1905 and 1983 illustrate changes.

667. East Africa. (Library of Nations). Time-Life; dist. by Silver Burdett, 1987. 160 p. ill. $19.

Gr 9+. * BR 6: Mar/Apr 1988. Uganda, Kenya, and Tanzania are the subjects of this lavishly illustrated work that covers history, government, economy, and resources.

668. Fage, J. D. History of Africa. Knopf, 1979. 534 p. maps. $25.

Adult. B 75; Dec 15 1978. B 83: Sep 1 1986. LJ 103: Nov 1 1978. This comprehensive history of Africa from prehistoric to modern times includes maps.

669. Fichter, George S. Bulge of Africa: Senegal, Guinea, Ivory Coast, Togo, Benin, and Equatorial Guinea. (First Book). Watts, 1981. 64 p. $7.

Gr 6-8. + - B 77: Jul 15/Aug 1981. SLJ 27: Aug 1981. This introductory overview of 7 nations in western Africa covers their history, culture, government, and people.

670. Foster, F. Blanche. East Central Africa: Kenya, Uganda, Tanzania, Rwanda, and Burundi. (First Book). Watts, 1981. 60 p. $7.

Gr 6-8. + - B 77: Jul 15/Aug 1981. SLJ 27: Aug 1981. The 5 nations in east central Africa are presented in this overview that covers history, culture, government, and people.

671. Fradin, Dennis B. Famines. (Disaster!). Childrens Press, 1986. 60 p. ill. $9.

Gr 4-8. B 83: Sep 1 1986. SLJ 33: Jan 1987. Fradin's overview of the causes and effects of famines throughout history emphasizes African famine.

672. Georges, D. V. Africa. (New True Book). Childrens Press, 1986. 44 p. maps. $12.

Gr 2-4. SLJ 33: May 1987. A short history of Africa is included in this colorful work that covers African geography, resources, wildlife, industry, technology, and people.

673. Gilfond, Henry. Countries of the Sahara: Chad, Mali, Mauritania, Niger, Upper Volta, and Western Sahara. (First Book). Watts, 1981. 64 p. $7.

Gr 6-8. + - B 77: Jul 15/Aug 1981. SLJ 27: Aug 1981. The nations of the Sahara desert are introduced in this overview that covers history, culture, geography, government, and people.

674. Gilfond, Henry. Gambia, Ghana, Liberia, and Sierra Leone. (First Book). Watts, 1981. 61 p. $7.

Gr 6-8. + - B 77: Jul 15/Aug 1981. SLJ 27: Aug 1981. This introductory overview of the west African nations of Gambia, Ghana, Liberia, and Sierra Leone covers history, culture, geography, government, and people.

675. Hornburger, Jane M. African Countries and Cultures: A Concise Illustrated Dictionary. McKay, 1981. 215 p. ill. $13.

Gr 7+. HB 57: Oct 1981. LJ 107: May 15 1982. SLJ 28: Nov 1981. In dictionary format, brief, illustrated entries cover all aspects of African history, culture, and politics. Succinct biographies are also included.

676. Jacobs, Francine. Fire Snake: The Railroad That Changed East Africa. Morrow, 1980. 95 p. $8. Lib. ed. $8.

Gr 5-10. B 77: Oct 1 1980. HB 56: Oct 1980. In a lively account, Jacobs describes the construction of the "Lunatic Line," a railroad that stretches from Lake Victoria to the Indian Ocean, and shows life in Africa at the turn of the 20th century.

677. Jones, Schuyler. Pygmies of Central Africa. (Original Peoples). Rourke, 1989. 48 p. ill. $14.

Gr 4-8. B 85: May 15 1989. + - SLJ 35: Jul 1989. Pygmy history and culture are introduced in this illustrated work.

678. Kodjo, Edem. Africa Tomorrow. Continuum; dist. by Harper, 1987. 312 p. $23.

Gr 9+. B 83: Jun 15 1987. LJ 112: Jul 1987. Kodjo analyzes the historical reasons for the underdevelopment of Africa and gives reasons for his belief that Africa can have a strong and prosperous future.

679. Lamb, David. Africans, The. Random, 1983. 384 p. $18.

Gr 9+. B 79: Jan 15 1983. LJ 108: Mar 1 1983. This readable portrait of Africa's 53 nations and more than 2000 tribes is lively and perceptive in conveying the complexity and contradictions of the continent.

680. Lauber, Patricia. Congo: River into Central Africa. (Rivers of the World). Garrard, 1964. 96 p. ill. $4.

Gr 4-7. Metzner. The Congo (Zaire) River has played an important historic role in the development of central Africa. Lauber discusses the history and culture of the people who have lived on its banks.

681. Lipschutz, Mark R. Dictionary of African Historical Biography. Aldine, 1978. 292 p. maps. $20.

Gr 9+. B 76: Jan 1 1980. Biographies of Africans and non-Africans important in African history through 1960 are included, with emphasis on those that precede 1900. Indexing is by subject and variant forms of a name.

682. Lipschutz, Mark R. Dictionary of African Historical Biography. 2nd ed. University of California Press, 1986. 328 p. $40.

Gr 9+. B 83: Apr 1 1987. The 1st edition of this work was a broad collection of biographies of sub-Saharan leaders prominent before 1960. This 2nd edition includes the biographies in the 1st edition plus a 32-page supplement that covers heads of state, 1960-1980.

683. Mazrui, Ali A. Africans: A Triple Heritage. Little, Brown, 1986. 336 p. ill. $30.

Gr 9+. B 82: Aug 1986. LJ 112: Jan 1987. Mazrui discusses the western, Islamic, and indigenous influences on African culture and shows how African culture has influenced western culture. Specific subjects such as sports and religion are included in this well-illustrated work.

684. McEvedy, Colin. Atlas of African History. Facts on File, 1980. 142 p. maps. $18.

Gr 9+. B 77: Feb 15 1981. This synthesis of African culture and history includes 59 maps, with factual narrative.

685. Rohr, Janelle. Problems of Africa. (Opposing Viewpoints Series). Greenhaven Press, 1986. 240 p. ill. $13. Pb $7.

Gr 9+. + - B 83: Mar 15 1987. BR 6: May 1987. - SLJ 33: Feb 1987. Rohr presents a wide range of western views of African problems, including famine and apartheid.

686. Murray, Jocelyn. Cultural Atlas of Africa. Facts on File, 1981 240 p. ill. $30.

Gr 9+. B 78: May 1 1982. LJ 106: Aug 1981. Numerous photos and maps that show changing boundaries and physical geography enrich the text that covers African culture from ancient to modern times.

687. Newman, Gerald. Zaire, Gabon, and the Congo. (First Book). Watts, 1981. 66 p. ill. $7.

Gr 6-8. + - B 77: Jul 15/Aug 1981. SLJ 27: Aug 1981. The history, people, government, and culture of three nations in west central Africa are covered in Newman's brief, illustrated overview.

688. Oliver, Roland. Cambridge Encyclopedia of Africa, The. Cambridge University Press, 1981. 492 p. ill. $35.

Gr 9+. B 78: Mar 15 1982. B 83: Sep 1 1986. LJ 107: May 1 1982. Oliver covers Africa as a whole, discussing the African past, contemporary Africa, and the relations of Africa with the world, and includes an overview of each nation.

689. Oliver, Roland. Short History of Africa, A. 6th ed. Facts on File, 1989. 303 p. $25.

Gr 10+. * BR 8: Nov/Dec 1989. This account of African history shows the rise and fall of various African empires, colonization, and the rise of independent nations.

690. Pedler, Frederick J. Main Currents of West African History 1940-1978. Barnes & Noble, 1980. 301 p. maps. $25.

Gr 9+. B 76: Apr 1 1980. Pedler shows how former colonies of Britain, France, and Portugal in west Africa became independent countries after World War II and why these 13 nations are so different in their cultural and political lives.

691. Moorehead, Alan. White Nile. Random, 1961. 385 p. ill. Pb $13.

Gr 10+. * B 57: Feb 1 1961. B 83: Sep 1 1986. LJ 86: Jan 1 1961. Burton, Livingstone, and other great explorers of the Victorian period are introduced, and the exploration of Africa and the response to it are examined. This well-written account is supported by fine maps, pictures and drawings.

692. Rowell, Trevor. Scramble for Africa, The. (Living Through History). Batsford; dist. by David & Charles, 1987. 72 p. ill. $18.

Gr 9+. SLJ 34: Feb 1988. This account of the partitioning of Africa is told primarily through biographies of explorers and empire-builders. These accounts represent several nationalities and include numerous quotes, illustrations, and a chronology.

693. Smith, Fredrika S. Stanley, African Explorer. Rand McNally, 1968. 240 p. ill. $17.

Gr 7+ Metzner. | - LJ 93: Apr 15 1968. This account of Stanley's explorations is primarily based on his writings.

694. Stewart, John. African States and Rulers. McFarland, 1989. 408 p. $45.

Gr 10+. + - BR 8: Nov/Dec 1989. LJ May 15 1989. This encyclopedic listing includes official and alternative names of African nations, with brief histories, and lists of rulers with dates.

695. Steyn, H. P. Bushmen of the Kalahari, The. (Original Peoples). Rourke, 1989. 48 p. ill. $11.

Gr 5-10. SLJ 35: Apr 1989. Photos and maps clarify this introduction to the history and culture of the San people (Bushmen) and their efforts to adapt to modern civilization.

696. Taylor, L. B. South East Africa: Zimbabwe, Zambia, Malawi, Madagascar, Mauritius, and Reunion. (First Book). Watts, 1981. 63 p. ill. $7.

Gr 6-8. + - B 77: Jul 15/Aug 1981. SLJ 27: Aug 1981. This illustrated work introduces the history, geography, government, culture, and people of the nations of south east Africa.

697. Van der Post, Laurens. Testament to the Bushmen. Viking, 1985. 176 p. ill. $20.

Gr 9+. B 81: Jan 1 1985. LJ 110: Apr 1 1985. Colorful photos and a clear text reveal traditional and modern activities of the Bushmen and their current problems.

698. Whitaker, Jennifer Seymour. How Can Africa Survive? Harper, 1988. 243 p. $20.

Gr 9+. B 84: May 15 1988. * LJ 113: Sep 15 1988. Whitaker provides insight into the problems of Africa in the 1980s in this account that considers history, economics, and tradition.

699. Woods, Harold. Horn of Africa: Ethiopia, Sudan, Somalia, and Djibouti. (First Book). Watts, 1981. 64 p. ill. $7.

Gr 6-8. + - B 77: Jul 15/Aug 1981. SLJ 27: Aug 1981. Information on the region and on individual nations covers history, government, culture, and people. Photos are included.

Botswana

700. Alverson, Marianne. Under African Sun. University of Chicago Press, 1987. 235 p. ill. $20.

Gr 9+. LJ 112: Apr 1 1987. Alverson's account of her years living in Botswana provide insight into its culture and the arrogance of developed nations concerning solutions to Botswana's problems.

Burundi

701. Wolbers, Marian F. Burundi. (Places and Peoples of the World). Chelsea House, 1989. 120 p. ill. $13.

Gr 6-8. B 86: Oct 15 1989. Burundi's history, geography, economy, culture, and people are covered in this illustrated overview.

Cameroon

702. Hathaway, Jim. Cameroon in Pictures. (Visual Geography Series). Lerner, 1989. 64 p. ill. $12.

Gr 5-8. B 86: Sep 15 1989. Photos, maps, and charts augment this overview of Cameroon's history, geography, resources, government, and cities.

Central African Republic

703. Central African Republic in Pictures. (Visual Geography Series). Lerner, 1989. 64 p. ill. $10.

Gr 6+. + - SLJ 35: Jul 1989. This introduction to the history and government of the Central African Republic includes photos.

Egypt

704. Cross, Wilbur. Egypt. (Enchantment of the World). Childrens Press, 1982. 124 p. ill. $10.

Gr 4-8. B 79: Apr 1 1983. + - B 86: Sep 1 1989. SLJ 29: Apr 1983. SLJ 30: Nov 1983. The contrasts of modernized Egypt with ancient villages and the influence of petroleum and cotton are shown in numerous photos. Coverage includes history, geography, culture, agriculture, and people. Maps.

705. David, A. Rosalie. Egyptian Kingdoms, The. (Making of the Past). Peter Bedrick, 1988. 160 p. ill. $20.

Gr 9+. * BR 8: May/Jun 1989. SLJ 35: Mar 1989. + - VOYA 12: Apr 1989. Egyptian history and culture from ancient times to the 20th century are presented in this illustrated overview that includes numerous photos.

706. Feinstein, Steve. Egypt in Pictures. Rev. ed. (Visual Geography Series). Lerner, 1988. 64 p. ill. $10.

Gr 5-8. B 85: Feb 1 1989. B 86: Sep 1 1989. SLJ 35: May 1989. Egypt's history, geography, culture, economy, resources, cities, government, people, and contemporary problems are introduced in this illustrated work that includes maps and charts.

707. Harper, Paul. Suez Crisis, The. (Flashpoints). Rourke, 1987. 78 p. ill. $11.

Gr 7-10. SLJ 33: Aug 1987. Photos and maps enhance this balanced explanation of the multinational interests in the Middle East that erupted into the Suez Crisis in 1956.

708. Lye, Keith. Take a Trip to Egypt. Watts, 1985. 32 p. ill. $11.

Gr 2-3. B 86: Sep 1 1989. + - SLJ 30: Feb 1984. For the beginning reader, a simple introduction to Egypt's history, geography, economy, government, culture, and people. Photos and a map are included.

709. Mahmoud, Zaki Naguib. Land and People of Egypt. Rev. ed. (Portraits of the Nations Series). Harper, 1960; 1972. 128 p. ill. $12.

Gr 6+. Metzner. * B 56: Feb 15 1960. HB 36: Feb 1960. * LJ 84: Dec 15 1959. This readable account of Egyptian history, current to the early 1970s, is written by an Egyptian.

710. Wucher King, Joan. Historical Dictionary of Egypt. (African Historical Dictionaries). Scarecrow, 1984. 719 p. $48.

Gr 10+. B 81: Jun 15 1985. Emphasis is on Islamic Egypt, from 640 A.D. to 1982. Arranged alphabetically are biographies and articles on all aspects of Egyptian life. Number 36 of the series.

Egypt–0-476

711. Asimov, Isaac. Egyptians, The. Houghton, 1967. 288 p. ill. $12.

Gr 7+. Metzner. HB 44: Apr 1968. LJ 93: Jan 15 1968. Asimov sorts out the 30 Egyptian dynasties and other complications of Egyptian history in this readable, illustrated work that extends to the fall of the Roman Empire.

712. Baines, John. Atlas of Ancient Egypt. Facts on File, 1980. 240 p. ill. $30.

Gr 9+. B 77: Jun 1 1981. This colorful work, which covers Egypt from 6500 B.C. to the end of the Roman Empire, includes 36 maps and over 500 plates along with the explanatory text.

713. Bowman, Alan K. Egypt after the Pharaohs: 332 BC-AD 642 from Alexander to the Arab Conquest. University of California Press, 1986. 264 p. ill. $25.

Gr 9+. B 83: Jan 1 1987. A lively and well-illustrated account of Egyptian political and social life during the Greco-Roman era.

714. David, Rosalie. Ancient Egypt. (History as Evidence). Warwick; dist. by Watts, 1984. 37 p. ill. $9.

Gr 4-7. B 81: Mar 1 1985. SLJ 31: Mar 1985. Emphasis is on the Pharaohs, politics, trade, war, religion, and daily life in this concise and colorful work.

715. Perl, Lila. Mummies, Tombs, and Treasure: Secrets of Ancient Egypt. Clarion, 1987. 120 p. ill. $15.

Gr 4-8. * B 83: Jun 15 1987. BC 40: Jun 1987. * BR 6: Sep/Oct 1987. HB 63: Sep/Oct 1987. SLJ 33: Aug 1987. * SE 52: Apr/May 1988. In addition to a wealth of detail about mummies, their preparation, and religious significance, Perl presents information on ancient Egyptian history.

716. Robinson, Charles Alexander. Ancient Egypt. (First Book). Watts, 1984. 63 p. ill. $9.

Gr 4-7. B 81: Oct 15 1984. BC 38: Dec 1984. New photos and a time chart add to the value of this authoritative work on the history of ancient Egypt that emphasizes culture and the daily life of the ordinary person.

717. Romer, John. Ancient Lives: Daily Life in Egypt of the Pharaohs. Holt, 1984. 235 p. ill. $19.

Gr 9+. LJ 110: Feb 1 1985. SLJ 31: Mar 1985. * VOYA 8: Jun 1985. In his carefully researched biography of a 3000-year-old Egyptian village, Romer provides rich details about the lives of villagers, scribes, priests, and tombmakers. Colorful photos, a chronology of pharaohs, and maps enhance the work.

718. Romer, John. People of the Nile: Everyday Life in Ancient Egypt. Crown, 1982. 224 p. ill. $20.

Gr 9+. B 79: Apr 1 1983. SLJ 29: Apr 1983. Romer presents a lively and well-illustrated political and cultural history of ancient Egypt based on his BBC television series.

719. Santrey, Laurence. Ancient Egypt. Troll, 1985. 29 p. ill. $8. Pb $2.

Gr 3-5. + - SLJ 32: Feb 1986. Santrey's brief account of the highlights of the history of ancient Egypt centers on the importance of the Nile.

720. Stead, Miriam. Ancient Egypt. Rev. ed. (Civilization Library). Gloucester Press; dist. by Watts, 1985. 32 p. ill. $10.

Gr 5-7. SLJ 32: Mar 1986. This overview of the history of ancient Egypt emphasizes the role of religion in the culture.

721. Ventura, Piero. In Search of Tutankhamun. Silver Burdett, 1985. 47 p. ill. $12. Lib. ed. $8.

Gr 4-9. + - HB 62: Jul/Aug 1986. SLJ 32: Aug 1986. The way of life and the major historic events of ancient Egypt are presented along with accounts of major archaeological discoveries.

Egypt–0-476–Social Life and Customs

722. Burland, Cottie A. Ancient Egypt. (Great Civilizations). Defour, 1974. 93 p. ill. $7.

Gr 4-8. Metzner. Burland's brief, illustrated overview of life in ancient Egypt covers architecture, education, clothing, industry, and culture.

723. Millard, Anne. Ancient Egypt. (Modern Knowledge Library). Watts, 1979. 44 p. ill. Lib. ed. $7.

Gr 5-7. B 76: Dec 1 1979. SLJ 26: Jan 1980. Highlights of the history of ancient Egypt are presented, but Millard emphasizes daily social activities, work, and religious life.

724. Watson, Lucilla. Egyptians, The. (First History). Rourke, 1987. 24 p. ill. $8.

Gr 1-3. + - SLJ 33: Aug 1987. Watson's introduction to ancient Egyptian town and country life, government, and religion, also discusses the contributions of Egypt to world history.

Egypt–Biographies

725. Carroll, Raymond. Anwar Sadat. (Impact Biography). Watts, 1982. 118 p. ill. $9.

Gr 7+. B 79: Nov 1 1982. SLJ 29: Nov 1982. Sadat's childhood, his political career, his administration as president of Egypt, and his assassination are covered in this biography that includes quotes from Sadat's writing.

726. DeChancie, John. Gamal Abdel Nasser. (World Leaders Past & Present). Chelsea House, 1987. 111 p. ill. $17.

Gr 6+. B 84: Dec 15 1987. B 86: Sep 1 1989. + - SLJ 34: Feb 1988. Following World War II Nasser led Egypt to independence after centuries of foreign domination. Quotes, maps, photos, and a chronology augment the accessible text.

727. Rosen, Deborah Nodler. Anwar el-Sadat: A Man of Peace. (People of Distinction). Childrens Press, 1986. 152 p. ill. $9.

Gr 4-8. B 83: Feb 15 1987. B 86: Sep 1 1989. SLJ 33: Feb 1987. Rosen introduces Sadat's rise from a youth of poverty to the presidency of Egypt. Photos of significant persons in his life and maps that explain the territorial conflicts of the region are included.

728. Sullivan, George. Sadat: The Man Who Changed Mid-East History. Walker, 1981. 124 p. ill. $9. Lib. ed. $10.

Gr 5+. B 78: Feb 1 1982. BC 35: Jan 1982. LJ 106: Nov 15 1981. * SE 46: Apr 1982. SLJ 28: Mar 1982. VOYA 5: Apr 1982. This biography emphasizes Sadat's political activities that range from terrorist to a leader in the effort to establish peace in the Middle East.

Egypt–Exploration and Explorers

729. Percefull, Aaron W. Nile, The. (First Book). Watts, 1984. 61 p. ill. $9.

Gr 5-8. B 81: Dec 15 1984. B 86: Sep 1 1989. + - SLJ 31: Nov 1984. The exploration of the Nile and the changes that have occurred along the river are presented. Includes photos.

Egypt–Fiction

730. DePaola, Tomie. Bill and Pete Go Down the Nile. Putnam, 1987. 32 p. ill. $13.

Gr K-3. B 83: May 1 1987. SLJ 34: Sep 1987. A bit of Egyptian history and lore are incorporated in this humorous story of Bill and Pete, who capture a couple of bad guys on a class trip down the Nile.

731. Stolz, Mary. Zekmet, the Stone Carver: A Tale of Ancient Egypt. Harcourt, 1988. 32 p. ill. $14.

Gr 2-6. B 84: May 15 1988. BC 41: May 1988. * SLJ 35: May 1988. Skillful artwork in the Egyptian style enhances this imaginative account of how the Sphinx may have come to be.

Egypt–Kings, Queens, Rulers, etc.

732. Hoobler, Dorothy. Cleopatra. (World Leaders Past & Present). Chelsea House, 1986. 115 p. ill. $17.

Gr 6+. B 83: Feb 1 1987. SLJ 33: Feb 1987. Highly illustrated with photos and maps, this biography of the legendary Cleopatra shows how she used her genius and beauty in attempts to realize her ambition of world domination. Numerous photos enrich the readable text.

733. Langley, Andrew. Cleopatra and the Egyptians. (Life and Times). Bookwright Press; dist. by Watts, 1986. 58 p. ill. $11.

Gr 5-7. SLJ 33: Nov 1986. This brief, illustrated overview of Cleopatra's life presents a picture of daily life at that time.

Egypt–Kings, Queens, Rulers, etc.–Fiction

734. Carter, Dorothy S. His Majesty, Queen Hatshepsut. Lippincott, 1987. 248 p. ill. Lib. ed. $14.

Gr 7+. BC 41: Nov 1987. BR 6: Mar/Apr 1988. * SLJ 34: Oct 1987. + - VOYA 10: Dec 1987. Details of the royal life enhance this fictional biography of Hatshepsut, the only female pharaoh of Egypt (ca. 1503-1482 B.C.).

Egypt–Social Life and Customs

735. Aliki. Mummies Made in Egypt. Crowell, 1979. 32 p. ill. $9.

Gr 2-5. B 76: Dec 15 1979. BC 33: Feb 1980. HB 55: Dec 1979. * SE 44: Apr 1980. SLJ 26: Jan 1980. Ancient Egyptian history, culture, and religion are examined in this well-illustrated examination of the mummy-making process.

736. Bendick, Jeanne. Egyptian Tombs. Watts, 1989. 64 p. ill. $11.

Gr 3-6. B 85: Apr 15 1989. BC 42: Apr 1989. SLJ 35: May 1989. Life in ancient Egypt and the beliefs that led to the construction of the pyramids are introduced in this well-illustrated work. A glossary is appended.

737. Katan, Norma Jean. Hieroglyphs: The Writing of Ancient Egypt. Atheneum, 1981. 96 p. ill. $9.

Gr 4-6. SLJ 28: Jan 1982. The significance of hieroglyphics to the ancient Egyptians is examined, along with the education of scribes and many beliefs of the Egyptians.

738. Scott, Geoffrey. Egyptian Boats. (Carolrhoda On My Own Books). Carolrhoda, 1981. 48 p. ill. $6.

Gr 2-4. BC 35: Jul/Aug 1982. SLJ 28: Feb 1982. Insight into the ancient Egyptian culture and way of life is provided in this simple, illustrated account of the many types and functions of boats used for everyday and ceremonial activities.

739. Stead, Miriam. Egyptian Life. Harvard University Press, 1986. 72 p. ill. $8.

Gr 9+. SLJ 33: Mar 1987. Stead uses photos and illustrations to support her idea that the Egyptians were happy people who looked forward to continuing their enjoyable life after death.

740. Unstead, R. J. Egyptian Town, An. (See Inside). Warwick; dist. by Watts, 1986. 32 p. ill. $11.

Gr 4-6. BR 6: May/Jun 1987. SLJ 33: Feb 1987. This illustrated introduction to life in ancient Egypt shows how towns were organized and the ways of life of the ruling and servant classes.

Egypt–Technology and Civilization

741. Woods, Geraldine. Science in Ancient Egypt. (First Book). Watts, 1988. 92 p. ill. $10.

Gr 5-8. B 84: May 1 1988. BR 7: Sep/Oct 1988. + - SLJ 35: May 1988. The ancient Egyptians made many advances in agriculture, architecture, astronomy, crafts, mathematics, medicine, and writing. Photos, other illustrations, and a glossary are included.

Ethiopia

742. Abebe, Daniel. Ethiopia in Pictures. Rev. ed. (Visual Geography Series). Lerner, 1988. 64 p. ill. $10.

Gr 5-8. B 85: Feb 1 1989. The effects of drought and famine in Ethiopia are covered along with the nation's history, geography, climate, economy, and culture. Photos, maps, and charts are included.

743. Fradin, Dennis B. Ethiopia. (Enchantment of the World). Childrens Press, 1988. 125 p. ill. $23.

Gr 4-9. B 85: Feb 15 1989. SLJ 35: Mar 1989. This balanced work covers Ethiopia's history, geography, government, politics, culture, and severe economic problems. Maps, photos, and drawings enrich the text.

744. Kleeberg, Irene Cumming. Ethiopia. (First Book). Watts, 1986. 63 p. ill. $9.

Gr 5-8. + - B 82: May 1 1986. - SLJ 32: Aug 1986. This introduction to Ethiopia's history, religions, languages, culture, political problems, poverty, and famine includes photos.

745. Lye, Keith. Take a Trip to Ethiopia. Watts, 1986. 32 p. ill. $10.

Gr 2-5. B 82: May 15 1986. Photos on each page and a brief informative text introduce Ethiopian history, geography, industry, and cities.

Ethiopia–Fiction

746. Levitin, Sonia. Return, The. Atheneum, 1987. 183 p. $13.

Gr 6-10. * B 83: Apr 15 1987. BC 40: Mar 1987. BR 6: Nov/Dec 1987. * SE 52: Apr/May 1988. * SLJ 33: May 1987. VOYA 10: Jun 1987. Hunger and prejudice forced a number of Ethiopian Jews to flee their homes and become a part of operation Moses, a secret airlift that flew thousands of them to Israel. Their experience is realistically portrayed in this story of Desta, an orphan.

Ethiopia–Kings, Queens, Rulers, etc.

747. Negash, Askale. Haile Selassie. (World Leaders Past & Present). Chelsea House, 1989. 112 p. ill. $17.

Gr 7+. B 86: Oct 1 1989. BR 8: Nov/Dec 1989. SLJ 35: Sep 1989. Numerous photos and background information augment this balanced account of the personal and public life of the Emperor of Ethiopia.

Gabon

748. Perriman, Andrew. Gabon. (Let's Visit Places and Peoples of the World Series). Chelsea House, 1988. 96 p. ill. $13.

Gr 4-6. B 85: Apr 1 1989. Photos and maps augment this clear account of Gabon's history, geography, culture, people, and problems.

Ghana

749. Barnett, Jeanie M. Ghana. (Places and Peoples of the World). Chelsea House, 1988. 104 p. ill. $13.

Gr 5-7. B 85: Feb 15 1989. Ghana's current problems are introduced along with the nation's history, people, culture, economy, and geography.

750. Ghana in Pictures. (Visual Geography Series). Lerner, 1988. 64 p. ill. $10.

Gr 5-8. B 84: Aug 1988. The history of Ghana through 1987 is covered as well as its geography, resources, government, cities, and culture. Numerous photos, maps, and charts are included.

751. Hintz, Martin. Ghana. (Enchantment of the World). Childrens Press, 1987. 127 p. ill. $20.

Gr 4-9. B 84: Oct 15 1987. SLJ 34: Dec 1987. This overview of Ghanan history, culture, geography, and politics begins with a chapter on the life of a village schoolboy. Photos and maps are included.

Ghana–Biographies

752. Kellner, Douglas. Kwame Nkrumah. (World Leaders Past & Present). Chelsea House, 1987. 111 p. ill. $17.

Gr 9+. B 83: Aug 1987. SLJ 34: Sep 1987. A balanced biography of Nkrumah's personal and political life.

Ivory Coast

753. Cote d'Ivoire (Ivory Coast) in Pictures. (Visual Geography Series). Lerner, 1988. 64 p. ill. $10.

Gr 5-8. B 84: Apr 15 1988. SLJ 35: Nov 1988. This introduction to Cote d'Ivoire covers history, geography, resources, economy, cities, culture, religion, education, and health. Numerous photos, maps, and charts are included.

Kenya

754. Bentsen, Cheryl. Maasai Days. Summit, 1989. 276 p. $20.

Gr 10+. B 86: Sep 1 1989. LJ 114: Aug 1989. The fierce and proud Maasai people are torn between their wish to benefit from modern practices and their strong desire to retain traditional beliefs and activities. Numerous quotes enhance the text.

755. Kaula, Edna M. Land and People of Kenya. Rev. ed. (Portraits of the Nations Series). Harper, 1964; 1973. 160 p. ill. $12.

Gr 5-9. Metzner. B 70: Mar 15 1974. LJ 99: Sep 15 1974. Kenya's history, politics, economy, and social life are covered in this illustrated work.

756. Kenya in Pictures. (Visual Geography Series). Lerner, 1988. 64 p. ill. $10.

Gr 5-8. B 84: Apr 15 1988. SLJ 35: Nov 1988. This introduction to Kenya's history, land, government, people, and economy is supplemented by photos, maps, and charts.

757. Lye, Keith. Take a Trip to Kenya. Watts, 1985. 32 p. ill. $10.

Gr 2-4. B 82: Jan 1 1986. SLJ 32: Apr 1986. This introduction to Kenyan history, geography, economy, and culture includes photos, maps, and a page of stamps and currency.

758. Maren, Michael. Land and People of Kenya. (Portraits of the Nations Series). Lippincott, 1989. 192 p. ill. $15. Lib. ed. $15.

Gr 7+. B 86: Sep 15 1989. SLJ 35: Oct 1989. In an illustrated overview Maren presents Kenya's history, geography, people, resources, and culture.

759. Stein, R. Conrad. Kenya. (Enchantment of the World). Childrens Press, 1985. 127 p. ill. $20.

Gr 4-6. B 82: Mar 1 1986. SLJ 32: May 1986. Kenya's national park system and its wildlife are included in this overview of Kenya's history, geography, industry, and culture.

760. Winslow, Zachery. Kenya. (Let's Visit Places and Peoples of the World Series). Chelsea House, 1987. 93 p. ill. $12.

Gr 6-9. + - SLJ 34: Feb 1988. History, geography, politics, economy, and urban life are included in this illustrated work about Kenya.

Kenya Fiction

761. Whitnell, Barbara. Song of the Rainbird, The. St. Martin's, 1984. 367 p. $15.

Gr 9+. B 81: Nov 15 1984. SLJ 31: Jan 1985. Forty turbulent years of Kenya's history provide the background for the story of Kate, who went there in 1906 from England, her half-caste adopted daughter, and their friends and family.

Lesotho

762. Tonsing-Carter, Betty. Lesotho. Chelsea House, 1988. 95 p. ill. $12.

Gr 4-6. B 85: Dec 1 1988. This straightforward account of Lesotho's history, geography, industry, government, economy, and people includes maps and numerous photos.

Liberia

763. Smith, James Wesley. Sojourners in Search of Freedom: The Settlement of Liberia by Black Americans. University Press of America, 1987. 242 p. $25.

Gr 10+. SE 52: Feb 1988. In the early 19th century the United States government supported a movement by free blacks to emigrate and form their own nation on the west coast of Africa. This is an account of their experiences and accomplishments.

764. Sullivan, Jo M. Liberia in Pictures. (Visual Geography Series). Lerner, 1988. 64 p. ill. $10.

Gr 5-8. B 84: Aug 1988. SLJ 35: Oct 1988. An abundance of photos, maps, and charts enriches this work that covers Liberian history, geography, resources, people, cities, and problems of the 1980s.

Libya

765. Brill, Marlene Targ. Libya. (Enchantment of the World). Childrens Press, 1988. 127 p. ill. $22.

Gr 4-7. + - B 84: May 15 1988. Brill's straightforward introduction to Libya's history, geography, culture, politics, government, and economy includes maps and colorful photos.

766. Tames, Richard. Take a Trip to Libya. Watts, 1989. 32 p. ill. $11.

Gr 1-3. B 86: Sep 1 1989. + - SLJ 35: Jun 1989. This brief, illustrated work provides an overview of basic information about Libya and its history.

Libya–Biographies

767. Blundy, David. Qaddafi and the Libyan Revolution. Little, Brown, 1987. 240 p. ill. $18.

Gr 10+. LJ 112: Sep 1 1987. A thorough, objective, and readable biography of the Libyan leader who supports terrorism as a tool of foreign policy.

768. Kyle, Benjamin. Muammar El-Qaddafi. (World Leaders Past & Present). Chelsea House, 1987. 112 p. ill. $17.

Gr 6-10. B 83: Jun 15 1987. B 86: Sep 1 1989. SLJ 33: Aug 1987. This anecdotal biography of Qaddafi also presents recent Libyan history and its relations with its Arab neighbors. Captioned photos and quotes are a highlight of this balanced account.

769. Lawson, Don. Libya and Qaddafi. Rev. ed. (Impact Book). Watts, 1987. 128 p. ill. $12.

Gr 6+. B 83: Jun 15 1987. B 86: Sep 1 1989. BR 6: Sep/Oct 1987. SLJ 33: Jun/Jul 1987. VOYA 10: Aug/Sep 1987. In this revised edition, Lawson explores Libya's history, its role in the Middle East, and the impact of chief of state Muammar Qaddafi on Libyan domestic and foreign policies.

Madagascar

770. Madagascar in Pictures. Rev. ed. (Visual Geography Series). Lerner, 1988. 64 p. ill. $10.

Gr 5-8. B 85: Feb 1 1989. SLJ 35: May 1989. This concise overview covers Madagascar's history, culture, economy, and contemporary society. It is enriched by numerous photographs, charts, and maps.

771. Stevens, Rita. Madagascar. (Places and Peoples of the World). Chelsea House, 1987. 111 p. ill. $12.

Gr 6-8. B 84: Feb 1 1988. Stevens introduces Madagascar's history, politics, economy, culture, and people.

Malawi

772. O'Toole, Thomas. Malawi in Pictures. Rev. ed. (Visual Geography Series). Lerner, 1988. 64 p. ill. $10.

Gr 5-8. B 85: Feb 1 1989. SLJ 35: Feb 1989. Photos, maps, and charts augment this account of the history, geography, government, economy, people, resources, culture, cities, and contemporary problems of Malawi.

773. Sanders, Renfield. Malawi. (Places and Peoples of the World). Chelsea House, 1987. 103 p. ill. $12.

Gr 6-8. B 84: Feb 1 1988. Malawi's history, geography, culture, economy, resources, and people are introduced in this illustrated work.

Morocco

774. Hintz, Martin. Morocco. (Enchantment of the World). Childrens Press, 1985. 127 p. ill. $15.

Gr 4-8. + - B 82: Dec 1 1985. + - B 86: Sep 1 1989. + - SLJ 32: Jan 1986. Maps and a reference section are included in this illustrated introduction to Moroccan history, economy, culture, government, and geography.

775. Lye, Keith. Take a Trip to Morocco. Watts, 1988. 32 p. ill. $10.

Gr 2-3. B 84: May 1 1988. + - B 86: Sep 1 1989. Colorful illustrations highlight this overview of Moroccan history, geography, culture, and government.

776. Morocco in Pictures. (Visual Geography Series). Lerner, 1989. 64 p. ill. $10.

Gr 5-8. B 86: Sep 1 1989. SLJ 35: Aug 1989. This illustrated introduction to Morocco covers the nation's history, government, economy, people, and contemporary problems.

Mozambique

777. James, R. S. Mozambique. (Places and Peoples of the World). Chelsea House, 1987. 103 p. ill. $12.

Gr 7-9. B 84: Feb 1 1988. Mozambique's history, politics, economy, social structure, and people are introduced in this illustrated work.

Namibia

778. Gould, D. E. Namibia. Chelsea House, 1988. 96 p. ill. $13.

Gr 4-6. B 85: Apr 1 1989. This straightforward account of Namibia's history, geography, industry, government, economy, and people includes maps and numerous photos.

Nigeria

779. Feinstein, Steve. Nigeria in Pictures. (Visual Geography Series). Lerner, 1988. 64 p. ill. $10.

Gr 5-8. B 84: Aug 1988. Nigerian history, government, geography, resources, and culture are covered in this illustrated work that includes maps, photos, and charts.

780. Forman, Brenda-Lu. Land and People of Nigeria. (Portraits of the Nations Series). Harper, 1964. 160 p. ill. $12.

Gr 5-9. Metzner. HB 41: Feb 1965. LJ 89: Dec 15 1964. The history, geography, culture, religion, and language of each of the regions of Nigeria are covered up to the 1960s. Includes glossary.

781. Nelson, Harold D. Nigeria: A Country Study. (Area Handbook Series). U. S. Government Printing Office, 1982. 358 p. ill. $12.

Gr 10+. B 83: Sep 1 1986. Historical and current information on Nigeria is supplemented by photos, maps, and tables.

Rwanda

782. Pomeray, J. K. Rwanda. (Places and Peoples of the World). Chelsea House, 1988. 104 p. ill. $12.

Gr 5+. B 85: Feb 15 1989. BR 7: Sep/Oct 1988. + - VOYA 11: Oct 1988. Ethnic rivalries and other contemporary problems of Rwanda are explained in this illustrated account that covers the nation's history, economy, and geography.

Senegal

783. Gellar, Sheldon. Senegal: An African Nation between Islam and the West. (Profiles: Nations of Contemporary Africa). Westview, 1982. 145 p. ill. $22.

Gr 11+. B 83: Sep 1 1986. Maps and tables augment this account of Senegal's history, culture, economy, foreign relations, and government.

784. Lutz, William. Senegal. (Places and Peoples of the World). Chelsea House, 1987. 104 p. ill. $12.

Gr 6-8. B 84: Feb 1 1988. Senegal's history, geography, culture, politics, and people are introduced in this illustrated work.

785. Senegal in Pictures. (Visual Geography Series). Lerner, 1988. 64 p. ill. $10.

Gr 5-10. B 84: Apr 15 1988. SLJ 35: Nov 1988. Information on Senegal's geography, culture, and people is included along with its history, government, and the outlook for its economic future. Photos, maps, and charts augment the text.

Sierra Leone

786. Milsome, John. Sierra Leone. Chelsea House, 1988. 95 p. ill. $12.

Gr 4-6. B 85: Dec 1 1988. The history, geography, people, industry, resources, politics, and economics of Sierra Leone are introduced in this well-illustrated work.

Somalia

787. Godbeer, Deardre. Somalia. Chelsea House, 1988. 95 p. ill. $12.

Gr 4-6. B 85: Dec 1 1988. This straightforward account of Somalia's history, geography, industry, government, economy, and people includes maps and numerous photos.

Somalia–Social Life and Customs

788. Baez, Joan. One Bowl of Porridge: Memoirs of Somalia. John Daniel, 1986. 96 p. ill. Pb $8.

Gr 9+. B 83: Sep 1 1986. LJ 111: Oct 1 1986. The mother of folk singer Joan Baez recounts her experiences as a volunteer worker at health and food stations in Somalia where refugees from famine and war sought help.

South Africa

789. Canesso, Claudia. South Africa. (Places and Peoples of the World). Chelsea House, 1989. 119 p. ill. $13.

Gr 5+. * BR 8: Sep/Oct 1989. SLJ 35: Jul 1989. VOYA 12: Aug 1989. This clear and informative overview of South Africa's history, geography, government, culture, and economy includes photos, a map, and a glossary.

790. De Villiers, Marq. White Tribe Dreaming: As Witnessed by Eight Generations of an Afrikaner Family. Viking, 1988. 410 p. ill. $20.

Gr 9+. + - B 84: Feb 1 1988. LJ 113. Feb 1 1988. De Villiers traces the history of white society in South Africa from the 17th century, showing the development of apartheid.

791. Evans, Michael. South Africa. (Issues). Watts, 1988. 32 p. ill. $11.

Gr 4-9. B 84: May 1 1988. BC 41: Jun 1988. BR 7: May/Jun 1988. SLJ 34: Aug 1988. Photos or maps appear on every page in this brief introduction to South Africa that covers history, daily life, apartheid, politics, and labor.

792. Griffiths, Ieuan. Crisis in South Africa, The. (Flashpoints). Rourke, 1988. 76 p. ill. $12.

Gr 6-9. SLJ 35: Feb 1989. Photos are used to help clarify the development of the racial policies of South Africa. The impact of these policies on international issues is also discussed.

793. Harris, Sarah. Sharpeville. (Day That Made History). Batsford; dist. by David & Charles, 1989. 64 p. ill. $18.

Gr 6+. + - SLJ 35: Feb 1989. When blacks protested passport laws in 1960, the overreaction of the police led to shooting. Harris examines the causes, events, and results of the violence.

794. Harris, Sarah. Timeline: South Africa. (Weighing Up the Evidence). Dryad, 1988. 64 p. ill. $18.

Gr 5+. B 85: Jan 15 1989. - BR 7: Nov/Dec 1988. + - SLJ 35: Jan 1989. Harris presents a succinct, chronological account of events in the history of South Africa and quotes from speeches and writings that show the development of political attitudes.

795. Harrison, David. White Tribe of Africa: South Africa in Perspective. (Perspectives on Southern Africa). University of California Press, 1982. 315 p. ill. $18.

Gr 10+. LJ 107: Apr 1 1982. This readable overview of the history of the South African white population is based on a BBC film series and includes photos, quotes, and a glossary. Number 31 of the series.

796. Lapping, Brian. Apartheid: A History. Braziller, 1987. 197 p. ill. $20.

Gr 9+. B 83: Jun 1 1987. LJ 112: Apr 15 1987. This history of Afrikaner nationalism shows the development of apartheid and covers the political, social, and economic causes and results of this policy.

797. Lawson, Don. South Africa. (First Book). Watts, 1986. 88 p. ill. $10.

Gr 5+. + - B 82: Apr 15 1986. BC 39: May 1986. + - SE 51: Feb 1987. + - SLJ 32: Aug 1986. VOYA 9: Dec 1986. Emphasis is on the practice of apartheid, its causes and effects, in this account of South African history since the 17th century.

798. Leach, Graham. South Africa: No Easy Path to Peace. Routledge & Kegan Paul, 1986. 226 p. ill. $25.

Gr 9+. B 82: Jun 15 1986. LJ 111: Jul 1986. Journalist Leach combines history, observation, and interviews to provide an informative account of the political situation in South Africa to 1985.

799. Lee, Emanoel. To the Bitter End: A Photographic History of the Boer War, 1899-1902. Viking; Penguin, 1985; 1986. 226 p. ill. $20. Pb $11.

Gr 10+. HT 21: Nov 1987. LJ 111: May 1 1986. Vivid and balanced, this photo essay shows all aspects of the Boer War. The author was a photographer who spent 20 years collecting the photos and interviewing survivors.

800. Omer-Cooper, J. D. History of Southern Africa. Heinemann, 1987. 297 p. ill. $20.

Gr 9+. B 84: Sep 15 1987. This history of South Africa presents the experiences of blacks and whites, and analyzes political, social, and economic forces. Photos and maps are included.

801. Omond, Roger. Apartheid Handbook, The. Penguin, 1986. 231 p. Pb $5.

Gr 9+. B 82: Jan 1 1986. LJ 111: Jan 1986. Using a question and answer format, Omond explores such topics as pass laws, race classification, health, education, the church, the press, and security services.

802. Pascoe, Elaine. South Africa: Troubled Land. Watts, 1987. 128 p. ill. $12.

Gr 6+. * B 84: Jan 1 1988. + - SLJ 34: Feb 1988. * VOYA 11: Jun 1988. Pascoe's history of South Africa begins before the Europeans came, covers the British and Dutch conflict, the discovery of gold and diamonds, the development of apartheid, and the major leaders and events of the late 20th century.

803. Paton, Alan. Land and People of South Africa. Rev. ed. (Portraits of the Nations Series). Harper, 1955; 1972. 160 p. ill. $12.

Gr 5-9. Metzner. LJ 98: Mar 15 1973. Written by a noted expert, this readable, illustrated history of South Africa is current to the early 1970s.

804. Stein, R. Conrad. South Africa. (Enchantment of the World). Childrens Press, 1986. 127 p. ill. $15.

Gr 4-8. B 83: Apr 1 1987. + - SLJ 33: Jun/Jul 1987. Stein introduces South African history, geography, politics, and culture and discusses the impact of apartheid on the nation. Photos and maps are included.

805. Tessendorf, K. C. Along the Road to Soweto: A Racial History of South Africa. Atheneum, 1989. 152 p. ill. $14.

Gr 6+. BC 43: Oct 1989. VOYA 12: Oct 1989, * Dec 1989. This history of South Africa from the days before European colonization to the present provides a clear background for understanding contemporary problems.

806. Villet, Barbara. Blood River: The Passionate Saga of South Africa's Afrikaners and of Life in Their Embattled Land. Everest, 1982. 213 p. ill. $17.

Gr 9+. B 78: Jun 15 1982. LJ 107: Jun 1 1982. Villet presents a readable history of the Afrikaners, the white rulers of South Africa, from their point of view.

807. Watson, R. L. South Africa in Pictures. (Visual Geography Series). Lerner, 1988. 64 p. ill. $10.

Gr 5-8. B 84: Aug 1988. SLJ 35: Oct 1988. South Africa's political problems and its noted leaders are introduced along with basic information on the nation's history, geography, resources, cities, government, and culture. Photos, maps, and charts are included.

808. Wilson, Monica. History of South Africa to 1970, A. Westview, 1983. 476 p. ill. $35. Pb $14.

Gr 9+. B 81: Nov 15 1984. This illustrated history of South Africa begins in pre-colonial days and covers events to modern times.

South Africa–Biographies

809. Benson, Mary. Nelson Mandela. (Profiles). Hamilton; dist. by David & Charles, 1987. 58 p. ill. $10.

Gr 4-8. B 84: Sep 1 1987. BC 41: Sep 1987. BR 6: Nov/Dec 1987. SLJ 34: Sep 1987. The evolution of Mandela's political philosophy and his determination to continue the struggle for racial equality are shown in this simple, balanced biography.

810. Benson, Mary. Nelson Mandela. Norton, 1986. 230 p. ill. $17. Pb $8.

Gr 9+. B 82: Jan 15 1986. LJ 111: Mar 15 1986. Benson quotes freely from Mandela's speeches and letters in this biography that shows the development of his political beliefs. Includes photos.

811. Bentley, Judith. Archbishop Tutu of South Africa. Enslow, 1988. 96 p. ill. $14.

Gr 6-10. B 85: Feb 1 1989. + - BC 42: Nov 1988. + - BR 7: Jan/Feb 1989. SLJ 35: Nov 1988. A chronology and glossary augment this account of Tutu's growing up under apartheid and his religious and political leadership in efforts to achieve racial equality.

812. Biko, Steve. I Write What I Like. Harper, 1979. 216 p. $11.

Gr 9+. B 81: Nov 15 1984. LJ 104: Feb 15 1979. This collection of Steve Biko's writing and speeches shows his visionary leadership of South Africa's Black Consciousness Movement, and includes a memoir by the editor.

813. Boesak, Allan A. If This Is Treason, I Am Guilty. Eerdmans, 1987. 134 p. $8.

Gr 9+. VOYA 10: Feb 1988. Boesak is a noted opponent of apartheid in South Africa. This is a collection of his speeches and sermons delivered from 1982 to 1986.

814. Derrida, Jacques. For Nelson Mandela. Seaver Books; dist. by Holt, 1987. 256 p. $18.

Gr 9+. + - B 84: Sep 15 1987. VOYA 11: Apr 1988. Twenty-three international writers pay tribute to Mandela through essays, fiction, drama, and poetry that speak of his life, the evils of apartheid, and the ongoing struggle for human dignity and freedom.

815. Greene, Carol. Desmond Tutu: Bishop of Peace. (Picture-Story Biographies). Childrens Press, 1986. 31 p. ill. $8.

Gr 2-5. B 83: Jan 15 1987. SLJ 34: Sep 1987. Greene's pictorial biography of the black South African teacher who became a priest and led a civil rights struggle. Includes a timeline.

816. Hargrove, Jim. Nelson Mandela: South Africa's Silent Voice of Protest. (People of Distinction). Childrens Press, 1989. 136 p. ill. $15.

Gr 4-9. B 85: Aug 1989. SLJ 35: Sep 1989. Hargrove's balanced chronological biography of the leader of the African National Congress includes quotations and photos.

817. Harrison, Nancy. Winnie Mandela. Braziller, 1986. 181 p. ill. $15.

Gr 9+. B 82: Jan 1 1986. LJ 111: Feb 15 1986. Banned, imprisoned, and tortured, still Winnie Mandela serves with her husband as a leader of anti-apartheid forces. Her story is the story of racism in South Africa.

818. Haskins, Jim. Winnie Mandela: Life of Struggle. Putnam, 1988. 173 p. ill. $15.

Gr 7+. + - B 84: May 1 1988. * BC 41: Jun 1988. IID 64: Sep/Oct 1988. * SE 53: Apr/May 1989. SLJ 35: Jun/Jul 1988. * VOYA 11: Aug 1988. Winnie Mandela's life of increasing political activity and sacrifice are seen in this fast-paced biography that includes quotes and photos.

819. Hoobler, Dorothy. Nelson and Winnie Mandela. (Impact Biography). Watts, 1987. 128 p. ill. $12.

Gr 6+. * B 83: Apr 15 1987. B 83: Aug 1987. BC 40: May 1987. BR 6: Nov/Dec 1987. * SLJ 33: May 1987. * VOYA 10: Aug/Sep 1987. This biography of the Mandelas is also the story of the African National Congress and their efforts to achieve racial justice in South Africa. Includes photos.

820. Makeba, Miriam. Makeba: My Story. New American Library, 1988. 248 p. ill. $19.

Gr 9+. B 84: Jan 15 1988. LJ 113: Feb 15 1988. VOYA 12: Feb 1989. A noted South African singer tells the effects of apartheid on her life and of her experiences as an internationally renowned musician and a representative to the United Nations.

821. Mandela, Nelson. Struggle Is My Life: His Speeches and Writings Brought Together with Historical Documents and Accounts of Mandela in Prison by Fellow Prisoners. Rev. ed. Pathfinder, 1986. 249 p. ill. $23.

Gr 9+. B 83: Sep 15 1986. LJ 111: Dec 1986. This compilation includes Mandela's major speeches and writings, comments from fellow prisoners, documents, articles, and photos.

822. Mandela, Winnie. Part of My Soul Went with Him. Norton, 1985. 163 p. ill. $17.

Gr 9+. B 82: Feb 1 1986. B 82: May 15 1986. SE 51: Feb 1987. SLJ 33: Nov 1986. Interviews and letters form the basis of this autobiographical account of Winnie Mandela's personal life and the development of her beliefs and leadership in the anti-apartheid movement.

823. Mathabane, Mark. Kaffir Boy in America: An Encounter with Apartheid. Scribner, 1989. 288 p. $20.

Gr 10+. B 85: May 1 1989. LJ 114: Jun 1 1989. In his sequel to Kaffir Boy, Mathabane describes the culture shock of coming to America, his experiences as a tennis player, and his opposition to racism and apartheid.

824. Mathabane, Mark. Kaffir Boy: The True Story of a Black Youth's Coming of Age in Apartheid South Africa. Macmillan, 1986. 354 p. ill. $19.

Gr 9+. B 82: Mar 15 1986. LJ 111: Apr 15 1986. SLJ 33: Dec 1986. Mathabane tells his own story of growing up black under apartheid and of struggling against both white and black opposition to his desire to become a tennis player.

825. Meltzer, Milton. Winnie Mandela: The Soul of South Africa. (Women of Our Time). Viking, 1986. 64 p. ill. $10.

Gr 4-8. B 83: Sep 1 1986. BC 40: Oct 1986. - SLJ 33: Dec 1986. This introduction to Mandela's life shows her education and her growing involvement in anti-apartheid political activities.

826. Ramusi, Molapatene Collins. Soweto, My Love: A Testimony to Black Life in South Africa. Holt, 1989. 262 p. maps. $23.

Gr 10+. * BR 8: Sep/Oct 1989. VOYA 12: Aug 1989, Oct 1989. A member of the Batlokwa tribe, Ramusi became an attorney and activist for freedom. His memoir reveals the details of his struggle for the freedom of his people.

827. Tutu, Desmond. Words of Desmond Tutu, The. Newmarket, 1989. 112 p. ill. $13.

Gr 7+. BR 8: Nov/Dec 1989. LJ 114: May 1 1989. VOYA 12: Jun 1989, Oct 1989. Photos and a chronology enrich this topically arranged collection of excerpts from Tutu's speeches and writings. The introduction is written by Desmond Tutu's daughter, Naomi Tutu.

828. Vail, John. Nelson and Winnie Mandela. (World Leaders Past & Present). Chelsea House, 1988. 112 p. ill. $17.

Gr 7+. B 85: Oct 15 1988. BR 8: May/Jun 1989, Sep/Oct 1989. SLJ 35: Mar 1989. + - VOYA 12: Feb 1989. In telling the story of Nelson and Winnie Mandela, Vail recounts the history of the struggle against apartheid since World War II.

829. Wepman, Dennis. Desmond Tutu. Watts, 1989. 154 p. ill. $13.

Gr 7-10. + - B 86: Sep 1 1989. Quotations, anecdotes, a chronology, and photos supplement this overview of the personal and political life of Bishop Desmond Tutu.

830. Winner, David. Desmond Tutu. (People Who Have Helped the World). Gareth Stevens, 1989. 68 p. ill. $13.

Gr 5-9. B 85: Aug 1989. SLJ 35: Nov 1989. This introduction to Tutu's life is enriched by photos and illustrations, maps, quotations, a chronology, and a glossary. It addresses the causes and effects of apartheid.

831. Woods, Donald. Biko. Rev. and expanded ed. Holt, 1987. 418 p. $19.

Gr 10+. VOYA 11: Apr 1988. Woods, a South African journalist, presents the biography and philosophy of his friend Steve Biko, the Bantu anti-apartheid leader whom Woods believes was murdered in prison. This is the basis for the movie Cry Freedom.

South Africa–Fiction

832. Courtenay, Bruce. Power of One, The. Random, 1989. 524 p. $20.

Gr 10+. + - B 85: Apr 15 1989. * BR 8: Nov/Dec 1989. * LJ 114: May 1 1989. * VOYA 12: Dec 1989. During World War II an English-born South African boy takes up boxing to overcome the injustices he has suffered. As he gains experience and skill the reader meets a succession of well-drawn characters who provide a good sense of time and place.

833. Gordon, Sheila. Waiting for the Rain. Orchard, 1987. 214 p. $13.

Gr 6+. * B 83: Aug 1987. BC 40: Jul 1987. HB 63: Sep/Oct 1987. SE 52: Apr/May 1988. + - SLJ 33: Aug 1987. VOYA 10: Dec 1987. The friendship between a white boy and a black boy grows and changes over 9 years until the policies of apartheid force them onto opposite sides of a violent confrontation.

834. Hope, Christopher. Separate Development, A. Scribner, 1981. 199 p. $11.

Gr 9+. B 78: Jan 1 1982. LJ 106: Dec 15 1981. SLJ 28: Apr 1982. Living in a nation where one's value and rights are based on skin color is the theme of this novel about Moto, whose olive skin and crinkly hair leave him displaced even though his parents are white.

835. Jones, Toeckey. Go Well, Stay Well: A Novel. Harper, 1980. 240 p. $9.

Gr 7+. B 76: May 1 1980. BC 33: Jun 1980. HB 56: Jun 1980. In spite of the restrictions of apartheid, a white girl and a black girl strike up a friendship, which can be maintained only at a price.

836. Mendels, Ora. Mandela's Children. Little, Brown, 1987. 282 p. $17.

Gr 9+. B 83: Dec 1 1986. LJ 111: Dec 1986. A naturalized American, Ruth Harris returns to her native South Africa, which she left 20 years ago. Her mission is to convince the son of her former friend to leave before his anti-apartheid activities result in imprisonment.

837. Michener, James A. Covenant, The. Random, 1980. 878 p. $16.

Gr 10+. + - B 77: Sep 1 1980. + - LJ 105: Oct 15 1980. Michener traces the development of South Africa through his account of several generations of fictional families.

838. Naidoo, Beverley. Journey to Jo'burg: A South African Story. Lippincott, 1986. 75 p. ill. $10.

Gr 3-7. + - B 82: Mar 15 1986. + - BC 39: May 1986. * SE 51: Apr/May 1987. * SLJ 33: Aug 1986. VOYA 9: Aug/Oct 1986. The illness of a little sister sends Naledi and Tiro from their small village to Johannesburg to find their mother. Their story shows the cruel social conditions imposed by apartheid.

839. Paton, Alan. Cry, The Beloved Country. Scribner, 1948. 278 p. $18. Pb $5.

Gr 10+. B 82: May 15 1986. B 44: Feb 1 1948. * HB 24: Nov 1948. * LJ 73: Feb 1 1948. A humble and wise Zulu minister who traveled to the city to visit his sick sister found that his daughter had become a prostitute and his son was accused of murder. A novel of hope, courage, and faith.

840. Sacks, Margaret. Beyond Safe Boundaries. Dutton, 1989. 155 p. $14.

Gr 7+. * B 85: May 15 1989. BC 42: Jul/Aug 1989. BR 8: Nov/Dec 1989. HB 65: Jul/Aug 1989. VOYA 12: Aug 1989. This story of a Jewish family in South Africa during the 1950s and 1960s reveals the contradictions of life in a divided nation.

South Africa–Race Relations

841. Apartheid: The Facts. International Defense and Aid Fund, 1983. 112 p. Pb $7.

Gr 10+. B 83: Sep 1 1986. SE 51: Feb 1987. This handbook on all aspects of South Africa's policies of racial discrimination includes maps, tables, graphs, and a glossary.

842. Finnegan, William. Crossing the Line: A Year in the Land of Apartheid. Harper, 1986. 432 p. $23.

Gr 9+. * B 83: Sep 1 1986. LJ 111: Sep 15 1986. The school boycott of 1980 that resulted in violence is recorded by Finnegan, an American who was teaching near Cape Town. His account shows the maturing of his political awareness.

843. Frederikse, Julie. South Africa: A Different Kind of War, from Soweto to Pretoria. Harper, 1987. 192 p. ill. Pb $13.

Gr 9+. B 83: Jun 1 1987. B 83: Aug 1987. SLJ 33: Aug 1987. Oral history combined with photos, pamphlets, posters, newspaper clippings, and songs provide an account of daily life under apartheid from 1976 to 1986.

844. Gordimer, Nadine. Lifetimes Under Apartheid. Knopf, 1986. 115 p. ill. $30.

Gr 9+. * B 83: Feb 1 1987. * B 83: Aug 1987. LJ 112: Mar 1 1987. Photos of 35 years of life under apartheid are enriched by brief selections from Gordimer's fiction.

845. Laure, Jason. South Africa: Coming of Age Under Apartheid. Farrar, 1980. 180 p. ill. $14.

Gr 7+. B 77: Oct 1 1980. B 81: Nov 15 1984. BC 34: Dec 1980. * SE 45: Apr 1981. * SLJ 27: Feb 1981. SLJ 28: Sep 1981. VOYA 3: Feb 1981. Photo essays of 8 young South Africans of different ethnic or social groups show contemporary culture and reveal much of the nation's history.

846. Lelyveld, Joseph. Move Your Shadow: South Africa, Black and White. Times Books, 1985. 384 p. map. $18.

Gr 9+. B 82: Sep 15 1985. * LJ 110: Nov 15 1985. Lelyveld is a South African who was forced to leave in the 1960s. He has been a reporter for the New York Times, and returned to South Africa in the 1980s. He reports on his interviews with leaders and common people and on the changes he found.

847. Magubane, Peter. Soweto: The Fruit of Fear. Eerdmans, 1986. 100 p. ill. $30. Pb $15.

Gr 9+. B 83: Dec 1 1986. B 83: Aug 1987. VOYA 10: Aug/Sep 1987. Outstanding photos document this account of the 1976 uprising in Soweto, its causes, and its fearful results.

848. Manning, Richard. They Cannot Kill Us All: An Eyewitness Account of South Africa. Houghton, 1987. 255 p. $17.

Gr 9+. B 84: Sep 1 1987. BR 7: Sep/Oct 1988. LJ 112: Nov 1 1987. Manning records interviews with persons representing all facets of the South African political spectrum and his own candid reactions to what he observed before the government expelled him for his work as a Newsweek reporter.

849. Mermelstein, David. Anti-Apartheid Reader: South Africa and the Struggle Against White Racist Rule. Grove, 1987. 544 p. $23. Pb $13.

Gr 9+. B 83: Jul 1987. + - LJ 112: Jul 1987. Excerpts from speeches, interviews, articles, and books clarify both sides of the apartheid issue and provide an account of United States

foreign policy toward South Africa. A chronology, a glossary, and maps are included.

850. Meyer, Carolyn. Voices of South Africa: Growing Up in A Troubled Land. Harcourt, 1986. 220 p. $15.

Gr 7+. + - B 83: Sep 15 1986. BC 40: Nov 1986. HB 63: May/Jun 1987. * SE 51: Apr/May 1987. SLJ 33: Nov 1986. Meyer spent five weeks in South Africa interviewing persons of all racial groups. She presents the history of the apartheid conflict along with excerpts and anecdotes from interviews.

851. Neuhaus, Richard John. Dispensations: The Future of South Africa as South Africans See it. Eerdmans, 1986. 314 p. $17.

Gr 9+. B 82: Apr 1 1986. LJ 111: Jul 1986. These interviews with South Africans represent the full range of political beliefs and present ideas not commonly heard in the United States.

852. North, James. Freedom Rising. Macmillan, 1985. 435 p. $20.

Gr 9+. * B 81: Feb 1 1985. B 82: Oct 1 1985. B 82: Jan 15 1986. LJ 110: May 1 1985. VOYA 9: Feb 1987. North, a white journalist, traveled throughout South Africa for over 4 years and interviewed ordinary persons from a wide range of social groups. These accounts are informative about the nation's political and social history.

853. Tatum, Lyle. South Africa: Challenge and Hope. Rev. ed. Watts, 1987. 214 p. $14.

Gr 7+. B 83: Feb 15 1987. B 83: Aug 1987. Charts, maps, and statistics supplement this discussion of conditions in South Africa, including the divestment movement, international relations, and apartheid.

854. Turnley, David C. Why Are They Weeping? South Africans Under Apartheid. Stewart, Tabori, & Chang; dist. by Workman, 1988. 192 p. ill. $35. Pb $20.

Gr 9+. * B 85: Jan 1 1989. + - LJ 114: Feb 1 1989. Daily life and political violence are recorded in Turnley's photo-essay about South Africa in the mid-1980s.

855. Uhlig, Mark A. Apartheid in Crisis. Random, 1986. 331 p. Pb $6.

Gr 9+. B 83: Sep 1 1986. This collection of speeches and articles on both sides of the apartheid issue provides a balanced introduction for the general reader.

856. Wilson, Francis. South Africa: The Cordoned Heart. Norton, 1986. 186 p. ill. $25. Pb $15.

Gr 9+. B 82: May 15 1986. * LJ 111: May 15 1986. This powerful collection of photographic essays covers such varied topics as black migrant labor, poverty, forced removals, and overcrowding, all contrasted with white wealth.

857. Woods, Donald. South African Dispatches: Letters to My Countrymen. Holt, 1987. 188 p. $17

Gr 9+. B 83: Dec 1 1986. BR 6: May/Jun 1987. LJ 111: Dec 1986. + - SE 52: Jan 1988. SLJ 33: Jun/Jul 1987. * VOYA 9: Feb 1987. Woods was a noted journalist in South Africa until he was officially banned by the government. This collection of his biting articles written between 1975 and 1977 exposes the cruel contradictions of apartheid.

South Africa–Social Life and Customs

858. Magubane, Peter. Black Child. Knopf, 1982. 102 p. ill. $17. Pb $9.

Gr 9+. B 78: Jun 15 1982. SLJ 28: Aug 1982. LJ 107: Jun 15 1982. VOYA 5: Oct 1982. This photo-essay shows the reality of growing up black in South Africa.

South Africa–Venda

859. Stevens, Rita. Venda. (Places and Peoples of the World). Chelsea House, 1989. 96 p. ill. $12.

Gr 7+. SLJ 35: Nov 1989. Venda is one of the "homeland nations" established in 1979 by South Africa for black Africans. Stevens' overview covers social, political, and geographical issues.

South Africa–Zulus

860. Ngubane, Harriet. Zulus of Southern Africa. (Original Peoples). Rourke, 1987. 48 p. ill. $13.

Gr 4-6. B 84: Jan 15 1988. Colorful illustrations enhance this introduction to the Zulu people, their religion, culture, and modern problems.

861. Stanley, Diane. Shaka, King of the Zulus. Morrow, 1988. 40 p. ill. $13.

Gr K-5. * B 85: Nov 1 1988. BC 42: Nov 1988. HB 65: Jan/Feb 1989. * SE 53: Apr/May 1989. This colorfully illustrated biography of the 19th-century military genius and Zulu (Bantu) chief provides information on the customs and activities of his people. Zululand is now a region of South Africa.

Sudan

862. Sudan in Pictures. Rev. ed. (Visual Geography Series). Lerner, 1988. 64 p. ill. $10.

Gr 5-8. B 85: Feb 1 1989. The history, geography, government, culture, economy, and people of Sudan are introduced in this well-illustrated text.

Swaziland

863. Conway, Jessica. Swaziland. Chelsea House, 1989. 96 p. ill. $13.

Gr 4-6. B 85: Apr 1 1989. This straightforward account of Swaziland's history, geography, industry, government, economy, and people includes maps and numerous photos.

Tanzania

864. Crofts, Marylee S. Tanzania in Pictures. Rev. ed. (Visual Geography Series). Lerner, 1988. 64 p. ill. $10.

Gr 5-8. B 85: Feb 1 1989. SLJ 35: Feb 1989. Crofts' account of the history, geography, people, economy, resources, culture, cities, and contemporary problems of Tanzania is augmented by photos, maps, and charts.

865. McCulla, Patricia E. Tanzania. (Places and Peoples of the World). Chelsea House, 1988. 112 p. ill. $13.

Gr 5-7. B 85: Feb 15 1989. Photos, a map, and a glossary enhance this overview of Tanzania's history, ethnic groups, geography, and the nation's troubled economy.

Tanzania–Biographies

866. Saitoti, Tepilit Ole. Worlds of a Maasai Warrior: An Autobiography. Random, 1985. 184 p. $17.

Gr 9+. B 82: Dec 1 1985. B 82: May 15 1986. LJ 110: Dec 1985. Saitoti describes his life growing up in a traditional Maasai village, his education in Europe and the United States, and his return home.

Togo

867. Winslow, Zachery. Togo. (Places and Peoples of the World). Chelsea House, 1987. 96 p. ill. $12.

Gr 6-8. B 84: Feb 1 1988. Winslow's introduction to Togo covers its history, including slavery and colonialism, as well as its geography, politics, social structure, and ethnic groups.

Tunisia

868. Tunisia in Pictures. (Visual Geography Series). Lerner, 1989. 64 p. ill. $10.

Gr 6+. SLJ 35: Sep 1989. Numerous photos, charts, and maps enhance this introduction to Tunisia's history, geography, economy, politics, and culture.

Uganda

869. Creed, Alexander. Uganda. (Places and Peoples of the World). Chelsea House, 1987. 96 p. ill. $12.

Gr 6-8. + - B 84: Feb 1 1988. This introduction to Uganda covers history, economy, ethnic groups, politics, social structure, and geography.

Uganda–Princes and Princesses

870. Nyabongo, Elizabeth. Elizabeth of Toro: The Odyssey of an African Princess. Simon & Schuster, 1989. 238 p. ill. $20. Pb $10.

Gr 10+. B 86: Sep 1 1989. + - LJ 114: Sep 1 1989. Nyabongo is a princess from Uganda. She is also a lawyer, an actress, and a foreign minister for her country. Her account of her life includes information on Ugandan history and politics.

Zambia

871. Holmes, Timothy. Zambia. Chelsea House, 1988. 96 p. ill. $12.

Gr 4-6. B 85: Dec 1 1988. This straightforward account of Zambia's history, geography, industry, government, economy, and people includes maps and numerous photos.

Zimbabwe

872. Barnes-Svarney, Patricia. Zimbabwe. (Places and Peoples of the World). Chelsea House, 1989. 128 p. ill. $13.

Gr 5+. + - B 86: Oct 15 1989. BR 8: Nov/Dec 1989. Zimbabwe's history, geography, culture, economy, government, and people are introduced. The text is supplemented by photos and a glossary.

873. Laure, Jason. Zimbabwe. (Enchantment of the World). Childrens Press, 1988. 128 p. ill. $22.

Gr 4-8. * B 84: Aug 1988. SLJ 35: Sep 1988. This balanced overview of Zimbabwe's history, culture, resources, industry, economy, and daily life includes photos, maps, and a chronology.

874. Lye, Keith. Take a Trip to Zimbabwe. Watts, 1987. 32 p. ill. $10.

Gr 1-4. B 84: Nov 15 1987. + - SLJ 34: Jun/Jul 1988. Photos, charts, and maps augment the brief text that introduces Zimbabwe's history, geography, economy, resources, and culture.

875. O'Toole, Thomas. Zimbabwe in Pictures. (Visual Geography Series). Lerner, 1988. 64 p. ill. $10.

Gr 5+. B 84: Apr 15 1988. SLJ 34: Jun/Jul 1988. O'Toole's illustrated introduction to Zimbabwe's history, geography, economy, politics, and culture includes photos, charts, and maps.

876. Stark, Al. Zimbabwe: A Treasure of Africa. (Discovering Our Heritage). Dillon Press, 1986. 160 p. ill. $12.

Gr 4-8. B 82: Jun 15 1986. BR 5: Sep/Oct 1986. SLJ 32: May 1986. History, geography, culture, resources, and people are covered in this illustrated introduction that shows the similarities between Zimbabwe and the United States.

Asia and Oceania

General

877. Batchelor, John. Euphrates, The. (Rivers of the World). Silver Burdett, 1981. 67 p. ill. $8.

Gr 4-8. B 78: Sep 1 1981. + - BC 35: Sep 1981. SLJ 28: Nov 1981. In a journey downstream readers are introduced to the history, geography, culture, resources, and religions of the area. Photos, maps, and a glossary are included.

878. Coblence, Jean-Michel. Asian Civilizations. (Human Story). Silver Burdett, 1988. 77 p. ill. $16.

Gr 5-8. B 85: Jan 1 1989. + - SLJ 35L: Feb 1989. Coblence traces the ancient history of China, Japan, India, Korea, Indonesia, and other Asian countries. A timeline, photos, and maps are included.

879. Constable, George. Arabian Peninsula. (Library of Nations). Time-Life; dist. by Silver Burdett, 1985. 160 p. ill. $14

Gr 7+. * BR 4: Mar/Apr 1986. Pictorial essays and a well-written text cover the history of the peninsula, the Bedouin way of life, and the rise of Islam, the changes caused by oil wealth, and the complexities of the region.

880. De Lee, Nigel. Rise of the Asian Superpowers from 1945. (Conflict in the 20th Century). Watts, 1987. 62 p. ill. $13.

Gr 6+. B 84: Jan 15 1988. BR 7: Sep/Oct 1988. SLJ 34: Feb 1988. The post-World War II political and military development of China, Japan, Korea, India, Pakistan, and Bangladesh are explored, using helpful biographical sketches, charts, and illustrations.

881. Evans, Michael. Gulf Crisis, The. (Issues). Gloucester Press; dist. by Watts, 1988. 32 p. ill. $12.

Gr 4-8. SLJ 35: Mar 1989. This brief overview of the Persian Gulf crisis shows its economic, political, and religious causes, and its effect on international affairs. Well-illustrated, this account is balanced and complete through 1987.

882. Goldston, Robert C. Sword of the Prophet: A History of the Arab World from the Time of Mohammed to the Present Day. Dial, 1979. 246 p. maps. $9.

Gr 8+. B 76: Nov 15 1979. BC 33: Feb 1980. This readable chronological history of Arab political and economic history covers events from 570 A.D. through the 1970s.

883. Hinton, Harold C. Far East and Western Pacific 1983, The. (World Today Series). Stryker-Post, 1983. 99 p. ill. Pb $4.

Gr 7+. B 80: Mar 1 1984. Current through 1983, these illustrated profiles of national history, culture, and economy cover Australia, Burma, Cambodia, China, the Philippines, Thailand, Vietnam, and other nations of the Far East.

884. Lightfoot, Paul. Mekong, The. (Rivers of the World). Silver Burdett, 1981. 65 p. ill. $8.

Gr 4-8. B 78: Sep 1 1981. B 83: Oct 1 1986. SLJ 28: Nov 1981. The Mekong flows from Tibet, forms the boundary between Thailand and Laos, and crosses Laos, Cambodia, and Vietnam. This account shows the river's economic importance and the cultures of those who live on its banks.

885. Pandey, B.N. South and South-East Asia, 1945-1979: Problems and Policies. (Making of the 20th Century). St. Martin's, 1980. 236 p. $20.

Gr 11+. HT 11: Aug 1981. This comparative analysis of the political history of the region of South and South-East Asia shows how the non-aligned position of these nations influenced the Cold War.

886. Polk, William Roe. Arab World, The. 4th ed. (American Foreign Policy Library). Harvard University Press, 1980. 456 p. ill. $23. Pb $9.

Gr 9+. B 77: Dec 15 1980. The history of the Arab nations and their relations with the United States is discussed, showing the impact of the oil economy and cultural changes.

887. Rice, Edward. Babylon, Next to Nineveh; Where the World Began. Four Winds, 1979. 204 p. ill $9.

Gr 6+. BC 33: Feb 1980. SLJ 26: Jan 1980. Rice's sweeping history of the Mesopotamian area covers conquests by the Babylonians, Assyrians, Greeks, and Romans. His selection of events provides a clear overview of the importance of the region from ancient to modern times.

888. Weingarten, Violet. Jordan: River of the Promised Land. (Rivers of the World). Garrard, 1967. 96 p. Pb $4.

Gr 4-7. Metzner. The Jordan forms the boundary between Israel and Syria, flows across Jordan, and separates Israel and Jordan before it empties into the Dead Sea. Weingarten discusses the history and culture of the people who have lived on its banks since ancient times.

General–Exploration and Explorers

889. Ceserani, Gian Paolo. Marco Polo. Putnam, 1982. 34 p. ill. $10.

Gr 2-7. B 78: May 1 1982. BC 35: May 1982. HB 58: Jun 1982. SLJ 28: May 1982. SLJ 30: Nov 1983. This oversized picture book presents a rich picture of the explorations of Marco Polo and the societies he visited.

890. Demi. Adventures of Marco Polo, The. Holt, 1982. 29 p. ill. $7.

Gr 1-4. - BC 35: Jun 1982. SLJ 28: Apr 1982. Marco Polo's travels and the sights he saw are portrayed by bright drawings. Endpaper maps show the entire journey, while other maps show portions of the 24-year trip.

891. Discovering Marco Polo. SPICE, 1982. 98 p. $13.

Gr 7+. SE 50: Feb 1986. Primary sources are used to introduce the history and culture of Central America as seen by Marco Polo.

892. Greene, Carol. Marco Polo: Voyager to the Orient. (People of Distinction). Childrens Press, 1987. 109 p. ill. $12.

Gr 4-7. + - B 84: Nov 1 1987. + - SLJ 34: Dec 1987. Polo's life is traced from his boyhood, and his travels are discussed in a balanced, illustrated account.

893. Severin, Tim. Tracking Marco Polo. Peter Bedrick; dist. by Harper, 1986. 164 p. ill. $15.

Gr 9+. B 82: Mar 1 1986. LJ 111: Mar 15 1986. The author led a photographic expedition that retraced Marco Polo's journey. He combines Polo's account with his own narrative and photos for an informative tour of Asia, past and present.

General–Islamic Countries

894. Beshore, George. Science in Early Islamic Culture. Watts, 1988. 69 p. ill. $11.

Gr 5-8. B 85: Dec 15 1988. B 86: Sep 1 1989. SLJ 35: Jun 1989. As the Islamic empire grew the conquerors preserved and expanded the science of the nations they controlled, and they were responsible for the spread of Arabic numerals, several important medical discoveries, and the scientific method of research.

General–Kings, Queens, Rulers, etc.

895. Wepman, Dennis. Tamerlane. (World Leaders Past & Present). Chelsea House, 1987. 111 p. ill. $16.

Gr 6-10. B 83: Jul 1987. SLJ 33: Aug 1987. Tamerlane ruled a Mongol empire from 1369 to 1405. He controlled land in Turkestan, Afghanistan, Persia, India, and Asia Minor, and was noted for his savagery.

General–Middle East

896. Adams, Michael. Middle East, The. (Handbooks to the Modern World). Facts on File, 1988. 865 p. maps. $45.

Gr 9+. BR 7: May/Jun 1988. For each nation in the Middle East this is a handy reference to history, politics, economy, social affairs, and statistics.

897. Carter, Jimmy. Blood of Abraham, The. Houghton, 1985. 227 p. maps. $16.

Adult. + - B 81: Apr 1 1985. * LJ 110: May 1 1985. Carter's country-by-country examination of the historic causes of conflict in the Middle East also discusses the current impasse and provides suggestions for the future.

898. Draper, Thomas. Israel and the Middle East. Wilson, 1983. 233 p. map. Pb $7.

Gr 10+. BR 2: Nov/Dec 1983. Articles by government officials, news reporters, and others analyze the causes of the Middle East conflict and efforts at peace.

899. Ferrara, Peter. East vs. West in the Middle East. (Impact Book). Watts, 1982. 90 p. map. $9.

Gr 7+. B 79: Jul 1983. * BR 2: Jan/Feb 1984. SLJ 30: Sep 1983. Ferrara details the history of conflict within the Middle East and the problems between that region and the west. He presents a clear picture of many varied points of view.

900. Frank, Harry. Discovering the Biblical World. Rev. ed. Hammond, 1988. 288 p. ill. $30. Pb $17.

Gr 9+. * BR 6: Mar/Apr 1988. An updated, nonsectarian account of the lives and history of the ancient people of the Middle East, this includes maps, pictures, and drawings to enhance the text.

901. Haskins, James. Leaders of the Middle East. Enslow, 1985. 176 p. ill. $14.

Gr 7+. B 81: Jul 1985. BR 4: Mar/Apr 1986. BR 5: Nov/Dec 1986. + - SLJ 32: Sep 1985. VOYA 9: Apr 1986. Following an overview of Middle East history are 9 biographies of contemporary leaders, including Arafat, Assad, Begin, Fahd, Hussein, Khomeini, Mubarak, Qaddafi, and Zia.

902. Leone, Bruno. Middle East, The. (Opposing Viewpoints Series). Greenhaven Press, 1982. 167 p. ill. $11.

Gr 7+. B 79: Jan 15 1983. The Arab, Israeli, and Palestinian positions on the many causes of the Middle East conflict are presented, including the wide range of ideas within each camp.

903. Messenger, Charles. Middle East, The. (Conflict in the 20th Century). Watts, 1988. 64 p. ill. $13.

Gr 6+. B 84: Jun 15 1988. B 86: Sep 1 1989. * BR 7: Sep/Oct 1988. Colorful photos and maps augment this balanced introduction to the history of the region and the important events of the 20th century. Included is information on influential Arab groups.

904. Middle East and North Africa, 1986. 32nd ed. Europa Publications Limited; dist. by Gale, 1985. 863 p. ill. $125.

Gr 10+. B 82: Aug 1986. Articles on the region as a whole, regional organizations, each nation of the Middle East, and statistics are included.

905. Middle East, The. 6th ed. (Congressional Quarterly). Congressional Quarterly, 1986. 317 p. ill. Pb $14.

Gr 9+. B 82: Aug 1986. BR 5: Sep/Oct 1986. Included are readable articles on the region and on each of the Middle East nations, biographies of notable 20th-century persons, a chronology, and maps and tables.

906. Rohr, Janelle. Middle East, The. (Opposing Viewpoints Series). Greenhaven Press, 1987. 237 p. ill. $14. Pb $7.

Gr 9+. B 84: Jan 15 1988. Excerpts from articles, speeches, and books present a balanced account of the views of the Palestinians, Israelis, Iranians, Americans, and others on the Middle East conflict.

907. Spencer, William. Islamic States in Conflict. (Impact Book). Watts, 1983. 90 p. map. $9.

Gr 7+. + - B 79: May 15 1983. BC 36: Jun 1983. BR 2: Jan/Feb 1984. SLJ 29: May 1983. This straightforward account of Islamic history shows how the political, cultural, and religious differences in Islamic nations have caused the current schisms.

908. Westwood, J. N. History of the Middle East Wars, The. Exeter Books; dist. by Bookthrift, 1984. 189 p. ill. $13.

Gr 9+. B 81: Jan 15 1985. This balanced coverage of the wars in the Middle East since 1945 includes maps and illustrations.

909. Wormser, Michael. Middle East, The. 5th ed. (Congressional Quarterly). Congressional Quarterly, 1981. 275 p. ill. Pb $9.

Gr 9+. B 78: Mar 1 1982. Events in the Middle East crisis are clearly presented up to the death of Egyptian President Anwar al-Sadat in 1981. A chronology, maps, charts, and profiles on each nation have been updated.

General–Middle East–Social Life and Customs

910. Graham-Brown, Sarah. Images of Women: The Portrayal of Women in Photography of the Middle East, 1860-1950. Columbia University Press, 1988. 273 p. ill. $40.

Gr 10+. LJ 113: Dec 1988. This photo essay shows the lives of women in the Middle East and how they changed between 1860 and 1950.

General–Oceania

911. Craig, Robert D. Historical Dictionary of Oceania. Greenwood, 1981. 392 p. maps. $55.

Adult. B 79: Nov 1 1982. LJ 107: Apr 1 1982. This authoritative dictionary focuses on the political, economic, and social history of all the Pacific islands.

912. Hereniko, Vilsoni. South Pacific Islanders. (Original Peoples). Rourke, 1987. 48 p. ill. $13.

Gr 4-6. B 84: Jan 15 1988. This highly illustrated history of the people of the south Pacific islands includes a glossary.

General–Oceans, Seas, etc.

913. Hargreaves, Pat. Indian Ocean, The. (Seas and Oceans). Silver Burdett, 1981. 65 p. ill. $8.

Gr 4-8. B 77: Jul 15/Aug 1981. SLJ 28: Mar 1982. Graphs, maps, diagrams, photos, and a glossary augment this account of the history, exploration, resources, and people of the nations along the shores of the Indian Ocean.

914. Hargreaves, Pat. Red Sea and Persian Gulf, The. (Seas and Oceans). Silver Burdett, 1981. 67 p. ill. $8.

Gr 4-8. B 77: Jul 15/Aug 1981. SLJ 28: Mar 1982. Graphs, maps, diagrams, photos, and a glossary augment this account of the history, exploration, resources, and people of the nations that have existed along the shores of the Red Sea and the Persian Gulf.

General–Refugees

915. Wain, Barry. Refused: The Agony of the Indochina Refugees. Simon & Schuster, 1982. 256 p. $17.

Gr 9+. B 78: Feb 1 1982. + - LJ 107: Feb 15 1982. Journalist Wain describes the various groups within the 1 3/4 million refugees who left, or were forced out of, Indochina, and the treatment they received from Hanoi, other Asian governments, and the United States.

General–Southeast Asia

916. Beckett, Ian. Southeast Asia from 1945. (Conflict in the 20th Century). Watts, 1987. 62 p. ill. $13.

Gr 6-9. B 83: Jun 15 1987. Beckett describes the growing nationalism following World War II, the Vietnamese War, and the continuing strife in the region.

917. Clark, James. Southeast Asia, Learning about Peoples and Cultures. (Peoples and Cultures Series). McDougal-Littel, 1983. 104 p. ill. $6.

Gr 6-9. B 83: Oct 1 1986. Clark examines the history and culture of Southeast Asia, emphasizing the late 1970s and early 1980s, including the impact of war on people and nations.

918. Southeast Asia. (Library of Nations). Time-Life; dist. by Silver Burdett, 1987. 160 p. ill. Lib. ed. $19.

Gr 9+. * BR 6: Mar/Apr 1988. Vivid colorful photos, maps, and graphs enrich this readable presentation of the history, government, economy, and resources of Brunei, Malaysia, the Philippines, Singapore, and Thailand.

919. Withington, William. Southeast Asia. Rev. ed. (Fideler/Gateway Global Community Series). Gateway Press, 1988. 160 p. ill. $17.

Gr 5-9. B 85: Dec 1 1988. The history, geography, government, resources, economy, culture, and way of life of the people in Southeast Asia are covered in this updated work. A glossary is included.

Afghanistan

920. Afghanistan in Pictures. (Visual Geography Series). Lerner, 1989. 64 p. ill. $10.

Gr 5 8. B 85: May 1 1985. SLJ 35: Jul 1989. The political situation in Afghanistan up to the withdrawal of Soviet troops is covered, along with the nation's history, geography, climate, economy, and culture. Photos, maps, and charts are included.

921. Bonner, Arthur. Among the Afghans. (Central Asia Book Series). Duke, 1987. 358 p. ill. $28.

Gr 9+. B 84: Nov 1 1987. LJ 112: Nov 1 1987. Bonner describes the revolution of Afghan politics since the 1950s and provides eyewitness accounts of the war between Afghan rebels and the Soviet-supported communist government.

922. Chaliand, Gerard. Report from Afghanistan. Viking, 1982. 87 p. ill. $14.

Gr 9+. B 78: Jul 1982. LJ 107: Jun 15 1982. An experienced observer of Third World politics, journalist Chaliand presents a clearly written primer on the Soviet invasion of Afghanistan and the role of western nations in the rebellion.

923. Clifford, Mary Louise. Land and People of Afghanistan, The. (Portraits of the Nations Series). Lippincott, 1989. 224 p. ill. $15. Lib. ed. $15.

Gr 6-9. B 86: Sep 15 1989. * SLJ 35: Sep 1989. VOYA 12: Aug 1989. Afghanistan's current political problems are included in this illustrated account of the nation's history, geography, and multi-ethnic culture.

924. Gilfond, Henry. Afghanistan. (First Book). Watts, 1980. 64 p. ill. $7.

Gr 6-7. B 77: Mar 1 1981. Colorful photos enrich this brief introduction to Afghan history, customs, politics, geography, and people.

925. Goodwin, Jan. Caught in the Crossfire. Dutton, 1987. 467 p. ill. $19.

Gr 9+. B 83: Mar 15 1987. * BR 6: Sep/Oct 1987. LJ 113: Mar 15 1987. VOYA 10: Oct 1987. Goodwin traveled extensively in Afghanistan disguised as a resistance fighter. She also met government officials, visited refugee camps, and talked with families of Soviet soldiers who died in Afghanistan, to provide her account of the 1980s civil war.

926. Griffiths, John C. Conflict in Afghanistan, The. (Flashpoints). Rourke, 1988. 77 p. ill. $12.

Gr 6-9. SLJ 35: Feb 1989. The reasons for the Soviet invasion of Afghanistan and the impact of this decision on the international scene are presented in this well-illustrated introduction.

927. Hodson, Peregrine. Under a Sickle Moon: A Journey through Afghanistan. Atlantic; dist. by Little, Brown, 1987. 240 p. ill. Pb $8.

Gr 9+. B 84: Nov 1 1987. LJ 112: Sep 15 1987. British journalist Hodson recounts Afghan history along with the story of his own perilous adventures in 1984 as he traveled with the resistance fighters who were battling the Soviets.

928. Howarth, Michael. Afghanistan. Chelsea House, 1988. 96 p. ill. $12.

Gr 4-6. B 85: Jan 1 1989. This straightforward account of Afghanistan's history, geography, industry, government, economy, and people includes maps and numerous photos.

929. Isby, David C. War in a Distant Country: Afghanistan: Invasion and Resistance. Arms and Armour; dist. by Sterling, 1989. 128 p. ill. $25.

Gr 9+. B 86: Sep 1 1989. Maps and photos supplement this account of the Soviet occupation of Afghanistan. Background of the events leading up to the invasion is included.

930. Newell, Nancy Peabody. Struggle for Afghanistan, The. Cornell University Press, 1981. 237 p. ill. $15.

Gr 11+. LJ 106: Apr 15 1981. Newell's survey of Afghan history, geography, and society explains the causes of the Soviet invasion of Afghanistan in 1979.

Australia

931. Arnold, Caroline. Australia Today. (First Book). Watts, 1987. 96 p. ill. $10.

Gr 4-8. B 84: Jan 1 1988. BR 6: Jan/Feb 1988. + - SLJ: Dec 1987. A brief history is presented along with information on the land, resources, wildlife, government, economy, and contemporary life of Australia.

932. Australia. (Children of the World). Gareth Stevens, 1988. 64 p. ill. $13.

Gr 3-5. + - SLJ 35: Sep 1988. An abundance of photos enriches this introduction to Australia which illustrates the daily life of an Australian child and includes a section on the nation's history, government, resources, and geography.

933. Clark, Manning. Ashton Scholastic History of Australia, The. Ashton Scholastic, 1988. 160 p. ill. $20.

Gr 4-8. B 85: Oct 15 1988. This readable well-illustrated history of Australia is a condensation of a 6-volume work for adults.

934. Fabian, Sue. Children in Australia: An Outline History. Melbourne, 1980. 248 p. ill. $20.

Gr 5-8. B 85: Oct 15 1988. This profusely illustrated history of the treatment of children in Australia ranges from the days before European settlement to 1980.

935. Holder, Robyn. Aborigines of Australia. (Original Peoples). Rourke, 1987. 48 p. ill. $13.

Gr 4-6. B 84: Jan 15 1988. The native people of Australia are introduced in this highly illustrated work.

936. Kelly, Andrew. Australia. (Countries of the World). Bookwright Press; dist. by Watts, 1989. 48 p. ill. Lib. ed. $13.

Gr 4-8. B 85: May 15 1989. SLJ 35: May 1989. The history, geography, government, economy, culture, and people of Australia are introduced in this colorfully illustrated work. A glossary is included.

937. Keneally, Thomas. Australia: Beyond the Dreamtime. Facts on File, 1987; 1989. 248 p. $25.

Gr 10+. BR 8: Sep/Oct 1989. Australian history, culture, and current problems are explored in 3 segments written by native authors.

938. Lepthien, Emilie U. Australia. (Enchantment of the World). Childrens Press, 1982. 127 p. ill. $10.

Gr 4-8. B 79: Apr 1 1983. SLJ: Apr 1983. Colorful photos and maps augment this account of the history, industry, and culture of Australia. The Australian aborigines are introduced and an account is given of their ancient and modern ways of living.

939. Miller, James. Koori: A Will to Win. Angus & Robertson; dist. by Salem House, 1987. 302 p. ill. $17.

Gr 9+. SLJ 33: Apr 1987. Miller explores the history of the Australian aborigines, shows how their society was destroyed by European settlers, and explains efforts to establish their rights.

940. Moore, Robert. Living in Sydney. (City Life). Silver Burdett, 1987. 45 p. ill. $14.

Gr 5-8. B 84: Feb 1 1988. + - BC 41: Feb 1988. BR 7: Sep/Oct 1988. This introduction to Sydney presents its history and other basic information along with color photos and an account of everyday life in the city.

941. Pepper, Susan. Passport to Australia. Watts, 1987. 48 p. ill. $12.

Gr 3-6. B 83: May 15 1987. + - SLJ 33: Aug 1987. Colorful photos, maps, and charts are included in this brief introduction to Australian history, government, and culture.

942. Shaw, John. Concise Encyclopedia of Australia, The. 2nd ed. G. K. Hall, 1989. 848 p. ill. $54.

Gr 9+. B 85: Aug 1989. Historical, geographic, cultural, economic, and biographical information are included in this balanced encyclopedia which includes numerous photos, maps, and charts.

943. Stark, Al Australia: A Lucky Land. (Discovering Our Heritage). Dillon Press, 1987. 151 p. ill. $13.

Gr 5+. B 84: Feb 15 1988. BR 7: May/Jun 1988. SLJ 34: Mar 1988. The history of Australia, its culture, customs, traditions, and noted persons are all covered. Photos, maps, and a glossary are included.

944. Terrill, Ross. Australians, The. Simon & Schuster, 1987. 342 p. $20.

Gr 9+. B 84: Sep 1 1987. * LJ 112: Aug 1987. Terrill, an Australian journalist, adroitly merges history, geography, and a sociological and psychological examination of the people in this portrait of his native land.

945. Watson, Don. Story of Australia, The. Melbourne, 1984. 202 p. ill. $20.

Gr 5-8. B 85: Oct 15 1988. Timelines and illustrations augment this history of Australia which emphasizes the aborigines.

Australia–Biographies

946. Morgan, Sally. My Place. Seaver Books; dist. by Holt, 1988. 358 p. $20.

Gr 9+. B 84: Aug 1988. BR 7: Mar/Apr 1989. LJ 113: Oct 1 1988. * VOYA 12: Apr 1989. Morgan was raised to believe she was white, but at age 15 she discovered her aboriginal roots. As she researched the history of her family she came to know the suffering of her people since the early 1900s.

Australia–Fiction

947. Beatty, Patricia. Jonathan Down Under. Morrow, 1982. 219 p. $9.

Gr 5-9. B 79: Jan 1 1983. + - BC 36: Mar 1983. HB 59: Feb 1983. * SE 47: Apr 1983. SLJ 29: Nov 1982. *VOYA 6: Apr 1983. The story of the 1851 Australian gold rush is told through the adventures of Jonathan Cole and his father.

948. Collins, Alan. Jacob's Ladder. Dutton, 1989. 149 p. $14.

Gr 7+. B 85: Jun 1 1989. BC 42: May 1989. - BR 8: Nov/Dec 1989. HB 65: Sep/Oct 1989. + - SLJ 35: Oct 1989. * VOYA 12: Aug 1989. Jacob is one of many Jewish orphans sent from Europe to Australia for safety before World War II began. Although he is safe, Jacob still faces anti-Semitism and the problems of growing up without a family.

949. Cox, David. Bossyboots. Crown, 1987. 25 p. ill. $11.

Gr K-3. B 83: Apr 15 1987. BC 40: Apr 1987. HB 63: Jul/Aug 1987. + - SLJ 33: Jun/Jul 1987. An amusing story about a bossy little girl and a stage coach robber, set in the frontier days of the Australian outback.

950. Dengler, Sandy. Code of Honor. Bethany House, 1988. 255 p. $7.

Gr 7+. + - VOYA 12: Apr 1989. These adventures of indentured servant Samantha Connolly are set in Australia at the turn of the 20th century.

951. Wales, Robert. Harry. Watts, 1985. 277 p. $17.

Gr 9+. BR 5: Sep/Oct 1986. + - VOYA 9: Aug/Oct 1986. In 1882 a pair of rustlers risked the gallows in their attempt to herd 1500 head of cattle over a thousand miles of the Australian Outback in this dramatic story that provides a good sense of time and place.

Bangladesh

952. Laure, Jason. Joi Bangla!: The Children of Bangladesh. Farrar, 1974. 153 p. ill. $10.

Gr 7+. SLJ 28: Sep 1981. Photos enrich these stories of 9 children whose lives were affected by the 1971 revolution that created their new nation.

953. McClure, Vimala. Bangladesh: Rivers in a Crowded Land. (Discovering Our Heritage). Dillon Press, 1989. 128 p. ill. $13.

Gr 5-8. B 86: Nov 1 1989. Photos, recipes, and folk stories enrich this clear account of the history of Bangladesh and the culture of its people.

954. Wright, R. E. Bangladesh. Chelsea House, 1988. 96 p. ill. $12.

Gr 4-6. B 85: Jan 1 1989. The history, geography, and daily life of Bangladesh are covered in this illustrated overview.

Bhutan

955. Foster, Leila Merrell. Bhutan. (Enchantment of the World). Childrens Press, 1989. 128 p. ill. $23.

Gr 5-7. B 85: Aug 1989. Bhutan's history, culture, economy, and geography are introduced in this illustrated work.

956. Kamatsu, Yoshio. Bhutan. (Children of the World). Gareth Stevens, 1988. 64 p. ill. $13.

Gr 2-4. + - B 85: Dec 15 1988. BC 42: Dec 1988. The daily life of a Bhutanese child and his family is the focus of this work, which includes a section on his nation's history, geography, politics, and culture.

Burma

957. Morieda, Takashi. Burma. (Children of the World). Gareth Stevens, 1987. 64 p. ill. $13.

Gr 3-7. B 83: Jun 1 1987. SLJ 34: Nov 1987. Following an account of the daily life of a Burmese child is an introduction to Burma's history, government, culture, and economy. Photos, a glossary, and a map are included.

China

958. Bloodworth, Dennis. Chinese Looking Glass, The. Rev. and expanded ed. Farrar, 1980. 448 p. $15. Pb $9.

Gr 9+. B 77: Sep 1 1980. This anecdotal history of China also covers social and political customs and trivia, presented in a way that promotes understanding.

959. Clayre, Alasdair. Heart of the Dragon, The. Houghton, 1985. 281 p. ill. $30.

Gr 9+. B 81: May 15 1985. * LJ 110: May 1 1985. SLJ 32: Oct 1985. This topically arranged survey of China's cultural and political history is profusely illustrated and includes maps and a chronology.

960. Dudley, William. China: Opposing Viewpoints. (Opposing Viewpoints Series). Greenhaven Press, 1988. 236 p. ill. $15.

Gr 9+. B 85: Feb 1 1989. SLJ 35: Feb 1989. An overview of 19th- and 20th-century Chinese history precedes an examination of several viewpoints on modern Chinese economic reforms, human rights concerns, foreign policy, and U.S. policy on China. A chronology, cartoons, and quotations enrich this useful work.

961. Fairbank, John King. Great Chinese Revolution: 1800 to the Present. Harper, 1986. 400 p. maps. $20.

Gr 10+. * LJ 111: Sep 1 1986. LJ 112: Jan 1987. The complex struggle of the Chinese since 1800 to break the grips of the past and become a modern nation is recounted in this lively survey by a noted scholar.

962. Feinstein, Steve. China in Pictures. (Visual Geography Series). Lerner, 1989. 64 p. ill. $10.

Gr 5-8. B 85: May 1 1989. SLJ 35: Jul 1989. This introduction to China's history, geography, and culture includes photos.

963. Filstrup, Chris. China: From Emperors to Communes. (Discovering Our Heritage). Dillon Press, 1983. 160 p. ill. $10.

Gr 4-8. B 79: Jul 1983. B 81: Feb 1 1985. * BR 2: Nov/Dec 1983. SLJ 30: Sep 1983. A map, photos, glossary, and a ready-reference section are included in this overview of Chinese geography, history, folklore, holidays, education, and sports.

964. Loescher, Gil. China: Pushing toward the Year 2000. Harcourt, 1981. 160 p. ill. $11.

Gr 6-8. B 78: Sep 15 1981. The political development of China is traced from the 8th century to the 1949 Chinese communist revolution.

965. Major, John S. Land and People of China, The. (Portraits of the Nations Series). Lippincott, 1989. 288 p. ill. $15. Lib. ed. $15.

Gr 6+. B 86: Sep 15 1989. + - SLJ 35: Oct 1989. VOYA 12: Aug 1989. Photos enrich this view of Chinese history that shows how events have been affected by the nation's culture, society, and religions. Recent political and foreign policy decisions are also discussed.

966. McLenighan, Valjean. China: A History to 1949. (Enchantment of the World). Childrens Press, 1983. 127 p. ill. $13.

Gr 5-8. B 80: Mar 1 1984. B 81: Feb 1 1985. + - SLJ 30: May 1984. McLenighan's overview of Chinese history, culture, and technological innovation is augmented by maps and colorful photos.

967. McLenighan, Valjean. People's Republic of China. (Enchantment of the World). Childrens Press, 1984. 143 p. ill. $15.

Gr 5-9. B 81: May 15 1985. + - SLJ 31: Aug 1985. A chronology, a "Quick Facts" section, and colorful photos enrich this overview of Chinese history, culture, economy, and geography.

968. Merton, Anna. China: The Land and Its People. Rev. ed. (Silver Burdett Countries). Silver Burdett, 1987. 43 p. ill. $15.

Gr 4-6. SLJ 33: Aug 1987. Photos augment this introduction to the history, geography, culture, government, and industry of China.

969. Miyazima, Yasuhiko. China. (Children of the World). Gareth Stevens, 1988. 64 p. ill. $13.

Gr 3-5. + - SLJ 35: Sep 1988. This introduction to China includes a section on a typical family, numerous photos, and a brief section on Chinese history, resources, government, and climate.

970. Morton, William Scott. China: Its History and Culture. Lippincott, 1980. 304 p. ill. $13.

Gr 9+. B 77: Dec 15 1980. LJ 105: Sep 1 1980. This comprehensive account of Chinese history and culture from ancient to modern times is arranged in compact and readable chapters.

971. Murphey, Rhoads. China. (Fideler/Gateway Global Community Series). Gateway Press, 1988. 192 p. ill. $17.

Gr 5-9. B 85: Dec 1 1988. Current to 1987, Murphey's work covers Chinese history, lifestyles, economy, government, geography, and climate.

972. O'Neill, Hugh B. Companion to Chinese History. Facts on File, 1987. 397 p. maps. $25.

Gr 9+. B 84: Dec 15 1987. LJ 112: Sep 1 1987. Chinese history from ancient times to 1985 is covered in this handbook of brief entries that cover persons, events, dynasties, literature, and religion.

973. Perl, Lila. Red Star and Green Dragon: Looking at New China. Morrow, 1983. 129 p. ill. $9.

Gr 5-8. B 79: Jun 15 1983. HB 59: Oct 1983. * SE 48: May 1984. * SLJ 30: Sep 1983. VOYA 6: Dec 1983. In 5 chapters Perl presents a concise look at Chinese history, geography, culture, way of life, and politics, including current problems.

974. Roberson, John R. China: From Manchu to Mao (1699-1976). Atheneum, 1980. 191 p. ill. $11.

Gr 5-10. * B 77: Oct 15 1980. B 82: Feb 1 1985. SLJ 27: Jan 1981. SLJ 28: Sep 1981. In this readable overview of the last 3 centuries of Chinese history Roberson emphasizes the events of the 20th century and presents a clear picture of the role of China in international politics.

975. Rodzinski, Witold. Walled Kingdom: A History of China from Antiquity to the Present. Free Press/Macmillan, 1984. 450 p. maps. $20.

Gr 9+. SLJ 31: Apr 1985. Four thousand years of Chinese economic, cultural, political, and social history are presented, supplemented by chronological tables and 20 historical maps.

976. Salisbury, Harrison E. China: 100 Years of Revolution. Holt, 1983. 139 p. ill. $35.

Gr 9+. B 80: Sep 15 1983. LJ 108: Sep 1 1983. The major events and personalities in China from the 1830s through the coming to power of Mao Tse-tung in the 1940s are presented in this readable introduction.

977. Sizer, Nancy Faust. China: A Brief History. Independent School Press, 1981. 199 p. Pb $7.

Gr 10+. * SE 50: Feb 1986. Primary source materials accompany this introduction to Chinese history.

978. Spencer, Cornelia. Yangtze: China's River Highway. (Rivers of the World). Garrard, 1963. 96 p. ill. $4.

Gr 4-7. Metzner. China's principal river, the Yangtze is over 3000 miles in length and has been of great importance in the development of the nation. Spencer discusses the history and culture of the people who have lived on its banks.

979. Woodruff, John. China in Search of Its Future: Years of Great Reform, 1982-87. University of Washington Press, 1989. 270 p. ill. $20.

Gr 10+. B 86: Sep 1 1989. SLJ 35: Sep 1989. Woodruff explores 20th-century political and cultural events in China to provide a useful background for recent events.

China–0-1912

980. Burland, Cottie A. Ancient China. (Great Civilizations). Defour, 1974. 144 p. ill. $7.

Gr 4-8. Metzner. An illustrated overview of life in ancient China, including architecture, education, clothing, industry, and culture.

981. Fisher, Leonard Everett. Great Wall of China, The. Macmillan, 1986. 30 p. ill. $12.

Gr 2-6. * B 82: Mar 15 1986. * BC 39: Apr 1986. HB 63: Nov 1987. * SE 51: Apr/May 1987. * SLJ 32: May 1986. Large, powerful illustrations detail the building of the Wall. Its purpose and subsequent history are told in the brief text. A map and translations of Chinese characters are included.

982. Goff, Denise. Early China. Rev. ed. (Civilization Library). Gloucester Press; dist. by Watts, 1986. 32 p. ill. $10.

Gr 3-5. B 83: Dec 15 1986. An abundance of colorful photos enhances this introduction to the history, government, religion, art, industry, science, and family life of ancient China.

983. Hughes-Stanton, Penelope. Ancient Chinese Town, An. Rev. ed. (See Inside). Warwick; dist. by Watts, 1986. 32 p. ill. $11.

Gr 4-8. BR 6: May/Jun 1987. SLJ 33: Feb 1987. A timeline and glossary add to this well-illustrated book that clearly introduces life in an ancient Chinese town and shows the differing lives of the rich and the poor.

984. Hughes-Stanton, Penelope. See Inside an Ancient Chinese Town. Warwick; dist. by Watts, 1979. 29 p. ill. $7.

Gr 4-6. SLJ 26: Jan 1980. As the everyday life and customs of the ancient Chinese are presented, their contributions to modern life become clear. Highly illustrated with reproductions of works of art, photos, maps, charts, and diagrams.

985. Kan, Lai Po. Ancient Chinese, The. Silver Burdett, 1981. 61 p. ill. $8.

Gr 5+. B 78: Nov 15 1981. SLJ 28: Aug 1982. This visual introduction to life in ancient China covers history, farming, art, education, commerce, technology, and beliefs. It includes timelines, maps, and a glossary.

986. Nancarrow, Peter. Early China and the Wall. (Cambridge Topic Book). Lerner, 1980. 52 p. ill. Lib. ed. $5.

Gr 4-9. + - B 77: Sep 15 1980. SLJ 27: Mar 1981. This concise and highly illustrated history of ancient China from the Stone Age to the 1st century A.D. includes discussions of early writing, art and ironwork, and the building of the Great Wall.

China–0-1912–Social Life and Customs

987. Knox, Robert. Ancient China. (Modern Knowledge Library). Warwick; dist. by Watts, 1979. 44 p. ill. $7.

Gr 2-4. * SE 44: Apr 1980. + - SLJ 26: Sep 1979. Colorful illustrations supplement the brief text that introduces ancient Chinese culture, social life, government, and economy.

China–1912-1949

988. Botjer, George F. Short History of Nationalist China, A. Putnam, 1980. 312 p. $16.

Gr 10+. B 76: Mar 1 1980. + - LJ 105: Feb 15 1980. Describes the rise of the Nationalist Party at the end of the empire in 1912, their struggles in World War II, and their loss of power to the communist party in 1949.

989. Fritz, Jean. China's Long March: 6,000 Miles of Danger. Putnam, 1988. 124 p. ill. $15.

Gr 6+. * B 84: Mar 1 1988. * BC 41: Apr 1988. HB 64: May/Jun 1988. SE 53: Apr/May 1989. SLJ 35: May 1988. * VOYA 11: Jun 1988. Fritz interviewed survivors of this incredible march to present a readable account of life in China during the 1930s and the struggles of more than 90,000 soldiers and civilians seeking to elude the enemy as they crossed 6000 miles of rugged, mountainous terrain.

990. Hoyt, Edwin P. Rise of the Chinese Republic: From the Last Emperor to Deng Xiaoping. McGraw-Hill, 1988. 384 p. ill. $20.

Gr 9+. B 85: Nov 15 1988. Hoyt presents the complex background of the conflict between the Chinese nationalists and communists and a readable account of the events that resulted in a communist victory.

991. Kidd, David. Peking Story. Clarkson N. Potter, 1988. 207 p. ill. Pb $12.

Gr 9+. B 84: Jan 15 1988. SLJ 35: Oct 1988. A teacher of English at a university in Peking from 1946 to 1950, Kidd married into an aristocratic family. This is the story of their experiences at the beginning of the communist revolution.

992. Lawson, Don. Long March: China under Chairman Mao. Harper, 1983. 192 p. ill. $11. Lib. ed. $11.

Gr 6+. B 79: May 1 1983. BR 2: Mar/Apr 1984. HB 59: Jun 1983. * SE 48: May 1984. SLJ 30: Sep 1983. VOYA 6: Aug 1983. Lawson explores the growth of the power of Mao Tse-tung and the Chinese Communist Party and its conflict with Chiang Kai-shek as he presents a detailed account of the 6000-mile march that involved nearly 100,000 men, women, and children.

993. Wei, Katherine. Second Daughter: Growing Up in China, 1930-1949. Little, Brown, 1984. 243 p. ill. $17.

Gr 9+. + - B 80: Aug 1984. LJ 109: Aug 1984. An unsentimental memoir of growing up in China during the 1930s and 1940s, when World War II and the communist revolution destroyed the old social order.

China–1949-1999

994. Bingham, Marjorie W. Women in Modern China: Transition, Revolution and Contemporary Times. Gary E. McCuen, 1980. 106 p. ill. $7. Teachers guide $2.

Gr 10+. SE 50: Feb 1986. Quotations and illustrations enhance this brief work on the historical, social, and cultural role of women in China, with emphasis on the 20th century.

995. Bredsdorff, Jan. To China and Back. Pantheon; dist. by Random, 1980. 256 p. $10.

Gr 9+. B 76: Apr 1 1980. LJ 105: May 1 1980. The author taught English in Chinese schools in the 1960s and 1970s. He provides insight into life in China during Mao's chairmanship and the changes after his death.

996. Carter, Alden R. Modern China. (First Book). Watts, 1986. 90 p. ill. $10.

Gr 4-9. B 82: Jun 1 1986. + - BR 5: Sep/Oct 1986. SLJ 32: Aug 1986. Following an overview of Chinese history is an examination of 20th-century China, including politics, education, and social life. Includes numerous photos.

997. China. (Library of Nations). Time-Life; dist. by Silver Burdett, 1985. 160 p. ill. $15.

Gr 7+. B 81: Apr 1 1985. Emphasis is on the history and culture of China following World War II, arranged in 7 pictorial essays.

998. Cohen, David. Day in the Life of China, A. Collins, 1989. 224 p. ill. $45.

Gr 9+. B 86: Sep 1 1989. April 15, 1989, the day Chinese students began their demonstrations in Tiananmen Square, was coincidentally the day that an international team of photographers had arranged to photograph life in modern China. The result is a visual record of the many changes taking place there.

999. Dures, Alan. Postwar World: China since 1949. Batsford; dist. by David & Charles, 1988. 63 p. ill. $20.

Gr 6-9. + - SLJ 35: Mar 1989. Following a brief overview of Chinese history before World War II is an introduction to Chinese history and politics since that time. Photos, a timeline, and mini-biographies are included.

1000. Hacker, Jeffery H. New China, The. (Impact Book). Watts, 1986. 120 p. ill. $11.

Gr 7+. B 83: Sep 1 1986. * BR 5: Nov/Dec 1986. + - SLJ 33: Sep 1986. Following a brief overview of Chinese history is an examination of political and economic changes in China following the Cultural Revolution. Includes photos.

1001. Poole, Frederick King. Album of Modern China, An. (Picture Album). Watts, 1981. 89 p. ill. $9.

Gr 5-9. B 77: Jul 15/Aug 1981. + - SLJ 28: Nov 1981. A profusely illustrated introduction to China following World War II, showing political, economic, and social changes.

1002. Rau, Margaret. Our World: The People's Republic of China. Rev. ed. Messner, 1981. 128 p. ill. $8.

Gr 4-8. B 78: Apr 15 1982. SE 50: Feb 1986. This overview of the history of communist China includes an examination of the impact of the Cultural Revolution, problems with Vietnam, unrest over civil rights, and efforts at modernization.

1003. Ross, Stewart. China Since 1945. (Witness History Series). Bookwright Press; dist. by Watts, 1989. 64 p. ill. $13.

Gr 9+. B 85: Jun 1 1989. SLJ 35: Aug 1989. This succinct illustrated work presents the highlights of Chinese history from the end of World War II to the present. A glossary and brief biographies of noted persons are included.

1004. Terzani, Tiziano. Behind the Forbidden Door. Holt, 1986. 262 p. $17.

Gr 9+. B 82: Aug 1986. LJ 111: Jun 1 1986. Terzani lived and traveled in China from 1980 to 1984. He read and spoke Chinese and examined the effects of 3 decades of communism on China, including its material progress, corruption, and the destruction of tradition.

China–1949-1999–Fiction

1005. Vander Els, Betty. Leaving Point. Farrar, 1987. 212 p. $13.

Gr 5-9. B 84: Dec 15 1987. BC 41: Jan 1988. HB 64: Mar 1988. * SE 52: Apr/May 1988. SLJ 34: Feb 1988. VOYA 11: Apr 1988. This powerful sequel to Bomber's Moon shows the change in attitudes of the Chinese people toward Ruth's missionary family when the communists came to power. It makes the issue personal when Ruth's friendship with a girl who believes in communism is tested.

China–1949-1999–Social Life and Customs

1006. Mathews, Jay. One Billion: A China Chronicle. Random, 1983. 353 p. $18.

Gr 9+. B 80: Sep 1 1983. LJ 108: Nov 1 1983. Work on the farm and in a factory, food, language, medicine, art, humor, marriage and sex, and other aspects of contemporary Chinese life are presented in this accurate and readable work by American journalists who worked in China.

1007. Meyer, Charles. China Observed. Oxford University Press, 1981. 182 p. ill. $35.

Gr 9+. B 78: Dec 1 1981. SLJ 28: Mar 1982. Brief appendices cover Chinese history and other basic information, but the main body of the book is a colorful photo essay on modern China, its people, civilization, and countryside. Includes maps.

1008. Mosher, Steven W. Broken Earth: The Rural Chinese. Free Press, 1983. 317 p. ill. $18.

Gr 10+. BR 3: May/Jun 1984. LJ 108: Sep 1 1983. Mosher spent over a year in a Chinese village researching this anecdotal and readable book. It presents a historical perspective on current problems, including corruption, low standards of living, poor education, and birth control.

1009. Rau, Margaret. Holding up the Sky. Young People in China. Dutton, 1983. 136 p. ill. $12.

Gr 6+. * B 79: Apr 15 1983. + - BC 37: Dec 1983. HB 59: Aug 1983. SLJ 30: Oct 1983. In describing the daily lives of 12 Chinese young adults, Rau shows work styles, the treatment of minorities, the impact of the government on daily life, and contrasts urban and rural life. Historical and geographical information is interwoven.

1010. Rau, Margaret. Minority Peoples of China, The. Messner, 1982. 128 p. ill. $9.

Gr 5-9. B 79: Dec 1 1982. B 81: Feb 1 1985. BC 36: Nov 1982. + - SLJ 29: Dec 1982. Separate chapters profile the customs and living conditions of 10 of China's 56 minority groups. Each account focuses on the life of a child of the minority group featured.

1011. Schell, Orville. To Get Rich Is Glorious: China in the Eighties. Pantheon, 1985. 210 p. $16.

Gr 9+. B 81: Feb 15 1985. * LJ 110: Feb 15 1985. An informed and readable account of the changes that the relaxation of economic controls brought about in China during the mid-1980s.

China–Biographies

1012. Baker, Nina. Sun Yat-sen. Vanguard, 1946. 247 p. ill. $13.

Gr 4-6. Metzner. B 43: Nov 1 1946. LJ 71: Dec 15 1946. This readable presentation of the life of the founder of modern China clarifies the history of the turbulent years that led to the founding of a republic in China.

1013. Barlow, Jeffrey. Sun Yat-Sen. (World Leaders Past & Present). Chelsea House, 1987. 112 p. ill. $17.

Gr 6+. B 84: Sep 1 1987. SLJ 34: Oct 1987. The complex story of China's struggle to become a modern nation is told in this biography of Sun Yat-sen the dominant political leader in the early 1920s. Includes photos.

1014. Chang, Jung. Mme Sun Yat-sen. (Lives of Modern Women). Penguin, 1986. 143 p. ill. Pb $5.

Gr 9+. B 83: Nov 1 1986. This brief, readable biography is about the wife of Sun Yat-sen. After his death in 1925 she continued to work to bring about his dreams of a democratic and powerful China.

1015. Dolan, Sean. Chiang Kai-Shek. (World Leaders Past & Present). Chelsea House, 1988. 111 p. ill. $17.

Gr 7+. + - BR 7: Nov/Dec 1988. + - SLJ 35: Nov 1988. * VOYA 12: Feb 1989. Pictures and quotes augment this biography of Chiang Kai-Shek that presents an overview of 20th-century Chinese history.

1016. Dunster, Jaok. China and Mao Zedong. (Cambridge Topic Book). Lerner, 1983. 35 p. ill. $7.

Gr 5+. B 80: Oct 15 1983. SLJ 30: Nov 1983. In telling the story of Mao's life, Dunster also provides an account of the complex cultural, political, and social changes in China before, during, and after World War II.

1017. Duton, Alan. Mao Tse-Tung. (World Leaders in Context). Batsford, 1980. 80 p. ill. $15.

Gr 7+. SLJ 27: Apr 1981. This brief account of Mao's life and the forces that shaped him includes quotes, photos, notes on contemporaries, a chronology, and a glossary.

1018. Fisher, Lois. Peking Diary: A Personal Account of Modern China. St. Martin's, 1980. 256 p. ill. $11.

Gr 9+. SLJ 26: Apr 1980. Although Lois Fisher knew no Chinese, she accompanied her journalist husband to China in the 1970s and lived among the ordinary people. She tells of her daily experiences, the purge of the Gang of Four, the 1976 earthquake, and the death of Mao Tse-tung.

1019. Franz, Uli. Deng Xiaoping. Harcourt, 1988. 322 p. $20.

Gr 10+. * LJ 113: Oct 15 1988. A balanced and detailed biography of a Chinese leader who was close to Mao for much of his career.

1020. Fritz, Jean. China Homecoming. Putnam, 1985. 143 p. ill. $13.

Gr 6+. * B 81: Aug 1985. BC 38: Jul/Aug 1985. BR 4: Mar/Apr 1986. HB 61: Sep 1985. * SE 50: Apr/May 1986. * SLJ 31: Aug 1985. * VOYA 8: Oct 1985. In Homesick, Fritz told of her youth in China and her wish to come to the United

States. Here she tells of her return to China as a successful writer, of visiting her childhood home, and of the changes she saw.

1021. Garza, Hedda. Mao Zedong. (World Leaders Past & Present). Chelsea House, 1987. 112 p. ill. $17.

Gr 7-10. B 84: Mar 15 1988. This biography emphasizes Mao's political life. It is enriched by numerous photos and quotes by and about him.

1022. Hoobler, Dorothy. Zhou Enlai. (World Leaders Past & Present). Chelsea House, 1986. 115 p. ill. $16.

Gr 8+. SLJ 33: Nov 1986. The personality, achievements, and significance of Zhou (Chou) are examined in this highly illustrated work.

1023. Humphrey, Judy. Genghis Khan. (World Leaders Past & Present). Chelsea House, 1987. 111 p. ill. $17.

Gr 6+. B 84: Nov 15 1987. + - SLJ 34: Dec 1987. Set within the context of the times is a biography of the ferocious Mongolian warrior Genghis Khan, who was known by his followers for his wisdom, courage, loyalty, and military cunning.

1024. Kolpas, Norman. Mao. (Leaders Series). McGraw-Hill, 1981. 69 p. ill. $8.

Gr 7+. B 78: Dec 15 1981. SLJ 28: Mar 1982. Emphasis is on Mao's political leadership in this highly illustrated account of the man and his times.

1025. Liang, Heng. Son of the Revolution. Knopf; dist. by Random, 1983. 302 p. ill. $15. Pb $6.

Gr 9+. B 82: May 15 1986. LJ 108: Feb 15 1983. HB 59: Jun 1983. SLJ 29: Aug 1983. The author and his family were victims of the many changes in policy in China from the 1950s through the early 1980s. Both parents were "disciplined," and the teenage boy, who was sent to the countryside, later went to college and married an American.

1026. Lo, Ruth Earnshaw. In the Eye of the Typhoon. Harcourt, 1980. 289 p. ill. $13.

Gr 9+. B 77: Dec 1 1980. LJ 105: Oct 1 1980. An American woman married to a Chinese professor, Lo found her family caught up in the tumult of the Cultural Revolution. Her vivid account of these years is augmented by illustrations and a glossary.

1027. Lubetkin, Wendy. Deng Xiaoping. (World Leaders Past & Present). Chelsea House, 1988. 112 p. ill. $17.

Gr 9+. B 84: Jun 15 1988. BR 7: May/Jun 1988. + - SLJ 34: Aug 1988. This biography of China's leader is also a history of modern China. Photos and a chronology are included.

1028. Milton, Joyce. Friend of China, A. Hastings House, 1980. 126 p. ill. $9.

Gr 7+. BC 34: Jun 1981. * SE 45: Apr 1981. SLJ 27: Apr 1981. Agnes Smedley went to China in 1928 as a journalist and stayed there. She worked for feminine liberation, improved medical service, and reported on the war with Japan and the communist revolution.

1029. Poole, Frederick King. Mao Zedong. (Impact Biography). Watts, 1982. 120 p. ill. $9.

Gr 7-9. B 79: Feb 1 1983. This readable and highly illustrated biography of Mao Tse-tung provides a clear commentary that places Mao within the context of his times and shows his continuing influence.

1030. Power, Brian. Ford of Heaven, The. Michael Kesend, 1984. 192 p. ill. $17.

Gr 9+. B 81: Dec 15 1984. LJ 110: Jan 1985. Born of European parents and nurtured by a Chinese nanny, Power lived in Tientsien during the 1920s and 1930s. He presents a lively account of living in two cultures in a tumultuous time.

1031. Purcell, Hugh. Mao Tse-Tung. (History Makers Series). St. Martin's, 1977. 99 p. ill. $7.

Gr 7+. SE 50: Feb 1986. Numerous photos and quotes enrich this simple account of Mao's life and leadership.

1032. Rius. Mao for Beginners. (Pantheon Documentary Comic Book). Pantheon, 1980. 171 p. ill. Pb $3.

Gr 9+. SLJ 27: Dec 1980. This lively introduction to Mao Tse-tung is presented by an internationally famous cartoonist.

1033. Rowland-Entwistle, Theodore. Confucius and Ancient China. (Life and Times). Bookwright Press; dist. by Watts, 1987. 61 p. ill. $12.

Gr 4-8. + - SLJ 33: Aug 1987. This brief introduction to Confucius places his life and teaching in historical context. Includes photos.

1034. Terrill, Ross. Mao: A Biography. Harper, 1980. 450 p. ill. $18.

Gr 9+. B 76: Jul 1 1980. * LJ 105: Jun 1 1980. A solid, balanced, and readable biography of the leader of the Chinese communist revolution who sought to free the peasants and create an egalitarian society.

1035. Wales, Nym. My China Years: A Memoir. Morrow, 1984. 349 p. ill. $18.

Gr 9+. B 80: Apr 15 1984. LJ 109: Apr 15 1984. SLJ 31: Jan 1985. The author and her husband were journalists in China during the 1930s and were friends of Teilhard de Chardin and Mao Tse-tung. Her memoirs are a lively account of life in pre-revolutionary China.

1036. Wilson, Dick. People's Emperor: A Biography of Mao Tse-tung. Doubleday, 1980. 530 p. ill. $18.

Gr 9+. B 76: Mar 15 1980. + - LJ 105: Jun 15 1980. Extensive excerpts from Mao's writing and speeches are incorporated in this biography that shows his influence on the political life and history of China.

China–Fiction

1037. Bosse, Malcolm. Warlord, The. Simon & Schuster, 1983. 717 p. $18.

Gr 11+. B 79: Apr 1 1983. BR 2: Jan/Feb 1984. LJ 108: May 15 1983. The struggles among the communists, nationalists, and warlords in 1927 China provide the setting for this complex and realistic book.

1038. Broome, Susannah. Pearl Pagoda: A Novel. Simon & Schuster, 1980. 352 p. ill. $13.

Gr 9+. B 77: Nov 15 1980. LJ 105: Oct 1 1980. Megan traveled to mid-19th-century China by clipper ship to marry her missionary fiance, but finds that he has mysteriously died. A story of adventure and romance that presents a good picture of life at that time.

1039. Buck, Pearl. Good Earth, The. Crowell; Pocket Books, 1931. 316 p. $17. Pb $4.

Gr 8+. B 82: May 15 1986. This classic concerns Wong Lung and his wife, O-Lan, who helps him rise from peasant to land-owner, only to be cast aside when he becomes wealthy.

1040. Lord, Bette Bao. Spring Moon: A Novel of China. Harper; Avon, 1981. 464 p. $16. Pb $4.

Gr 10+. B 82: May 15 1986. LJ 106: Oct 15 1981. SLJ 28: Apr 1982. This saga of an upper class Chinese family presents a picture of changes in Chinese society from 1890 to the 1970s.

1041. Montalbano, William D. Death in China, A. Atheneum, 1984. 320 p. $15.

Gr 10+. B 80: Apr 1 1984. LJ 109: Apr 1 1984. An archae-ological dig at the burial site of Emperor Qin, who ruled 2200 years ago, is the setting for a thriller that provides an accurate account of the modern Chinese way of life.

1042. Paterson, Katherine. Rebels of the Heavenly Kingdom. Dutton; Avon, 1983. 227 p. $12. Pb $3.

Gr 7+. + - B 79: Jun 15 1983. B 81: Feb 1 1985. BC 36: Jul 1983. + - HB 59: Aug 1983. * SE 48: May 1984. + - SLJ 30: Sep 1983. * VOYA 7: Apr 1984. The Taiping Rebellion (1850-1853) was an attempt by a group of peasants to destroy the Manchu Dynasty and establish a just and peaceful nation. But when murder and other violence were used for that purpose, Wong Lee and Mei Lin became disillusioned.

1043. Yep, Laurence. Mountain Light. Harper, 1985. 256 p. $12. Lib. ed. $12.

Gr 6+. B 82: Sep 15 1985. BC 39: Nov 1985. SLJ 32: Jan 1986. VOYA 8: Dec 1985. In this sequel to the Serpent's Children, Cassia and her friends Squeaky Lau and Tiny con-tinue the struggle against the Manchu in a story that presents much of China's history and its culture in the 1850s.

1044. Yep, Laurence. Serpent's Children, The. Harper, 1984. 277 p. $13. Lib. ed. $13.

Gr 5+. B 81: Feb 1 1985. BC 37: Mar 1984. BR 3: Sep/Oct 1984. HB 60: Aug 1984. + - SLJ Aug 1984. VOYA 7: Aug 1984. This novel of a Chinese peasant family is set at the time of the rebellion against the Manchu and the British. Yep's story shows why some Chinese came to America and why others clung to traditional ways in spite of poverty.

China–Kings, Queens, Rulers, etc.

1045. Guisso, R. W. L. First Emperor of China, The. Birch Lane Press, 1989. 216 p. ill. $25.

Gr 9+. B 86: Oct 1 1989. LJ 114: Oct 1 1989. Emperor from 259 to 210 B.C., Ch'in Shih-Huang built the Great Wall, and a tomb of over 7000 life-sized terra cotta soldiers and horses, and had hundreds of scholars buried alive. This profusely il-lustrated book is based on the movie.

China–Nepal

1046. Lye, Keith. Take a Trip to Nepal. Watts, 1988. 32 p. ill. $11.

Gr 2-4. B 85: Nov 1 1988. + - SLJ 35: Jan 1989. Colorful photos and a map augment this introduction to basic informa-tion about the history, geography, and sociology of Nepal.

1047. Nepal in Pictures. (Visual Geography Series). Lerner, 1989. 64 p. ill. $10.

Gr 6-9. SLJ 35: Jul 1989. The religion and culture of Nepal are emphasized in this illustrated work that also covers the na-tion's history and geography.

1048. Watanabi, Hitomi. Nepal. (Children of the World). Gareth Stevens, 1987. 63 p. ill. $13.

Gr 3-6. B 83: Jul 1987. SLJ 34: Oct 1987. Nepalese history, agriculture, arts, climate, geography, government, industry, and religion are covered along with information on the life of a Nepalese child.

China–Social Life and Customs

1049. Aero, Rita. Things Chinese. Doubleday, 1980. 256 p. ill. $25. Pb $11.

Gr 9+. B 77: Dec 15 1980. + - LJ 105: Dec 1 1980. This alphabetic reference to over 370 historical and cultural terms includes illustrations.

1050. Ebrey, Patricia Buckley. Chinese Civilization and Society. Free Press, 1981. 492 p. $20. Pb $10.

Gr 9+. * HT 15: Nov 1981. * HT 17: Feb 1984. LJ 105: Dec 15 1980. Excerpts from diaries, letters, newspaper articles, histories, essays, stories, and folklore provide a lively introduc-tion to Chinese culture from ancient to modern times. Ar-ranged chronologically.

1051. Juliano, Annette. Treasures of China. Richard Marek, 1981. 192 p. ill. $35

Gr 11+. LJ 106: Dec 15 1981. Juliano has examined art ob-jects and monuments as the basis for this survey of the culture of traditional China.

China–Technology and Civilization

1052. Beshore, George. Science in Ancient China. (First Book). Watts, 1988. 95 p. ill. $10.

Gr 5-8. B 84: May 1 1988. BR 7: Sep/Oct 1988. SLJ 34: Apr 1988. Illustrations enhance this account of technological and scientific innovations in China from ancient times to the middle of the 16th century.

1053. Silverberg, Robert. Wonders of Ancient Chinese Science. Hawthorn, 1969. 126 p. ill. $4.

Gr 7+. B 81: Feb 1 1985. LJ 94: Nov 15 1969. The compass, explosives, paper, the umbrella, and the wheelbarrow are among the many inventions and discoveries of the ancient Chinese included in this survey that covers the 4th to the 13th centuries.

China–Tibet

1054. Avedon, John F. In Exile from the Land of Snows: The First Full Account of the Dalai Lama and Tibet since the Chinese Conquest. Knopf, 1984. 384 p. ill. $19.

Gr 9+. B 80: Apr 15 1984. + - LJ 109: Apr 15 1984. An overview of the history of Tibet and the traditions surrounding the Dalai Lama precedes an account of the Chinese conquest of Tibet in 1950 and efforts to maintain Tibetan culture in exile.

1055. Brook, Elaine. Land of the Snow Lion: An Adventure in Tibet. Dodd, 1987. 238 p. ill. $19.

Gr 7+. VOYA 11: Jun 1988. Brook was one of the first westerners allowed in Tibet after 30 years of Chinese control. In telling of her adventures she incorporates Tibetan history and culture.

1056. Tung, Rosemary Jones. Portrait of Lost Tibet, A. Holt, 1980. 224 p. ill. $20.

Gr 9+. B 77: Nov 1 1980. An informative text and a profusion of photos taken in 1942 reveal the theocratic, medieval society of Tibet before it was annexed by China.

China–Women

1057. Rau, Margaret. Young Women in China. Enslow, 1989. 160 p. ill. $17.

Gr 7+. B 86: Nov 1 1989. BC 43: Dec 1989. SLJ 35: Dec 1989. Rau's account of the social status and responsibilities of Chinese women since ancient times concludes with interviews with modern Chinese women that show how ancient traditions still affect their lives.

Hong Kong

1058. Fairclough, Chris. We Live in Hong Kong. (Living Here). Watts, 1986. 60 p. ill. $11.

Gr 5-8. B 82: May 15 1986. Interviews with 26 persons show everyday life in Hong Kong and present information on its history, culture, and geography.

India

1059. Galbraith, Catherine Atwater. India: Now and through Time. Rev. ed. Houghton, 1980. 160 p. ill. $14.

Gr 6+. * SE 45: Apr 1981. SLJ 27: Jan 1981. SLJ 28: Sep 1981. This lively overview of India's history, people, geography, social system, and culture includes over 100 photos, a map, legends and anecdotes.

1060. India in Pictures. (Visual Geography Series). Lerner, 1989. 64 p. ill. Lib. ed. $10.

Gr 5-8. B 85: May 1 1989. SLJ 35: Sep 1989. Emphasis is on history and geography in this illustrated work that also covers India's resources, cities, and economy.

1061. Karan, P.P. India. (Fideler/Gateway Global Community Series). Gateway Press, 1988. 144 p. ill. $17.

Gr 5-9. B 85: Dec 1 1988. India's history, geography, government, resources, economy, culture, and way of life are introduced in this updated work. Includes a glossary.

1062. Sarin, Amita Vohra. India: An Ancient Land, a New Nation. (Discovering Our Heritage). Dillon Press, 1984. 175 p. ill. $11.

Gr 5-9. B 81: May 1 1985. * BR 4: Sep/Oct 1985. SLJ 31: May 1985. Following a section of basic facts, Sarin discusses the history and culture of India, explaining the difficulties caused by the diverse ethnic groups and languages. Lists of noted Indian-Americans and embassies, a glossary, photos, and a map are included.

1063. Traub, James S. India: The Challenge of Change. Rev. ed. Messner, 1985. 167 p. ill. $11.

Gr 6-9. B 82: Mar 1 1986. SLJ 32: Feb 1986. Traub presents information on the history, religion, and geography of India in order to explain the complexities of modernization of industry, farming, and culture.

1064. Wigner, Annabel. Elizabeth and Akbar: Portraits of Power. (World of Change). Dufour, 1987. 52 p. $7.

Gr 6-8. + - BR 7: May/Jun 1988. Based on letters, pamphlets, pictures, and records, this is an account of the early relationship between England and India.

India–Biographies

1065. Allen, Charles. Lives of the Indian Princes. Crown, 1985. 352 p. ill. $25.

Gr 10+. B 81: May 1 1985. LJ 110: May 1 1985. Photos and quotes enhance this composite picture of the lives of princes of the 118 Indian states that existed at the time of independence.

1066. Butler, Francelia. Indira Gandhi. (World Leaders Past & Present). Chelsea House, 1987. 115 p. ill. $17.

Gr 6-10. SLJ 33: May 1987. Numerous quotes, photos, drawings, and maps enhance this biography that shows the importance of Gandhi's father, Jawaharlal Nehru, and her hero, Mahatma Gandhi, in forming her political beliefs.

1067. Cheney, Glenn Alan. Mohandas Gandhi. (Impact Biography). Watts, 1983. 114 p. ill. $9.

Gr 7+. B 79: Jun 1 1983. BC 36: Jul/Aug 1983. BR 2: Jan/Feb 1984. This straightforward account of Gandhi's life explains how his beliefs developed, his impact on the history of India, and how he influenced others, including Martin Luther King, Jr.

1068. Currimbhoy, Nayana. Indira Gandhi. (Impact Biography). Watts, 1985. 116 p. ill. $10.

Gr 7+. B 81: Dec 15 1985. BR 5: May/Jun 1986. SLJ 32: Jan 1986. Currimbhoy presents a balanced biography of Indira Gandhi, who was a charismatic, pragmatic, and controversial prime minister of India.

1069. Faber, Doris. Mahatma Gandhi. Messner, 1986. 122 p. ill. $10.

Gr 9+. B 83: Dec 15 1986. SE 51: Apr/May 1987. SLJ 33: Dec 1986. Gandhi's beliefs and the high points of his life are covered in this illustrated introduction that is based on Gandhi's autobiography.

1070. Finck, Lila. Jawaharlal Nehru. (World Leaders Past & Present). Chelsea House, 1987. 112 p. ill. $16.

Gr 6-10. B 83: Jun 1 1987. SLJ 33: Aug 1987. In telling of Nehru's life Finck also tells the story of India's independence movement and the early days as a sovereign nation. Includes photos.

1071. Fishlock, Trevor. Indira Gandhi. (Profiles). Hamilton; dist. by David and Charles, 1987. 61 p. ill. $9.

Gr 5-8. B 83: Jun 1 1987. SLJ 33: Apr 1987. This concise biography of a woman who was an important figure in world politics for 20 years, and the leader of her nation at the time of her assassination, is illustrated with drawings.

1072. Gold, Gerald. Gandhi: A Pictorial Biography. Newmarket; dist. by Scribner, 1983. 192 p. ill. $17. Pb $10.

Gr 7+. + - LJ 108: Mar 1 1983. SLJ 29: Aug 1983. Gandhi's role in the political life of India is clearly shown in this biography, intended to accompany Attenborough's film on Gandhi. Photos from his life and from the movie are included.

1073. Haskins, James. India under Indira and Rajiv Gandhi. Enslow, 1989. 104 p. ill. $16.

Gr 9+. B 85: Jul 1989. BC 42: Jul/Aug 1989. SLJ 35: Aug 1989. VOYA 12: Oct 1989. This account of the political activities of Indira and Rajiv Gandhi, prime ministers of India, also provides information on India's history and customs.

1074. Hunter, Nigel. Gandhi. (Great Lives). Bookwright Press; dist. by Watts, 1987. 32 p. ill $11.

Gr 4-7. + - SLJ 34: Dec 1987. A simple introduction to the highlights of Gandhi's life and achievements.

1075. Kytle, Calvin. Gandhi, Soldier of Nonviolence: An Introduction. Rev. ed. Seven Locks Press; dist. by Dodd, 1983. 203 p. ill. $14. Pb $9.

Gr 7+. B 79: Jun 1 1983. This revision of Kytle's 1969 biography of Gandhi incorporates many new photos and quotes within a readable text.

1076. Mehta, Ved. Ledge between the Streams, The. Norton, 1984. 544 p. ill. $17.

Gr 9+. * B 80: Mar 15 1984. B 82: May 15 1986. LJ 109: Mar 15 1984. The author was a blind boy growing up in India during the struggle for independence and the partition into Hindu India and Muslim Pakistan. This memoir covers his struggles for education and personal independence during a tumultuous period of his nations' history.

1077. Nicholson, Michael. Mahatma Gandhi: The Man Who Freed India and Led the World in Nonviolent Change. Gareth Stevens, 1988. 68 p. ill. $13.

Gr 5-8. B 85: Feb 15 1989. + - SLJ 35: Feb 1989. This profusely illustrated biography that introduces Gandhi's life and contributions to the world includes a chronology and a glossary.

1078. Rawding, F.W. Gandhi and the Struggle for India's Independence. (Cambridge Topic Book). Lerner, 1982. 51 p. ill. $6.

Gr 6-10. B 78: Feb 1 1982. SLJ 28: Apr 1982. This balanced introduction of Gandhi's political life and the forces that shaped his philosophy is augmented by illustrations, photos, and diagrams.

1079. Shirer, William L. Gandhi, a Memoir. Simon & Schuster, 1980. 255 p. ill. $13.

Gr 10+. B 76: Jan 15 1980. HT 15: Feb 1982. LJ 104: Dec 15 1979. Journalist Shirer had many interviews with Gandhi in the 1930s and provides insight into Gandhi's character and the nature of nonviolent revolution.

1080. Spink, Kathryn. Gandhi. (Profiles). Hamilton; dist. by David and Charles, 1984. 63 p. ill. $8.

Gr 5-9. + - B 81: Feb 1 1985. SLJ 31: Oct 1984. This illustrated introduction to Gandhi shows the development of his philosophy and his work for the independence of India.

India–Fiction

1081. Markandaya, Kamala. Nectar in a Sieve. New American Library, 1955. 248 p. Pb $3.

Gr 9+. B 51: Feb 15 1955. B 51: Apr 15 1955. B 82: May 15 1986. * LJ 80: Apr 1 1955. Rukmani, married at age 12 to a tenant farmer who was a stranger to her, came to love him and they struggled together to raise their family and conquer poverty and national disaster. A powerful novel of daily life.

Indonesia

1082. Fairclough, Chris. We Live in Indonesia. (Living Here). Watts, 1986. 60 p. ill. $11.

Gr 5-8. B 82: May 15 1986. Interviews with 26 persons show everyday life in Indonesia and include discussions of the nation's history, culture, and geography.

1083. Lye, Keith. Take a Trip to Indonesia. Watts, 1985. 32 p. ill. $9.

Gr 2-5. B 81: May 15 1985. SLJ 32: Oct 1985. This introduction to Indonesian history, geography, natural resources, economy, and culture includes photos, maps, and a page of stamps and currency.

1084. Smith, Datus C. Land and People of Indonesia, The. Rev. ed. (Portraits of the Nations Series). Lippincott; dist. by Harper, 1961; 1983. 128 p. ill. $11. Lib. ed. $11.

Gr 5-9. Metzner. * B 57: Jul 15 1961. B 79: Aug 1983. * LJ 86: Jun 15 1961. + - SLJ 30: Sep 1983. This overview of Indonesia's history, geography, culture, and resources emphasizes Indonesia's struggle for independence.

1085. Tozuka, Takako. Indonesia. (Children of the World). Gareth Stevens, 1987. 63 p. ill. $13.

Gr 3-6. B 83: Jun 1987. SLJ 34: Oct 1987. Indonesian history, agriculture, arts, climate, geography, government, industry, and religion are covered, along with information on the life of an Indonesian child.

Iran

1086. Forbis, William H. Fall of the Peacock Throne: The Story of Iran. Harper, 1980. 320 p. $16.

Gr 9+. B 76: Jan 15 1980. LJ 104: Dec 15 1979. Forbis reviews the history of the Persian empire, the traditional roles of the monarchy and religion, and the effects of oil money and rapid westernization in his analysis of the causes of the overthrow of the Shah.

1087. Hiro, Dilip. Iran under the Ayatollahs. Routledge & Kegan Paul, 1985. 416 p. $40.

Gr 9+. B 82: Jan 15 1986. A summary of Iranian history through the fall of the Shah is followed by a detailed account of events in Iran since Khomeini came to power in 1979.

1088. Husain, Akbar. Revolution in Iran, The. (Flashpoints). Rourke, 1988. 76 p. ill. $12.

Gr 6-9. B 85: Dec 1 1988. SLJ 35: Feb 1989. Husain clarifies the historical, cultural, and religious reasons for the revolution in Iran that brought the ayatollah to power.

1089. Iran in Pictures. (Visual Geography Series). Lerner, 1989. 64 p. ill. $10.

Gr 5-8. B 85: May 1 1989. SLJ 35: Aug 1989. Iranian culture, religion, history, economy, geography, and government are introduced in this concise illustrated work. Maps and charts are included.

1090. Irving, Clive. Crossroads of Civilization: 3000 Years of Persian History. Barnes & Noble, 1980. 223 p. ill. $20.

Gr 9+. B 76: May 15 1980. LJ 105: Apr 1 1980. This dramatic and well-illustrated history of Persia covers the years from 559 B.C. to 1941, the beginning of the modern age of Iran.

1091. Kahn, Margaret. Children of the Jinn: In Search of the Kurds and Their Country. Seaview; dist. by Harper, 1980. 303 p. $11.

Gr 9+. B 76: Apr 1 1980. LJ 105: Apr 15 1980. Kahn lived among the Kurds in Iran for a year, studying their culture, history, and language. She explains what she learned and expresses concern about their survival under the Iranian government.

1092. Lengyel, Emil. Iran. (First Book). Watts, 1978; 1981. 72 p. ill. $8.

Gr 4-8. * SE 46: Apr 1982. Iran's geography, cities, culture, and history to 1980 are introduced in this illustrated work.

1093. Mannetti, Lisa. Iran and Iraq: Nations at War. (Impact Book). Watts, 1986. 87 p. ill. $11.

Gr 7+. B 82: Jun 1 1986. B 86: Sep 1 1989. BR 5: Nov/Dec 1986. SLJ 33: Sep 1986. The causes and events of the Iraqi-Iranian conflict are explained in this well-organized, illustrated work.

1094. Pahlavi, Mohammed Reza. Answer to History. Stein & Day, 1980. 204 p. $13.

Gr 9+. B 77: Oct 1 1980. LJ 105: Nov 15 1980. Shortly before his death the deposed Shah of Iran wrote these memoirs. They present his view of the events leading up to the revolution.

1095. Saikal, Amin. Rise and Fall of the Shah, The. Princeton University Press, 1980. 279 p. ill. $15.

Gr 9+. B 76: Jun 1 1980. LJ 105: Apr 15 1980. Saikal examines the domestic and foreign policies of Shah Mohammed

Rezi Pahlavi as he worked to make Iran a regional and world power.

1096. Sullivan, William H. Mission to Iran. Norton, 1981. 320 p. ill. $15.

Gr 9+. B 78: Nov 1 1981. LJ 106: Nov 1 1981. Sullivan served as the last ambassador from the United States to Iran. He describes the events in Iran from 1977 through 1979 and the impact of U.S. foreign policy.

1097. Tames, Richard. Take a Trip to Iran. Watts, 1989. 32 p. ill. $11.

Gr 1-3. + - SLJ 35: Jun 1989. Colorful photos augment this brief introduction to Iran's history, culture, geography, resources, and people.

1098. Watson, Jane W. Iran: Crossroads of Caravans. (Living in Today's World). Garrard, 1966. 112 p. ill. Pb $8.

Gr 3-6. Metzner. Because of its location Iran (formerly Persia) has been an important part of the trade route between Europe and China. Conflict over control of it has been a source of war since ancient times.

Iran–Biographies

1099. Cockcroft, James. Mohammed Reza Pahlavi: Shah of Iran. (World Leaders Past & Present). Chelsea House, 1988. 112 p. ill. $17.

Gr 6+. BR 8: May/Jun 1989, Sep/Oct 1989. - SLJ 35: Jan 1989. Voya 12: Apr 1989. Cockcroft's biography of the Shah emphasizes the political aspects of his reign, especially his relationship with the United States.

1100. Gordon, Matthew S. Ayatollah Khomeini. (World Leaders Past & Present). Chelsea House, 1987. 116 p. ill. $16.

Gr 7+. + - B 83: Apr 15 1987. SLJ 33: May 1987. Gordon presents a history of Islam and Iran in order to provide the setting for the revolution that brought Khomeini to power. His leadership and the Iran-Iraq war are also covered.

1101. Llywelyn, Morgan. Xerxes. (World Leaders Past & Present). Chelsea House, 1987. 111 p. ill. $17.

Gr 6-10. B 84: Nov 15 1987. + - SLJ 34: Dec 1987. Under Xerxes, Persian art was highly developed, and he was a wise administrator, but his military losses to the Greeks caused significant problems for his kingdom.

1102. Shawcross, William. Shah's Last Ride: The Fate of an Ally. Simon & Schuster, 1988. 380 p. ill. $20.

Gr 9+. B 85: Oct 15 1988. + - LJ 113: Oct 15 1988. Shawcross recalls the last few months of the Shah's despotic reign and the events that caused his downfall.

Iran–Fiction

1103. Gilmore, Kate. Remembrance of the Sun. Houghton, 1986. 246 p. $14.

Gr 7+. B 83: Dec 1 1986. BC 40: Dec 1986. + - BR 5: Jan/Feb 1987. + - LJ 111: Nov 1986. VOYA 9: Dec 1986. Set in the last year of the Shah's reign, this story of a love affair between an American girl and an Iranian boy who is involved in the revolution provides detail on Iranian culture and the political situations that led to Khomeini's rule.

Iraq

1104. Docherty, J.P. Iraq. Chelsea House, 1988. 96 p. ill. $12.

Gr 4-6. B 85: Jan 1 1989. This straightforward account of Iraq's history, geography, industry, government, economy, and people includes maps and numerous photos.

1105. Moss, Carol. Science in Ancient Mesopotamia. (First Book). Watts, 1988. 71 p. ill. $11.

Gr 5-7. B 85: Dec 15 1988. SLJ 35: Jun 1989. Moss' description of ancient scientific achievements, such as the invention of the wheel and developments in agriculture, mathematics, medicine, and astronomy, is illustrated with numerous photos.

1106. Tames, Richard. Take a Trip to Iraq. Watts, 1989. 32 p. ill. $11.

Gr 1-3. + - SLJ 35: Jun 1989. Colorful photos augment this brief introduction to Iraq's history, culture, geography, resources, and people.

Israel

1107. Banks, Lynne Reid. Letters to My Israeli Sons: The Story of Jewish Survival. Watts, 1980. 276 p. maps. $11.

Gr 10+. LJ 106: Jan 15 1981. This informed capsule version of Jewish history concentrates on the era since World War II.

1108. Bergman, Denise. Through the Year in Israel. David & Charles, 1983. 71 p. ill. $15.

Gr 6+. + - B 80: Feb 15 1984. SLJ 30: Mar 1984. Israeli history and culture are examined in this British series that examines topics by the months of the year. Includes photos, statistics, timelines, maps, and tables.

1109. Burstein, Chaya. Kid's Catalog of Israel, A. Jewish Publication Society, 1988. 279 p. ill. Pb $13.

Gr 3-8. B 85: Dec 1 1988. * SE 53: Apr/May 1989. SLJ 35: Jan 1989. This lively account of Israel's history, geography, and culture includes short biographies, descriptions of holidays, craft ideas, songs, and recipes.

1110. Carmi, Giora. And Shira Imagined. Jewish Publication Society, 1988. 32 p. ill. $14.

Gr K-3. * SE 53: Apr/May 1989. + - SLJ 35: Apr 1989. Famous places in Israel, past and present, are seen as a little girl travels through the land and imagines that her stuffed animals live there.

1111. Dan, Uri. To the Promised Land: The Birth of Israel, 40th Anniversary. Doubleday, 1988. 240 p. ill. $25.

Gr 9+. B 84: Apr 1 1988. LJ 113: May 1 1988. This account of the struggle from 1897 to 1948 to establish the nation of Israel is illustrated with over 200 archival photos.

1112. Feinstein, Steve. Israel in Pictures. (Visual Geography Series). Lerner, 1988. 64 p. ill. $10.

Gr 5-8. B 84: Aug 1988. The history of Israel through 1987 is covered along with its geography, resources, government, cities, and culture. Numerous photos, maps, and charts are included.

1113. Fisher, Leonard Everett. Wailing Wall, The. Macmillan, 1989. 32 p. ill. $15.

Gr 2-6. * B 86: Sep 1 1989. BC 43: Sep 1989. SLJ 35: Oct 1989. Through the story of the Wailing Wall Fisher tells of the frequently violent history of Jerusalem.

1114. Hasan, Sana. Enemy in the Promised Land: An Egyptian Woman's Journey into Israel. Pantheon, 1987. 324 p. $19.

Gr 9+. B 83: Jan 1 1987. What began as a 6-week trip to Israel by an Egyptian woman became a 3-year obsession with Israel that led Hasan to work among the people and interview both notable and ordinary people. She presents a view of Israel through the eyes of an Arab.

1115. Hillel, Shlomo. Operation Babylon. Doubleday, 1987. 302 p. $20.

Gr 9+. B 84: Nov 1 1987. LJ 112: Nov 15 1987. Over 100,000 Iraqi Jews immigrated to Palestine between 1947 and 1952 in defiance of a British ban. Hillel's account provides insight into the culture of Iraqi Jews and the Zionist movement.

1116. Hoffman, Gail. Land and People of Israel. Rev. ed. (Portraits of the Nations Series). Harper, 1963. 124 p. ill. $12.

Gr 5-9. Metzner. B 46: Mar 15 1950. * HB 26: May 1950. LJ 75: Jul 1950. This account of the early days of modern Israel presents a concise introduction to the nation's history and clarifies its problems and achievements.

1117. Hohlfelder, Robert L. King Herod's Dream: Caesarea on the Sea. Norton, 1988. 140 p. ill. $30.

Gr 9+. B 84: Feb 15 1988. LJ 113: Mar 15 1988. The history of ancient Caesarea, and life in this port city that prospered for over 1200 years, are examined by archaeologists who excavated the site.

1118. Jones, Helen Hinckley. Israel. (Enchantment of the World). Childrens Press, 1986. 124 p. ill. $15.

Gr 4-6. B 83: Apr 1 1987. SLJ 33: May 1987. The history section of this work covers ancient times to the creation of an independent nation. Also covered are Israel's geography, resources, government, economy, culture, and cities.

1119. Kuskin, Karla. Jerusalem, Shining Still. Harper, 1987. 27 p. ill. $13. Lib. ed. $13.

Gr 1-7. * B 84: Oct 1 1987. BC 41: Dec 1987. HB 63: Nov/Dec 1987. * SLJ 34: Nov 1987. This accessible account of the 4000 years of Jerusalem's history is told in poetic prose that is enriched by woodcuts.

1120. Lawton, Clive. Passport to Israel. Watts, 1988. 48 p. ill. $12.

Gr 4-9. B 85: May 15 1988. SLJ 34: Aug 1988. Colorful illustrations, maps, charts, and graphs add to the appeal of this introduction to Israel. A brief history and other basic facts are included, but emphasis is on how people live in Israel today.

1121. Mann, Peggy. Israel in Pictures. (Visual Geography Series). Sterling, 1980. 64 p. ill. $5. Pb $3.

Gr 5-7. SLJ 27: Feb 1981. An abundance of photos enriches this concise account of Israel's history, culture, geography, and government.

1122. Perlmutter, Amos. Israel: The Partitioned State. Scribner, 1985. 301 p. ill $20.

Gr 11+. B 82: Oct 1 1985. LJ 110: Oct 1 1985. From ancient to modern times Israel's borders have been a matter of dispute. Perlmutter presents the historic debates and argues that the final resolution rests on Arab good will.

1123. Raphael, Chaim. Road from Babylon: The Story of Sephardi and Oriental Jews. Harper, 1986. 294 p. ill. $25.

Gr 10+. B 82: Dec 1 1985. Raphael examines the historic causes of conflict between two major groups in Israel, the Sephardic Jews, whose ancestors lived in Spain, Portugal, and North Africa, and the Ashkenazi Jews, whose ancestors lived in Eastern Europe.

1124. Shamir, Maxim. Story of Israel in Stamps. Wilshire, 1969. 75 p. ill. Pb $1.

Gr 3-7. Metzner. Using the illustrations on stamps, Shamir recounts the history of Israel.

1125. Sirof, Harriet. Junior Encyclopedia of Israel, The. Jonathan David, 1980. 476 p. ill. $17.

Gr 5-9. B 76: Jul 1 1980. This profusely illustrated encyclopedia covers the people, places, and events of ancient and modern Israel.

1126. Stefoff, Rebecca. West Bank/Gaza Strip. (Places and Peoples of the World). Chelsea House, 1988. 104 p. ill. $12.

Gr 5-8. BR 7: Sep/Oct 1988. SLJ 34: Aug 1988. Conflicting claims to this small area, which is about 5 miles wide and 26 miles long, have occurred throughout history and continue today. This work introduces the history, culture, and terrain of the area.

1127. Taitz, Emily. Israel: A Sacred Land. (Discovering Our Heritage). Dillon Press, 1987. 159 p. ill. $13.

Gr 5+. B 84: Feb 15 1988. BR 7: May/Jun 1988. SLJ 34: Jun/Jul 1988. An overview of Israeli history and contemporary problems accompanies information on everyday social life and customs. Photos, a glossary, and a map are included.

1128. Worth, Richard. Israel and the Arab States. (Impact Book). Watts, 1983. 90 p. maps. $9.

Gr 7-10. B 79: Jun 15 1983. BR 2: Jan/Feb 1984. SLJ 30: Sep 1983. Worth examines the relationships of Israel with its neighbors and introduces the primary leaders on both sides since 1948.

Israel–Biographies

1129. Adler, David A. Our Golda: The Story of Golda Meir. Viking, 1984. 52 p. ill. $11.

Gr 3-7. B 80: Jul 1984. + - BC 38: Nov 1984. HB 60: Jun 1984. * SE Apr 1985. SLJ 30: May 1984. Anecdotes enhance this introduction to the woman who was Israel's prime minister in the early 1970s. The development of her character is set in the context of Jewish history in the 20th century.

1130. Amdur, Richard. Chaim Weizmann. (World Leaders Past & Present). Chelsea House, 1988. 112 p. ill. $17.

Gr 7+. B 85: Sep 15 1988. BR 7: Nov/Dec 1988. As president of the World Zionism Organization, Weizmann was a leader in establishing the new nation of Israel in 1948, and became its first president. This balanced biography is well illustrated.

1131. Amdur, Richard. Menachem Begin. (World Leaders Past & Present). Chelsea House, 1987. 112 p. ill. $17.

Gr 6-10. B 84: Nov 15 1987. Amdur's balanced introduction to the multi-faceted Israeli prime minister includes photos.

1132. Bar-Zohar, Michael. Ben-Gurion: A Biography. Centennial ed. Adama, 1986. 342 p. ill. $18.

Gr 10+. BR 5: Mar/Apr 1987. The author of several biographies of Israel's first prime minister has updated the 1977 edition of this title with an essay on Ben-Gurion's place in the history of Israel. Includes photos.

1133. Benziman, Uzi. Sharon–An Israeli Caesar. Adama, 1985. 276 p. $18.

Gr 10+. BR 5: Sep/Oct 1986. Benziman presents a balanced biography of Ariel Sharon, a courageous, charismatic, and dictatorial former defense minister of Israel who continues to wield great political influence.

1134. Davidson, Margaret. Golda Meir Story, The. Rev. ed. Scribner, 1981. 228 p. ill. $11.

Gr 4-9. B 77: Jul/Aug 1981. B 82: Sep 15 1985. + - BC 34: Jun 1981. * SE 46: Apr 1982. SLJ 28: Feb 1982. This balanced and accessible biography includes some fictionalized dialogue. It focuses on Meir's early life and her contributions to Israel.

1135. Herzog, Chaim. Heroes of Israel: Profiles of Jewish Courage. Little, Brown, 1989. 304 p. $20.

Gr 9+. B 86: Sep 15 1989. LJ 114: Sep 1 1989. Bravery in moral and military activities is the criterion for inclusion in this collective biography that includes Jewish persons from ancient to modern times.

1136. Jordan, Ruth. Daughter of the Waves: Memories of Growing Up in Pre-War Palestine. Taplinger, 1983. 224 p. ill. $11.

Gr 9+. LJ 106: May 1 1981. SLJ 30: Sep 1983. Information on Arab-Jewish relations and the cultural and political life of the time is included in this personal account of life in Palestine in the 1920s and 1930s.

1137. Keller, Mollie. Golda Meir. (Impact Biography). Watts, 1983. 119 p. ill. $9.

Gr 6-10. B 79: Jul 1983. BR 2: Nov/Dec 1983. SLJ 29: Aug 1983. The energetic Golda Meir dedicated her life to the establishment of Israel and to her children. This balanced biography covers the major events in her life within their historical setting. Illustrated.

1138. Kotler, Yair. Heil Kahane. Adama, 1986. 254 p. $18.

Gr 9+. - LJ 111: Apr 1 1986. VOYA 9: Dec 1986. Kahane is a leader of the militaristic Jewish Defense League. The author believes that he seeks to destroy the democratic structure of Israel.

1139. Krantz, Hazel. Daughter of My People: Henrietta Szold and Hadassah. (Jewish Biography Series). Lodestar, 1987. 117 p. ill. $15.

Gr 9+. B 84: Nov 1 1987. BC 41: Jan 1988. SLJ 34: Jan 1988. VOYA 11: Jun 1988. On a trip to Palestine in 1910, Henrietta Szold became aware of the region's critical need for medical care, and established a hospital. During and after World War II she provided for 10,000 Jewish refugee children.

1140. Martin, Ralph G. Golda: Golda Meir, the Romantic Years. Scribner, 1988. 356 p. ill. $20.

Gr 9+. B 85: Oct 1 1988. + - LJ 113: Nov 1 1988. Martin's biography of Meir covers her life to 1948, revealing details of her personal life and the development of her political philosophy.

1141. Peres, Shimon. From These Men: Seven Founders of the State of Israel. Wyndham Books/Simon & Schuster, 1980. 214 p. $11.

Gr 10+. LJ 105: Mar 1 1980. These sketches on the lives of seven Israeli heroes also provide a view of national history. Included are David Ben-Gurion, Levi Eshkol, Berl Katznelson, Moshe Haviv, Nathan Alterman, Ernst David Bergmann, and Yonatan Netanyahu.

1142. Silver, Eric. Begin: The Haunted Prophet. Random, 1984. 278 p. ill. $18.

Gr 9+. B 81: Dec 1 1984. LJ 110: Jan 1985. Silver shows the origins and results of Begin's nationalistic ideology as he traces Begin's life from his Polish childhood through his time as prime minister of Israel.

1143. Silverstein, Herma. David Ben-Gurion. (Impact Biography). Watts, 1988. 128 p. ill. $12.

Gr 6+. B 84: Mar 1 1988. + - BR 7: Sep/Oct 1988. + - SLJ 35: May 1988. * VOYA 11: Aug 1988. This detailed account of Ben-Gurion's life and his leadership of Israel explains the various political factions within Israel.

1144. Slater, Robert. Golda: The Uncrowned Queen of Israel: A Pictorial Biography. Jonathan David, 1981. 277 p. ill. $17.

Gr 9+. + - B 78: Dec 15 1981. LJ 106: Nov 1 1981. Slater includes many previously unpublished photos in this biography, which covers Meir's personal life and her career as ambassador and prime minister.

1145. Vail, John J. David Ben-Gurion. (World Leaders Past & Present). Chelsea House, 1987. 112 p. ill. $17.

Gr 6+. B 84: Oct 15 1987. * BR 7: Sep/Oct 1988. + - SLJ 34: Feb 1988. Emphasis is on Ben-Gurion's career as a military strategist and political leader. This illustrated biography of Israel's first prime minister is also an overview of the 20th-century history of Israel.

Israel–Fiction

1146. Bergman, Tamar. Boy from Over There, The. Houghton, 1988. 180 p. $13.

Gr 5-9. * B 84: Apr 1 1988. B 85: Apr 1 1989. BC 41: Apr 1988. * BR 7: Jan 1989. SLJ 34: Jun/Jul 1988. * VOYA 11: Dec 1988. Avramic and Rina are young survivors of the Holocaust who must adjust to life on a kibbutz during the 1948 war, which was fought to establish the nation of Israel.

1147. Steiner, Connie Colker. On Eagles' Wings and Other Things. Jewish Publication Society, 1987. 32 p. ill. $13.

Gr 5-8. B 84: Apr 1 1988. Steiner's compact story concerns four Jewish children who came from different nations to make their homes in the new nation of Israel in the late 1940s.

Israel–Jewish-Arab Relations

1148. Anderson, Bob. Israel. (Opposing Viewpoints Series). Greenhaven Press, 1988. 266 p. ill. $15. Pb $8.

Gr 9+. B 85: Jan 15 1989. The historical reasons for the conflict between the Israelis and the Palestinians are explored and various points of view are presented. Cartoons and critical thinking activities are included.

1149. Binur, Yoram. My Enemy, My Self. Doubleday, 1989. 240 p. ill. $19.

Gr 9+. B 85: Jan 1 1989. Binur, a Jewish journalist, posed as an Arab to examine the relationship between Jews and Arabs in Israel, and reports the depressing results of his experiences.

1150. Carroll, Raymond. Palestine Question, The. (Impact Book). Watts, 1983. 90 p. map. $9.

Gr 7+. B 79: Jun 15 1983. * BR 2: Jan/Feb 1984. SLJ 30: Sep 1983. Carroll presents a brief but lively and balanced overview of the history of both Arab and Jewish claims to the land at the east end of the Mediterranean.

1151. Dimbleby, Jonathan. Palestinians, The. Quartet; dist. by Horizon, 1980. 256 p. ill. $25.

Gr 9+. B 76: Jul 1 1980. LJ 105: Jun 1 1980. Dimbleby clarifies the Palestinian point of view in a history of the Palestinian people that is enriched by quotes and photos.

1152. Grossman, David. Yellow Wind, The. Farrar, 1988. 188 p. $16.

Gr 9+. B 84: Apr 1 1988. LJ 113: Apr 15 1988. Grossman's examination of the moral dilemma caused by the symbiotic relationship between the Jewish and Palestinian people, and of the West Bank crisis, shows that both peoples are victims.

1153. Halter, Marek. Jester and the Kings: A Political Autobiography. Little, Brown, 1989. 273 p. $20.

Gr 10+. LJ 114: Jun 15 1989. VOYA 12: Dec 1989. Halter tells of his experiences in World War II and his involvement with political groups trying to find a peaceful settlement to conflicting claims in the Middle East. His work brought him into contact with leaders on both sides of the struggle.

1154. Harper, Paul. Arab-Israeli Issue, The. (Flashpoints). Rourke, 1987. 77 p. ill. $11.

Gr 7-10. SLJ 33: Aug 1987. This balanced introduction to the 1967 war and its aftermath explores the possibilities of a peaceful resolution to the continuing conflict. Photos and maps are included.

1155. Laquer, Walter. Israel-Arab Reader: A Documentary History of the Middle East Conflict. 4th ed. Facts on File, 1985. 704 p. map. $22.

Gr 9+. B 81: Jun 15 1985. * VOYA 8: Feb 1986. All sides of the Arab-Israeli conflict are presented in this balanced collection of documents.

1156. McDowall, David. Palestinians, The. (Issues). Gloucester Press; dist. by Watts, 1986. 29 p. ill. $11.

Gr 5-9. + - BC 40: Mar 1987. BR 5: Mar/Apr 1987. SLJ 33: May 1987. This brief outline of the history, culture, and religion of the Palestinians discusses their search for a land of their own. It includes colorful photos, graphics, and a chronology.

1157. Regan, Geoffrey. Israel and the Arabs. Lerner, 1986. 48 p. $9.

Gr 7-10. B 86: Sep 1 1989. Regan examines Great Britain's role in the Arab-Israeli conflict from 1800 through the Suez crisis in 1956.

1158. Reich, Walter. Stranger in My House: Jews and Arabs in the West Bank. Holt, 1984. 127 p. maps. $13.

Gr 9+. B 81: Nov 1 1984. Interviews with Jewish and Palestinian settlers in the West Bank show the conflicting claims and dreams that center on this small, strategic land.

1159. Shehadeh, Raja. Samed: Journal of a West Bank Palestinian. Watts, 1984. 172 p. Pb $10.

Gr 9+. BR 3: Jan/Feb 1985. Shehadeh tells of his experiences as a West Bank Palestinian and pleads for reason, rather than violence, on both sides.

1160. Shipler, David K. Arab and Jew: Wounded Spirits in a Promised Land. Times Books, 1986. 608 p. $23.

Gr 9+. B 83: Sep 1 1986. Shipler's detailed account of how varied facets of the Arab and Jewish communities view each other is balanced and perceptive.

1161. Stefoff, Rebecca. Yasir Arafat. (World Leaders Past & Present). Chelsea House, 1988. 111 p. ill. $17.

Gr 6+. B 85: Nov 1 1988. B 86: Sep 1 1989. BR 7: Nov/Dec 1988. SLJ 35: Dec 1988. This balanced, illustrated biography of PLO leader Arafat also presents a clear account of the history and activities of the PLO and of the Arab-Jewish conflict. Includes photos.

1162. Tawil, Raymonda Hawa. My Home, My Prison. Holt, 1980. 265 p. $13.

Gr 9+. * B 76: Jan 1 1980. LJ 105: Jan 15 1980. Tawil is a Palestinian journalist, wife, and mother. Her autobiography is a personal account of a woman in a male-dominated society as well as a record of the suffering of Palestinians in an occupied territory.

1163. Turki, Fawaz. Soul in Exile: Lives of a Palestinian Revolutionary. Monthly Review Press, 1988. 155 p. $26. Pb $10.

Gr 9+. B 84: Mar 15 1988. * LJ 113: Apr 15 1988. When he was 8 Turki and his Palestinian family were deprived of home and national identity when their part of Palestine became Israel (1948). Turki's lyrical prose tells the Palestinian story.

1164. Wallach, John. Still Small Voices. Harcourt, 1989. 286 p. ill. $17.

Gr 9+. B 85: Mar 1 1989. LJ 114: Mar 15 1989. This photo album presents profiles of varied residents of the West Bank and Gaza Strip who represent a wide range of opinion about Arab-Jewish relations.

Israel–Military History

1165. Brown, Ashley. Strike from the Sky. (Villard Military Series). Villard, 1986. 96 p. ill. $5.

Gr 9+. BR 5: Jan 1987. * VOYA 10: Apr 1987. This highly illustrated account of the Israeli parachute corps includes an account of the raid on Entebbe.

Israel–Social Life and Customs

1166. Ashabranner, Brent. Gavriel and Jemal: Two Boys of Jerusalem. Dodd, 1984. 94 p. ill. $11.

Gr 4-7. B 81: Feb 1 1985. B 82: Sep 1 1989. BC 38: Dec 1984. HB 61: Mar/Apr 1985. SLJ 31: Jan 1985. * SE 49: Apr 1985. An Israeli and a Palestinian boy lived within blocks of one another, but grew up in cultures a world apart. Their daily lives and beliefs are described and unfamiliar terms are explained.

1167. Clayton-Felt, Josh. To Be Seventeen in Israel: Through the Eyes of an American Teenager. Watts, 1987. 96 p. ill. $12.

Gr 7+. - BR 6: May/Jun 1987. BC 40: May 1987. SLJ 33: Jun/Jul 1987. + - VOYA 10: Aug/Sep 1987. The author is an American youth who spent 5 weeks in Israel. He reports on the daily activities of Israeli teens and includes many photos.

Japan

1168. Bird, Isabella. Unbeaten Tracks in Japan. Beacon, 1880; 1987. 332 p. ill. Pb $10.

Gr 9+. SLJ 34: Feb 1988. Twenty-five years after Japan was opened to westerners in 1853, Isabella Bird explored from Tokyo north to Hokkaido. Her journal describes the people, culture, and landscape that she saw. Photos and drawings are included.

1169. Bolitho, Harold. Meiji Japan. (Cambridge Topic Book). Lerner, 1980. 51 p. ill. $5.

Gr 4-6. SLJ 27: Mar 1981. Bolitho's graphic introduction to ancient Japan examines the results of the opening of trade following the visits of Commodore Perry and Townsend Harris.

1170. Davidson, Judith. Japan: Where East Meets West. (Discovering Our Heritage). Dillon Press, 1983. 142 p. ill. $10.

Gr 4-8. B 79: Jul 1983. * BR 2: Nov/Dec 1983. SLJ 29: Aug 1983. A summary of useful reference material is followed by an overview of the geography, history, and culture of Japan and information on Japanese immigrants to the United States. Photos and a glossary are included.

1171. Dolan, Edward F. New Japan, The. Watts, 1983. 118 p. ill. $10.

Gr 6+. B 80: Dec 15 1983. + - BR 2: Mar/Apr 1984. * SE 48: May 1984. SLJ 30: Jan 1984. * VOYA 7: Jun 1984. How Japan rose from the physical and economic disaster of World War II to become an economic superpower is explained in this account of Japanese corporate and family life, education, culture, and religion.

1172. Greene, Carol. Japan. (Enchantment of the World). Childrens Press, 1983. 127 p. ill. $13.

Gr 5-8. B 80: Mar 15 1984. + - SLJ 30: May 1984. Colorful maps and photos enhance this introduction to Japanese history, culture, geography, economy, and resources.

1173. Hunter, Janet. Concise Dictionary of Modern Japanese History. University of California Press, 1984. 347 p. maps. $33. Pb $11.

Gr 10+. LJ 109: Dec 1984. Some 650 brief entries cover events, notable persons, and political topics in Japanese history from 1850 to 1980.

1174. Jacobsen, Karen. Japan. (New True Book). Childrens Press, 1982. 45 p. ill. $7.

Gr 1-4. B 79: Mar 1 1983. + - SLJ 30: Sep 1983. SLJ 30: Nov 1983. Maps, diagrams, and colorful photos enhance this introduction to Japan and its people.

1175. Japan in Pictures. (Visual Geography Series). Lerner, 1989. 64 p. ill. $12.

Gr 5-8. B 86: Sep 15 1989. Photos, maps, and charts augment this introduction to Japan's history, geography, climate, resources, and government.

1176. Lewis, Brenda Ralph. Growing Up in Samurai Japan. Batsford; dist. by David & Charles, 1981. 72 p. ill. $15.

Gr 5-9. B 78: Mar 15 1982. - SLJ 28: May 1982. The feudal system that was the samurai period in Japan lasted from the 1100s to 1853. Lewis covers the culture of the period in this illustrated work that includes a timeline and chronology.

1177. Morris, Ivan. World of the Shining Prince: Court Life in Ancient Japan. Penguin, 1975. 348 p. ill. $8.

Gr 10+. LJ 89: Sep 1 1964. SE 45: May 1981. Tenth-century Japanese society is discussed in chapters covering such topics as politics, religion, superstitions, and beauty. A glossary is included.

1178. Pitts, Forrest R. Japan. (Fideler/Gateway Global Community Series). Gateway Press, 1988. 160 p. ill. $17.

Gr 5-9. B 85: Dec 1 1988. Japan's history, geography, government, resources, economy, culture, and way of life are covered in this updated work that includes a glossary.

1179. Reischauer, Edwin O. Japanese, The. Harvard University Press, 1977. 443 p. ill. $20. Pb $10.

Gr 12+. LJ 102: May 1 1977. SE 45: May 1981. An overview of Japanese geography, resources, and history is followed by a detailed discussion of their social organization and values, the political system, and international relations.

1180. Roberson, John R. Japan: From Shogun to Sony 1543-1984. Atheneum, 1985. 198 p. ill. $14.

Gr 7+. B 82: Oct 15 1982. BC 39: Nov 1985. HB 61: Nov/Dec 1985. SLJ 32: Dec 1985. Photos, maps, and a glossary enhance this clear and concise history of Japan from its first encounter with the west in 1543. Social conditions, arts, religion, and philosophy are included in a discussion of Japan's internal politics and international role.

1181. Sansom, George. Japan: A Short Cultural History. Century, 1931; 1978. 584 p. ill. Pb $13.

Gr 10+. B 28: Mar 1932. SE 45: May 1981. This anecdotal history of Japan from ancient times to 1868 emphasizes social, economic, and religious events rather than political happenings.

1182. Spry-Leverton, Peter. Japan. Facts on File, 1988. 192 p. ill. $23.

Gr 9+. B 84: Feb 15 1988. * BR 7: Sep/Oct 1988. This highly illustrated account of Japanese history and culture shows how the Japanese preserve the past while they move to the fore in business and education.

1183. Steel, Anne. Samurai Warrior. (How They Lived). Rourke, 1988. 32 p. ill. $13.

Gr 3-6. B 85: Nov 15 1988. SLJ 35: Jun 1989. Medieval society in Japan is clearly presented in this illustrated work.

1184. Stefoff, Rebecca. Japan. (Places and Peoples of the World). Chelsea House, 1988. 112 p. ill. $12.

Gr 6-8. B 84: May 15 1988. Japanese history, culture, geography, economy, cities, and resources are covered in this overview that is augmented by maps, photos, and a glossary.

1185. Tames, Richard. Japan in the Twentieth Century. (Twentieth Century World History). Batsford, 1981. 96 p. ill. $15.

Gr 5-9. SLJ 28: May 1982. This well organized, illustrated overview of the 20th century history of Japan includes maps.

1186. Tames, Richard. Japan: The Land and Its People. Rev. ed. (Silver Burdett Countries). Silver Burdett, 1987. 43 p. ill. $15.

Gr 4-7. + - B 84: Nov 15 1987. - SLJ 34: Feb 1988. Tames' large-sized pictorial work presents a brief overview of Japan's history, geography, industry, culture, and social life.

1187. Tames, Richard. Japanese, The. (Today's World). Batsford; dist. by David & Charles, 1983. 72 p. ill. $15.

Gr 8+. B 79: Apr 15 1983. BR 1: Mar/Apr 1983. From a British publisher, this is an examination of social, cultural, and economic changes in Japan following World War II.

1188. Tames, Richard. Passport to Japan. Watts, 1988. 48 p. ill. $13.

Gr 4-8. B 85: Feb 1 1989. SLJ 35: Jan 1989. A brief history of modern Japan is included in this introduction to Japanese culture, daily life, economy, and geography.

1189. Vaughan, Josephine B. Land and People of Japan. Rev. ed. (Portraits of the Nations Series). Harper, 1952; 1972. 128 p. ill. $12.

Gr 5-9. Metzner. B 48: Feb 15 1952. HB 28: Aug 1952. A clear and readable illustrated introduction to the history of Japan and the lives of the Japanese people.

Japan–Biographies

1190. Morris, Ivan. Nobility of Failure: Tragic Heroes in the History of Japan. Holt, 1975. 500 p. ill. not avail.

Gr 12+. LJ 101: Feb 15 1976. SE 45: May 1981. Morris presents portraits of heroic individuals in Japanese history from ancient times through World War II.

Japan–Fiction

1191. Haugaard, Erik Christian. Samurai's Tale, The. Houghton, 1984. 234 p. $13.

Gr 6-10. B 80: Apr 1 1984. BC 37: Jun 1984. * HB 60: Apr 1984. * SE 49: Apr 1985. SLJ 30: May 1984. Taro, son of a samurai, is the only survivor when his family is killed. He gradually proves himself worthy of samurai training and serves his master well, in this exciting story of 16th-century Japan.

1192. Matsubara, Hisako. Cranes at Dusk. Doubleday, 1985. 253 p. $16.

Gr 7+. B 81: Mar 15 1985. B 82: Oct 1 1985. B 82: May 15 1986. * BC 38: May 1985. LJ 110: Mar 1 1985. SLJ 31: May 1985. The tragedies at the end of World War II, the American occupation, and the conflict between her traditionalist mother and her free-thinking father complicate the life of 10-year-old Saya.

1193. Namioka, Lensey. Valley of the Broken Cherry Trees. Delacorte, 1980. 218 p. $9.

Gr 6-9. B 76: Apr 15 1980. BC 33: Jun 1980. HB 56: Jun 1980. SLJ 26: Aug 1980. A sense of the period pervades this samurai adventure set in 16th century Japan, involving a struggle between two warlords.

1194. Say, Allen. Bicycle Man, The. Houghton, 1982. 42 p. ill. $12.

Gr K-3. * B 79: Sep 15 1982. B 83: Mar 1 1987. HB 58: Dec 1982. * SE 47: Apr 1983. In 1945 the author was a first grader. On the day of a family picnic at his school two Americans, one white and one black, joined the festivities and entertained with a spectacular display of bicycle riding.

Japan–Kings, Queens, Rulers, etc.

1195. Behr, Edward. Hirohito: Behind the Myth. Villard, 1989. 448 p. ill. $23.

Gr 9+. B 86: Sep 15 1989. Behr's biography of Hirohito examines his role in the events leading up to World War II and the reasons why the United States allowed him to remain as emperor following the war.

1196. Severns, Karen. Hirohito. (World Leaders Past & Present). Chelsea House, 1988. 112 p. ill. $17.

Gr 6-10. B 84: Jun 1 1988. This generously illustrated biography explores Japan's role in World War II as it presents an account of the life of the emperor.

Japan–Social Life and Customs

1197. Collcutt, Martin. Cultural Atlas of Japan. Facts on File, 1988. 240 p. $40.

Gr 8+. BR 8: Mar/Apr 1989. + - LJ 114: Feb 1 1989. SLJ 35: May 1989. A chronology, a glossary, gazetteer, and a list of rulers augment this work that provides much information about Japanese culture and history. Special essays discuss the tea ceremony, samurai society, Kabuki Theater, and similar topics.

1198. Meyer, Carolyn. Voice from Japan, A. Harcourt, 1988. 212 p. $15.

Gr 7+. B 85: Nov 15 1988. BC 42: Nov 1988. HB 65: Jan/Feb 1989. * SE 53: Apr/May 1989. SLJ 35: Nov 1988. Brief information on Japanese history and culture provides the background for Meyer's readable observations on contemporary Japanese life.

Jordan

1199. Jordan in Pictures. Rev. ed. (Visual Geography Series). Lerner, 1988. 64 p. ill. $10.

Gr 5-8. B 85: Feb 1 1989. B 86: Sep 1 1989. SLJ 35: Feb 1989. Emphasis is on history and geography in this illustrated work that also covers Jordan's resources, cities, and economy.

1200. Whitehead, Susan. Jordan. Chelsea House, 1988. 96 p. ill. $12.

Gr 4-6. B 85: Jan 1 1989. The history, geography, and daily life of Jordan are covered in this illustrated overview.

1201. Wright, David K. Jordan. (Children of the World). Gareth Stevens, 1988. 64 p. ill. $13.

Gr 3-5. B 86: Sep 1 1989. Contemporary political concerns, customs, culture, and the everyday life of city and rural dwellers are covered in this illustrated work.

Jordan–Kings, Queens, Rulers, etc.

1202. Matusky, Gregory. King Hussein. (World Leaders Past & Present). Chelsea House, 1987. 111 p. ill. $16.

Gr 6-10. B 83: Jul 1987. SLJ 33: May 1987. This balanced biography of Jordan's king covers the last 100 years of his nation's history, and has photos on nearly every page.

Kampuchea

1203. Canesso, Claudia. Cambodia. (Places and Peoples of the World). Chelsea House, 1989. 96 p. ill. $13.

Gr 6-8. + - B 86: Oct 15 1989. Cambodia's history, geography, culture, economy, government, and people are introduced. The text is supplemented by numerous photos.

Kampuchea–Biographies

1204. Mam, Teeda Butt. To Destroy You Is No Loss. Atlantic; dist. by Little, Brown, 1987. 289 p. maps. $18.

Gr 9+. SLJ 34: Dec 1987. Mam documents her experiences and those of her nation when the Khmer Rouge reversed national values, executed educated persons, and forced city dwellers to become farm laborers.

1205. May, Someth. Cambodian Witness: The Autobiography of Someth May. Random, 1987. 287 p. $18.

Gr 9+. B 83: Jan 15 1987. May tells the story of his family's experiences at the hands of the Khmer Rouge during the civil war of the 1970s.

1206. Picq, Laurence. Beyond the Horizon: Five Years with the Khmer Rouge. St. Martin's, 1989. 224 p. $16.

Gr 10+. B 85: Jul 1989. + - LJ 114: May 15 1989. Initially a loyal supporter of the Khmer Rouge, Picq saw the horrors of the revolution and was eventually able to escape with her daughter.

Korea

1207. Farley, Carol. Korea: A Land Divided. (Discovering Our Heritage). Dillon Press, 1983. 143 p. ill. $10.

Gr 3-6. B 80: Jul 1984. SLJ 31: Sep 1984. This overview of Korean history, geography, folklore, and culture includes a ready-reference section, information on Korean immigration to the United States, photos, a map, the Korean alphabet, and a glossary.

1208. Kubota, Makoto. South Korea. (Children of the World). Gareth Stevens, 1987. 63 p. ill. $13.

Gr 3-6. B 83: Jul 1987. SLJ 34: Oct 1987. One section of this work is an account of the daily life of a South Korean boy. Another section provides reference information on history, culture, geography, industry, and agriculture. Photos, maps, and a glossary are included.

1209. Lye, Keith. Take a Trip to South Korea. Watts, 1985. 32 p. ill. $10.

Gr 2-4. B 82: Jan 1 1986. SLJ 32: Apr 1986. Korean history, geography, economy, and culture are introduced in this work that includes photos, maps, and a page of illustrations of stamps and currency.

1210. McNair, Sylvia. Korea. (Enchantment of the World). Childrens Press, 1986. 127 p. ill. $20.

Gr 4-6. B 82: Aug 1986. SLJ 33: Oct 1986. Colorful photos enhance this well-organized presentation of Korean history, geography, culture, economy, and government.

1211. Shepheard, Patricia. South Korea. Chelsea House, 1988. 96 p. ill. $12.

Gr 4-6. B 85: Jan 1 1989. The history and geography of South Korea, and the daily life of its people, are examined in this highly illustrated work.

1212. Winchester, Simon. Korea: A Walk through the Land of Miracles. Prentice-Hall, 1988. 224 p. ill. $18.

Gr 9+. B 84: Apr 1 1988. LJ 113: Apr 1 1988. The author walked across Korea and interviewed many people in an effort to learn how a nation that was in chaos following the war in the 1950s became a major world economic power in the 1980s.

Korea–1950-1953

1213. Edwards, Richard. Korean War, The. (Flashpoints). Rourke, 1988. 76 p. ill. $12.

Gr 6-9. SLJ 35: Feb 1989. This well-illustrated work clarifies the political and military causes and events of the Korean War, 1950-1953.

1214. Hastings, Max. Korean War, The. Simon & Schuster, 1987. 364 p. ill. $23.

Gr 9+. B 84: Oct 15 1987. LJ 112: Dec 1987. Hastings' overview of the Korean War includes excerpts from interviews with Chinese and North Korean veterans.

Korea–Biographies

1215. Hyun, Peter. Man Sei! The Making of a Korean American. University of Hawaii Press, 1986. 186 p. ill. $18.

Gr 9+. B 83: Dec 15 1986. The Korean movement for independence from Japan early in the 20th century is portrayed in this autobiography that tells of Hyun's father's political activities and his own boyhood.

Kuwait

1216. Mulloy, Martin. Kuwait. Chelsea House, 1989. 96 p. ill. $13.

Gr 4-6. B 85: Apr 1 1989. Maps and colorful photos enhance this overview of Kuwait's contemporary problems, and its history, geography, and culture.

Laos

1217. Goldfarb, Mace. Fighters, Refugees, Immigrants: A Story of the Hmong. Carolrhoda, 1982. 39 p. ill. $10.

Gr 4-8. B 79: Jan 15 1983. B 81: Jul 1985. B 83: Oct 1 1986. SLJ 29: Nov 1982. The Hmong were farmers in the mountains of Laos. They fought for the United States in the Vietnamese War and were later driven from their homes to refugee camps in Thailand.

Lebanon

1218. Lebanon in Pictures. Rev. ed. (Visual Geography Series). Lerner, 1988. 64 p. ill. $10.

Gr 5-8. B 85: Feb 1 1989. B 86: Sep 1 1989. SLJ 35: May 1989. This concise overview covers Lebanese history, culture, economy, and contemporary society. It is enriched by numerous photos, graphs, charts, and maps.

1219. Mackey, Sandra. Lebanon: Death of a Nation. Congdon & Weed; dist. by Contemporary, 1989. 298 p. $23.

Gr 10+. B 85: Jul 1989. * BR 8: Nov/Dec 1989. LJ 114: Jul 1989 Mackey clearly explains the historical, cultural, and political causes of the conflict in Lebanon. Numerous quotes clarify the ideas of persons on different sides of the struggle.

1220. Shapiro, William E. Lebanon. (Impact Book). Watts, 1984. 88 p. ill. $10.

Gr 7+. B 81: Dec 15 1984. B 86: Sep 1 1989. SLJ 31: Mar 1985. * VOYA 8: Apr 1985. A balanced account of Lebanese history since World War II, including photos and a 6-page chronology.

1221. Tames, Richard. Take a Trip to Lebanon. Watts, 1989. 32 p. ill. $11.

Gr 1 3. + - SLJ 35: Jun 1989. This brief, illustrated work provides an overview of basic information about Lebanon and its history.

1222. Winder, Viola H. Land and People of Lebanon. Rev. ed. (Portraits of the Nations Series). Harper, 1965; 1973. 160 p. ill. $12.

Gr 5-9. Metzner. LJ 90: Sep 15 1965. Lebanese history from ancient times to the early 1970s is introduced along with the nation's geography and culture.

Lebanon–Biographies

1223. Cutting, Pauline. Children of the Siege. St. Martin's, 1989. 208 p. ill. $16.

Gr 9+. B 85: Feb 1 1989. When fierce fighting in Lebanon cut off supplies of food and medicine to the Palestinian refugee camp where she was a surgeon, Cutting and her associates risked death to broadcast a plea for help.

1224. Gordon, Matthew S. Gemayels, The. (World Leaders Past & Present). Chelsea House, 1988. 112 p. ill. $17.

Gr 5+. B 84: Aug 1988. B 86: Sep 1 1989. * BR 7: Sep/Oct 1988. * VOYA 12: Feb 1989. A review of the history of Lebanon provides the background for understanding the leadership of the Jumayyil (Gemayel) family in Lebanon since World War II.

1225. Newman, Barbara. Covenant: Love and Death in Beirut. Crown, 1989. 242 p. ill. $19.

Gr 9+. + - LJ 114: Apr 1 1989. SLJ 35: Oct 1989. VOYA 12: Oct 1989. Newman's account of events in Lebanon in the 1980s is intertwined with her account of her romance with the assassinated president-elect of Lebanon, Bashi Gemayel.

Macao

1226. Williams, Jeff. Macao. (Places and Peoples of the World). Chelsea House, 1988. 96 p. ill. $12.

Gr 4-9. BR 7: Sep/Oct 1988. + - SLJ 34: Aug 1988. A brief account of Macao's history, government, geography, economy, and culture is included in this work that emphasizes current problems.

Malaysia

1227. Elder, Bruce. Take a Trip to Malaysia. Watts, 1985. 32 p. ill. $9.

Gr 2-5. B 81: May 15 1985. SLJ 32: Oct 1985. Photos on every page, maps, and a page of facts enrich this simple introduction to Malaysian history, culture, government, occupations, education, sports, and religion.

1228. Malaysia in Pictures. (Visual Geography Series). Lerner, 1989. 64 p. ill. $10.

Gr 5-8. B 85: May 1 1989. This introduction to the history, government, economy, and people of Malaysia is enriched by photos, maps, and charts.

1229. Oshihara, Yuzuro. Malaysia. (Children of the World). Gareth Stevens, 1987. 64 p. ill. $13.

Gr 3-7. B 83: Jun 1 1987. SLJ 34: Nov 1987. Reference information is provided on Malaysian history, government, agriculture, education, industry, and culture. In addition the daily life of Yati, an 11-year-old Malaysian girl and her family is told with many photos.

1230. Wee, Jessie. We Live in Malaysia and Singapore. (Living Here). Watts, 1985. 60 p. ill. $11.

Gr 4-8. + - B 82: Jan 15 1986. + - SLJ 32: Apr 1986. Interviews with adults and young people are used to show life in Malaysia and Singapore and to present information on the area's history, government, culture, and customs.

1231. Wright, David K. Malaysia. (Enchantment of the World). Childrens Press, 1988. 128 p. ill. $22.

Gr 4-7. + - B 84: Aug 1988. + - SLJ 35: Oct 1988. A colorful introduction to Malaysian history, culture, government, and geography.

New Zealand

1232. Armitage, Ronda. New Zealand. (Countries of the World). Bookwright Press; dist. by Watts, 1988. 48 p. ill. $13.

Gr 3-5. B 85: Feb 1 1989. + - SLJ 35: Feb 1989. A brief, well-illustrated introduction to New Zealand's history, geography, economy, culture, and people.

1233. Kaula, Edna M. Land and People of New Zealand. Rev. ed. (Portraits of the Nations Series). Harper, 1964; 1972. 160 p. ill. $12.

Gr 5-9. Metzner. LJ 86: Jun 15 1964. Photos, maps, and other illustrations enrich this account of New Zealand's history, geography, and daily life. The Maori culture is also discussed.

1234. Marsh, Ngaio. New Zealand. Aeonean Press, 1942; 1976. 128 p. ill. $20.

Gr 7+. Metzner. LJ 89: Dec 15 1964. A balanced account of the history of New Zealand and its Maori people to the 1970s.

1235. McLauchlan, Gordon. Bateman New Zealand Encyclopedia. David Bateman; dist. by Sheridan House, 1984. 656 p. ill. $40.

Gr 9+. + - B 81: Feb 1 1985. A comprehensive and highly illustrated reference on New Zealand history, geography, resources, culture, and notable persons.

1236. Yanagi, Akinobu. New Zealand. (Children of the World). Gareth Stevens, 1987. 63 p. ill. $13.

Gr 3-7. B 83: Jun 1 1987. SLJ 34: Dec 1987. Life in New Zealand is introduced through Hanish, a 10-year-old who lives on a farm. Also included is information on New Zealand's history, agriculture, arts, climate, government, industry, and religions.

New Zealand–Maoris

1237. Higham, Charles. Maoris, The. (Cambridge Topic Book). Lerner, 1983. 51 p. ill. $7.

Gr 5-8. B 80: Oct 1 1983. SLJ 30: Nov 1983. The history and culture of the Maori people are introduced in this highly illustrated and well-written account.

1238. Wiremu, Graham. Maoris of New Zealand, The. Rourke, 1989. 48 p. ill. Lib. ed. $14.

Gr 5-9. B 85: May 15 1989. SLJ 35: Apr 1989. Maori history, culture, religion, and adaptation to modern society are presented in this well-illustrated work that includes reproductions of historic art.

Pakistan

1239. Lang, Robert. Land and People of Pakistan. Rev. ed. (Portraits of the Nations Series). Harper, 1968. 160 p. ill. $12.

Gr 5-9. Metzner. B 64: Jun 15 1968. A well-organized account of Pakistan's history, geography, economy, politics, religion, and society.

1240. Lye, Keith. Take a Trip to Pakistan. Watts, 1985. 32 p. ill. $9.

Gr 2-4. B 81: May 15 1985. Photos on each page and a brief informative text introduce Pakistani history, geography, industry, and cities.

1241. Pakistan in Pictures. (Visual Geography Series). Lerner, 1989. 64 p. ill. $12.

Gr 5-8. B 86: Sep 15 1989. Information on the people of Pakistan is included in this balanced account of the nation's history, culture, geography, government, and cities. Photos are included.

Pakistan–Biographies

1242. Easwaran, Eknath. Man to Match His Mountains: Badshan Khan, Nonviolent Soldier of Islam. Nilgiri; dist. by Random, 1985. 216 p. ill. $14. Pb $8.

Gr 9+. B 81: Feb 15 1985. B 83: Sep 15 1986. LJ 110: Feb 1 1985. As Gandhi was advocating peaceful rebellion among Hindus in India, Khan was leading the Muslims in an effort to use nonviolent means to gain independence for the area that became Pakistan.

Philippines

1243. Bjener, Tamiko. Philippines. (Children of the World). Gareth Stevens, 1987. 64 p. ill. $13.

Gr 3-6. B 83: Jul 1987. SLJ 34: Oct 1987. A section on Philippine history, geography, agriculture, arts and crafts, climate, government, industry, and language follows an easy-to-read account of the daily life of a typical Filipino child.

1244. Bresnan, John. Crisis in the Philippines: The Marcos Era and Beyond. Princeton University Press, 1986. 284 p. $30.

Adult. LJ 111: Dec 1986. These essays on Philippine history, economics, politics, security, and social conditions emphasize the Marcos government.

1245. Cordero-Fernando, Gilda. We Live in the Philippines. (Living Here). Watts, 1986. 60 p. ill. $11.

Gr 5-8. B 82: May 15 1986. Aspects of Philippine history, geography, economy, and religion are covered in interviews with 26 Filipinos. Photos, maps, facts, and a glossary are included.

1246. Hahn, Emily. Islands: America's Imperial Adventure in the Philippines. Coward, McCann, 1981. 384 p. ill. $15.

Gr 10+. B 78: Oct 15 1981. LJ 106: Oct 15 1981. Hahn recounts the reasons for United States involvement with the Philippines and the political disputes of the colonial days. Vignettes on the major personalities involved clarify the issues.

1247. Johnson, Bryan. Four Days of Courage: Untold Story of the People Who Brought Marcos Down. Free Press, 1987. 290 p. $20.

Gr 9+. B 83: Jun 1 1987. LJ 112: Jun 1 1987. This account of the 1986 revolution that toppled Ferdinand Marcos and brought Corazon Aquino to power is based on observations and interviews.

1248. Lawson, Don. Marcos and the Philippines. (Impact Book). Watts, 1984. 88 p. ill. $10.

Gr 7-10. B 81: Dec 1 1984. * BR 4: May/Jun 1985. * VOYA 8: Apr 1985. This clear and balanced introduction to Philippine history, and Marcos' role in that history following World War II, also covers Philippine geography and culture.

1249. Lawson, Don. New Philippines, The. 2nd ed. (Impact Book). Watts, 1986. 128 p. ill. $11.

Gr 7-10. B 83: Nov 15 1986. * BR 5: Jan/Feb 1987. Philippine geography, economy, and history through Aquino's rise to power are covered in a balanced, well-illustrated account. This edition updates Lawson's Marcos and the Philippines.

1250. Lepthien, Emilie U. Philippines, The. (Enchantment of the World). Childrens Press, 1984. 128 p. ill. $13.

Gr 4-9. B 81: Sep 1 1984. SLJ 31: Dec 1984. Vivid color photos, maps, and a reference section augment this introduction to Philippine history, geography, politics, and culture.

1251. Lye, Keith. Take a Trip to the Philippines. Watts, 1985. 32 p. ill. $10.

Gr 2-4. B 82: Jan 1 1986. SLJ 32: Apr 1986. This introduction to Philippine history, geography, economy, and culture includes photos, a page of illustrations of stamps and currency, and maps.

1252. Simons, Lewis M. Worth Dying For. Morrow, 1987. 352 p. ill. $19.

Gr 9+. B 83: Aug 1987. * LJ 112: Aug 1987. A balanced account of the events that led to the fall of Marcos and the rise of Corazon Aquino to the presidency.

Philippines–Biographies

1253. Chua-Eoan, Howard. Corazon Aquino. (World Leaders Past & Present). Chelsea House, 1987. 112 p. ill. $17.

Gr 6-10. B 84: Apr 15 1988. A brief account of Marcos' rise to power is followed by an introduction to Benigno Aquino whose widow, Corazon, rose to power following his assassination. Chua-Eoan provides a clear account of Philippine politics and events.

1254. Ellison, Katherine. Imelda: Steel Butterfly of the Philippines. McGraw-Hill, 1988. 304 p. ill. $18.

Gr 9+. B 85: Oct 15 1988. LJ 113: Oct 15 1988. Ellison describes Marcos' use of her beauty and political savvy to increase her own and her husband's power.

1255. Haskins, James. Corazon Aquino: Leader of the Philippines. Enslow, 1988. 127 p. ill. $14.

Gr 5-10. B 84: Apr 15 1988. + - BC 41: Jul 1988. BR 7: Sep/Oct 1988. SLJ 34: Mar 1988. This clearly written political biography of the Philippines' first woman president includes maps and photos.

1256. Komisar, Lucy. Corazon Aquino: The Story of a Revolution. Braziller, 1987. 290 p. maps. $16.

Gr 9+. B 83: May 15 1987. + - LJ 112: May 15 1987. SLJ 34: Sep 1987. The events of Corazon Aquino's life and her presidency are set within the context of Philippine history.

1257. Lepthien, Emilie U. Corazon Aquino: President of the Philippines. (Picture-Story Biographies). Childrens Press, 1988. 31 p. ill. $11.

Gr 2-5. B 84: May 15 1988. SLJ 34: Aug 1988. Numerous photos and a timeline are included in this basic introduction to the life of the Philippine president.

1258. Nadel, Laurie. Corazon Aquino: Journey to Power. Messner, 1987. 127 p. ill. $10.

Gr 6-9. B 84: Sep 1 1987. SLJ 34: Oct 1987. - VOYA 10: Feb 1988. This profile of Aquino shows the development of her political skills and her handling of the complex political situation in the Philippines up to 1987.

1259. Nance, John. Lobo of the Tasaday. Pantheon, 1982. 53 p. ill. $10. Lib. ed. $10.

Gr 3-7. B 78: Jul 1982. BC 35: Jun 1982. HB 58: Aug 1982. * SE 47: Apr 1983. SLJ 29: Sep 1982. Through the story of Lobo, a Tasaday boy, the culture and beliefs of the Tasaday tribe are introduced, along with the story of their first introduction to industrialized civilization.

1260. Rosca, Ninotchka. Endgame: The Fall of Marcos. Watts, 1987. 195 p. $19.

Gr 10+. * BR 6: Mar/Apr 1988. SLJ 35: Sep 1988. A chronology and glossary augment this account of the end of Marcos' regime. Included are excerpts of interviews with participants.

1261. Scariano, Margaret M. Picture Life of Corazon Aquino, The. Watts, 1987. 64 p. ill. $10.

Gr 4-7. B 84: Jan 15 1988. + - SLJ 34: Feb 1988. An illustrated introduction to the Philippine president, her policies, and her accomplishments.

1262. Siegel, Beatrice. Cory: Corazon Aquino and the Philippines. Dutton, 1988. 118 p. ill. $16.

Gr 6-8. B 84: Aug 1988. BR 7: Nov/Dec 1988. SLJ 34: Feb 1988. * VOYA 11: Dec 1988. Philippine history, politics, and sociology are the focus of this biography that explores the lives of Corazon Aquino and her assassinated husband Benigno.

1263. Slack, Gordy. Ferdinand Marcos. (World Leaders Past & Present). Chelsea House, 1988. 112 p. ill. $17.

Gr 6-10. B 85: Sep 1 1988. BR 7: Nov/Dec 1988. * VOYA 11: Oct 1988. Following a brief summary of Philippine history through World War II is an account of Marcos' personal and political life, showing how, at the time the Philippine president was forced from power, he had a personal fortune of over $10 billion.

Saudi Arabia

1264. Gordon, Eugene. Saudi Arabia in Pictures. Rev. ed. (Visual Geography Series). Sterling, 1980. 64 p. ill. $5. Pb $3.

Gr 5-7. SLJ 27: Feb 1981. Numerous photos enhance this account of Saudi Arabia's history, culture, geography, and government.

1265. Lye, Keith. Take a Trip to Saudi Arabia. Watts, 1985. 32 p. ill. $9.

Gr 2-3. B 81: Apr 15 1985. B 86: Sep 1 1989. Photos of stamps and currency and other pictures enhance this introduction to Saudi Arabia that covers history, geography, economy, culture, and contemporary issues.

1266. McCarthy, Kevin. Saudi Arabia: A Desert Kingdom. (Discovering Our Heritage). Dillon Press, 1986. 125 p. ill. $12.

Gr 4-9. B 82: May 1 1986. B 86: Sep 1 1989. BR 5: Sep/Oct 1986. SLJ 32: Mar 1986. This account of the culture, history, and geography of Saudi Arabia includes photos and anecdotes.

1267. Saudi Arabia in Pictures. (Visual Geography Series). Lerner, 1989. 64 p. ill. $10.

Gr 5-9. B 86: May 1 1989. SLJ 35: Sep 1989. The history, geography, resources, government, and cities of Saudi Arabia are introduced in this work that includes numerous photos, maps, and charts.

Saudi Arabia–Social Life and Customs

1268. Gray, Seymour Jerome. Beyond the Veil: The Adventures of an American Doctor in Saudi Arabia. Harper, 1983. 368 p. $17.

Gr 10+. B 79: Jan 15 1983. LJ 108: Jan 1 1983. Historical and political notes are interjected in this account of social and cultural life in Saudi Arabia as observed by an American physician. Includes glossary.

Singapore

1269. Elder, Bruce. Take a Trip to Singapore. Watts, 1985. 32 p. ill. $9.

Gr 2-5. B 81: May 15 1985. SLJ 32: Oct 1985. Photos on every page, maps, and a page of facts enrich this simple introduction to the history, culture, government, occupations, education, sports, and religion of Singapore.

Sri Lanka

1270. Fyson, Nance Lui. Sri Lanka. (Islands). Batsford; dist. by David & Charles, 1989. 64 p. ill. $18.

Gr 6-9. + - SLJ 35: May 1989. Sri Lankan history, culture, economy, and geography are introduced in this profusely illustrated work that includes photos, maps, and diagrams.

1271. Sri Lanka in Pictures. (Visual Geography Series). Lerner, 1989. 64 p. ill. $10.

Gr 6+. SLJ 35: Aug 1989. Photos, maps, and graphs supplement this introduction to Sri Lanka's history, geography, culture, economy, and politics.

Syria

1272. Beaton, Margaret. Syria. (Enchantment of the World). Childrens Press, 1988. 125 p. ill. $23.

Gr 4-9. B 85: Feb 15 1989. SLJ 35: Mar 1989. This balanced work covers Syria's history, geography, economy, government, politics, and culture. Current political problems and Syria's relations with Israel are also covered. Maps, photos, and drawings enrich the text.

1273. Copeland, Paul W. Land and People of Syria. Rev. ed. (Portraits of the Nations Series). Harper, 1964; 1972. 160 p. ill. $12.

Gr 5-9. Metzner. LJ 89: Jun 15 1964. A readable introduction to Syria's history, geography, transportation, foreign relations, and people.

1274. Hopwood, Derek. Syria 1945-1986: Politics and Society. Allen & Unwin, 1988. 190 p. maps. $45.

Gr 10+. LJ 113: May 15 1988. Hopwood presents an overview of Syrian history and culture since ancient times and then explores more deeply all aspects of Syrian cultural and political life since 1945.

1275. Lye, Keith. Take a Trip to Syria. Watts, 1988. 32 p. ill. $11.

Gr 2-4. B 85: Nov 1 1988. B 86: Sep 1 1989. + - SLJ 35: Jan 1989. Colorful photos and a map augment this introduction to basic information about the history, geography, and sociology of Syria.

1276. Mulloy, Martin. Syria. Chelsea House, 1988. 96 p. ill. $12.

Gr 4-6. + - B 85: Jan 1 1989. This overview of Syrian history, culture, and geography is augmented by numerous photos.

Syria—Biographics

1277. Ma'oz, Moshe. Assad: The Sphinx of Damascus: A Political Biography. Weidenfeld & Nicholson, 1988. 221 p. $19.

Gr 9+. B 84: Aug 1988. * LJ 113: Sep 15 1988. A short account of Syrian history helps provide the context for this biography of Hafiz al Assad, president of Syria, who is seen as a rising force in Middle East politics in the late 1980s.

Taiwan

1278. Wee, Jessie. Taiwan. (Let's Visit Places and Peoples of the World Series). Chelsea House, 1987. 96 p. ill. $12.

Gr 5-8. + - SLJ 34: Aug 1988. This introduction to the history, culture, economy, and politics of Taiwan includes photos and maps.

1279. Yu, Ling. Taiwan in Pictures. (Visual Geography Series). Lerner, 1989. 64 p. ill. $12.

Gr 5-8. B 86: Sep 15 1989. The history, government, geography, cities, and resources of Taiwan are covered in this illustrated overview.

Thailand

1280. Lye, Keith. Take a Trip to Thailand. Watts, 1986. 32 p. ill. $10.

Gr 2-5. B 82: May 15 1986. Photos on each page and a brief informative text introduce Thai history, geography, industry, and cities.

1281. Thailand in Pictures. (Visual Geography Series). Lerner, 1989. 64 p. ill. $12.

Gr 5-8. B 86: Sep 15 1989. Thai history, government, cities, geography, resources, culture, and ethnic groups are introduced in this account, supplemented by photos, maps, and charts.

1282. McNair, Sylvia. Thailand. (Enchantment of the World). Childrens Press, 1987. 127 p. ill. $20.

Gr 4-6. B 84: Oct 15 1987. Colorful photos enrich this readable and well-organized presentation of Thai history, geography, resources, and art.

1283. Orihara, Kei. Thailand. (Children of the World). Gareth Stevens, 1988. 64 p. ill. $13.

Gr 2-4. + - B 85: Dec 15 1988. + - BC 42: Dec 1988. The daily life of a Thai child and his family is the focus of this work, which includes a section on his nation's history, geography, politics, and culture.

Turkey

1284. Feinstein, Steve. Turkey in Pictures. (Visual Geography Series). Lerner, 1988. 64 p. ill. $10.

Gr 5-9. B 84: Aug 1988. SLJ 35: Sep 1988. Maps, charts, colorful photos, and reproductions of art works enrich this balanced introduction to Turkey's history, government, geography, economy, culture, and people.

1285. Lye, Keith. Take a Trip to Turkey. Watts, 1987. 32 p. ill. $10.

Gr 1-4. B 84: Nov 15 1987. + - SLJ 34: Jun/Jul 1988. Maps and other colorful illustrations enhance the brief text that introduces Turkey's history, geography, resources, culture, and cities.

1286. Spencer, William. Land and People of Turkey. Rev. ed. (Portraits of the Nations Series). Harper, 1972. 160 p. ill. $12.

Gr 5-9. Metzner. B 55: Feb 15 1959. + - LJ 83: Dec 15 1958. This examination of Turkish history also covers its climate, land, resources, and people.

Turkey–Biographies

1287. Kherdian, David. Road from Home: The Story of an Armenian Girl. Greenwillow, 1979. 238 p. $13.

Gr 7-10. B 82: May 15 1986. BC 33: Jan 1980. * SE 49: Sep 1985. * SE 50: Apr 1986. The author's Armenian mother was a child when she and her family were forced, along with other Armenians, on a deadly march out of Turkey in 1915. Most of her family were killed, and she eventually came to America.

1288. Tachau, Frank. Kemal Ataturk. (World Leaders Past & Present). Chelsea House, 1987. 111 p. ill. $17.

Gr 6-10. B 84: Jan 1 1988. SLJ 34: Mar 1988. Photos enhance this account of Ataturk's childhood, military career, and rise to political power to become the first president of the Turkish republic (1923).

Turkey–Fiction

1289. Holland, Cecelia. Belt of Gold, The. Knopf, 1984. 320 p. $16.

Gr 10+. B 80: Feb 1 1984. LJ 109: Feb 15 1984. The details of daily life are clearly presented in this novel of political intrigue set in Byzantium (Constantinople) in the 9th century.

Vietnam

1290. Chanda, Nayan. Brother Enemy: The War After the War. Harcourt, 1986. 422 p. $25.

Gr 9+. B 83: Nov 1 1986. LJ 111: Dec 1986. A long-time correspondent in Indochina examines the tragedies that followed the fall of Saigon in 1975 and includes interviews with Chinese, Cambodian, and Vietnamese officials and observers.

1291. Chanoff, David. Portrait of the Enemy. Random, 1986. 288 p. $18.

Gr 9+. B 83: Oct 1 1986. LJ 111: Oct 15 1986. Using interviews, Chanoff shows the fears, doubts, courage, and dedication of 36 North Vietnamese, Viet Cong, and American adversaries during the Vietnamese War.

1292. Cole, Wendy M. Vietnam. (Places and Peoples of the World). Chelsea House, 1989. 112 p. ill. $13.

Gr 5+. B 85: Aug 1989. * BR 8: Sep/Oct 1989. VOYA 12: Oct 1989. Cole presents a clear picture of Vietnamese culture in her work which also covers the nation's history, government, geography, resources, and economy.

1293. Page, Tim. Ten Years After: Vietnam Today. Knopf, 1987. 114 p. ill. $30. Pb $19.

Gr 9+. B 84: Nov 1 1987. + - LJ 112: Dec 1987. This collection of photos of Vietnam in the 1980s shows the devastation caused by the war, the beauty of the land, and the tenacity of its people.

1294. Wright, David K. Vietnam. Childrens Press, 1989. 128 p. ill. $23.

Gr 4-7. B 85: Aug 1989. Colorful photos and a chronology enhance this introduction to Vietnam's history, geography, customs, and the nation's problems following the war that ended in 1975.

Vietnam–Biographies

1295. Hayslip, Le Ly. When Heaven and Earth Changed Places: Vietnamese Woman's Journey from War to Peace. Doubleday, 1989. 384 p. $19.

Gr 10+. B 85: May 15 1989. LJ 114: May 15 1989. The author was a child guerilla and blackmarketeer during the Vietnamese War. Twenty years later she wrote of her experiences.

1296. Huynh, Quang Nhuong. Land I Lost: Adventures of a Boy in Vietnam. Harper, 1982. 115 p. ill. $10.

Gr 3-8. B 78: Jun 15 1982. B 81: Jul 1985. B 82: Sep 15 1985. BC 36: Oct 1982. BR 1: Jan 1983. HB 58: Jun 1982. * SE 47: Apr 1983. + - SLJ 29: Nov 1982. Episodic chapters recount the author's memories of growing up in a pre-war Vietnamese village. Though many of the stories concern wild animals, there is much information about customs, traditions, and beliefs.

1297. Lloyd, Dana Ohlmeyer. Ho Chi Minh. (World Leaders Past & Present). Chelsea House, 1986. 116 p. ill. $17.

Gr 6-10. B 83: Feb 1 1987. A well-illustrated introduction to the life of the enigmatic Vietnamese president who was regarded by some as a ruthless dictator and by others as a patriot.

1298. Truong, Nhu Tang. Viet Cong Memoir, A. Harcourt, 1985. 325 p. maps. $18.

Gr 9+. B 81: Apr 15 1985. LJ 110: Jun 1 1985. The son of a wealthy family in South Vietnam, Truong worked for the Viet Cong throughout the war. This memoir recounts his experiences and gradual disillusionment with the brutality of the regime.

Vietnam–Fiction

1299. Anderson, Rachel. War Orphan, The. Oxford University Press; dist. by Merrimack Publishers' Circle, 1986. 256 p. $14.

Gr 6+. + - B 83: Sep 1 1986. + - BC 40: Oct 1986. BR 5: Sep/Oct 1986. - SLJ 33: Oct 1986. English teenager Simon finds it difficult to adjust after his parents adopt Ha, a Vietnamese war orphan, especially when the trauma of Ha's experiences fill Simon's dreams.

1300. Clark, Ann Nolan. To Stand Against the Wind. Viking, 1978. 136 p. $8.

Gr 5-9. + - B 75: Dec 15 1978. B 83: Oct 1 1986. + - BC 32: Apr 1979. HB 55: Feb 1979. + - SLJ 25: Oct 1978. The details of Vietnamese culture and custom are revealed in this story, told through flashbacks, of events that befell a Vietnamese family.

1301. Wartski, Maureen Crane. Boat to Nowhere, A. Westminster, 1980. 192 p. ill. $10.

Gr 6-9. * SE 45: Apr 1981. SLJ 105: Apr 1980. Three children flee by boat from Vietnam to escape persecution and star-

vation. This is a prequel to A Long Way from Home, which finds the children trying to adjust to life in the United States.

Europe

General

1302. Cook, Chris. Longman Handbook of Modern European History, 1763-1985, The. Longman, 1987. 435 p. maps. $40. Pb $20.

Gr 9+. B 84: Feb 1 1988. For each European nation Longman's handbook provides chronologically arranged information on heads of state; military, economic, and social history; and biographies. Maps are included.

1303. Dornberg, John. Eastern Europe: A Communist Kaleidoscope. Dial, 1980. 302 p. $10.

Gr 7+. * B 76: Apr 15 1980. HB 56: Aug 1980. SLJ 27: Sep 1980. In a balanced presentation Dornberg covers the histories of Bulgaria, Czechoslovakia, Hungary, Poland, and Romania. He dispels many myths and clarifies how each nation differs in its politics, economy, culture, and relations with the U.S.S.R.

1304. Dukes, Paul. History of Europe 1648-1948: The Arrival, the Rise, the Fall. Sheridan House, 1985. 552 p. maps. $43. Pb $23.

Gr 9+. B 82: Apr 15 1986. Dukes examines the political and diplomatic events that resulted in European domination of the world and the later events that led to the demise of European influence.

1305. Haigh, Christopher. Cambridge Historical Encyclopedia of Great Britain and Ireland, The. Cambridge University Press, 1985. 392 p. ill. $35.

Gr 9+. B 82: Oct 15 1985. B 82: Apr 15 1986. LJ 110: Nov 1 1985. SLJ 32: May 1986. This survey of British and Irish history from 100 B.C. to 1975 covers government, politics, international relations, economy, and culture, and is enhanced by maps, charts, photos, and a listing of notable persons.

1306. Lyttle, Richard B. Land Beyond the River: Europe in the Age of Migration. Atheneum, 1986. 175 p. ill. $13.

Gr 6-10. B 82: Aug 1986. * SE 51: Apr/May 1987. + - SLJ 32: Apr 1986. VOYA 9: Feb 1987. Lyttle's concise examination of the effects of the migrations of European tribes covers the Angles and Saxons, Goths, Gypsies, Huns, Moslems, Vandals, and Vikings.

1307. Mayne, Richard. Western Europe. Facts on File, 1986. 699 p. maps. $40.

Gr 10+. B 82: Aug 1986. Recent history of the nations of western Europe is included, along with information on geography, demography, economy, government, politics, living conditions, and noted persons. Essays discuss topics of concern in each nation.

1308. Schopflin, George. Soviet Union and Eastern Europe, The. (Handbooks to the Modern World). Facts on File, 1986. 637 p. maps. $40.

Gr 9+. B 82: Aug 1986. For each nation information is presented on many topics, including recent history, geography,

economy, social welfare, and government. Brief biographies, statistical data, and analysis of current issues are also included.

1309. Shoemaker, M. Wesley. Soviet Union and Eastern Europe 1988, The. 19th ed. Stryker-Post, 1988. 154 p. ill. Pb $7.

Gr 9+. B 85: Feb 1 1989. This work, which includes historical and contemporary information about a variety of topics concerning the Soviet Union and Eastern Europe, is updated annually.

1310. Thompson, Wayne C. Western Europe 1983. (World Today Series). Stryker-Post, 1983. 404 p. ill. $10.

Gr 7+. B 80: Mar 1 1984. These profiles of European nations cover history, culture, economy, and politics. They include photos, maps, and ready-reference data.

General–0–476

1311. Boardman, John. Oxford History of the Classical World, The. Oxford University Press, 1986. 882 p. ill. $40.

Gr 9+. * B 83: Jan 1 1987. LJ 112: Jan 1987. Noted specialists contributed to this attractive, comprehensive account of history, social life and culture, architecture, and noted persons from the time of Homer to the fall of Rome.

1312. Grant, Michael. Guide to the Ancient World: A Dictionary of Classical Place Names. Wilson, 1986. 728 p. maps. $65.

Gr 10+. B 83: Mar 1 1987. BR 5: Mar/Apr 1987. VOYA 10: Jun 1987. Entries cover battle sites, cities, towns, lakes, mountains, and important rivers of the Greek, Roman, and Etruscan world from 1000 B.C. to 500 A.D.

General 0-476–Fiction

1313. Bosse, Malcolm. Captives of Time. Doubleday, 1987. 268 p. $15.

Gr 9+. B 84: Jan 1 1988. B 85: Nov 1 1988. BC 41: Jan 1988. BR 6: Nov/Dec 1987. * SE 52: Apr/May 1988. * SLJ 34: Nov 1987. VOYA 10: Dec 1987. The brutality of the Middle Ages is presented through the adventures of 16-year-old Anne and her mute brother, who are orphaned and must travel across plague-infested Europe to find an unknown uncle.

General–0–476–Social Life and Customs

1314. Caselli, Giovanni. Roman Empire and the Dark Ages, The. (History of Everyday Things). Peter Bedrick; dist. by Harper, 1985. 48 p. ill. $13.

Gr 5-10. B 82: Nov 15 1985. BR 4: Mar/Apr 1986. SLJ 32: Jan 1986. Tools, clothing, furniture, and other objects of daily living from Celtic through Roman times are presented in this densely illustrated work.

General–0476-1492

1315. Adams, Brian. Atlas of the World in the Middle Ages. Watts, 1981. 61 p. ill. Lib. ed. $9.

Gr 5-8. B 77: May 1 1981. Photos, charts, and a chronology are included. The maps trace the changes in nations, religions, technology, and trade from the fall of Rome to 1453.

1316. Cardini, Franco. Europe 1492: Portrait of a Continent Five Hundred Years Ago. Facts on File, 1989. 240 p. ill. $50.

Gr 10+. B 86: Nov 1 1989. - LJ 114: Sep 1 1989. This popular, illustrated overview of politics, art, social life, economics, and religion in Europe in the year that Columbus sailed presents a picture of European life at that time.

1317. Caselli, Giovanni. Middle Ages, The. (History of Everyday Things). Peter Bedrick; dist. by Publishers Group West, 1988. 48 p. ill. $15.

Gr 4-8. B 85: Dec 15 1988. SLJ 35: Nov 1988. Detailed, captioned drawings of everyday things and a brief text present an overview of the major topics of the time, including technology, knights, cathedrals, crusades, travel, and entertainment.

1318. Holmes, George. Oxford Illustrated History of Medieval Europe, The. Oxford University Press, 1988. 398 p. ill. $35.

Gr 9+. B 84: Jul 1988. * LJ 113: Aug 1988. The primary events of medieval Europe that shaped modern western civilizations are explored in 6 lively essays enriched by charts, maps, illustrations, and a chronology.

1319. Matthew, Donald. Atlas of Medieval Europe. Facts on File, 1983. 240 p. ill. $35.

Gr 9+. B 80: Nov 15 1983, Apr 15 1984. + - LJ 108: Dec 15 1983. This colorful and heavily illustrated history of medieval Europe that covers cultural, religious, and political history includes maps, photos, reproductions of artwork, a glossary, and a gazetteer.

1320. Miquel, Pierre. Days of Knights and Castles, The. (Silver Burdett Picture Histories). Silver Burdett, 1981. 64 p. ill. $8.

Gr 5-8. + - B 77: Jul 15/Aug 1981. - SLJ 28: Jan 1982. A broad perspective of the European feudal system is provided along with unusual facts, key dates, a glossary, and numerous illustrations.

1321. Oleksy, Walter. Black Plague, The. (First Book). Watts, 1982. 88 p. ill. $8.

Gr 5+. B 79: Sep 15 1982. SLJ 29: Jan 1983. Olesky introduces the black and bubonic plagues, their causes, treatments, and impact on civilization.

1322. Sabbagh, Antoine. Europe in the Middle Ages. (Human Story). Silver Burdett, 1988. 77 p. ill. $16.

Gr 5-8. B 85: Feb 15 1989. + - SLJ 35: Feb 1989. Colorful illustrations, maps, and a chronology enhance this introduction to the lives of persons at all levels of medieval society.

General–0476-1492–Fiction

1323. Anno, Mitsumasa. Anno's Medieval World. Philomel, 1980. 49 p. ill. $10. Lib. ed. $10.

Gr 3-6. + - B 77: Feb 1 1981. B 79: Jun 1 1983. * BC 34: Dec 1980. HB 57: Apr 1981. SLJ 27: Dec 1980. SLJ 33: May 1987. Anno shows how the people of one small medieval village gradually changed their attitude toward the world as they learned that it was round.

1324. Lasker, Joe. Tournament of Knights, A. Harper, 1986. 32 p. ill. $13.

Gr 1-6. * B 83: Oct 15 1986. BC 40: Oct 1986. The risks, rules, weapons, and details of tournaments are clarified in this well-illustrated story.

General–0476-1492–Military History

1325. Matthews, John. Warriors of Christendom: Charlemagne, El Cid, Barbarossa, Richard Lionheart. Firebird; dist. by Sterling, 1989. 192 p. ill. $25.

Gr 9+. B 85: Feb 15 1989. Four heroes of European military history are profiled in a balanced, illustrated work.

1326. Newark, Tim. Barbarians: Warriors and Wars of the Dark Ages. Blandford; dist. by Sterling, 1985; 1989. 144 p. ill. $18. Pb $13.

Gr 9+. B 85: Apr 15 1989. SLJ 32: Nov 1985. The military leaders and campaigns of the tribes who overran Europe from the 6th through the 13th centuries are the focus of this lively work that includes color plates.

1327. Oakeshott, Ewart. Dark Age Warrior. Dufour, 1984. 135 p. map. $12.

Gr 7+. B 81: Jan 1 1985. BR 4: Sep/Oct 1985. SLJ 31: Mar 1985. Enhanced by detailed line drawings of weapons is an informative account of the armor, weaponry, and battle techniques of the tribes that invaded Europe following the fall of the Roman Empire.

1328. Perin, Patrick. Barbarian Invasions of Europe, The. (Silver Burdett Picture Histories). Silver Burdett, 1986. 64 p. ill. $15.

Gr 5+. BR 6: Jan/Feb 1988. - SLJ 34: Feb 1988. Profusely illustrated, Perin's introduction to the nomadic behavior and customs of the tribes that occupied Europe after the fall of Rome includes a glossary and a chronology.

1329. Windrow, Martin. Invaders, The. (Living Past). Arco, 1980. 61 p. ill. $7.

Gr 5+. B 76: Mar 1 1980. * SE 44: Oct 1980. SLJ 27: Sep 1980. This colorful introduction to the battles and settlements of the Dark Ages and the Crusades includes information on noted persons, a glossary, and a timeline.

General–0476-1492–Social Life and Customs

1330. Brown, Reginald Allen. Castles: A History and Guide. Blandford; dist. by Sterling, 1981. 192 p. ill. $20.

Gr 9+. B 78: Oct 15 1981. LJ 106: Dec 1 1981. This profusely illustrated survey of European castles from the 9th to the 15th centuries shows how they were built, their function, and the daily lives of their occupants.

1331. Cairns, Conrad. Medieval Castles. (Cambridge Topic Book). Lerner, 1989. 52 p. ill. $9.

Gr 6-10. + - SLJ 35: Aug 1989. This brief, illustrated history of European castles, 650 A.D. to 1580, describes their functional design.

1332. Caselli, Giovanni. Irish Pilgrim, An. (Everyday Life of). Peter Bedrick, 1987. 29 p. ill. $10.

Gr 4-7. BR 6: Sep/Oct 1987. + - SLJ 34: Sep 1987. Seventh-century European society is seen through the eyes of an Irish monk on a pilgrimage to Rome. A pictorial glossary is included.

1333. Corbin, Carole Lynn. Knights. (First Book). Watts, 1989. 64 p. ill. $11.

Gr 3-6. + - BC 42: Apr 1989. SLJ 35: May 1989. The daily activities of knights are covered in this brief, illustrated work.

1334. Duby, Georges. History of Private Life, II: Revelations of the Medieval World. Harvard University Press, 1988. 660 p. ill. $40.

Gr 9+. B 84: Feb 15 1988. * LJ 113: Mar 1 1988. This detailed account of daily life during the Middle Ages covers social conventions, architecture, literature, and the developing concepts of individuality.

1335. Duby, Georges. Revelations of the Medieval World. (History of Private Life.) Harvard University Press, 1988. 660 p. ill. $40.

Gr 9+. B 84: Feb 15 1988. * LJ 113: Mar 1 1988. The domestic lives of ordinary people from the 11th century to the Renaissance are presented in the 2nd of a 5-volume illustrated set.

1336. Fradon, Dana. Sir Dana: A Knight, as Told by His Trusty Armor. Dutton, 1988. 40 p. ill. $14.

Gr 3-6. B 85: Oct 15 1988. * SE 53: Apr/May 1989. In this entertaining and informative work a talking suit of armor is the source of much information about life in medieval Europe.

1337. Gibson, Michael. Knights, The. (Living Past). Arco, 1980. 61 p. ill. $7.

Gr 5-9. B 76: Mar 1 1980. * SE 44: Oct 1980. SLJ 27: Sep 1980. Profusely illustrated with colorful photos, drawings, and maps, this account of the daily activities of knights covers their duties, armor, equipment, and tournaments, and provides information on castles.

1338. Gies, Frances. Knight in History, The. Harper, 1984. 214 p. ill. $15.

Adult. B 81: Sep 15 1984. LJ 109: Oct 15 1984. The realities of knighthood are presented in this account of the origins of knighthood; the first Crusade; the economic, political, social, and military roles of knights; and episodes showing knightly virtues and misdeeds.

1339. Hartman, Gertrude. Medieval Days and Ways. Macmillan, 1937. 332 p. ill. $17.

Gr 6+. B 34: Nov 15 1937. * HB 13: Nov 1937. LJ 62: Nov 1 1937. * LJ 62: Nov 15 1937. Clear and simply written, this introduction to village and castle life in the Middle Ages includes illustrations from contemporary prints and wood cuts.

1340. Hunt, Jonathan. Illuminations. Bradbury, 1989. 40 p. ill. $17.

Gr 1-4. B 86: Sep 15 1989. + - BC 43: Oct 1989. + - SLJ 35: Sep 1989. Using a highly illustrated alphabet to guide the format, Hunt explores events and objects of the Middle Ages.

1341. Lasker, Joe. Merry Ever After: The Story of Two Medieval Weddings. Viking; Penguin, 1976. 48 p. ill. $10. Pb $4.

Gr 4-9. B 79: Jun 1 1983. + - HB 53: Feb 1977. SLJ 23: Nov 1976. Lasker's profusely illustrated account of the festivities surrounding two 15th-century weddings contrasts the lives of the wealthy with those of peasants.

1342. Lewis, Brenda Ralph. Growing Up in the Dark Ages. Batsford, 1980. 72 p. ill. $15.

Gr 4-6. + - SLJ 27: Mar 1981. This brief, illustrated introduction to life in the Dark Ages emphasizes what life was like for children.

1343. MacDonald, Fiona. Middle Ages, The. (Everyday Life). Silver Burdett, 1985. 61 p. ill. $10.

Gr 4-8. + - B 81: Aug 1985. + - BR 4: Mar/Apr 1986. - SLJ 32: Sep 1985. VOYA 8: Aug 1985. Two-page spreads cover many varied aspects of European life in the Middle Ages, including housing, family life, trade, and religion.

1344. Ross, Stewart. Crusading Knight, A. (How They Lived). Rourke, 1987. 28 p. ill. $9.

Gr 4-7. SLJ 33: Jun/Jul 1987. This illustrated introduction to the life of a knight covers his weapons, food, and clothing, and presents a picture of life during the Middle Ages.

1345. Scarry, Huck. Looking into the Middle Ages. (Pop-Up Book). Harper, 1985. 12 p. ill. $11.

Gr 3-6. B 82: Sep 15 1985. + - BC 38: Jun 1985. SLJ 32: Oct 1985. Pop-up pictures show a wealth of detail about knights and castle life.

1346. Smith, Beth. Castles. (First Book). Watts, 1988. 96 p. $10.

Gr 4-9. B 84: May 1 1988. BC 41: Jun 1988. * BR 7: Nov/Dec 1988. SLJ 35: Nov 1988. Diagrams, photos, and drawings enhance this account of castle design, castle warfare, and life within castles.

1347. Unstead, R. J. Castle, A. (See Inside). Warwick; dist. by Watts, 1986. 32 p. ill. $10.

Gr 4-8. BR 6: May/Jun 1987. SLJ 33: Feb 1987. Unstead's illustrated introduction to life in a medieval castle features cutaway views that show architectural design and illustrations that show the ways of life of the ruling and servant classes.

1348. Vaughan, Jenny. Castles. (Easy-Read Fact Book). Watts, 1984. 32 p. ill. $9.

Gr 2-5. B 80: Jun 15 1984. BC 37: May 1984. SLJ 31: Sep 1984. Illustrations, diagrams, and color photos show many different kinds of castles. The text discusses feudal society and the use and design of castles.

1349. Windrow, Martin. Medieval Knight, The. (Soldier Through the Ages). Watts, 1985. 32 p. ill. $10.

Gr 4-7. B 82: Mar 15 1986. BR 5: Jan/Feb 1987. SLJ 32: Mar 1986. The feudal system and castle life, the desire for personal glory, and the introduction of standing armies are all introduced in this abundantly illustrated work that includes a glossary and a timeline.

General–0476-1492–Women

1350. Labarge, Margaret Wade. Small Sound of the Trumpet: Women in Medieval Life. Beacon; dist. by Harper, 1986. 271 p. ill. $22.

Gr 10+. LJ 111: Oct 15 1986. SLJ 33: Mar 1987. Labarge examined the lives of European women from all classes involved in all types of activities and occupations during the Middle Ages. Personal details, humor, and rich illustrations enhance this lively book.

General–1492-1789

1351. Arciniegas, German. America in Europe: A History of the New World in Reverse. Harcourt, 1986. 291 p. $17.

Gr 11+. LJ 111: Feb 1 1986. The effects of the discovery of the New World on European science, culture, diet, and politics are discussed.

1352. Cairns, Trevor. Old Regime and the Revolution, The. (Cambridge Introduction to History). Lerner, 1980. 99 p. ill. $7.

Gr 7+. SLJ 27: Feb 1981. Cairns' readable and well-organized overview shows the turbulent events of 18th-century Europe.

1353. Goodenough, Simon. Renaissance, The. (Living Past). Arco, 1980. 61 p. ill. $7.

Gr 5+. B 76: Mar 1 1980. * SE 44: Oct 1980. SLJ 27: Sep 1980. This colorful introduction to the Renaissance includes information on noted persons, a glossary, and a timeline.

1354. Pierre, Michel. Renaissance, The. (Events of Yesteryear). Silver Burdett, 1987. 69 p. ill. $15.

Gr 7+. * BR 6: Jan/Feb 1988. - SLJ 34: Mar 1988. In a profusely illustrated work, Pierre introduces events of the western world between 1450 and 1510.

1355. Williams, E. N. Facts On File Dictionary of European History: 1485-1789. Facts on File, 1980. 509 p. $23.

Gr 10+. B 77: Feb 1 1981. Williams' balanced and concise dictionary covers significant ideas, people, and events of European history from the time of Columbus through the French Revolution.

General–1492-1789–Kings, Queens, Rulers, etc.

1356. Miller, John. Bourbon and Stuart: Kings and Kingship in France and England in the Seventeenth Century. Watts, 1987. 272 p. ill. $20.

Gr 9+. B 84: Sep 1 1987. BR 6: Jan/Feb 1988. Miller's examination of the 17th-century British and French monarchies explores their political and financial problems and explains how each survived a climate of change.

General–1492-1789–Social Life and Customs

1357. Caselli, Giovanni. Renaissance and the New World, The. (History of Everyday Things). Peter Bedrick; dist. by Harper, 1986. 48 p. ill. $13.

Gr 6+. B 82: Apr 15 1986. SLJ 32: Aug 1986. This tour of Europe from 1400 to 1780 presents a visual account of daily life, including clothing, furniture, homes, tools, and weapons. Numerous maps and diagrams are included.

1358. Chartier, Roger. History of Private Life, III: Passions of the Renaissance. Harvard University Press, 1989. 611 p. ill. $40.

Gr 9+. B 85: Feb 15 1989. All aspects of social life in Europe during the Renaissance are discussed, including religion and child care.

1359. Grant, Neil. Eighteenth Century, The. (Everyday Life). Silver Burdett, 1984. 61 p. ill. $10.

Gr 6+. SLJ 31: Oct 1984. VOYA 7: Aug 1984. Detailed illustrations with explanatory captions emphasize 18th-century daily life, including amusements, fashion, food, medicine, occupations, religion, and transportation. A summary of political events is included.

1360. Middleton, Haydn. Sixteenth Century, The. (Everyday Life). Silver Burdett, 1984. 61 p. ill. $10.

Gr 6+. SLJ 31: Oct 1984. VOYA 7: Aug 1984. Detailed illustrations with explanatory captions emphasize 16th-century daily life, including amusements, fashion, food, medicine, occupations, religion, and transportation. A summary of political events is included.

1361. Taylor, Laurence. Seventeenth Century, The. (Everyday Life). Silver Burdett, 1984. 61 p. ill. $10.

Gr 6+. SLJ 31: Oct 1984. VOYA 7: Aug 1984. Detailed illustrations with explanatory captions emphasize 17th-century daily life, including amusements, fashion, food, medicine, occupations, religion, and transportation. A summary of political events is included.

General–1789-1900

1362. Cairns, Trevor. Power for the People. (Cambridge Introduction to History). Lerner, 1980. 99 p. ill. $7.

Gr 7+. SLJ 27: Feb 1981. Readable and well-organized, this overview shows the impact of shifting political and cultural events in 19th-century Europe.

General–1789-1900–Social Life and Customs

1363. Chamberlin, E. R. Nineteenth Century, The. (Everyday Life). Silver Burdett, 1984. 61 p. ill. $10.

Gr 6+. SLJ 31: Oct 1984. VOYA 7: Aug 1984. Detailed illustrations with explanatory captions emphasize 19th-century daily life, including amusements, fashion, food, medicine, occupations, religion, and transportation. A summary of political events is included.

General–1900-1999

1364. Banyard, Peter. Rise of the Dictators, 1919-1939, The. (Conflict in the 20th Century). Watts, 1986. 62 p. ill. $12.

Gr 5-10. B 83: Jan 15 1987. BR 5: Mar/Apr 1987. SLJ 33: Apr 1987. Banyard describes how the devastation in Europe following World War I and the Depression of the 1930s encouraged the rise of Hitler, Mussolini, and Franco. Maps, charts, graphs, and photos are included.

1365. Cook, Chris. European Political Facts, 1918-1984. New ed. Facts on File, 1986. 280 p. $25.

Gr 9+. B 83: Sep 15 1986. For each European nation a summary of recent political history is provided in addition to statistical data and brief essays on international organizations, defense, population, justice, and similar topics.

1366. Lane, Peter. Europe Since 1945: An Introduction. Barnes & Noble, 1985. 303 p. $24.

Gr 10+. + - HT 20: Aug 1987. Primary documents, tables, maps, and cartoons enrich this concise history of political, diplomatic, and economic events in Europe from 1945 to the 1980s.

1367. Morris, L. P. Eastern Europe Since 1945. (Studies in Modern History). Heinemann, 1984. 211 p. Pb $10.

Gr 11+. HT 19: May 1986. Morris' concise examination of post-World War II political events in the region that encompasses Poland, Czechoslovakia, Hungary, Romania, and Yugoslavia includes maps and statistical charts.

1368. Richards, Michael D. Europe, 1900-1980: A Brief History. Forum Press, 1982. 265 p. Pb $12.

Gr 9-11. + - HT 16: Feb 1983. This concise, chronological overview of 20th-century European history emphasizes social and cultural events.

General 1900-1999–Fiction

1369. Rabon, Israel. Street, The. Schocken, 1985. 184 p. $15.

Gr 9+. B 81: May 1 1985. The author was one of many homeless persons following World War I. His novel, first published in Yiddish in 1928, describes the fate of many like him.

General–Arms and Armor

1370. Funcken, Liliane. Age of Chivalry, Part 1: The 8th to the 15th Century: Helmets and Mail; Tournaments and Heraldic Bearings; Bows and Crossbows. (Arms and Uniforms). Prentice-Hall, 1983. 102 p. ill. $18. Pb $9.

Gr 9+. B 79: May 15 1983. VOYA 6: Dec 1983. Part 1 of this profusely illustrated trilogy emphasizes the military uniforms, armaments, tournaments, and heraldry of the European Middle Ages.

1371. Funcken, Liliane. Age of Chivalry, Part 2: Castles, Forts and Artillery, 8th to 15th Century; Armour, 12th to 15th Century; Infantry of the Renaissance; Cav-

alry of the Renaissance; the Slavs and the Orientals at the End of the Renaissance. (Arms and Uniforms). Prentice-Hall, 1983. 109 p. ill. $18. Pb $9.

Gr 7+. B 79: May 15 1983. Part 2 of this profusely illustrated trilogy emphasizes the armour, artillery, castles, forts, infantry, and cavalry of the European Middle Ages and Renaissance.

1372. Funcken, Liliane. Age of Chivalry, Part 3. The Renaissance: Arms, Horses and Tournaments; Helmets and Armor; Tactics and Artillery. (Arms and Uniforms). Prentice-Hall, 1983. 104 p. ill. $18. Pb $9.

Gr 7+. B 79: May 15 1983. Part 3 of this profusely illustrated trilogy emphasizes European armor and armaments and the military clothing and tactics that were used during the Renaissance.

General–Bibliographies

1373. Horak, Stephen M. Soviet Union and Eastern Europe: A Bibliographic Guide to Recommended Books. Libraries Unlimited, 1985. 373 p. $28.

Gr 10+. B 82: Jan 15 1986. + - BR 4: Mar/Apr 1986. LJ 110: May 1 1985. + - VOYA 8: Aug 1985. This annotated guide to over 1500 titles is arranged topically.

1374. Povsic, Frances F. Eastern Europe in Children's Literature: An Annotated Bibliography of English Language Books. (Bibliographies and Indexes in World Literature). Greenwood, 1986. 200 p. $35.

Gr K-8. B 83: Mar 1 1987. Historical fiction, biographies, and autobiographies are included in this annotated bibliography of titles published in the 20th century.

General–Biographies

1375. Aronson, Theo. Grandmama of Europe: The Crowned Descendants of Queen Victoria. Merrimack Publishers' Circle, 1974. 353 p. ill. $12.

Gr 10+. B 82: Dec 1 1985. This lively composite biography of the descendants of Queen Victoria who occupied 10 European thrones includes numerous quotes.

General–Diseases

1376. Day, James. Black Death, The. (Great Disasters). Bookwright Press; dist. by Watts, 1989. 32 p. ill. $11.

Gr 3-6. B 86: Oct 1 1989. SLJ 35: Nov 1989. Well-illustrated, this work shows the effects of the plague on the people of 14th-century Europe and how the disease influenced European history.

General–Kings, Queens, Rulers, etc.

1377. Finestone, Jeffrey. Last Courts of Europe: A Royal Album 1860-1914. Vendome, dist. by Viking, 1981. 256 p. ill. $30.

Gr 9+. B 82: Dec 1 1985. This photo album shows how life was lived by Austrian, British, Prussian, and Russian royalty from 1860 to World War I.

1378. Gurney, Gene. Kingdoms of Europe: An Illustrated Encyclopedia of Ruling Monarchs from Ancient Times to the Present. Crown, 1982. 627 p. ill. $20.

Gr 9+. B 78: May 15 1982. LJ 107: May 15 1982. This informative overview that covers European monarchies from Roman to modern times includes illustrations based on artwork from stamps, coins, portraits, and photos.

1379. Mondadori, Arnoldo. Great Dynasties. Mayflower, 1980. 343 p. ill. $23.

Gr 9+. B 76: Jul 15 1980. Mondadori has brought together authoritative accounts of 16 dynasties that ruled Austria, France, Germany, Great Britain, Italy, Portugal, Russia, and Spain, showing how each came to power, their strengths and weaknesses, and the reasons why they lost, or retained, power.

1380. Opfell, Olga S. Queens, Empresses, Grand Duchesses, and Regents: Women Rulers of Europe, A.D. 1328-1989. McFarland, 1989. 282 p. ill. $26.

Gr 10+. B 86: Oct 1 1989. BR 8: Nov/Dec 1989. LJ 114: May 1 1989. These balanced and illustrated biographies cover 39 women rulers in Europe from 1328 through 1989.

General–Maps

1381. McEvedy, Colin. Penguin Atlas of Recent History: Europe Since 1815. Penguin, 1982. 95 p. ill. Pb $6.

Gr 9+. B 79: Apr 1 1983. Clearly drawn maps and a concise text cover European military and political history and population changes from 1815 to 1980.

General–Women

1382. Anderson, Bonnie S. History of Their Own: Women in Europe from Prehistory to the Present. Harper, 1988. 2 vol. ill. $28 ea.

Gr 9+. + - LJ 113: Oct 15 1988. SLJ 35: Jan 1989. The social and work experiences of European women since the 18th century are examined in this illustrated work that is appropriate for reference work.

1383. Bingham, Marjorie W. Women in Ancient Greece and Rome. (Women in World Area Studies). Glenhurst, 1983. 123 p. $7.

Gr 7+. VOYA 7: Aug 1984. This well-researched work is a concise account of the role of women in Greece and Rome, 200 B.C.-1453 A.D.

Albania

1384. Lear, Aaron E. Albania. (Let's Visit People and Places of the World Series). Chelsea House, 1987. 92 p. ill. $12.

Gr 6-9. + - SLJ 34: Mar 1988. This illustrated overview covers Albanian history, geography, culture, economy, and noted persons.

Austria

1385. Greene, Carol. Austria. (Enchantment of the World). Childrens Press, 1986. 126 p. ill. $20.

Gr 4-6. B 82: Aug 1986. SLJ 33: Oct 1986. This colorfully illustrated introduction to Austria covers history, noted persons, geography, culture, and economy.

1386. Lye, Keith. Take a Trip to Austria. Watts, 1987. 32 p. ill. $10.

Gr 2-4. B 84: Nov 15 1987. Photos on each page and a brief, informative text introduce Austrian history, geography, industry, and cities.

1387. Wohlrabe, Raymond A. Land and People of Austria. Rev. ed. (Portraits of the Nations Series). Harper, 1956; 1972. 120 p. ill. $12.

Gr 5-9. Metzner. HB 32: Oct 1956. * LJ 81: Dec 15 1956. Wohlrabe's readable, illustrated introduction covers Austrian culture, politics, geography, and history to the early 1970s.

Austria–Biographies

1388. Clare, George. Last Waltz in Vienna: The Destruction of a Family 1842-1942. Holt, 1982. 274 p. $16.

Gr 10+. B 78: Apr 1 1982. HB 58: Oct 1982. LJ 107: Mar 15 1982. SLJ 28: May 1982. Clare charts the chronicle of his distinguished Austrian Jewish family from the 19th century through the Holocaust in an effective personal history.

1389. Herzstein, Robert Edwin. Waldheim: The Missing Years. Arbor House, 1988. 303 p. ill. $19.

Gr 9+. B 84: May 15 1988. * LJ 113: Jun 15 1988. Herzstein presents a carefully researched account of Kurt Waldheim's complicity in World War II atrocities, which was hidden as he rose to power in European politics following the war.

Austria–Fiction

1390. Carter, Peter. Children of the Book. Oxford University Press; dist. by Merrimack Publishers' Circle, 1984. 271 p. $14.

Gr 7+. B 81: Dec 1 1984. BC 38: Nov 1984. + - SLJ 31: Mar 1985. The 1683 siege of Vienna by the Turks is recounted in this complex story that clarifies the issues of the times.

Austria–Kings, Queens, Rulers, etc.

1391. Haslip, Joan. Emperor and the Actress: The Love Story of Emperor Franz Josef and Katharina Schratt. Dial, 1982. 284 p. ill. $19.

Gr 10+. B 79: Dec 1 1982. B 82: Dec 1 1985. LJ 107: Dec 1 1982. Haslip based her colorful account of the friendship between Emperor Franz Josef and Katarina Schratt on numerous letters.

Belgium

1392. Hargrove, Jim. Belgium. (Enchantment of the World). Childrens Press, 1988. 128 p. ill. $22.

Gr 4-7. B 84: Aug 1988. The diversities of life in Belgium are covered in this colorful introduction to the nation's history, geography, politics, social customs, and cultural interests.

1393. Loder, Dorothy. Land and People of Belgium. Rev. ed. (Portraits of the Nations Series). Harper, 1957; 1973. 128 p. ill. $12.

Gr 5-9. Metzner. B 53: May 15 1957. * HB 33: Aug 1957. * LJ 82: May 15 1957. Loder's readable, illustrated introduction to Belgium covers culture, geography, and history to the early 1970s.

Bulgaria

1394. Popescu, Julian. Bulgaria. (Let's Visit People and Places of the World Series). Chelsea House, 1987. 96 p. ill. $12.

Gr 5-8. + - SLJ 34: Aug 1988. About one-half of Popescu's work covers Bulgarian history. The remainder provides an overview of Bulgarian culture, economy, and contemporary politics.

Czechoslovakia

1395. Lye, Keith. Take a Trip to Czechoslovakia. Watts, 1986. 32 p. ill. $10.

Gr 2-4. B 83: Oct 15 1986. SLJ 33: Feb 1987. Photos on each page and a brief, informative text introduce Czechoslovakian history, geography, industry, and cities.

Czechoslovakia–Biographies

1396. Kovtun, George J. Masaryk and America: Testimony of a Relationship. Library of Congress. European Division, 1988. 89 p. ill. Pb $3.

Gr 11+. B 84: Jul 1988. Reminiscences of Thomas Masaryk and selections from his letters, speeches, and writings commemorate the life of Czechoslovakia's first president.

Denmark

1397. Lye, Keith. Take a Trip to Denmark. Watts, 1985. 32 p. ill. $9.

Gr 2-4. B 81: May 15 1985. Photos on each page and a brief, informative text introduce Denmark's history, geography, industry, and cities.

Denmark–Fiction

1398. Collins, Meghan. Maiden Crown. Houghton, 1979. 230 p. map. $9.

Gr 7+. B 76: Dec 1 1979. + - BC 33: Mar 1980. HB 56: Apr 1980. SLJ 26: Nov 1979. VOYA 2: Feb 1980. Sophie, a 12th-century Russian princess, married Valdemar, King of Denmark. This story is based on her struggle to find happiness in the face of court intrigue and accusations of murder.

Denmark–Greenland

1399. Anderson, Madelyn Klein. Greenland: Island at the Top of the World. Dodd, 1983. 127 p. ill. $11.

Gr 5-9. * B 80: Nov 1 1983. BC 37: Jan 1984. SLJ 30: Nov 1983. The history and strategic importance of Greenland, its economy and culture, and information on Arctic exploration are clearly presented and enhanced by maps, photos, and drawings.

1400. Lepthien, Emilie U. Greenland. (Enchantment of the World). Childrens Press, 1989. 128 p. ill. Lib. ed. $23.

Gr 5-7. B 85: Aug 1989. Greenland's history, economy, culture, and geography are presented in this illustrated work.

1401. Levine, Charlotte. Danish Dependencies. (Places and Peoples of the World). Chelsea House, 1989. 102 p. ill. $13.

Gr 5+. * BR 8: Sep/Oct 1989. Photos and a map augment this introduction to Greenland and the Faroe Islands, dependencies of Denmark. Topics covered include history, government, geography, culture, economy, and people.

Denmark–Greenland–Fiction

1402. Newth, Mette. Abduction, The. Farrar, 1989. 248 p. $14.

Gr 9+. B 86: Dec 1 1989. BC 43: Nov 1989. * SLJ 35: Dec 1989. Newth tells the story of the treatment of Greenland's Inuit people by the Norwegians who "discovered" their land in the early 1600s.

Finland

1403. Berry, Erick. Land and People of Finland. Rev. ed. (Portraits of the Nations Series). Harper, 1959; 1972. 128 p. ill. $12.

Gr 5-9. Metzner. * B 55: May 1 1959. * LJ 84: Apr 15 1959. Finnish culture, social life, economy, and history to the early 1970s are covered in Berry's readable, illustrated overview.

1404. Hintz, Martin. Finland. (Enchantment of the World). Childrens Press, 1983. 128 p. ill. $12.

Gr 5-7. B 79: Aug 1983. + SLJ 30: Sep 1983. A quick-reference section, map, and numerous photos enhance this introduction to Finnish history, geography, customs, industry, and noted persons.

1405. James, Alan. Lapps: Reindeer Herders of Lapland. (Original Peoples). Rourke, 1989. 48 p. ill. Lib. ed. $14.

Gr 5-8. B 85: May 15 1989. SLJ 35: Apr 1989. Colorful photos and helpful maps augment the lively text that covers the history and culture of the Lapp people of northern Finland.

1406. Lye, Keith. Take a Trip to Finland. Watts, 1986. 32 p. ill. $10.

Gr 2-5. B 82: May 15 1986. Photos on each page and a brief, informative text introduce Finnish history, geography, industry, and cities.

France

1407. Balerdi, Susan. France: The Crossroads of Europe. (Discovering Our Heritage). Dillon Press, 1984. 142 p. ill. $10.

Gr 4-6. B 80: Jul 1984. + - SLJ 30: Aug 1984. Photos and a map enhance this work on French history, geography, holidays, sports, education, and daily life. A chapter on French immigration to the United States concludes the book.

1408. Bishop, Claire. Here is France. Farrar, 1969. 240 p. ill. $11.

Gr 7+. Metzner. LJ 94: Nov 15 1969. Typical French attitudes toward many subjects are revealed in Bishop's illustrated introduction to French history, politics, culture, food, religion, and language.

1409. Blackwood, Alan. France. (Countries of the World). Bookwright Press; dist. by Watts, 1988. 48 p. ill. $13.

Gr 3-6. B 85: Feb 1 1989. - SLJ 35: Feb 1989. This introduction to French history, geography, economy, government, customs, and social life is enriched by colorful photos.

1410. Geraghty, Tony. March or Die: A New History of the French Foreign Legion. Facts on File, 1987. 352 p. ill. $20.

Gr 9+. B 84: Dec 1 1987. Maps and illustrations supplement this balanced look at the achievements of the French Foreign Legion and its role in French foreign policy.

1411. Goubert, Pierre. Course of French History, The. Watts, 1988. 495 p. ill. $23.

Gr 9+. B 84: Dec 15 1987. BR 7: May/Jun 1988. LJ 112: Dec 1987. Goubert examines how the common people lived in his social, economic, and political history of France from 987 to the 1980s.

1412. Harris, Jonathan. Land and People of France, The. (Portraits of the Nations Series). Lippincott, 1989. 256 p. ill. $15. Lib. ed. $15.

Gr 9+. B 86: Sep 15 1989. SLJ 35: Dec 1989. + - VOYA 12: Aug 1989. French history, government, geography, and culture are covered in this illustrated work that uses numerous French words and phrases in the context of the book.

1413. Hills, C. A. R. Seine, The. (Rivers of the World). Silver Burdett, 1981. 67 p. ill. $8.

Gr 5-8. B 78: Sep 1 1981. SLJ 28: Nov 1981. The economic importance of the Seine, its beauty and unique qualities, and the history of the people along its banks are introduced in this highly illustrated work.

1414. James, Ian. Inside France. Watts, 1989. 32 p. ill. $12.

Gr 3-6. B 85: Mar 15 1989. Colorful photos, a map, and statistics augment this brief introduction to French history, culture, geography, resources, and cities.

1415. Moss, Peter. France. (Enchantment of the World). Childrens Press, 1986. 125 p. ill. $15.

Gr 4-6. B 83: Apr 1 1987. SLJ 33: May 1987. A brief section on facts and noted persons, colorful photos, and maps augment the text that covers French history, resources, geography, government, economy, and culture.

1416. Tunnacliffe, Chantal. France: The Land and Its People. Rev. ed. (Silver Burdett Countries). Silver Burdett, 1987. 43 p. ill. $15.

Gr 4-6. SLJ 33: Aug 1987. Well-illustrated chapters cover French history, geography, government, family life, food, culture, sports, and leisure.

1417. Von Maltitz, Frances. Rhone: River of Contrasts. (Rivers of the World). Garrard, 1965. 96 p. ill. $4.

Gr 4-7. Metzner. The Rhone rises in Switzerland and travels through southeastern France. Von Maltitz discusses the history and culture of the people who have lived on its banks.

France–0-1789

1418. Caselli, Giovanni. Medieval Monk, A. Peter Bedrick, 1986. 30 p. ill. $10.

Gr 5-7. B 82: Apr 15 1986. BR 5: Mar/Apr 1987. SLJ 33: Dec 1986. Numerous illustrations enhance this account of a year in the life of a new monk in a Benedictine Chapel in France during the Middle Ages.

1419. Scherman, Katherine. Birth of France: Warriors, Bishops and Long-Haired Kings. Random, 1987. 313 p. $23.

Gr 10+. B 83: Aug 1987. LJ 112: Aug 1987. This detailed account of French nobility through the Dark Ages, from Clovis to Charlemagne, shows the brutality and decadence of the times.

1420. Wheeler, Daniel. Chateaux of France, The. Vendome; dist. by Viking, 1979. 211 p. ill. $45.

Gr 9+. B 76: Jan 15 1980. LJ 105: Feb 15 1980. The historical background of 77 pre-revolutionary French chateaux is presented along with anecdotes about their occupants and comments on their architectural features. Enhanced by striking photos.

France–0-1789–Fiction

1421. Chester, Deborah. Sign of the Owl, The. Four Winds, 1981. 219 p. $10.

Gr 7-10. + - B 77: Jul/Aug 1981. + - BC 35: Dec 1981. HB 57: Aug 1981. - SLJ 28: Sep 1981. Medieval France is the setting for this adventure, in which 15-year-old Wint and his 10-year-old cousin Jerilyn seek to out-do evil Uncle Claude.

1422. Skurzynski, Gloria. Minstrel in the Tower, The. (Stepping Stone Book). Random, 1988. 65 p. ill. Lib. ed. $6. Pb $2.

Gr 3-6. B 84: Jul 1988. BC 41: Jul 1988. SLJ 35: Sep 1988. Their father did not return from the Crusades and their mother is gravely ill, so Alice and Roger must travel across medieval France to seek help from their uncle in this fast-paced adventure.

France–1789-1799

1423. Bernier, Olivier. Words of Fire, Deeds of Blood: The Mob, the Monarchy, and the French Revolution. Little, Brown, 1989. 464 p. $22.

Gr 9+. B 85: Jun 15 1989. In presenting a French view of their revolution, Bernier argues that once France had adopted a democratic government it was inevitable that other nations in Europe would follow.

1424. Campling, Elizabeth. French Revolution, The. (Living Through History). Batsford; dist. by David & Charles, 1984. 72 p. ill. $15.

Gr 7+. SLJ 31: Feb 1985. Quotes, photos, maps, and drawings enhance this readable overview of the French Revolution. Brief biographies of the famous, infamous, and unknown are included.

1425. Cobb, Richard. Voices of the French Revolution. Salem House, 1988. 256 p. ill. $30.

Gr 9+. B 85: Oct 15 1988. VOYA 12: Apr 1989. This chronological account of the French Revolution is enriched by excerpts from memoirs, diaries, journals, speeches, letters, poems, and pamphlets written at the time. Short biographies of principal characters, a glossary, and numerous illustrations are included.

1426. Harris, Nathaniel. Fall of the Bastille, The. (Day That Made History). Batsford; dist. by David & Charles, 1987. 64 p. ill. $17.

Gr 6-10. * BR 6: Nov/Dec 1987. + - SLJ 34: Feb 1988. Archival illustrations are included in this analysis of the causes of the French Revolution, which erupted with the storming of the Bastille in 1789.

1427. Hibbert, Christopher. Days of the French Revolution. Morrow, 1980. 351 p. ill. $11.

Gr 9+. B 77: Sep 15 1980. LJ 105: Oct 1 1980. This readable account provides details of the events from July 14, 1789 to November 9, 1799. Its lively descriptions of events and principal persons are augmented by a glossary and a chronology.

1428. Luxardo, Herve. French Revolution, The. (Events of Yesteryear). Silver Burdett, 1987. 69 p. ill. $15.

Gr 7+. * BR 6: Jan/Feb 1988. + - SLJ 34: Mar 1988. The causes and events of the revolution are explored in this highly illustrated work that includes coverage of key persons.

1429. Paxton, John. Companion to the French Revolution. Facts on File, 1988. 256 p. ill. $25.

Gr 9+. B 84: Apr 15 1988. * BR 7: Sep/Oct 1988. LJ 113: Jan 1988. This alphabetical guide to the French Revolution covers the years 1769 to 1804. It includes entries on the causes, events, and results of the revolution, important people and places, a chronology, and maps.

France–1799-1815

1430. Chandler, David G. Waterloo: The Hundred Days. Macmillan, 1981. 224 p. ill. $19.

Gr 9+. B 77: May 1981. LJ 106: Jun 1 1981. The battle at Waterloo, its consequences, and the characters of the 3 commanders–Napoleon, the Duke of Wellington, and Blucher–are analyzed in Chandler's illustrated work that is clarified by numerous maps.

1431. Palmer, Alan. Encyclopaedia of Napoleon's Europe, An. St. Martin's, 1984. 300 p. ill. $23.

Gr 9+. B 81: May 15 1985. + - LJ 109: Dec 1984. Alphabetically arranged entries cover political, military, economic, and cultural events; noted groups; and individual persons from 1795 to 1815.

France–1945-1999

1432. Ardagh, John. Rural France: The People, Places, and Character of the Frenchman's France. Salem House; dist. by Merrimack Publishers' Circle, 1985. 224 p. ill. $20.

Gr 9+. B 81: Feb 1 1985. LJ 110: Jan 1985. Details of daily life and holidays in the French countryside are well illustrated in this work that covers a variety of topics, from waterways and forests to folk dancing and menus.

France–Biographies

1433. Boutet de Monvel, Louis Maurice. Joan of Arc. Viking, 1980. 55 p. ill. $13.

Gr 3-6. B 77: Dec 15 1980. B 79: Jun 1 1983. BC 34: Feb 1981. * HB 58: Feb 1982. SLJ 27: Jan 1981. This recent reprint of a beautifully illustrated 1896 French work about the young woman of faith who led French armies to victory over the English in 1429 is suitable for all ages.

1434. Bronner, Stephen Eric. Leon Blum. (World Leaders Past & Present). Chelsea House, 1987. 112 p. ill. $16.

Gr 9+. SLJ 33: Aug 1987. Blum was the first Jew and the first socialist to serve as premier of France (1946-1947). Photos and a capsule of world events place Blum's life in context.

1435. Carson, S. L. Maximilien Robespierre. (World Leaders Past & Present). Chelsea House, 1987. 112 p. ill. $17.

Gr 7+. B 84: Jan 15 1988. BR 7: Nov/Dec 1988. + - SLJ 34: Mar 1988. The political life of Robespierre, a zealous leader of the French Revolution, is examined in the context of the turbulent times. Cartoons and other illustrations are included.

1436. Dwyer, Frank. Georges Jacques Danton. (World Leaders Past & Present). Chelsea House, 1987. 111 p. ill. $16.

Gr 9-11. SLJ 34: Oct 1987. Danton was a leader in the French Revolution. He was determined to remove the aristocracy from power, but fell victim to the Reign of Terror. A chronology is included.

1437. Gottfried, Ted. Georges Clemenceau. (World Leaders Past & Present). Chelsea House, 1987. 112 p. ill. $17.

Gr 6-10. B 84: Nov 15 1987. SLJ 34: Mar 1988. A chronology augments this well-illustrated account of the life of the man who was the premier of France during World War I.

1438. Keeler, Stephen. Louis Braille. (Great Lives). Bookwright Press; dist. by Watts, 1986. 32 p. ill. $10.

Gr 3-7. B 83: Jan 1 1987. + - BC 40: Dec 1986. SLJ 33: Feb 1987. An abundance of illustrations, a chronology, and a glossary enhance this introduction to the life of Louis Braille, the inventor of the raised dot system that makes it possible for the blind to read.

1439. Ledwidge, Bernard. De Gaulle. St. Martin's, 1983. 448 p. ill. $18.

Gr 10+. B 79: Jan 15 1983. LJ 108: Jan 15 1983. This lengthy biography is a balanced and informed account of De Gaulle's military and political careers, written by a British diplomat who knew him.

1440. Nottridge, Harold. Joan of Arc. (Great Lives). Bookwright Press; dist. by Watts, 1988. 32 p. ill. $11.

Gr 9-0. | SLJ 35: Jan 1989. The political and social climate of France are clarified in this illustrated introduction to the life and work of Joan of Arc.

1441. Provensen, Alice. Glorious Flight: Across the Channel with Louis Bleriot, July 25, 1909. Viking, 1983. 39 p. ill. $ 14.

Gr K-5. * B 80: Nov 1 1983. B 82: Sep 15 1985. * BC 37: Jan 1984. HB 59: Dec 1983. * SE 48: May 1984. SLJ 30: Dec 1983. This Caldecott winner is a humorous depiction of one man's obsession with the "flying machine."

1442. Schneider, Joyce Anne. Flora Tristan: Feminist, Socialist, and Free Spirit. Morrow, 1980. 255 p. $9. Lib. ed. $9.

Gr 7+. B 77: Dec 1 1980. BC 84: Feb 1981. HB 57: Apr 1981. * SE 45: Apr 1981. SLJ 27: Feb 1981. VOYA 4: Apr 1981. The tragic circumstances of Tristan's life caused her to become an ardent 19th-century French feminist and abolitionist who fought all political and economic injustice. This is an authentic and readable account of her life.

France–Colonies

1443. Stevens, Rita. French Overseas Departments and Territories. Chelsea House, 1987. 112 p. ill. $12.

Gr 6-9. SLJ 34: Jan 1988. The history and current problems of French colonial holdings are discussed and their administrative status is clarified in this illustrated work.

France–Kings, Queens, Rulers, etc.

1444. Aliki. King's Day, The. Crowell, 1989. 32 p. ill. $14. Lib. ed. $14.

Gr 2-5. * B 86: Sep 1 1989. * BC 43: Oct 1989. SLJ 35: Oct 1989. Colorful illustrations and a brief text reveal complex detail of the daily life of the Sun King, Louis XIV.

1445. Bernier, Olivier. Louis XIV: A Royal Life. Doubleday, 1987. 356 p. ill. $20.

Gr 9+. B 84: Nov 1 1987. + - LJ 112: Nov 1 1987. King at the age of 5, Louis XIV determined that he would become the most powerful and glorious monarch in Europe. Bernier's lively, illustrated biography shows how he succeeded and became known as the Sun King.

1446. Blackwood, Alan. Napoleon. (Great Lives). Bookwright Press; dist. by Watts, 1987. 32 p. ill. $10.

Gr 3-8. + - B 83: Jul 1987. SLJ 33: May 1987. This illustrated introduction to Napoleon's life includes numerous illustrations and maps. Events in his life are placed in the context of world affairs.

1447. Castries, Rene de La Croix, duc de. Lives of the Kings and Queens of France, The. Random, 1979. 272 p. ill. $20.

Gr 9+. B 76: Jan 15 1980. LJ 104: Nov 15 1979. The lives of French kings and their queens consort, and the major events of their reigns, are covered in this abundantly illustrated work.

1448. Gross, Albert C. Henry of Navarre. (World Leaders Past & Present). Chelsea House, 1988. 112 p. ill. $17.

Gr 6-10. B 84: Jun 15 1988. The illustrations and text present a balanced account of Henry IV and life in France during his reign (1589-1610).

1449. Haslip, Joan. Marie Antoinette. Weidenfeld & Nicholson, 1988. 328 p. ill. $20.

Gr 9+. B 84: Feb 15 1988. + - LJ 113: Mar 1 1988. This readable biography of Marie Antoinette shows clearly how her politically arranged marriage led to her unhappiness and alienation from the French people.

1450. Herold, J. Christopher. Horizon Book of the Age of Napoleon, The. (Power and Personality Series). Crown, 1962; 1983. 420 p. ill. Pb $15.

Gr 9+. BR 3: May/Jun 1984. This witty and highly illustrated account of Napoleon and the time in which he lived is a reissue of a 1962 publication.

1451. Masters, Anthony. Napoleon. (Leaders Series). McGraw-Hill, 1981. 69 p. ill. $8.

Gr 7-10. B 78: Dec 15 1981. + - SLJ 28: Mar 1982. Emphasis is on Napoleon's career in this introduction that has illustrations on nearly every page.

1452. Seward, Desmond. Marie Antoinette. St. Martin's, 1982. 297 p. ill. $13.

Gr 9+. B 78: Mar 15 1982. - LJ 107: Apr 1 1982. SLJ 29: Sep 1982. Seward examined correspondence and memoirs in writing this sympathetic reevaluation of the life of Marie Antoinette.

1453. Shor, Donnali. Napoleon Bonaparte. (Why They Became Famous). Silver Burdett, 1987. 64 p. ill. $14.

Gr 4-7. BR 6: Nov/Dec 1987. + - SLJ 33: Jun/Jul 1987. Napoleon's rise to power and the highlights of his rule are presented in this illustrated work that includes a chronology and information on noted contemporaries.

1454. Weider, Ben. Murder of Napoleon, The. Congdon & Lattes; dist. by St. Martin's, 1982. 266 p. $15.

Gr 9+. B 78: Apr 15 1982. LJ 107: Feb 15 1982. Napoleon's last years, spent in exile on St. Helena island, are documented, and evidence is presented that he died of arsenic poisoning.

1455. Weidhorn, Manfred. Napoleon. Atheneum, 1986. 142 p. $15.

Gr 7+. + - B 83: Nov 1 1986. SLJ 33: Feb 1987. + - VOYA 9: Feb 1987. Napoleon's political and military activities are the focus of this work that clarifies his accomplishments and the weaknesses that led to his failures.

1456. Zweig, Stefan. Marie Antoinette: The Portrait of an Average Woman. (Power and Personality Series). Crown, 1984. 476 p. $9.

Gr 10+. B 82: Dec 1 1985. BR 3: Nov/Dec 1984. This reprint of a 1933 edition shows Marie Antoinette as a spoiled 14-year-old bride who became a mature and courageous woman before she died on the guillotine at age 39.

Germany

1457. Dudman, John. Division of Berlin, The. (Flashpoints). Rourke, 1988. 76 p. ill. $12.

Gr 6-9. SLJ 35: Feb 1989. This balanced work explores the causes for the division of Berlin and the impact of the split on international politics.

1458. Einhorn, Barbara. West Germany. (Countries of the World). Bookwright Press; dist. by Watts, 1988. 48 p. ill. $13.

Gr 3-6. B 85: Feb 1 1989. - SLJ 35: Feb 1989. This introduction to German history, geography, economy, and social life is enriched by colorful photos.

1459. Gelb, Norman. Berlin Wall: Kennedy, Khrushchev, and a Showdown in the Heart of Europe. Times Books, 1987. 384 p. ill. $20.

Gr 9+. B 83: Dec 15 1986. B 84: Sep 1 1987. LJ 112: Feb 15 1987. Gelb presents a readable account of the reasons for the wall, details of its construction, its effect on German life, and escape attempts.

1460. Hintz, Martin. West Germany. (Enchantment of the World). Childrens Press, 1983. 127 p. ill. $12.

Gr 5-7. B 79: Aug 1983. SLJ 30: Sep 1983. A quick-reference section, map, and numerous photos enhance this introduction to the history, geography, customs, industry, resources, and noted persons of West Germany.

1461. James, Ian. Inside West Germany. Watts, 1989. 32 p. ill. $12.

Gr 3-6. B 85: Mar 15 1989. Colorful photos and a map augment this brief introduction to the history, economy, culture, and cities of West Germany.

1462. Jimbo, Terushi. West Germany. (Children of the World). Gareth Stevens, 1988. 64 p. ill. $12.

Gr 2-4. B 85: Dec 15 1988. Colorful photos complement the text that introduces the life of a German family. A brief section provides facts on German history, culture, government, and cities.

1463. Lye, Keith. Take a Trip to East Germany. Watts, 1987. 32 p. ill. $10.

Gr 2-5. B 83: Apr 15 1987. SLJ 33: Aug 1987. Photos on each page and a brief, informative text introduce East German history, geography, industry, and cities.

1464. McKenna, David. East Germany. (Let's Visit People and Places of the World Series). Chelsea House, 1988. 112 p. ill. $12.

Gr 6-8. B 84: May 15 1988. Conditions in East Germany in the mid-1980s are introduced along with the nation's history, geography, culture, economy, government, and cities.

1465. Pfeiffer, Christine. Germany: Two Nations, One Heritage. (Discovering Our Heritage). Dillon Press, 1987. 191 p. ill. $13.

Gr 4-7. B 84: Oct 1 1987. SLJ 34: Sep 1987. The geography, government, economy, and culture of East and West Germany

are covered along with an introduction to German history that covers both world wars and the division of the nation.

1466. Sharman, Tim. We Live in East Germany. (Living Here). Bookwright Press; dist. by Watts, 1986. 60 p. ill. $11.

Gr 5-8. B 82: May 15 1986. Interviews with East Germans reveal various aspects of life there in addition to information about the nation's history, economy, geography, and religions.

1467. Westerfeld, Scott. Berlin Airlift. (Turning Points in American History). Silver Burdett, 1989. 64 p. ill. $17. Pb $8.

Gr 6-10. B 86: Nov 1 1989. SLJ 35: Dec 1989. Westerfeld explores the reasons for the Soviet blockade of Berlin and the events and results of the air lift in which hundreds of planes flew to Berlin every day for over a year to meet the needs of the city.

Germany–0-1517

1468. Caselli, Giovanni. German Printer, A. (Everyday Life). Peter Bedrick; dist. by Harper, 1987. 29 p. ill. $10.

Gr 4-7. BR 6: Sep/Oct 1987. + - SLJ 34: Sep 1987. A picture glossary and a map are included in this introduction to a printer's apprentice and his friend, Albrecht Durer, whose father is a goldsmith.

Germany–0-1517–Fiction

1469. Skurzynski, Gloria. What Happened in Hamelin. Scholastic, 1979. 177 p. map. $8.

Gr 5-8. * B 76: Jan 1 1980. B 84: Mar 1 1988. BC 33: Feb 1980. HB 56: Feb 1980. + - SLJ 26: Jan 1980. Based on historical records, this is a readable account of the events in Hamelin, Germany, where the Pied Piper led all but two of the city's children away to be sold into servitude in 1284.

Germany–1918-1933

1470. Taylor, Simon. Rise of Hitler: Revolution and Counter-revolution in Germany, 1918-1933. Universe Books, 1983. 131 p. ill. $20.

Gr 9+. SLJ 30: Feb 1984. Based on recently discovered documentary material, this work examines the rise of fascism and the sequence of events that brought Hitler to power.

Germany–1918-1933–Fiction

1471. Vogel, Ilse-Margret. Tikhon. Harper, 1984. 112 p. ill. $11.

Gr 3-7. + - BC 37: Jun 1984. HB 60: Jun 1984. * SE 49: Apr 1985. SLJ 31: Sep 1984. A lonely and homesick Russian soldier, caught in Germany without identification following World War I, is befriended by a little girl and her farm family.

Germany–1945-1999

1472. Botting, Douglas. From the Ruins of the Reich: Germany, 1945-1949. Crown, 1985. 336 p. $18.

Gr 9+. B 82: Dec 15 1985. LJ 110: Nov 1 1985. Interviews with Germans and members of the occupying forces are the basis for this description of life in Germany immediately following World War II.

1473. Evans, Richard J. In Hitler's Shadow: West German Historians and the Attempt to Escape from the Nazi Past. Pantheon, 1989. 185 p. $17. Pb $7.

Gr 10+. B 85: Jun 15 1989. LJ 114: Jul 1989. Evans presents a balanced examination of the various ways in which contemporary Germans attempt to deal with the legacy of the Nazis.

1474. Sichrovsky, Peter. Born Guilty: Children of Nazi Families. Basic Books, 1988. 192 p. $18.

Gr 9+. * B 84: Jan 1 1988. * LJ 113: Jan 1988. Sichrovsky interviewed persons born following World War II whose parents were Nazi war criminals, showing how history affected their lives.

Germany–1945-1999–Fiction

1475. Benary-Isbert, Margot. Ark, The. Peter Smith, 1953. 246 p. $19.

Gr 7-9. Metzner. B 49: Mar 15 1953. * HB 29: Apr 1953. * HB 29: Apr 1953. * LJ 78: May 1 1953. The genuine experiences of a refugee family in war-ravaged West Germany following World War II are shown in this translation of a German story first published in 1948.

1476. Carter, Peter. Bury the Dead. Farrar, 1987. 374 p. $15.

Gr 8+. + - B 83: Mar 1 1987. HB 63: Sep/Oct 1987. * SLJ 33: Aug 1987. + - VOYA 10: Dec 1987. Fifteen-year-old East Berliner Erica is preparing for the high-jump championship when her close family life is disrupted by the appearance of an uncle who had been a Nazi official.

Germany–Biographies

1477. Agee, Joel. Twelve Years: An American Boyhood in East Germany. Farrar, 1981. 324 p. $15.

Gr 10+. B 77: May 15 1981. HB 57: Oct 1981. LJ 106: May 1 1981. The son of James Agee grew up in East Germany following World War II. His memoir provides a view of growing up in a communist country and of a boy's coming-of-age.

1478. Rose, Jonathan E. Otto von Bismarck. (World Leaders Past & Present). Chelsea House, 1987. 112 p. ill. $17.

Gr 6+. B 84: Sep 1 1987. BR 7: May/Jun 1988. + - SLJ 34: Jan 1988. Captioned illustrations and numerous quotes enrich this biography of the enigmatic Bismarck, who united Germany and became imperial chancellor. Suitable for students with some background in 19th-century European history.

1479. Viola, Tom. Willy Brandt. (World Leaders Past & Present). Chelsea House, 1987. 112 p. ill. $17.

Gr 9+. + - B 84: Apr 15 1988. Maps, photos, and a chronology supplement this biography of Brandt, who spent 12 years in the Resistance movement during WW II and later became chancellor of West Germany.

Germany–Kings, Queens, Rulers, etc.

1480. Benecke, Gerhard. Maximilian I (1459-1519): An Analytical Biography. Routledge & Kegan Paul, 1982. 205 p. $25.

Gr 10+. B 79: Apr 1 1983. B 82: Dec 1 1985. Maximilian used his political skills to rise from being a minor ruler to having great influence in Europe. This concise biography covers his career and describes life at the end of the Middle Ages.

1481. Kittredge, Mary. Frederick the Great. (World Leaders Past & Present). Chelsea House, 1987. 112 p. ill. $17.

Gr 6+. B 84: Nov 15 1987. BR 7: Nov/Dec 1988. + - SLJ 34: Dec 1987. As ruler of Prussia (1740-1786), Frederick the Great believed that any action that benefited his nation was correct. An active military leader, he did much to modernize Prussian agriculture, industry, and government.

Great Britain

1482. Fisher, Leonard Everett. Tower of London, The. Macmillan, 1987. 32 p. ill. $14.

Gr 3-6. B 84: Oct 15 1987. BC 41: Nov 1987. * SE 52: Apr/May 1988. SLJ 34: Jan 1988. British history is highlighted in concise, illustrated accounts of 13 dramatic episodes in the history of the Tower of London, from its construction in 1078 to modern times.

1483. James, Ian. Inside Great Britain. Watts, 1988. 32 p. $13.

Gr 3-6. B 85: Jan 15 1989. + - SLJ 35: Jan 1989. Maps and colorful photos enhance this concise introduction to British history, geography, industries, cities, culture, and social life.

1484. Jones, Christopher. Great Palace: The Story of Parliament. Parkwest Publications, 1985. 256 p. ill. $25.

Gr 9+. B 81: Aug 1985. LJ 110: Aug 1985. SLJ 32: Sep 1985. This attractive, colorful tour book and history of British legislative facilities takes the reader behind the scenes and explains traditions and methods of operation.

1485. Miller, Russell. East Indiamen, The. (Seafarers). Time-Life; dist. by Silver Burdett, 1981. 176 p. ill. $14.

Gr 9+. LJ 105: Dec 15 1980. For 3 centuries trade and travel between Britain and the East Indies had enormous economic, social, and political influence on both regions. This highly illustrated work emphasizes the ships and the social impact of their voyages.

1486. Morgan, Kenneth O. Oxford Illustrated History of Britain, The. Oxford University Press, 1984. 640 p. ill. $30.

Gr 9+. B 81: Nov 15 1984. LJ 109: Sep 15 1984. Morgan's profusely illustrated history of England, Scotland, Wales, and Ireland, from the time of the Roman occupation to the 20th century, covers economic, intellectual, political, and social topics.

1487. Munro, Roxie. Inside-Outside Book of London, The. Dutton, 1989. 48 p. ill. $14.

Gr 2-5. BC 43: Dec 1989. HB 65: Nov/Dec 1989. SLJ 35: Dec 1989. Exterior and interior views of London's historic buildings are presented in a colorful, picture book format.

1488. Newby, Howard. Country Life: A Social History of Rural England. Barnes & Noble, 1987. 250 p. $27.

Gr 10+. HT 21: Nov 1987. Life in rural England in the 18th, 19th, and 20th centuries, including the agricultural revolution, changes in estate management, and the growth of agribusiness is presented in a readable synthesis.

1489. Quennell, Marjorie. Everyday Life in Roman and Anglo-Saxon Times. Putnam, 1960; 1987. 225 p. ill. $21.

Gr 7-11. Metzner. * B 57: Oct 1 1960. * LJ 85: Apr 15 1960. This illustrated overview of English social, economic, cultural, and religious life covers from Roman through Norman times.

1490. Sproule, Anna. Great Britain. (Countries of the World). Bookwright Press; dist. by Watts, 1988. 48 p. ill. $13.

Gr 3-6. B 85: Feb 1 1989. + - SLJ 35: Feb 1989. This colorfully illustrated introduction to Great Britain covers history, geography, government, culture, and social life. A glossary is included.

1491. Sproule, Anna. Great Britain: The Land and Its People. Rev. ed. (Silver Burdett Countries). Silver Burdett, 1987. 43 p. ill. $15.

Gr 4-7. + - B 84: Nov 15 1987. - SLJ 34: Feb 1988. This brief overview of British history, culture, geography, and industry is presented in a large-sized pictorial format.

1492. Sproule, Anna. Living in London. (City Life). Silver Burdett, 1987. 45 p. ill. $14.

Gr 4-6. B 84: Feb 1 1988. BR 7: Sep/Oct 1988. The history of London and a view of life in the city are presented in this concise and well-illustrated work.

Great Britain–0-1066

1493. Abels, Harriette. Stonehenge. (Mystery of). Crestwood, 1987. 47 p. ill. $11.

Gr 4-7. + - SLJ 34: Mar 1988. This introduction to Stonehenge includes photos, a glossary, and an explanation of recent theories about its origins.

1494. Balfour, Michael David. Stonehenge and Its Mysteries. Scribner, 1980. 189 p. ill. $15.

Gr 9+. B 76: Apr 15 1980. LJ 105: May 15 1980. SLJ 27: Sep 1980. This well-illustrated survey of the history of Stonehenge covers its architecture and artistic aspects. A chronology of major discoveries is included.

1495. Chippindale, Christopher. Stonehenge Complete: History, Heritage, Archeology. Cornell University Press, 1983. 296 p. ill. $30.

Gr 10+. LJ 108: Sep 1 1983. The author has included important, interesting, or odd things that have been written or painted about Stonehenge, in a chronological arrangement.

1496. Clarke, Amanda. Battle of Hastings. David & Charles, 1988. 64 p. $18.

Gr 9+. BR 7: Nov/Dec 1988. Primary materials, maps, and photos enrich this readable account of the causes, events, and results of the significant Battle of Hastings.

1497. Dunrea, Olivia. Skara Brae: The Story of a Prehistoric Village. Holiday, 1986. 39 p. ill. $11.

Gr 3-8. B 82: Jun 15 1986. BC 39: May 1986. HB 62: Sep/Oct 1986. * SE 51: Apr/May 1987. SLJ 32: May 1986. The homes and objects of the Neolithic people who lived on Scotland's Orkney Islands from 3500 to 2400 B.C. are shown in clear and well-organized drawings augmented by a readable text.

1498. Fox, Aileen Mary. Roman Britain. Dufour, 1968. 46 p. ill. $14.

Gr 5-9. Metzner. B 65: May 15 1969. Fox's well-illustrated introduction to life in Britain following the Roman conquest covers such topics as daily life, religion, government, and road and building construction.

1499. Wood, Michael. In Search of the Dark Ages. Facts on File, 1987. 250 p. ill. $23.

Gr 11+. + - BR 6: Mar/Apr 1988. Photos and detailed maps aid in this account of the leaders, battles, and intrigues of the thousand years of British history between the end of the Roman Empire and the Norman conquest.

Great Britain–0-1066–Fiction

1500. Rees, David. Beacon for the Romans, A. Pergamon Press, 1981. 77 p. ill. $8.

Gr 4-6. SLJ 28: Aug 1982. As the last of the Romans occupying Britain prepare to leave in 410 A.D., a Roman boy meets a British boy. Through their conversation and the celebration of the Roman departure the Roman boy gains sympathy for the native point of view.

Great Britain–0-1066–Social Life and Customs

1501. Wilkins, Frances. Growing Up in Roman Britain. Batsford, 1980. 72 p. ill. $13.

Gr 6-10. SLJ 27: Oct 1980. Education, food, games, clothing, disease, religion, and other aspects of town and country life are covered in this illustrated introduction to early English history.

Great Britain–1066-1714

1502. Hallam, Elizabeth. Four Gothic Kings: The Turbulent History of Medieval England and the Plantagenet Kings. Weidenfeld & Nicholson, 1987. 320 p. ill. $35.

Gr 9+. B 84: Nov 15 1987. Excerpts from contemporary works provide insight into the cultural and political events and trends in England from 1216 to 1377.

1503. Hallam, Elizabeth. War of the Roses, The. Weidenfeld & Nicholson, 1988. 320 p. ill. $35.

Gr 9+. B 85: Nov 15 1988. This well-illustrated oversized work covers the events, people, and places of the hundred-year civil war (1377-1485). As a result of these struggles, the Tudors came to power and changed the development of the monarchy and the nation.

1504. Hodges, Cyril Walter. Battlement Garden: Britain from the War of the Roses to the Age of Shakespeare. (Mirror of Britain Series). Houghton, 1980. 144 p. ill. $11.

Gr 7+. B76: Mar 15 1980. BC 33: Jul/Aug 1980. HB 56: Apr 1980. * SE 45: Apr 1981. SLJ 26: Aug 1980. In this rich and lively social history of England during the days of Elizabeth I and Shakespeare, notable persons are introduced along with the political and social concerns of the day.

1505. Jarman, Rosemary Hawley. Crispin's Day: The Glory of Agincourt. Little, Brown, 1979. 223 p. ill. $15.

Gr 9+. B 78: Jan 1 1980. LJ 104: Nov 15 1979. Jarman presents a lively account of the battle of Agincourt which gave Henry V of England a claim to the French throne in 1415.

1506. Kelly, Rosemary. City at War: Oxford 1642-46. (World of Change). Thornes; dist. by Defour, 1988. 52 p. ill. Pb $7.

Gr 6-8. BR 7: May/Jun 1988. This account of life in the city of Oxford during the English Civil War is from a series written for British students.

1507. Matthews, Rupert. Fire of London, The. (Great Disasters). Bookwright Press; dist. by Watts, 1989. 32 p. ill. $11.

Gr 3-6. SLJ 35: May 1989. Numerous illustrations enrich this brief introduction to the events of the London fire in 1666. The fire burned for 5 days and destroyed most of the city.

1508. Morris, Robert. Bare Ruined Choirs: The Fate of a Welsh Abbey. (World of Change). Thorsons, 1987. 52 p. ill. Pb $7.

Gr 6-8. BR 7: May/Jun 1988. From 1534 to 1540 many Catholic abbeys in England were closed because of the Protestant movement. This British publication is based on documents from that time, including letters, pamphlets, and pictures.

1509. Smith, Leslie M. Making of Britain: The Middle Ages. Schocken, 1985. 216 p. ill. $24.

Gr 9+. B 81: Jul 1985. Essays cover many aspects of life in medieval Britain, including government, religion, the lives of peasants and nobility, and the growth of towns.

Great Britain–1066-1714–Biographies

1510. Miller, Helen Hill. Captains from Devon: The Great Elizabethan Seafarers Who Won the Oceans for England. Algonquin, 1985. 221 p. ill. $17.

Gr 9+. B 82: Oct 15 1985. SLJ 32: Mar 1986. Francis Drake, Walter Raleigh, John Hawkins, and other sea captains from Devon peninsula brought fame to themselves and England through their explorations and adventures which Miller presents in a readable, illustrated text.

Great Britain–1066-1714–Fiction

1511. Gray, Elizabeth Janet. Adam of the Road. Scholastic, 1942. 320 p. ill. $3.

Gr 4-8. Metzner. B 38: May 1 1942. * HB 18: May 1942. * LJ 67: May 15 1942. LJ 67: Oct 15 1942. This tale of a minstrel and his son in medieval England is rich in period details and enhanced by fine drawings.

1512. Greenberg, Joanne. King's Persons, The. Holt, 1963; 1985. 284 p. Pb $7.

Gr 9+. BR 4: Mar/Apr 1986. VOYA 9: Jun 1986. The 12th-century events that changed English acceptance of Jews to hatred, resulting in a massacre, are the setting for this solid historical novel.

1513. Hardwick, Mollie. Merrymaid, The. St. Martin's, 1985. 187 p. $13.

Gr 9+. B 81: Jun 1 1985. + - LJ 110: Jun 1 1985. SLJ 32: Nov 1985. The lives of 16th-century traveling minstrels included fun, adventure, persecution, and the threat of the plague. Hardwick's story is rich in historical and cultural detail.

1514. Harnett, Cynthia. Cargo of the Madalena, The. Lerner, 1960; 1984. 235 p. ill. $10.

Gr 7-9. * B 57: Oct 1 1960. B 81: Sep 15 1984. * HB 36: Dec 1960. HB 60: Sep 1984. * LJ 85: Sep 15 1960. This lively adventure and mystery about England's first printer is told by a young apprentice, and presents a good picture of 15th-century London. Originally published as Caxton's Challenge.

1515. Harnett, Cynthia. Great House, The. Lerner, 1984. 173 p. ill. $10.

Gr 5-9. B 81: Sep 15 1984. SE 33: May 1969. Details of 17th-century life enrich this story about the building of St. Paul's Cathedral in London.

1516. Harnett, Cynthia. Merchant's Mark. Lerner, 1952; 1984. 181 p. ill. $10.

Gr 7-9. B 49: Mar 15 1953. B 81: Sep 15 1984. This lively mystery presents a detailed picture of the wool industry in 15th-century England. Originally published as Nicholas and the Wool-Pack.

1517. Harnett, Cynthia. Sign of the Green Falcon, The. Lerner, 1953; 1984. 217 p. ill. $10.

Gr 7-9. B 81: Sep 15 1984. Fifteenth-century London is colorfully presented in this adventure, which involves young apprentices trying to foil a plot against the king.

1518. Harnett, Cynthia. Writing on the Hearth, The. Lerner, 1972; 1984. 299 p. ill. $10.

Gr 6-9. B 81: Sep 15 1984. This suspenseful story, set in 15th-century England, presents rich detail of the times. The peasant boy, Stephen, is educated by an earl and becomes involved in politics.

1519. Hilgartner, Beth. Murder for Her Majesty, A. Houghton, 1986. 241 p. $13.

Gr 5-9. B 83: Sep 15 1986. BC 40: Sep 1986. * BR 5: Mar/Apr 1981. * SE 51: Apr/May 1987. * SLJ 33: Oct 1986. VOYA 9: Dec 1986. After she witnesses her father's murder, Alice is disguised as a member of a boy's choir. The details of life in Elizabethan England enrich this adventure.

1520. King, Clive. Ninny's Boat. Macmillan, 1981. 243 p. map. $10.

Gr 6-9. B 78: Jan 1 1982. BC 35: Dec 1982. HB 58: Apr 1982. King's action-filled story of a young slave in 5th-century Britain is humorous and has lively characters.

1521. Marryat, Frederick. Children of the New Forest. Penguin, 1847; 1984. 304 p. ill. Pb $3.

Gr 4-6. Metzner. B 26: Jul 1930. Originally published in 1847, this is the story of 4 children from a Royalist family in the days of Cromwell. Following the deaths of their parents, the children seek refuge with a forester.

1522. Melnikoff, Pamela. Plots and Players: The Lopez Conspiracy. Peter Bedrick; dist. by Publishers Group West, 1989. 160 p. ill. $10.

Gr 5-9. B 85: Jul 1989. BR 8: Sep/Oct 1989. SLJ 35: Jul 1989. VOYA 12: Oct 1989. Details of life in Elizabethan England are woven into this story based on the life of the queen's physician. He was a Jew who, although it was illegal to be Jewish, was involved in espionage for the queen. Action centers around a young Shakespearean actor.

1523. Minard, Rosemary. Long Meg. Pantheon, 1982. 57 p. ill. $9. Lib. ed. $9.

Gr 3-6. B 79: Feb 1 1983. BC 36: Feb 1983. + - SLJ 29: Feb 1983. Long Meg is a legendary female Robin Hood who, dressed as a man, helped the army of Henry VIII defeat the French.

1524. Penman, Sharon Kay. Here Be Dragons. Holt, 1985. 704 p. $20.

Gr 10+. B 81: Jun 15 1985. LJ 110: Jul 1985. SLJ 32: Sep 1985. VOYA 9: Apr 1986. This detailed novel is based on the marriage of Joanna, daughter of King John, to Llewelyn, a Welsh warrior prince 20 years her senior. It spans 50 years and shows England's struggle to control Wales and Normandy.

1525. Phillips, Ann. Peace Child, The. Oxford University Press, 1988. 150 p. $14.

Gr 5-9. B 85: Dec 1 1988. HB 64: Nov/Dec 1988. SLJ 35: Nov 1988. Fourteenth-century England and the black plague provide the setting for this tale about a plucky heroine who learns the she was a "peace child" who had been exchanged at birth to ensure peace between warring rivals.

1526. Pyle, Howard. Men of Iron. Airmont, 1892. 328 p. ill. Pb $2.

Gr 6+. Metzner. Young Miles wins his knight's spurs and vanquishes his enemies in the days of Henry IV of England.

1527. Riley, Judith Merkle. Vision of Light, A. Delacorte, 1989. 442 p. $20.

Gr 9+. B 85: Nov 1 1988. * LJ 114: Jan 1989. This story of a 14th century-British midwife features rich characterizations and an authentic picture of the lives of women during medieval times.

1528. Russell, Jennifer Ellen. Threshing Floor, The. Paulist Press, 1987. 401 p. $17.

Gr 8+. BR 7: May/Jun 1988. + - LJ 112: Aug 1987. Life in 14th-century England is seen through this story of a noble family who lived at Keldacross. Their involvement with townspeople shows the impact of social class on individual lives.

1529. Sutcliff, Rosemary. Bonnie Dundee. Dutton, 1984. 204 p. $13.

Gr 7+. B 80: Aug 1984. * BC 38: Sep 1984. * BR 3: Mar/Apr 1985. HB 60: Sep/Oct 1984. SLJ 31: Sep 1984. Sutcliff presents an accurate picture of 17th-century Scottish history in a rousing story told by a follower of John Graham of Claverhouse. High adventure, personalities, and romance all add to the story.

1530. Sutcliff, Rosemary. Frontier Wolf. Dutton, 1981. 196 p. $12.

Gr 7+. B 77: Jul 1 1981. BC 34: Jul/Aug 1981. HB 57: Aug 1981. * SE 46: Apr 1982. SLJ 28: Sep 1981. VOYA 4: Oct 1981. Authentic historical background and high adventure are found in this story of Alexios, who is sent by his Roman commanders to lead a fierce band of native British warriors in the 4th century.

1531. Sutcliff, Rosemary. Song for a Dark Queen. Crowell, 1979. 182 p. $7.

Gr 6+. HB 55: Jun 1979. SE 44: Apr 1980. SLJ 25: Apr 1979. Bodacia, queen of a British tribe under Roman occupation, led a revolt against Roman tyranny. Celtic traditions and a strong sense of the times enrich the story.

1532. Turner, Ann. Way Home, The. Crown, 1982. 116 p. $9.

Gr 6+. B 79: Jan 1 1983. BC 36: Feb 1983. HB 59: Apr 1983. - SLJ 29: Feb 1983. * VOYA 6: Jun 1983. Fourteenth-century teenager Annie is a peasant girl with a harelip. Village superstition and her outspokenness result in her exile to a marsh, where she struggles to survive, only to find on her return that the plague has decimated the village.

1533. Van Woerkom, Dorothy. Pearl in the Egg: A Tale of the Thirteenth Century. Crowell, 1980. 118 p. ill. $9.

Gr 4-9. B 77: Jan 15 1981. BC 34: Feb 1981. * SE 45: Apr 1981. + - SLJ 27: Sep 1980. This story of a young medieval minstrel is based on the life of a real musician who performed at the court of the king.

1534. Walsh, Jill Paton. Parcel of Patterns, A. Farrar, 1983. 136 p. $11.

Gr 7+. B 80: Mar 1 1984. * BC 37: Mar 1984. HB 60: Apr 1984. + - SLJ 30: Feb 1984. * VOYA 7: Apr 1984. In 1665 the plague struck the small English village of Eyam. The details of daily life and the tragedy of the village which voluntarily isolated itself, are based on fact.

Great Britain–1066-1714–Social Life and Customs

1535. Harrison, Michael. Scolding Tongues: The Persecution of Witches. (World of Change). Thornes, 1987. 52 p. $7.

Gr 6-8. + - BR 7: May/Jun 1988. Excerpts from primary sources enrich this examination of the English witch trials.

1536. Jones, Madeline. Finding Out About Tudor and Stuart Towns. Batsford, 1982. 48 p. $12.

Gr 6-10. * BR 1: Jan/Feb 1983. + - SLJ 29: Feb 1983. All aspects of city life in England, 1485-1714, are discussed in this illustrated British publication. Included are churches, government, markets, schools, craftsmen, and merchants.

1537. Morgan, Gwyneth. Life in a Medieval Village. (Cambridge Topic Book). Lerner, 1982. 51 p. ill. $6.

Gr 5-7. B 78: Feb 1 1982. * SE 47: Apr 1983. The social and cultural life in a 13th-century English village is shown in this account of the lives of freeman John and his family.

1538. Sancha, Sheila. Castle Story, The. Crowell, 1982. 224 p. ill. $13.

Gr 7+. B 78: Aug 1982. + - BC 35: May 1982. + - BR 1: Sep/Oct 1982. HB 58: Jun 1982. SLJ 28: May 1982. This detailed reference on the structure and function of British castles from 1066 to the middle of the 16th century includes drawings and photos that show construction details and how the residents lived in peace and war.

1539. Sancha, Sheila. Luttrell Village: Country Life in the Middle Ages. Crowell, 1983. 64 p. ill. $13. Lib. ed. $13.

Gr 5+. B 79: May 15 1983. BC 36: Apr 1983. HB 59: Apr 1983. * SE 48: May 1984. SLJ 29: May 1983. * VOYA 6: Aug 1983. Emphasis is on the daily life of ordinary people in this illustrated account of English life in the 14th century.

1540. Sancha, Sheila. Walter Dragun's Town: Crafts and Trade in the Middle Ages. Crowell, 1989. 64 p. ill. $14. Lib. ed. $14.

Gr 5-7. B 86: Dec 1 1989. HB 65: Nov/Dec 1989. Sancha's illustrated account of life in a 13th-century English village is based on medieval documents. An epilogue and a glossary are included.

1541. Wilkins, Frances. Growing Up during the Norman Conquest. Batsford, 1980. 72 p. ill. $13.

Gr 6-10. SLJ 27: Oct 1980. Education, food, games, clothing, disease, religion, and other aspects of town and country life are covered in this illustrated introduction to early English history.

1542. Wright, Sylvia. Age of Chivalry: English Society, 1200-1400. Warwick; dist. by Watts, 1988. 40 p. ill. $14.

Gr 4-6. B 85: Jan 15 1989. Full-color photos and other illustrations enhance Wright's introduction to medieval culture and society in Britain.

Great Britain—1714-1837

1543. Brownlee, Walter. Navy That Beat Napoleon, The. (Cambridge Topic Book). Lerner, 1982. 52 p. ill. $6.

Gr 6-10. + - SLJ 28: Apr 1982. British ships, tactics, and weapons used in the battles against Napoleon (1803-1815) are introduced in this book that provides a sense of the lives of the sailors.

1544. Schwartz, Richard B. Daily Life in Johnson's London. University of Wisconsin Press, 1983. 196 p. ill. $25.

Gr 9+. B 80: Jun 1 1984. This lively account of the sociological aspects of life in 18th-century England includes information on medication, punishment for crimes, marriage, and the unusual activities that were considered entertainment.

1545. Vialls, Christine. Industrial Revolution Begins, The. (Cambridge Topic Book). Lerner, 1982. 52 p. ill. $6.

Gr 6-10. + - SLJ 28: Apr 1982. This simple account of the transformation of a peaceful British valley into an industrial complex, with coal mines and iron forges, shows the impact of social change on people's daily lives.

1546. Windrow, Martin. British Redcoat of the Napoleonic Wars, The. (Soldier Through the Ages). Watts, 1986. 32 p. ill. $11.

Gr 5-10. BR 5: Jan/Feb 1987. SLJ 33: Nov 1986. * SE 51: Apr/May 1987. Intended for students with some background on the Napoleonic wars, this account of the way of life of the British redcoat includes colorful illustrations, a glossary, and a timeline.

Great Britain—1714-1837—Fiction

1547. Calvert, Patricia. Hadder MacColl. Scribner, 1985. 134 p. $13.

Gr 5-9. B 82: Oct 15 1985. + - BC 39: Nov 1985. HB 62: Mar/Apr 1986. + - SLJ 32: Oct 1985. Calvert's effective portrayal of the Jacobite rebellion (1745-1746) centers on Hadder. She and her father cling to their belief that Scotland can be free from England, and they support Bonnie Prince Charlie, but her brother sees that this is a lost cause.

1548. Challoner, Robert. Give Fire! Century Hutchinson; dist. by David & Charles, 1987. 204 p. $19.

Gr 10+. LJ 112: Apr 1 1987. In a rousing sea adventure, Lord Charles Oakshott sails to Egypt to try to thwart Napoleon's plan to control the seas.

1549. Cornwell, Bernard. Sharpe's Regiment: Richard Sharpe and the Invasion of France, June to November 1813. Viking, 1986. 301 p. $17.

Gr 10+. B 82: Jul 1986. * BR 5: Jan/Feb 1987. SLJ 33: Nov 1986. Exciting and action-filled, Cornwell's 7th Richard Sharpe adventure is set in the early days of the campaign against Napoleon.

1550. Cornwell, Bernard. Sharpe's Siege: Richard Sharpe and the Winter Campaign, 1814. Viking, 1987. 319 p. $18.

Gr 10+. B 83: Apr 1 1987. + - BR 6: Nov/Dec 1987. Sharpe and his men must capture a French fort and destroy their supply lines in this fast-paced adventure of the Napoleonic wars. Sequel to Sharpe's Regiment.

1551. Cross, Gilbert B. Hanging at Tyburn, A. Atheneum, 1983. 233 p. $12.

Gr 7-10. + - B 80: Oct 1 1983. + - BC 37: Nov 1983. HB 60: Apr 1984. * SE 48: May 1984. SLJ 30: Dec 1983. Insight into English society in the 18th century is provided in this story about an orphan who works as an actor, miner, and account keeper and becomes involved in efforts to build a cross-country canal.

1552. Garfield, Leon. Smith. Dell, 1967; 1987. 224 p. Pb $5.

Gr 7+. Metzner. HB 43: Dec 1967. LJ 92: Nov 15 1967. This story of a 12-year-old pickpocket presents a vivid picture of the underworld in 18th-century London.

1553. Hendry, Frances. Quest for a Kelpie. Holiday, 1988. 152 p. $13.

Gr 6-10. B 84: Jul 1988. BC 41: May 1988. HB 64: Sep/Oct 1988. SLJ 35: Jun/Jul 1988. Beginning in 1743, this is the story of a Scottish fisherman's daughter who is involved in the rebellion of Bonnie Prince Charlie against the English king. Details of Scottish life and a glossary enhance the story.

1554. Kent, Alexander. Colors Aloft! Putnam, 1986. 286 p. $17.

Gr 9+. B 82: Jul 1986. VOYA 9: Dec 1986. In this high adventure seafaring yarn featuring British Admiral Bolitho in a battle against Napoleon's navy, Kent includes much information about naval life and the difficulties of command.

1555. Kent, Alexander. Success to the Brave. Putnam, 1983. 284 p. $14.

Gr 9+. B 80: Dec 15 1983. SLJ 30: Mar 1984. Following the 1802 Treaty of Amiens between Great Britain and France, Britain sent Richard Bolitho to return the island of San Felipe to the French. This story is told in a novel of sea battles, adventures, and romance.

1556. Wiseman, David. Thimbles. Houghton, 1982. 134 p. $9.

Gr 4-8. * B 78: Mar 15 1982. + - BC 35: Jul 1982. SLJ 28: Mar 1982. A thimble is the agent of time travel that moves Cathy back to 1819 where, as Kate, she becomes involved in a right to vote movement.

Great Britain—1837-1899

1557. Addy, John. Coal and Iron Community in the Industrial Revolution, A. (Then and There Series). Longman, 1978. 108 p. ill. $10.

Gr 9+. SE 46: May 1982. This account of the life and work of British coal miners is enhanced by pictures of homes, tools, and work scenes; maps; and charts.

1558. Gerrard, Roy. Favershams, The. Farrar, 1983. 30 p. ill. $11.

Gr K-4. B 79: Jul 1983. + - BC 37: Sep 1983. HB 59: Oct 1983. * SE 48: May 1984. SLJ 30: Sep 1983. This rhyming verse biography of a Victorian officer in India who returned to England to write and raise his family is notable for its illustrations, which show 19th-century English life in rich detail.

1559. Harris, Sarah. Finding Out About Railways. Batsford; dist. by David & Charles, 1982. 48 p. ill. $12.

Gr 6-10. * BR 1: Jan/Feb 1983. + - SLJ 29: Feb 1983. The development of the railroad in England during the 1800s was opposed by many persons. Harris discusses this in addition to costs, how the railroad affected the movement of freight and the development of towns, and what railroad travel was like in the early days.

1560. Hilcy, Michael. Victorian Working Women: Portraits from Life. Godine, 1980. 142 p. ill. $18.

Gr 10+. LJ 105: Jun 1 1980. Diaries and the growth of the photography business in the late 19th century made possible this highly illustrated account of the lives of working class women during Victorian times.

1561. Lasdun, Susan. Victorians at Home. Viking, 1981. 160 p. ill. $20.

Gr 9+. LJ 106: Nov 1 1981. Lasdun presents fascinating detail of the daily life and culture of upper- and middle-class Britons during the reign of Queen Victoria.

1562. Mitchell, Sally. Victorian Britain: An Encyclopedia. Garland, 1988. 986 p. ill. $125.

Gr 10+. B 85: May 15 1989. BR 8: May/Jun 1989. LJ 114: Mar 15 1989. The people, institutions, events, groups, and issues of Victorian Britain are covered in clearly written articles.

1563. Tann, Jennifer. Children at Work. (History in Focus). Batsford, 1981. 72 p. ill. $14.

Gr 9+. SLJ 28: Mar 1982. Tann includes many pictures in this examination of the working conditions of children in Great Britain from the late 18th century through the 19th century.

1564. Wiseman, David. Jeremy Visick. Houghton, 1981. 170 p. $8.

Gr 5-8. B 77: Jul 1 1981. BC 35: Sep 1981. HB 57: Apr 1981. * SE 46: Apr 1982. SLJ 27: Apr 1981. The harsh life of the Cornish copper miners is revealed as modern-day Matthew, doing a school assignment, seeks to learn about 12-year-old Jeremy Visick, whose body was never recovered after a mine accident.

Great Britain—1837-1899—Fiction

1565. Bloch, Robert. Night of the Ripper, The. Doubleday, 1984. 216 p. $15.

Gr 7+. * B 81: Oct 1 1984. - LJ 109: Sep 15 1984. SE 49: May 1985. VOYA 7: Feb 1985. The details of London street life in Victorian times provide the background for this novel based on the legend of Jack the Ripper.

1566. Carter, Peter. Sentinels, The. Oxford University Press, 1980. 247 p. $11.

Gr 7+. HB 57: Apr 1981. SLJ 28: Nov 1981. VOYA 4: Jun 1981. This dramatic sea adventure centers around Lyapo, a slave aboard a slave vessel, and John Spencer, a British sailor on an antislavery vessel.

1567. Cross, Gillian. Iron Way, The. Oxford University Press, 1979. 130 p. $9.

Gr 6-9. B 76: Jan 1 1980. + - SLJ 26: Feb 1980. The off-duty antics of the laborers (navvies) who were working on the new railroad antagonized the residents of a 19th-century English village and resulted in a tragic confrontation.

1568. Garfield, Leon. Young Nick and Jubilee. Delacorte, 1989. 138 p. $14.

Gr 4-8. B 86: Aug 1989. + - BC 43: Sep 1989. HB 65: Sep/Oct 1989. After orphaned Nick and Jubilee ran away from an orphanage they had to find a "father" to sponsor them so they could enter a charity school. Their story presents a lively picture of 19th-century London.

1569. Overton, Jenny. Ship from Simnel Street, The. Greenwillow, 1986. 144 p. $11.

Gr 6+. B 83: Nov 1 1986. BC 40: Oct 1986. + - BR 5: Nov/Dec 1986. + - SLJ 33: Nov 1986. * VOYA 9: Dec 1986. With her sister and her father gone, Susanah is left to run the family bakery, in this novel that details English life in a 19th-century village.

1570. Schlee, Ann. Ask Me No Questions. Holt, 1982. 228 p. $14.

Gr 5+. * B 78: Jul 1982. BC 35: May 1982. HB 58: Oct 1982. * SE 47: Apr 1983. SLJ 28: Apr 1982. Laura and Barty are sent to stay with a domineering aunt because of a cholera epidemic in London. They discover that next door is a "school" where the children of paupers are mistreated and starved while the headmaster prospers. Based on real events.

Great Britain–1837-1899–Social Life and Customs

1571. Ackroyd, Peter. Dickens' London: An Imaginative Vision. Headline; dist. by David & Charles, 1988. 192 p. ill. $25.

Gr 9+. B 85: Oct 15 1988. This description of London in the mid-1800s includes period photos and passages from Charles Dickens' work.

1572. Drabble, Margaret. For Queen and Country: Britain in the Victorian Age. Seabury, 1978. 144 p. ill. $9.

Gr 9+. HB 55: Apr 1979. * SE 44: Apr 1980. SLJ 25: May 1979. Information on the lives of ordinary British citizens is emphasized in this heavily illustrated work that also discusses Queen Victoria and her reign.

1573. Ford, Colin. Hundred Years Ago: Britain in the 1880s in Words and Photographs. Harvard University Press, 1983. 335 p. ill. $25.

Gr 10+. LJ 108: May 15 1983. This photo-essay examines all aspects of British social and cultural life during the height of the Victorian era.

1574. Jones, Madeline. Growing Up in Regency England. Batsford, 1980. 72 p. ill. $13.

Gr 6-10. SLJ 27: Oct 1980. This brief, illustrated work emphasizes what life was like for children in Regency England. Social life, education, health, work, and play are discussed.

1575. Rawcliffe, Michael. Finding Out About Victorian Towns. Batsford, 1982. 48 p. ill. $12.

Gr 6-10. * BR 1: Jan/Feb 1983. + - SLJ 29: Feb 1983. All aspects of city life in a Victorian town are discussed in this illustrated British publication. Included are education, family life, industry, shopping, sports, transportation, police, and prisons.

Great Britain–1900-1999

1576. Brittain, Vera. Chronicle of Youth: War Diary 1913-1917. Morrow, 1982. 383 p. ill. $16.

Gr 10+. B 79: Sep 1 1982. LJ 107: Jul 1982. Excerpts from Brittain's diaries present a powerful account of a young Englishwoman's experiences during World War I and her growth as a leading pacifist.

1577. Forrester, Helen. Minerva's Stepchild. Beaufort, 1981. 300 p. $11.

Gr 9+. BC 34: May 1981. HB 57: Jun 1981. SLJ 27: Apr 1981. VOYA 4: Aug 1981. Forrester's memories of severe deprivation during the Depression of the 1930s are recounted in a powerful account of poverty.

1578. Goodall, John S. Edwardian Holiday, An. Atheneum, 1979. 64 p. ill. $9.

Gr K+. BC 33: Apr 1980. + - SLJ 26: Feb 1980. This wordless book, which shows a family on holiday at the seashore, is full of detail about life in Edwardian England (1901-1910) and is suitable for all ages.

1579. Marwick, Arthur. Britain in Our Century: Images and Controversies. Thames & Hudson; dist. by Norton, 1985. 224 p. ill. $25.

Gr 9+. B 81: May 15 1985. + - LJ 110: Feb 1 1985. In his photo-essay on the economic, political, and social history of Great Britain since the turn of the century, Marwick shows the importance of photos and their correct interpretation.

1580. Warner, Marina. Crack in the Teacup: Britain in the 20th Century. (Mirror of Britain Series). Houghton, 1980. 160 p. ill. $11.

Gr 8-10. B 76: Mar 15 1980. HB 56: Apr 1980. * SE 45: Apr 1981. SLJ 26: Aug 1980. Social custom and everyday life are interwoven in this history of the events and people of Great Britain during the 20th century.

Great Britain–1900-1999–Fiction

1581. Allan, Mabel Esther. Mills Down Below, The. Dodd, 1981. 205 p. $8.

Gr 6-9. B 77: May 15 1981. BC 34: Jul/Aug 1981. * SE 46: Apr 1982. - SLJ 27: Apr 1981. The changing events of the summer of 1914 force 14-year-old Elinor to examine her family's values and consider women's rights and the class system.

1582. Howker, Janni. Isaac Campion. Greenwillow, 1987. 83 p. $11.

Gr 6+. * B 83: Jul 1987. BC 40: May 1987. * HB 63: Jul/Aug 1987. + - SLJ 33: Jun/Jul 1987. + - VOYA 10: Jun 1987. Following the tragic death of his favored older brother in 1901, 14-year-old Isaac must leave school to help his stern father in his business as a horse dealer. A moving picture of a working class family at the time.

1583. Hunter, Mollie. Hold on to Love. Harper, 1984. 251 p. $12.

Gr 7+. * B 80: May 1 1984. BC 37: Mar 1984. BR 3: May/Jun 1984. + - HB 60: Jun 1984. + - SLJ 30: May 1984. * VOYA 7: Jun 1984. This sequel to A Sound of Chariots continues the semi-autobiographical story of Bridie McShane, who is determined to achieve independence and become a writer. Set in Edinburgh just before World War II.

1584. Magorian, Michele. Back Home. Harper, 1984. 375 p. $14. Lib. ed. $14.

Gr 6-9. B 81: Dec 1 1984. + - BC 38: Nov 1984. + - HB 61: Jan/Feb 1985. VOYA 7: Feb 1985. Rusty spent the years of World War II in Connecticut. Her return to war-devastated

England is a severe shock to a girl who has become accustomed to American comfort and a free-spirited way of life.

1585. Smith, Rukshana. Sumitra's Story. Coward, McCann, 1983. 168 p. $10.

Gr 7-10. + - B 79: Apr 15 1983. B 82: May 15 1986. BC 36: Apr 1983. HB 59: Jun 1983. SLJ 29: Aug 1983. VOYA 6: Jun 1983. After Sumitra's family is forced from their home in Uganda and settle in London, she is torn by her parents' desire to retain traditional ways and her desire to live as other girls do in London in the 1980s.

1586. Temperley, Alan. Murdo's War. Cannongate; dist. by David & Charles, 1989. 256 p. $17.

Gr 9+. B 86: Oct 15 1989. + - BR 8: Nov/Dec 1989. This action-filled adventure set in 1943 centers on Hector, who discovers that a stranger is one of a network of German soldier/spies who intend to arm German POWs when Britain is invaded.

Great Britain–1900-1999–Military History

1587. Brown, Ashley. Undercover Fighters: The British 22nd SAS Regiment. (Villard Military Series). Villard, 1986. 96 p. ill. $5.

Gr 9+. BR 5: Jan 1987. VOYA 10: Apr 1987. A chronology is included in this highly illustrated account of the British 22nd Special Air Services Regiment, an elite British Army unit that was active in World War II and currently fights terrorism.

Great Britain–1900-1999–Social Life and Customs

1588. Bradley, Helen. Queen Who Came to Tea, The. Jonathan Cape; dist. by Merrimack Publishers' Circle, 1979. 32 p. $10.

Gr K+. HB 56: Apr 1980. SLJ 26: Apr 1980. The visit of Queen Alexandria to Manchester in 1901 is the topic of this nostalgic picture book that shows details of city life at the time. Suitable for all ages.

1589. Fyson, Nance Lui. Growing Up in Edwardian England. Batsford, 1980. 72 p. ill. $15.

Gr 7+. + - SLJ 27: Feb 1981. Fyson interviewed persons who were children of varied backgrounds during the reign of Edward VII (1901-1910), and shows what life was like at the time. An abundance of photos is included.

Great Britain–Biographies

1590. Bailey, Anthony. England, First and Last. Viking, 1985. 204 p. $15.

Gr 9+. B 81: Jun 15 1985. LJ 110: Jul 1985. During World War II young Bailey was sent from England to Ohio for safety. He told that story in his book America, Lost and Found. In England, First and Last, he tells of his post-war experiences as he tried, once again, to adjust.

1591. Brendon, Piers. Winston Churchill: A Biography. Harper, 1984. 234 p. ill. $17.

Gr 11+. LJ 109: Sep 15 1984. This short, readable biography captures the essence of Churchill.

1592. Brown, Pam. Florence Nightingale. (People Who Have Helped the World). Gareth Stevens, 1989. 68 p. ill. Lib. ed. $13.

Gr 5-9. B 85: Aug 1989. SLJ 35: Nov 1989. A chronology, glossary, maps, photos, drawings, and quotations all enrich this introduction to England's famous nurse.

1593. Concise Dictionary of National Biography, 1901-1970. Oxford University Press, 1982. 747 p. $35.

Gr 9+. B 80: Jun 15 1984. LJ 107: Sep 1 1982. Persons from all fields are represented in these brief biographies of British notable men and women who died between 1901 and 1970.

1594. Crawford, Anne. Europa Biographical Dictionary of British Women: Over 1,000 Notable Women from Britain's Past. Gale, 1983. 436 p. $55.

Gr 9+. B 81: Dec 1 1984. LJ 109: Jun 1 1984. Brief biographies are included on over 1000 notable deceased British women from all time periods and representing all walks of life.

1595. Faber, Doris. Margaret Thatcher: Britain's "Iron Lady." (Women of Our Time). Viking, 1985. 57 p. ill. $10.

Gr 4-7. B 82: Dec 15 1985. + - BC 39: Oct 1985. * SE 50: Apr/May 1986. - SLJ 32: Dec 1985. This brief introduction to Thatcher emphasizes her rise to political power. Major events of her administration and information on the British government are included.

1596. Foster, Genevieve. World of Captain John Smith. Scribner, 1959; 1978. 416 p. ill. $25.

Gr 5-11. Metzner. * B 56: Jan 15 1960. * HB 36: Feb 1960. * LJ 85: Mar 15 1960. This lively, illustrated work describes the world from 1580 to 1631, the life span of Captain John Smith.

1597. Gerrard, Roy. Sir Francis Drake: His Daring Deeds. Farrar, 1988. 32 p. ill. $13.

Gr K-4. * B 84: Aug 1988. + - BC 41: Jul 1988. HB 65: Jan/Feb 1989. * SLJ 34: Aug 1988. Lilting verses relate the highlights of Drake's life with humor, while watercolors show the detail of Drake's daily life from the time he went to sea at age 10.

1598. Haney, John. Charles Stewart Parnell. (World Leaders Past & Present). Chelsea House, 1989. 111 p. ill. $17.

Gr 8+. BR 8: Nov/Dec 1989. - VOYA 12: Dec 1989. This account of the public and private life of Charles Parnell, the Irish nationalist leader, includes numerous quotes and pictures.

1599. Haney, John. Clement Attlee. (World Leaders Past & Present). Chelsea House, 1987. 112 p. ill. $17.

Gr 9+. + - B 84: Apr 15 1988. Haney's biography of Attlee shows the political situation in Britain from World War I through Attlee's term as prime minister following World War II, when his socialist beliefs helped establish a welfare state. Photos and a chronology are included.

1600. Hook, Jason. Sir Francis Drake. (Great Lives). Bookwright Press; dist. by Watts, 1988. 32 p. ill. $12.

Gr 4-7. B 85: Jan 1 1989. Photos and a glossary enhance this balanced biography that introduces Drake, his explorations, piracy, and involvement in the battle against the Spanish Armada.

1601. Hughes, Libby. Madam Prime Minister. Dillon Press, 1989. 144 p. ill. $12.

Gr 3-7. D 06: Nov 1 1989. Photos enrich this balanced introduction to the life and political activities of Margaret Thatcher, the British prime minister.

1602. Keller, Mollie. Winston Churchill. (Impact Biography). Watts, 1984. 120 p. ill. $9.

Gr 6+. B 80: Jun 1 1984. BR 3: Sep/Oct 1984. SLJ 30: Aug 1984. VOYA 7: Dec 1984. Emphasis is on the development of Churchill's character and on his political life in this clearly written, illustrated biography.

1603. Longford, Elizabeth. Eminent Victorian Women. Knopf; dist. by Random, 1981. 256 p. ill. $23.

Gr 9+. B 78: Oct 15 1981. LJ 106: Nov 1 1981. SLJ 28: Apr 1982. Following an introduction to the status of 19th-century women are biographies of noted women, including Florence Nightingale, the Brontes, Annie Besant, Josephine Butler, and James Barry, a woman who, disguised as a man, served as a military physician.

1604. MacDonald, Fiona. Drake and the Armada. Hampstead Press, 1988. 47 p. map. $13.

Gr 6-9. + - SLJ 35: Apr 1989. MacDonald's fictionalized biography presents an account of Francis Drake's activities from the British point of view.

1605. Magill, Frank N. Great Lives from History: British and Commonwealth Series. Salem Press, 1987. 5 vol. $325.

Gr 7+. B 84: Jun 1 1988. Great Lives includes nearly 500 alphabetically arranged biographies that cover more than 1000 years of British history. Entries cover persons from all walks of life and include vital statistics, achievements, early life, life's work, and a bibliography.

1606. McGuirk, Carol. Benjamin Disraeli. (World Leaders Past & Present). Chelsea House, 1987. 112 p. ill. $17.

Gr 6+. B 83: Aug 1987. BR 7: May/Jun 1988. SLJ 34: Nov 1987. Quotations, a chronology, and illustrations augment this account of the personal and political life of the 19th-century British prime minister.

1607. Oxbury, Harold. Great Britons: Twentieth Century Lives. Oxford University Press, 1985. 370 p. ill. $30.

Gr 9+. B 82: May 1 1986. LJ 111: Feb 15 1986. Based on the Dictionary of National Biography, these brief biographies of British subjects who died between 1915 and 1980 are illustrated by photos, drawings, and cartoons, and indexed by occupation.

1608. Scott, Ronald McNair. Robert the Bruce: King of Scots. Peter Bedrick; dist. by Publishers Group West, 1989. 253 p. $24.

Gr 10+. B 85: May 1 1989. + - BR 8: Nov/Dec 1989. The history of Scotland from 1285 to 1329 is told in this biography of Robert the Bruce, King of Scotland.

1609. Shearman, Deidre. David Lloyd George. (World Leaders Past & Present). Chelsea House, 1987. 112 p. ill. $17.

Gr 7+. B 84: Jan 15 1988. David Lloyd George is introduced in this balanced, illustrated biography. He was an anti-imperialist who served as prime minister during World War I.

1610. Shor, Donnali. Florence Nightingale. (Why They Became Famous). Silver Burdett, 1987. 64 p. ill. Lib. ed. $14. Pb $7.

Gr 4-7. BR 6: Nov/Dec 1987. SLJ 33: Jun/Jul 1987. The reasons for Nightingale's commitment to health care and the difficulties she faced are shown in this balanced biography of the founder of modern nursing.

1611. Sinclair, Andrew. Sir Walter Raleigh and the Age of Discovery. Penguin, 1984. 127 p. ill. Pb $8.

Gr 9+. B 81: Nov 15 1984. This biography of Walter Raleigh, captain of Queen Elizabeth's guard, shows his activities within the context of his time.

1612. Stone, Norman. Makers of English History, The. Macmillan, 1987. 288 p. ill. $40.

Gr 9+. B 83: Jun 1 1987. Stone's illustrated work includes 45 essays about British leaders in all disciplines from the 7th to the 20th centuries.

1613. Tames, Richard. Makers of Modern Britain. Batsford; dist. by David & Charles, 1982. 168 p. ill. $25.

Gr 6+. * BR 2: May/Jun 1983. + - SLJ 29: Mar 1983. These brief biographies of over 100 noted Britains in all fields since 1700 include quotes, pictures, and information about the subjects' names and monuments to them.

1614. Turner, Dorothy. Florence Nightingale. (Great Lives). Bookwright Press; dist. by Watts, 1986. 32 p. ill. $10.

Gr 4-7. B 83: Jan 1 1987. SLJ 33: Feb 1987. Turner describes 19th-century Victorian society, in which nursing was not an honorable profession for women, and Nightingale's single-minded determination to aid the suffering.

1615. Wilson, John. Fairfax: A Life of Thomas, Lord Fairfax, Captain-General of All the Parliament's Forces in the English Civil War. Watts, 1985. 215 p. ill. $18.

Gr 10+. B 82: Sep 1 1985. - BR 4: Mar/Apr 1986. VOYA 9: Jun 1986. During the English civil war in the 1640s Thomas Fairfax was the commander of parliamentary forces. Wilson covers his military exploits and his efforts to find a middle ground between extremists on both sides. Maps are included.

1616. Young, Hugo. Iron Lady: A Biography of Margaret Thatcher. Farrar, 1989. 570 p. ill. $25.

Gr 10+. B 86: Sep 1 1989. LJ 114: Sep 1 1989. Young's balanced biography covers the evolution of Thatcher's political philosophy and the events of her administration as prime minister.

Great Britain–Colonies

1617. Kobler, Evelyn. United Kingdom Dependencies. Chelsea House, 1987. 126 p. ill. $12.

Gr 6-9. SLJ 34: Jan 1988. This informative and easy-to-read introduction covers the history and current status of British dependencies, including the Falklands and Pitcairn Island.

Great Britain–England

1618. Greene, Carol. England. (Enchantment of the World). Childrens Press, 1982. 127 p. ill. $10.

Gr 4-6. + - B 79: Apr 1 1983. + - BC 36: Mar 1983. + - SLJ 29: Apr 1983. This colorfully illustrated introduction to England covers history, noted persons, geography, resources, culture, and economy.

Great Britain–Espionage and Spies

1619. Cecil, Robert. Divided Life: A Biography of Donald Maclean. Morrow, 1989. 263 p. ill. $19.

Gr 10+. B 85: Mar 1 1989. * LJ 114: Feb 15 1989. Cecil explores Maclean's espionage career and examines the causes for his defection.

1620. Knightley, Phillip. Master Spy, The. Knopf, 1989. 304 p. ill. $20.

Gr 9+. B 85: Feb 1 1989. LJ 114: Apr 15 1989. Knightley interviewed Harold Philby before his death to add a personal element to this account of the life and activities of one of history's most successful spies.

1621. West, Nigel. Molehunt: Searching for Soviet Spies in MI5. Morrow, 1989. 320 p. ill. $20.

Gr 9+. B 85: Mar 1 1989. LJ 114: Mar 15 1989. West explores the post-World War II espionage of Soviet double agents and the defection of Donald Maclean and Guy Burgess.

Great Britain–Falkland Islands

1622. Strange, Ian J. Falklands: South Atlantic Islands. Dodd, 1985. 160 p. ill. $16.

Gr 6-9. B 82: Oct 15 1985. + - BC 39: Nov 1985. HB 61: Nov/Dec 1985. * SE 50: Apr/May 1986. + - SLJ 32: Oct 1985. * VOYA 9: Apr 1986. Strange has worked as a naturalist in the Falklands for over 20 years. He presents a history of the area and a well-illustrated view of the geography and wildlife.

Great Britain–Fiction

1623. Anno, Mitsumasa. Anno's Britain. Philomel, 1982. 42 p. ill. $11.

Gr 5-8. B 78: Jul 1982. * BC 35: Jun 1982. HB 58: Aug 1982. * HB 62: Nov 1986. * SE 47: Apr 1983. SLJ 29: Sep 1982. Anno's blue-clad wanderer meets historical and fictional characters and views British landmarks in this wordless book suitable for all ages.

1624. Rutherfurd, Edward. Sarum: The Novel of England. Crown, 1987. 897 p. $20.

Gr 9+. B 83: Jul 1987. LJ 112: Sep 1987. The sweep of British history is recounted in this rich tale of several families who lived near Salisbury from the days of Stonehenge to 1985.

Great Britain–Kings, Queens, Rulers, etc.

1625. Brooks, Polly Schoyer. Queen Eleanor: Independent Spirit of the Medieval World. Lippincott; dist. by Harper, 1983. 183 p. ill. $10. Lib. ed. $10.

Gr 6-9. B 80: Sep 15 1983. B 82: Sep 15 1985. BC 37: Jan 1984. BR 3: May 1984. HB 60: Feb 1984. * SE 48: May 1984. SLJ 30: Dec 1983. VOYA 6: Dec 1983. This balanced biography recounts the life of an English queen who had a great impact on the politics and culture of her time. She was the wife of King Henry I (ruled 1100-1135) and mother of King Richard the Lion Heart.

1626. Cannon, John. Oxford Illustrated History of the British Monarchy, The. Oxford University Press, 1988. 727 p. ill. $40.

Gr 9+. B 85: Nov 15 1988. The development of the British monarchy since post-Roman times is presented in this well-illustrated work that has several useful appendices.

1627. Chancellor, John. Life and Times of Edward I, The. Weidenfeld & Nicholson; dist. by Biblio Distribution Center, 1981. 224 p. ill. $18.

Gr 9+. B 77: Jun 15 1981. This balanced and well-illustrated introduction to Edward I, who ruled from 1272 to 1307, shows his strengths as a military leader and lawmaker, and his weaknesses in personal relationships.

1628. Donaldson, Frances Lonsdale. Edward VIII: The Road to Abdication. Abridged ed. Lippincott, 1980. 192 p. ill. $13.

Gr 9+. B 76: Dec 1 1979. HB 56: Feb 1980. This is an abridged and illustrated edition of Donaldson's authoritative biography of the king who, forced to choose between his throne and the woman he loved, abdicated and spent his life in exile.

1629. Dwyer, Frank. James I. (World Leaders Past & Present). Chelsea House, 1988. 112 p. ill. $17.

Gr 6-10. B 84: Jun 15 1988. On the abdication of his mother, Mary, Queen of Scots, James became King of Scotland; on the death of Elizabeth I he became King of England also, and ruled from 1603 to 1625. This informative, illustrated overview provides a sense of the times.

1630. Fraser, Antonia Pakenham. Royal Charles: Charles II and the Restoration. Knopf; dist. by Random, 1979. 560 p. ill. $17.

Gr 10+. B 76: Dec 1 1979. B 82: Dec 1 1985. This detailed biography is a readable account of the life of a frivolous young king who, after returning from exile, became a conscientious ruler and ruled from 1660 to 1685.

1631. Gibb, Christopher. Richard the Lionheart and the Crusades. (Life and Times). Bookwright Press; dist. by Watts, 1985. 60 p. ill. $11.

Gr 4-6. B 82: Feb 15 1986. Emphasis is on the purpose and realities of the Crusades in this work that introduces Richard I, who ruled from 1189 to 1199.

1632. Goodrich, Norma Lorre. King Arthur (475-542). Watts, 1986. 406 p. ill. $22.

Gr 10+. * BR 5: Sep/Oct 1986. + - LJ 111: Feb 1 1986. The author has searched ancient manuscripts to provide an account of the life and accomplishments of Arthur, the legendary 6th-century king of Britain.

1633. Gregg, Pauline. King Charles I, University of California Press, 1984. 496 p. ill. $27.

Gr 11+. B 80: May 15 1984. B 82: Dec 1985. HT 17: May 1984. LJ 108: Jun 1 1983. In a thorough and balanced biography, Gregg analyzes the life and reign of Charles I who ruled from 1625 to 1649. He tried to preserve his heritage when society was ripe for change.

1634. Hallam, Elizabeth. Plantagenet Chronicles, The. Weidenfeld & Nicholson, 1986. 352 p. ill. $30.

Gr 9+. B 83: Nov 15 1986. LJ 111: Dec 1986. This handsomely illustrated account of the reigns of Henry II, Richard the Lion Heart, and John (1154-1216), covers the political, social, and cultural events of the time.

1635. Hibbert, Christopher. Court of St. James's: The Monarch at Work from Victoria to Elizabeth II. Morrow, 1980. 254 p. ill. $13.

Gr 10+. LJ 105: May 15 1980. Court tradition, royal work habits, ceremonies, finances, and personal life are covered in this guide to British royalty from Victoria to Elizabeth II.

1636. Kaplan, Zoe Coralnik. Eleanor of Aquitaine. (World Leaders Past & Present). Chelsea House, 1986. 115 p. ill. $17.

Gr 6-10. B 83: Feb 1 1987. Eleanor of Aquitaine, queen consort of Henry II, one of the 12th century's most important persons, is the focus of this lavishly illustrated work. At a time when women were considered property, her strong will changed society.

1637. Lees-Milne, James. Last Stuarts: British Royalty in Exile. Scribner, 1984. 244 p. ill. $18.

Gr 9+. B 83: Jul 1984. LJ 109: Jul 1984. This chronicle begins in 1688 with the exile of James II to Italy and follows his descendants for over 200 years, showing how each did, or did not, further the family claim to the throne.

1638. Longford, Elizabeth. Royal House of Windsor, The. Rev. ed. Crown, 1984. 296 p. ill. $17.

Gr 9+. B 81: Nov 15 1984. Longford covers the reigns of George V, Edward VIII, George VI, and Elizabeth II and includes a good selection of photos and a genealogical table.

1639. Luke, Mary. Nine Days Queen: A Portrait of Lady Jane Grey. Morrow, 1986. 408 p. $19.

Gr 9+. B 82: May 15 1986. LJ 111: Jun 1986. Manipulated by her power-seeking family and friends, Lady Jane was proclaimed queen, but was quickly replaced by Mary Tudor. Luke presents a clear picture of Lady Jane her intrigue-filled times, and her brief reign in 1553.

1640. Magnus, Philip. King Edward the Seventh. Penguin, 1964. 528 p. Pb $6.

Gr 10+. B 82: Dec 1 1985. LJ 89: Jun 1 1964. Over 1200 quotes are included in this biography of the much maligned King who ruled from 1901 to 1910. Edward VII was the son of Victoria and was active in international affairs during her reign.

1641. Matthews, John. Boadicea: Warrior Queen of the Celts. (Heroes and Warriors). Firebird; dist. by Sterling, 1988. 48 p. ill. Pb $8.

Gr 9+. SLJ 35: Oct 1989. Boadicea was queen of the Iceni, a British tribe who revolted against their Roman rulers around 60 A.D. Boadicea committed suicide to avoid capture, but the rebellion led to improved conditions.

1642. May, Robin. Alfred the Great and the Saxons. (Life and Times). Bookwright Press; dist. by Watts, 1985. 59 p. ill. $11.

Gr 4-7. B 82: Sep 1 1985. - SLJ 32: Sep 1985. Saxon history from the 4th to the 11th centuries is introduced in this illustrated British publication.

1643. Plowden, Alison. Lady Jane Grey and the House of Suffolk. Watts, 1986. 201 p. ill. $16.

Gr 9+. B 82: Feb 15 1986. + - BR 5: Nov/Dec 1986. LJ 111: Feb 15 1986. SLJ 33: Sep 1986. VOYA 9: Aug/Oct 1986. As great-niece of Henry VIII, Lady Jane Grey reigned as a queen for 9 days before she was replaced by Mary Tudor and executed at the age of 16. This richly detailed account of her family includes numerous photos.

1644. Roll, Winifred. Mary I: The History of an Unhappy Tudor Queen. Prentice-Hall, 1980. 266 p. ill. $10.

Gr 7+. B 77: Sep 1 1980. HB 56: Oct 1980. SLJ 27: Mar 1981. Following the divorce of her parents, Henry VIII and Catherine of Aragon, Mary was a mistreated child. As queen (1553-1558), poor advice and her efforts to return England to Catholicism earned her the label "Bloody Mary." A clearly written biography.

1645. Rose, Kenneth. King George V. Knopf, 1984. 514 p. ill. $20.

Gr 11+. * B 80: Mar 1 1984. B 82: Dec 1 1985. LJ 109: Feb 15 1984. Rose's detailed, anecdotal biography explains how George V, who was unenthusiastically received as a new king, changed the public perception of the monarchy to such an extent that his death was deeply mourned. He reigned from 1910 to 1936.

1646. Ross, Josephine. Monarchy of Britain, The. Morrow, 1982. 192 p. ill. $17.

Gr 9+. B 79: Jan 15 1983. LJ 108: Jan 15 1983. This pictorial introduction to all British monarchs since 1066 is rich with anecdotes. It shows how the monarchy has evolved and succeeded.

1647. Seward, Desmond. Henry V: The Scourge of God. Viking, 1988. 239 p. ill. $20.

Gr 9+. B 84: Mar 15 1988. + - LJ 113: May 1 1988. Seward presents Henry V as an active king who was determined to legitimize his reign by military victory over France. He ruled from 1413 to 1422.

1648. Seward, Desmond. Richard III: England's Black Legend. Watts, 1984. 220 p. ill. $19.

Gr 10+. B 80: Feb 15 1984. HT 19: May 1986. + - LJ 109: May 1 1984. Richard III reigned 1483-1485. Seward's colorful biography acknowledges the conflicting legends, but concludes that Richard was a terrifying and evil ruler.

1649. Stewart, Bob. Macbeth: Scotland's Warrior King. (Heroes and Warriors). Firebird; dist. by Sterling, 1988. 48 p. ill. Pb $8.

Gr 9+. SLJ 35: Oct 1989. Shakespeare's play is based on a flawed biography of the Scottish king (1040-1057). Stewart's account separates fact from legend and presents a picture of life at that time.

1650. Williamson, David. Debrett's Kings and Queens of Britain. Salem House; dist. by Merrimack Publishers' Circle, 1986. 240 p. ill. $28.

Gr 9+. B 83: Nov 1 1986. This illustrated survey of British rulers since before Roman times covers their personalities and leadership styles, and explains the times in which each lived.

Great Britain–Kings, Queens, Rulers, etc.–Elizabeth I

1651. Erickson, Carolly. First Elizabeth, The. Summit; dist. by Simon & Schuster, 1983. 450 p. ill. $20.

Gr 9+. B 79: Feb 1 1983. B 82: Dec 1 1985. LJ 108: Mar 1 1983. Erickson presents a rich and vital account of the public and private lives of Elizabeth I who ruled England from 1558 to 1603.

1652. Plowden, Alison. Elizabeth Regina: The Age of Triumph 1588-1603. Times Books, 1980. 224 p. ill. $13.

Gr 9+. B 76: May 15 1980. LJ 105: Jun 1 1980. This last of Plowden's volumes on Elizabeth I focuses on the events from the Spanish Armada to her death.

1653. Pringle, Roger. Portrait of Elizabeth I: In the Words of the Queen and Her Contemporaries. Barnes & Noble, 1980. 128 p. ill. $11.

Gr 9+. B 77: Dec 1 1980. Excerpts from contemporary documents present a picture of Elizabeth I, her character, appearance, leisure activities, and strength as a monarch (1558-1603). Includes illustrations.

1654. Ridley, Jasper. Elizabeth I: The Shrewdness of Virtue. Viking, 1988. 356 p. ill. $25.

Gr 9+. B 84: Dec 15 1987. * LJ 113: Jan 1988. A balanced, carefully researched, and readable biography of Elizabeth I that puts her many accomplishments into perspective.

1655. Strachey, Lytton. Elizabeth and Essex. Harcourt, 1928. 296 p. ill. Pb $7.

Gr 11+. B 25: Jan 1929. B 82: Dec 1 1985. This lively biography emphasizes the personal relationships of the queen and members of her court.

1656. Turner, Dorothy. Queen Elizabeth I. (Great Lives). Bookwright Press; dist. by Watts, 1987. 32 p. ill. $11.

Gr 5-7. + - B 84: Dec 15 1987. Turner shows how Elizabeth I influenced England and the world. Photos, a chronology, and a glossary are included.

1657. White-Thomson, Stephen. Elizabeth I and Tudor England. (Life and Times). Bookwright Press; dist. by Watts, 1985. 60 p. ill. $11.

Gr 4-8. + - SLJ 32: Apr 1986. Life in Elizabethan England is the focus of this book that also summarizes the life of Elizabeth I.

1658. Zamoyska, Betka. Queen Elizabeth I. (Leaders Series). McGraw-Hill, 1981. 69 p. ill. $8.

Gr 6+. B 78: Nov 15 1981. + - SLJ 28: Mar 1982. Emphasis is on the queen's political role, but this well-illustrated work also presents a picture of life at court.

Great Britain–Kings, Queens, Rulers, etc.–Elizabeth II

1659. Campbell, Judith. Queen Elizabeth II: A Biography. Crown, 1980. 184 p. ill. $13.

Gr 9+. B 76: May 1 1980. LJ 105: Apr 15 1980. This balanced, general biography of Elizabeth II emphasizes her contributions to the stability of the monarchy at a time of great change. Numerous photos are included.

1660. Hamilton, Alan. Queen Elizabeth II. (Profiles). Hamilton; dist. by David & Charles, 1983. 64 p. ill. $8.

Gr 3-6. + - B 79: May 15 1983. BC 36: Jul/Aug 1983. SLJ 29: May 1983. Little-known facts add interest to this balanced introduction to Queen Elizabeth II. Pen-and-ink illustrations are included.

1661. Longford, Elizabeth. Queen: The Life of Elizabeth II. Knopf; Ballantine, 1983. 395 p. ill. $20. Pb $5.

Gr 9+. B 82: Dec 1 1985. LJ 108: Oct 1 1983. This lively biography of the queen is based on interviews with family and friends and written by a member of the aristocracy.

1662. Turner, Dorothy. Queen Elizabeth II. (Great Lives). Bookwright Press; dist. by Watts, 1985. 32 p. ill. $10.

Gr 4-6. + - B 82: Jan 15 1986. + - SLJ 32: Apr 1986. This chronological account of the life of Elizabeth II includes many photos, a family tree, and a glossary.

Great Britain–Kings, Queens, Rulers, etc.–Fiction

1663. George, Margaret. Autobiography of Henry VIII: With Notes by His Fool, Will Somers. St. Martin's, 1986. 960 p. $20.

Gr 10+. B 82: Jul 1986. LJ 111: Sep 15 1986. This massive, well-researched novel tells Henry VIII's story from his own viewpoint, showing how events changed his nature. Interspersed are comments by his faithful jester, who saw his weaknesses.

1664. Giardina, Denise. Good King Harry. Harper, 1984. 393 p. $16.

Gr 10+. B 80: May 15 1984. LJ 109: Apr 1 1984. Henry V (1387-1422) led an army that defeated the French at Agincourt. This fictional biography presents an accurate account of his life and medieval English society.

1665. Harnett, Cynthia. Stars of Fortune. Lerner, 1984. 220 p. ill. $10.

Gr 7-9. B 53: Feb 1 1957. B 81: Sep 15 1984. * HB 33: Feb 1957. The home of George Washington's English ancestors is the setting for this story about Queen Elizabeth I and her half-sister, Queen Mary.

1666. Hunter, Mollie. You Never Knew Her As I Did! Harper, 1981. 219 p. $10. Lib. ed. $10.

Gr 5+. B 78: Sep 1 1981. BC 35: Nov 1981. HB 57: Dec 1981. * SE 46: Apr 1982. * SLJ 28: Oct 1981. VOYA 4: Dec 1981. In the mid-16th century Mary, Queen of Scots was held captive in an effort to force her abdication. This story, told through the eyes of a 14-year-old boy, presents a strong account of the customs and political intrigue of those days.

1667. Kay, Susan. Legacy. Crown, 1986. 648 p. $18.

Gr 9+. B 82: Feb 15 1986. LJ 111: Apr 1 1986. A lively and detailed novel about Elizabeth I and the personalities and events of her reign.

1668. Luke, Mary. Ivy Crown, The. Doubleday, 1984. 456 p. $18.

Gr 10+. B 80: Mar 1 1984. LJ 109: Mar 1 1984. Luke's fictionalized biography of Catherine, the last of Henry VIII's six wives, presents an accurate picture of the queen, and a lively overview of court life.

1669. Penman, Sharon Kay. Falls the Shadow. Holt, 1988. 580 p. $19.

Gr 9+. B 84: Mar 15 1988. BR 7: May/Jun 1988. LJ 113: Jul 1988. SLJ 35: Sep 1988. The complex reign of Henry III included a Welsh uprising and a power struggle between the king and the aristocracy. Penman's novel includes strong characterizations and rich detail of the times.

1670. Plaidy, Jean. Battle of the Queens, The. (Plantagenet Saga). Putnam, 1981. 366 p. $11.

Gr 9+. B 77: Jul 1981. The fifth of the author's Plantagenet saga concerns Isabella, the widow of the evil King John, and the political and romantic intrigues between the English and French courts.

1671. Plaidy, Jean. Myself My Enemy. (Queens of England Series). Putnam, 1984. 396 p. $14.

Gr 9+. B 80: Oct 15 1983. The religious and political conflicts of 17th-century England are vividly recounted in this fictional first-person narrative by Henriette Marie, wife of Charles I.

1672. Plaidy, Jean. Passage to Pontefract. (Plantagenet Saga). Putnam, 1982. 366 p. ill. $13.

Gr 10+. B 79: Sep 1 1982. The rivalry between cousins Richard II and Henry IV is the focus of the 10th novel in the Plantagenet Saga.

1673. Plaidy, Jean. Plantagenet Prelude. Putnam, 1980. 333 p. ill. $11.

Gr 9+. B 76: Jun 1 1980. + - LJ 105: May 1 1980. A lively and colorful novel, based on the romance of King Henry II and his consort, Eleanor of Aquitaine.

1674. Plaidy, Jean. Princess of Celle, The. Putnam, 1985. 335 p. $16.

Gr 10+. B 81: Feb 1 1985. A victim of court intrigues, Sophia Dorothea, wife of the boorish George I, was imprisoned for 32 years.

1675. Plaidy, Jean. Queen in Waiting. Putnam, 1985. 399 p. $16.

Gr 9+. B 82: Oct 1 1985. The details of daily life and intrigue in the court of George I, at the turn of the 18th century, are soon in Plaidy's novel, which centers on the schemes of the king's son and daughter-in-law, Caroline.

1676. Plaidy, Jean. Queen of this Realm. (Queens of England Series). Putnam, 1985. 576 p. $16.

Gr 10+. + - B 81: Oct 15 1984. LJ 110: Feb 1 1985. A detailed story of the life and reign of Elizabeth I, presented in the form of a fictionalized memoir.

1677. Plaidy, Jean. Revolt of the Eaglets, The. Putnam, 1980. 330 p. $11.

Gr 9+. B 76: Jul 15 1980. Political plots and domestic squabbles marked the reign of Henry II, and Plaidy tells the story with a deft touch.

1678. Plaidy, Jean. Star of Lancaster, The. (Plantagenet Saga). Putnam, 1982. 320 p. ill. $13.

Gr 10+. B 79: Sep 1 1982. Detailed scenes of splendor at court and heroics on the battlefield enliven this account of royal intrigue and adventure involving Henry IV and his son, Henry V.

1679. Plaidy, Jean. Sun in Splendor, The. (Plantagenet Saga). Putnam, 1983. 365 p. $13.

Gr 10+. B 80: Dec 15 1983. In this final volume of the Plantagenet Saga Plaidy presents the story of the glamorous Edward IV and his brother, Richard, who lost the throne to Henry Tudor.

1680. Plaidy, Jean. Victoria Victorious. Putnam, 1986. 560 p. $18.

Gr 10+. LJ 111: Jan 1986. Plaidy's absorbing novel of the reign of Victoria shows a woman of powerful affection and antipathies.

1681. Plaidy, Jean. Vow on the Heron, The. (Plantagenet Saga). Putnam, 1982. 352 p. $13.

Gr 9+. B 78: May 1 1982. A richly detailed account of the events, personalities, and passions of the reign of Edward III, whose death in 1399 marked the beginning of the Hundred Years' War.

1682. Smith, Anthony C. H. Lady Jane. Holt, 1985. 186 p. $13.

Gr 9+. + - BR 4: Mar/Apr 1986. + - VOYA 8: Feb 1986. Events center around the marriage and 9-day reign of Lady Jane Grey, who was used by her family and put to death by political manipulators.

1683. Todd, Catherine. Bond of Honour. St. Martin's, 1982. 223 p. $12.

Gr 9+. B 78: Mar 1 1982. LJ 107: Feb 15 1982. SLJ 28: Feb 1982. The mental, political, and military battles of William the Conqueror in his struggle to become king of England are recorded in this dramatic novel.

Great Britain–Kings, Queens, Rulers, etc.–George VI

1684. Judd, Denis. King George VI, 1895-1952. Watts, 1983. 266 p. ill. $19.

Gr 10+. B 79: Apr 15 1983. B 82: Dec 1 1985. George VI, who came to power with the abdication of his brother, Edward VIII, was a modest king who restored dignity and confidence to the throne during his reign from 1936 to 1952. His story is told in this balanced and perceptive biography.

1685. Longford, Elizabeth. Queen Mother, The. Morrow, 1981. 184 p. ill. $18.

Gr 9+. LJ 106: Oct 1 1981. Longford's warm biography of the "Queen Mum," queen consort to George VI and mother of Elizabeth II, is illustrated with colorful photos.

1686. Morrow, Anne. Queen Mother, The. Stein & Day, 1985. 230 p. ill. $18.

Gr 10+. B 82: Dec 1 1985. LJ 110: Mar 1 1985. The popular "Queen Mum," as consort of King George VI, was important to the British following Edward's abdication and during World War II. This informative biography includes numerous photos.

1687. Mortimer, Penelope. Queen Elizabeth, a Portrait of the Queen Mother. St. Martin's, 1986. 288 p. ill. $18.

Gr 10+. B 82: Apr 15 1986. LJ 111: May 15 1986. Mortimer presents a balanced view of the popular wife of George VI and mother of Queen Elizabeth II, showing her contributions to the nation as well as her usually overlooked quirks of personality.

Great Britain–Kings, Queens, Rulers, etc.–Henry VIII

1688. Dwyer, Frank. Henry VIII. (World Leaders Past & Present). Chelsea House, 1987. 112 p. ill. $17.

Gr 6-10. B 84: Jan 15 1988. - SLJ 34: Mar 1988. In recounting the life of Henry VIII who ruled from 1509 to 1547, Dwyer shows his impact on the nation. A chronology and a glossary are included.

1689. Erickson, Carolly. Great Harry. Summit, 1980. 455 p. ill. $13.

Gr 9+. B 76: Apr 1 1980. + - LJ 105: May 1 1980. The personal life of Henry VIII is the focus of this lively biography of the English king, who changed from "prince charming" to tyrant.

1690. Erickson, Carolly. Mistress Anne. Summit, 1984. 277 p. $20.

Gr 11+ * B 80: Apr 1 1984. B 82: Dec 1 1985. LJ 109: May 1 1984. The life of the audacious Anne Boleyn, and the reasons for the attraction between her and Henry VIII, are revealed in this readable biography.

1691. Lofts, Norah Robinson. Anne Boleyn. Coward, McCann, 1979. 192 p. ill. $16.

Gr 9+. B 76: Jan 1 1980. + - LJ 104: Dec 15 1979. SLJ 26: Jan 1980. Attractive illustrations enrich this readable account of the personal and political maneuvering by Henry VIII to make Anne Boleyn his wife, and then later to dispose of her.

1692. Ridley, Jasper. Henry VIII. Viking, 1985. 473 p. ill. $25.

Gr 9+. B 81: Jun 15 1985. LJ 110: Jul 1985. Ridley is a prize-winning English historian. His biography of Henry VIII shows the influence of this calculating and tyrannical ruler on English government and everyday life.

1693. Starkey, David. Reign of Henry VIII: Personalities and Politics. Watts, 1986. 174 p. ill. $18.

Gr 10+. B 82: Apr 15 1986. + - BR 5: Sep 1986. + - LJ 111: Mar 1 1986. VOYA 9: Aug/Oct 1986. For the advanced student, an examination of the reign of Henry VIII which argues that the king was more manipulated than manipulator.

1694. Turner, Dorothy. Henry VIII. (Great Lives). Bookwright Press; dist. by Watts, 1988. 32 p. $12.

Gr 4-7. B 85: Jan 1 1989. SLJ 35: Jan 1989. This concise biography that presents the highlights of the life of Henry VIII and the formation of the Church of England is enriched by numerous illustrations, a list of important dates, and a glossary.

Great Britain–Kings, Queens, Rulers, etc.–Mary, Queen of Scots

1695. Fraser, Antonia. Mary Queen of Scots. Dell, 1969. 613 p. ill. Pb $6.

Gr 9+. B 82: Dec 1 1985. B 82: Jan 1 1986. Fraser's detailed biography captures a sense of the time and place and clearly shows the vibrant personality of Mary, Queen of Scots (1542-1587), whose personal life, and efforts to force Scotland to become Catholic, resulted in the loss of her throne.

1696. Stepanek, Sally. Mary, Queen of Scots. (World Leaders Past & Present). Chelsea House, 1987. 111 p. ill. $17.

Gr 6-10. + - B 83: Jun 1 1987. + - SLJ 34: Dec 1987. Illustrations and quotes augment this detailed biography of Mary, Queen of Scots, who struggled to keep Scotland Catholic.

1697. Turner, Dorothy. Mary, Queen of Scots. (Great Lives). Bookwright Press; dist. by Watts, 1988. 32 p. $12.

Gr 5-7. B 85: Jan 1 1989. This concise biography that presents the highlights of the life of Mary, Queen of Scots is enriched by numerous illustrations, a list of important dates, and a glossary.

Great Britain–Kings, Queens, Rulers, etc.–Victoria

1698. Plowden, Alison. Young Victoria, The. Stein & Day, 1981. 225 p. $13.

Gr 10+. B 77: Mar 1 1981. LJ 106: Feb 1 1981. Victoria was born 5th in line to the throne, but was crowned at age 18. Plowden shows the development of her character and the effects of becoming public property. She was queen from 1837 to 1901.

1699. Shearman, Deirdre. Queen Victoria. (World Leaders Past & Present). Chelsea House, 1987. 115 p. ill. $17.

Gr 6-10. SLJ 33: May 1987. This balanced, illustrated biography that presents the queen within the context of her time is enriched by the use of quotations. Victoria ruled from 1837 to 1901.

1700. Strachey, Lytton. Queen Victoria. Harcourt, 1921. 434 p. ill. Pb $6.

Gr 10+. B 17: Jul 1921. B 82: Dec 1 1985. This anecdotal biography is full of interesting trivia about Victoria's personal life.

Great Britain–Military History

1701. Smurthwaite, David. Ordnance Survey Complete Guide to the Battlefields of Britain, The. Rev. ed. Michael Joseph; dist. by Viking, 1987. 224 p. ill. Pb $15.

Gr 9+. B 84: Feb 15 1988. Smurthwaite explores the battlefields of Britain from Roman times through World War II. Maps, photos, and a variety of other illustrations enhance the text which presents both political and military information.

Great Britain–Northern Ireland

1702. Bartlett, Jonathan. Northern Ireland. Wilson, 1983. 167 p. Pb $7.

Gr 9+. BR 2: Nov/Dec 1983. Irish history from 1600 is presented, with emphasis on the conflict between the quest for home rule and British rule. Bartlett presents a balanced view, showing the role of the mass media in perpetuating fallacies.

1703. Buckland, Patrick. History of Northern Ireland, A. Holmes and Meier, 1981. 195 p. map. $23.

Gr 11+. HT 16: Feb 1983. This useful overview of the history of Northern Ireland provides background to its current political problems for advanced students.

1704. Cahill, Mary Jane. Northern Ireland. Chelsea House, 1987. 109 p. ill. $12.

Gr 5-8. + - SLJ 34: Aug 1988. This brief introduction to the history, culture, economy, and politics of Northern Ireland is illustrated.

1705. Conroy, John. Belfast Diary: War as a Way of Life. Beacon; dist. by Harper, 1987. 218 p. $19.

Gr 10+. B 84: Nov 15 1987. LJ 112: Nov 1 1987. Conroy is a journalist who spent 5 years in Northern Ireland. His first-hand account focuses on the desensitizing effects of sustained violence on ordinary citizens.

1706. Hewitt, James. Irish Question, The. (Flashpoints). Rourke, 1987. 77 p. ill. $11.

Gr 7-10. SLJ 33: Aug 1987. This balanced introduction to the conflict in Northern Ireland presents enough detail to clarify the issues. Photos included.

1707. Meyer, Carolyn. Voices of Northern Ireland: Growing Up in a Troubled Land. Harcourt, 1987. 212 p. $16.

Gr 7+. + - B 84: Dec 1 1987. + - BC 41: Nov 1987. HB 64: Jan/Feb 1988. + - SLJ 34: Nov 1987. * VOYA 11: Apr 1988. Meyer spent 6 weeks in Northern Ireland interviewing leaders and young people. She presents the history of the con-

tinuing conflict along with excerpts and anecdotes from interviews.

1708. O'Ballance, Edgar. Terror in Ireland: The IRA and the Heritage of Hate. Presidio, 1980. 257 p. $13.

Gr 9+. B 77: Dec 1 1980. + - LJ 106: Apr 1 1981. The history of the relations between the English and the citizens of Northern Ireland, and the causes for resentment, are explored in this presentation that includes excerpts from documents relevant to the struggle.

1709. Wigner, Annabel. Timeline: Ireland. (Weighing Up the Evidence). Batsford; dist. by David & Charles, 1989. 72 p. ill. $20.

Gr 7-10. SLJ 35: Jul 1989. This balanced account of the political, social, and historical causes of the conflict between the British and the Irish includes photos and a detailed timeline.

Great Britain–Northern Ireland–Fiction

1710. Alyn, Marjory. Sound of Anthems, The. St. Martin's, 1983. 211 p. $14.

Gr 6+. B 80: Dec 1 1983. SLJ 30: Feb 1984. + - VOYA 7: Apr 1984. The struggle between Catholics and Protestants for control of Northern Ireland, which had been overshadowed by World War II, resurfaced in 1945, to the confusion of 11-year-old Jennifer.

1711. Anderson, Linda. We Can't All Be Heroes, You Know. Ticknor & Fields , 1985. 195 p. $15.

Gr 10+. + - B 81: Jan 15 1985. LJ 110: Feb 1 1985. The difficulty of life in a town in Northern Ireland which is torn by violence is the theme of this novel about a young married couple whose happiness is threatened by the misery, hate, and rage around them.

1712. Sullivan, Mary Ann. Child of War. Holiday, 1984. 144 p. $11.

Gr 6+. + - B 81: Sep 1 1984. - BC 38: Dec 1984. * SE 49: Apr 1985. + - SLJ 31: Feb 1985. This vivid and bitter novel of the civil war in Northern Ireland focuses on 13-year-old Maeve. As she watches the destruction of her family and is drawn more into the war, Maeve seeks escape through fantasy.

Great Britain–Princes and Princesses

1713. Banks, David. Sarah Ferguson: The Royal Redhead. (Taking Part Books). Dillon Press, 1987. 64 p. ill. $10.

Gr 3-6. B 84: Jan 15 1988. + - SLJ 34: Mar 1988. This introduction to the royal princess includes quotes and photos.

1714. Barry, Stephen P. Royal Service: My Twelve Years as Valet to Prince Charles. Macmillan, 1983. 246 p. ill. $15.

Gr 9+. B 79: Apr 1 1983. LJ 108: May 1 1983. Barry was valet to Prince Charles for 12 years before Charles's marriage. His trivia-filled account reveals his affection for his employer.

1715. Brown, Michele. Prince Charles: A Biography. Crown, 1980. 184 p. ill. $13.

Gr 9+. B 77: Feb 15 1981. LJ 106: Feb 1 1981. Brown's profusely illustrated biography shows how the shy young prince grew to become a poised, well-rounded, mature man.

1716. Burnet, Alastair. In Private–In Public: The Prince and Princess of Wales. Summit, 1986. 159 p. ill. $15.

Gr 9+. B 83: Jan 15 1987. An eminent British journalist and photographer was allowed to document the day-by-day personal and public lives of Charles and Diana. Numerous snapshots show the private side of a very public couple.

1717. Clear, Celia. Royal Children. Crown, 1984. 128 p. ill. $13.

Gr 9+. B 81: Dec 15 1984. Clear's overview of what life is like for royal children, and the problems of raising royal children, emphasizes the British royal family from Queen Victoria to the birth of Prince Henry of Wales.

1718. Courtney, Nicholas. Prince Andrew. Little, Brown, 1983. 64 p. ill. $8.

Gr 9+. B 80: Jan 15 1984. This informal pictorial biography covers Andrew's education, naval career, and royal responsibilities.

1719. Darling, David J. Diana: The People's Princess. (Taking Part Books). Dillon Press, 1984. 62 p. ill. $9.

Gr 3-6. + - B 81: Apr 15 1985. - SLJ 31: Aug 1985. This introduction to the princess of Wales includes many photos.

1720. Erickson, Carolly. Bonnie Prince Charlie. Morrow, 1989. 348 p. ill. $20.

Gr 9+. B 85: Dec 1 1988. LJ 113: Dec 1988. The dramatic story of Bonnie Prince Charlie, the hope of the Stuarts to reclaim the crown from the Hanovers, provides exciting reading.

1721. Fox, Mary Virginia. Princess Diana. Enslow, 1986. 128 p. ill. $13.

Gr 6-10. B 83: Sep 1 1986. BC 40: Dec 1986. BR 5: Nov/Dec 1986. SLJ 33: Jan 1987. VOYA 9. Dec 1986. A clearly written and well-illustrated biography that tells of the princess' youth, her marriage to Prince Charles, and her public work.

1722. Greene, Carol. Diana, Princess of Wales. Childrens Press, 1985. 32 p. ill. $8.

Gr 2-4. SLJ 32: May 1986. A well-illustrated introduction to the princess of Wales.

1723. Junor, Penny. Charles. St. Martin's, 1988. 256 p. ill. $19.

Gr 9+. B 84: Mar 1 1988. LJ 113: Apr 1 1988. This well-written and objective examination of the life and character of the man destined to be the next king of Great Britain includes numerous photos.

1724. Junor, Penny. Diana, Princess of Wales. Doubleday, 1983. 223 p. ill. $15.

Gr 9+. B 80: Sep 1 1983. LJ 108: Jun 1 1983. VOYA 6: Feb 1984. This perceptive analysis extends through Diana's youth, her marriage to the prince, and the birth of Prince William.

1725. Martin, Ralph G. Charles & Diana. Putnam, 1985. 432 p. ill. $19.

Gr 9+. B 82: Nov 1 1985. LJ 110: Nov 1 1985. Information on the responsibilities and rituals of the monarchy is included in this detailed and balanced account of the lives of the prince and princess of Wales.

1726. Nesnick, Victoria Gilvary. Princess Diana: A Book of Questions and Answers. Evans; dist. by Little, Brown, 1988. 192 p. ill. $14.

Gr 5-9. B 85: Dec 15 1988. SLJ 35: Feb 1989. In question-and-answer format Nesnick reveals trivia about the daily life of the princess.

1727. Nugent, Jean. Prince Charles: England's Future King. (Taking Part Books). Dillon Press, 1982. 46 p. ill. $7.

Gr 3-6. B 78: Aug 1982. Large type and numerous photos enhance this introduction to Prince Charles and his bride, Princess Diana.

1728. Rasof, Henry. Picture Life of Charles and Diana, The. Watts, 1988. 64 p. ill. $10.

Gr 4-8. B 84: Mar 1 1988. + - SLJ 34: Jun/Jul 1988. This overview of the public and private lives of Charles and Diana includes numerous photos.

1729. Rhodes, Robert James. Prince Albert: A Biography. Knopf, 1984. 312 p. ill. $18.

Adult. * B 81: Nov 15 1984. B 82: Dec 1 1985. * LJ 109: Nov 15 1984. This well-written and well-researched biography shows Albert's contribution to British politics and to Victoria in her personal life and her responsibilities as monarch.

1730. Ross, Josephine. Princess of Wales, The. (Profiles). Hamilton, 1986. 59 p. ill. $9.

Gr 4-8. + - BR 5: Nov/Dec 1986. + - SLJ 33: Feb 1987. Ross' brief account of the life of Diana, Princess of Wales, is illustrated by black-and-white drawings.

Great Britain–Scotland–Fiction

1731. Porter, Jane. Scottish Chiefs. Scribner, 1809; 1982. 520 p. ill. $17.

Gr 7+. Metzner. Originally published in 1809, this work remains a popular account of the Scottish war for independence, 1287-1371.

Great Britain–Social Life and Customs

1732. Ferguson, Sheila. Village and Town Life. (History in Focus). Batsford; dist. by David & Charles, 1983. 72 p. ill. $15.

Gr 7-10. BC 36: Jul 1983. SLJ 30: Oct 1983. The changes in village and town life caused by political and economic events in England from the Middle Ages through the late 19th century are shown in this well-illustrated work.

1733. Goodall, John S. Above and Below Stairs. Atheneum, 1983. 60 p. ill. $10.

Gr 3-8. BC 37: Jan 1984. + - SLJ 30: Oct 1983. Goodall's pictorial account of the changing ways in which the British people have lived, worked, dressed, and designed their buildings covers from the Middle Ages to the 1980s.

1734. Goodall, John S. Story of an English Village, The. Atheneum, 1979. 58 p. ill. $9.

Gr 1-6. B 79: Jun 1 1983. B 83: Mar 1 1987. * SE 44: Apr 1980. Five hundred years of English village social life are shown in this wordless picture book that shows interior and exterior scenes since the 14th century.

1735. Harris, Sarah. Women at Work. (History in Focus). Batsford, 1981. 72 p. ill. $14.

Gr 9-10. SLJ 28: Mar 1982. Harris explores the world of British working women in the late 19th century and the 20th century, showing union growth, improvements, and continued injustices.

1736. Hartley, Dorothy. Lost Country Life. Pantheon; dist. by Random, 1979. 374 p. ill. $15.

Gr 9+. B 76: Apr 1 1980. LJ 105: Apr 15 1980. SLJ 27: Nov 1980. Arranged around the agricultural calendar is an extensive compendium of miscellaneous information on rural English life from the 12th through the 18th centuries.

1737. Hibbert, Christopher. English: A Social History, 1066-1945. Norton, 1987. 785 p. ill. $33.

Gr 9+. B 83: May 1 1987. LJ 112: May 15 1987. The daily social life and customs of all classes of English people from 1066 to 1945 are presented in rich detail.

Great Britain–Wales

1738. Lye, Keith. Take a Trip to Wales. Watts, 1986. 32 p. ill. $10.

Gr 2-4. B 83: Oct 15 1986. SLJ 33: Feb 1987. Photos on each page and a brief informative text introduce Welsh history, geography, industry, and cities.

1739. Sutherland, Dorothy B. Wales. (Enchantment of the World). Childrens Press, 1987. 127 p. ill. $20.

Gr 4-6. B 84: Oct 15 1987. SLJ 34: Feb 1988. Sutherland's balanced and well-illustrated introduction to Welsh history, resources, government, geography, and culture includes maps and lists of noted persons.

Great Britain–Wales–Fiction

1740. Llewellyn, Richard. How Green Was My Valley. Macmillan; Dell, 1940. 495 p. $18. Pb $5.

Gr 9+. B 36: Feb 1 1940. B 82: May 15 1986. * LJ 65: Feb 1 1940. The lives of Welsh coal miners during the days of Victoria provide the setting for this family chronicle.

Greece

1741. Asimov, Isaac. Greeks: A Great Adventure. Houghton, 1965. 320 p. ill. $14.

Gr 7+. Metzner. HB 41: Aug 1965. LJ 90: Jul 1965. Maps and illustrations enhance this readable and well-illustrated overview of Greek history and culture from ancient to modern times.

1742. Stein, R. Conrad. Greece. (Enchantment of the World). Childrens Press, 1988. 127 p. ill. $21.

Gr 4-7. B 84: May 15 1988. Greek history, culture, economy, government, and religion are covered in this illustrated work that includes maps and a section of facts.

Greece–0-323

1743. Amos, H. D. These Were the Greeks. Dufour, 1982. 224 p. ill. $13.

Gr 10+. D 77: Jan 1 1981. B 79: Sep 1 1982. Numerous photos, illustrations, maps, charts, and quotes enhance this well-organized introduction to ancient Greek culture, politics, military activities, and personalities.

1744. Connolly, Peter. Greek Armies, The. Silver Burdett, 1980. 77 p. ill. Lib. ed. $7.

Gr 6-8. B 76: Apr 15 1980. The accomplishments of the Greek armies from the siege of Troy through the final battle at Alexandria are clarified by maps, charts, diagrams, and drawings.

1745. Coolidge, Olivia. Golden Days of Greece, The. Crowell, 1968. 211 p. ill. $15.

Gr 5+. Metzner. HB 44: Dec 1968. LJ 94: Jan 15 1969. This illustrated history of Ancient Greece is both topical and chronological and emphasizes notable persons.

1746. Cotterell, Arthur. Minoan World, The. Scribner, 1981. 191 p. ill. $17.

Gr 9+. B 77: Jul 1 1981. LJ 106: Jan 15 1981. Photos and diagrams add to the value of this well-organized survey of Minoan society and history.

1747. Dover, Kenneth. Greeks, The. University of Texas Press, 1981. 133 p. ill. $18. Pb $9.

Gr 10+. HT 15: Aug 1982. The story of the ancient Greeks is told in a clear and readable text supplemented by outstanding illustrations.

1748. Edmonds, I. G. Mysteries of Homer's Greeks, The. Elsevier/Nelson, 1980. 144 p. ill. $8.

Gr 7+. B 77: Jan 1 1981. BC 34: Jun 1981. SLJ 27: May 1981. This account of the people and culture of the ancient Mycenaeans is based on archaeological discoveries, mythology, and the Homeric epics.

1749. Fagg, Christopher. Ancient Greece. (Modern Knowledge Library). Warwick; dist. by Watts, 1979. 44 p. ill. $7.

Gr 5-7. B 76: Dec 1 1979. + - SLJ 26: Jan 1980. Clear and colorful photos, diagrams, and illustrations enhance the brief text that introduces the history of ancient Greece and the culture and customs of its people.

1750. Gay, Kathlyn. Science in Ancient Greece. (First Book). Watts, 1988. 95 p. ill. $10.

Gr 5-8. B 84: May 1 1988. BR 7: Sep/Oct 1988. SLJ 35: May 1988. Numerous photos, charts, drawings, and diagrams enhance this account of scientific discoveries made by the ancient Greeks in the fields of anatomy, astronomy, geography, and mathematics, etc.

1751. Grant, Michael. Rise of the Greeks, The. Scribner, 1988. 390 p. map. $28.

Gr 9+. B 84: May 1 1988. Grant examines life in the independent city-states that later united to become the league that was Greece during its Golden Age.

1752. Horton, Casey. Ancient Greeks. (Civilization Library) Watts, 1984. 32 p. ill. $10.

Gr 4-8. B 81: Jan 15 1985. + - SLJ 31: Mar 1985. Attractive illustrations, a glossary, and a simple text introduce the history of the ancient Greeks and their contribution to western civilization.

1753. Jones, John Ellis. Ancient Greece. (History as Evidence). Warwick; dist. by Watts, 1984. 37 p. ill. $10.

Gr 6-8. B 80: May 1 1984. BR 3: Sep/Oct 1984. SLJ 30: Aug 1984. The history of ancient Greece is revealed through an examination of the ruins at Mycenae, Athens, Olympia, and Delos.

1754. Levi, Peter. Atlas of the Greek World. Facts on File, 1981. 239 p. ill. $30.

Gr 9+. B 77: Apr 1 1981. + - B 78: Jan 15 1982. LJ 106: Mar 1 1981. This atlas of ancient Greece from the Bronze Age to the Roman conquest includes photos and drawings. The text includes political and cultural information.

1755. Ling, Roger. Greek World, The. (Making of the Past Series). Peter Bedrick, 1988. 160 p. ill. $20.

Gr 9+. BR 8: May/Jun 1989. SLJ 35: Mar 1989. + - VOYA 12: Apr 1989. A photo-essay and a timeline that shows concurrent events in politics, science, literature, art, and other topics enhance this introduction to Greek history, economy, social life, religion, and architecture.

1756. Pluckrose, Henry. Ancient Greeks. (Small World). Gloucester Press; dist. by Watts, 1982. 28 p. ill. $8.

Gr 2-4. + - B 78: Jul 1982. SLJ 29: Oct 1982. The religion, Olympic games, and government of the ancient Greeks are emphasized in this colorful overview.

1757. Powell, Anton. Greece 1600-30 BC. (Great Civilizations). Watts, 1987. 32 p. ill. $11.

Gr 4-7. BR 6: Jan/Feb 1988. + - SLJ 34: Mar 1988. Numerous illustrations enrich this description of the four main historic periods of ancient Greece.

1758. Robinson, Charles Alexander. Ancient Greece. Rev. ed. (First Book). Watts, 1984. 64 p. ill. $9.

Gr 5-9. B 80: Aug 1984. SLJ 30: Aug 1984. This chronological introduction to the history of ancient Greece includes photos and maps. Greek democracy, myths, and culture are also covered.

1759. Rutland, Jonathan. Ancient Greek Town, An. Rev. ed. (See Inside). Warwick; dist. by Watts, 1986. 32 p. ill. $10.

Gr 4-8. BR 6: May/Jun 1987. SLJ 33: Feb 1987. Ancient Greek entertainment, religion, daily life, and the effects of social class are illustrated in cutaway pictures. A glossary is included.

1760. Ventura, Piero. In Search of Ancient Crete. Silver Burdett, 1985. 47 p. ill. $12. Lib. ed. $8.

Gr 4-9. + - HB 62: Jul/Aug 1986. SLJ 32: Aug 1986. The way of life and the major historical events of ancient Crete are presented along with an account of major archaeological discoveries.

1761. Ventura, Piero. In Search of Troy. Silver Burdett, 1985. 47 p. $12. Lib. ed. $8.

Gr 4-9. + - HB 62: Jul/Aug 1986. SLJ 32: Aug 1986. The way of life and the major historic events of ancient Troy are presented along with an account of major archaeological discoveries.

1762. Windrow, Martin. Greek Hoplite, The. (Soldier Through the Ages). Watts, 1985. 32 p. ill. $10.

Gr 4-7. B 82: Mar 15 1986. BR 5: Jan/Feb 1987. SLJ 32: Mar 1986. Detailed and colorful illustrations show the training and daily experiences of the common soldiers of ancient Greece. A glossary and a timeline are included.

1763. Wood, Michael. In Search of the Trojan War. Facts on File, 1986. 272 p. ill. $23.

Gr 10+. B 82: May 1 1986. LJ 111: Apr 15 1986. This readable and well-illustrated work examines the history behind the legend of Troy and the Trojan War.

1764. Woodford, Susan. Parthenon, The. (Cambridge Topic Book). Lerner, 1983. 51 p. ill. $7.

Gr 6+. B 80: Sep 15 1983. HT 15: Aug 1982. SLJ 30: Nov 1983. Abundant illustrations show the design of ancient Greek temples, the way they were built, and their importance to the people.

Greece–0-323–Fiction

1765. Ray, Mary. Shout Against the Wind. Faber, 1980. 175 p. ill. Pb $3.

Gr 8+. SLJ 28: Sep 1981. Ray's moving story tells of a family from Phylos whose society was destroyed when hordes of Dorian tribesmen attacked in 1200 B.C.

1766. Ray, Mary. Windows of Elissa, The. Faber, 1982. 183 p. $12.

Gr 6-8. + - B 78: May 15 1982. + - BC 35: Jul/Aug 1982. SLJ 29: Oct 1982. This story, rich in historic detail, relates the experiences of 2 sisters in Carthage during its 3-year siege in the 3rd century B.C.

Greece–1900-1999

1767. Rosen, Billi. Andi's War. Dutton, 1989. 136 p. $14.

Gr 6-10. BC 42: Apr 1989. HB 65: Jul/Aug 1989. SLJ 35: Jul 1989. VOYA 12: Aug 1989. Following World War II, communists and monarchists battled for control of Greece. Strong characterizations of children and adults highlight this story of life in wartime.

1768. Woodhouse, C. M. Rise and Fall of the Greek Colonels, The. Watts, 1985. 192 p. $17.

Gr 11+. + - BR 4: Mar/Apr 1986. The struggle for control of the Greek government from 1967 to 1974 resulted in military coups that have had a decisive impact on current Greek politics.

Greece–1900-1999–Fiction

1769. Fenton, Edward. Refugee Summer, The. Delacorte, 1982. 261 p. $11.

Gr 6-9. B 78: Apr 15 1982. BC 35: Apr 1982. HB 58: Jun 1982. * SLJ 28: Apr 1982. VOYA 5: Aug 1982. In 1922 5 young friends, two Americans, two Hungarians, and one Greek, have summer fun with their idealistic secret society until the realities of the Greek war with Turkey come to them by means of refugees and a diary.

Greece–Biographies

1770. Bowder, Diana. Who Was Who in the Greek World: 776 BC-30 BC. Cornell University Press, 1982. 227 p. ill. $30.

Gr 7+. B 79: Feb 1 1983. LJ 108: Jan 15 1983. VOYA 7: Feb 1985. Maps and photos enhance over 750 biographical entries about notable Greeks and persons important to them.

1771. Grant, Michael. Classical Greeks, The. Scribner, 1989. 358 p. $28.

Gr 9+. B 86: Oct 1 1989. Playwrights, poets, sculptors, politicians, generals, and philosophers are included in this collective biography of notable persons from ancient Greece.

1772. Ipsen, D. C. Archimedes: Greatest Scientist of the Ancient World. Enslow, 1989. 64 p. ill. $13.

Gr 5-10. BR 8: Sep/Oct 1989. SLJ 35: Jul 1989. Archimedes' contributions to technology are examined in this well-illustrated work.

1773. King, Perry Scott. Pericles. (World Leaders Past & Present). Chelsea House, 1987. 111 p. ill. $16.

Gr 7+. SLJ 34: Mar 1988. The achievements of Athens during its Golden Age are recounted in this biography of Pericles, the great statesman whose name stood for all that was best in ancient art and science.

Greece–Kings, Queens, Rulers, etc.

1774. Krensky, Stephen. Conqueror and Hero: The Search for Alexander. Little, Brown, 1981. 67 p. ill. $9. Pb $5.

Gr 6-9. B 78: Oct 1 1981. BC 35: Jan 1982. + - HB 57: Dec 1981. SLJ 28: Nov 1981. Background information sets the stage for this account of the years during which Alexander built his empire. Photos, drawings, and maps are included.

1775. Lasker, Joe. Great Alexander the Great, The. Viking, 1983. 32 p. ill. $14.

Gr 1-7. B 82: Sep 15 1985. BC 37: Apr 1984. HB 59: Dec 1983. SLJ 30: Feb 1984. Lasker's attractive pictorial biography of Alexander the Great has a brief text suitable for young students; the artwork will appeal to a wider audience.

Hungary

1776. Blackwood, Alan. Hungarian Uprising, The. (Flashpoints). Rourke, 1987. 77 p. ill. $11.

Gr 7-10. SLJ 33: Aug 1987. This brief account of the unsuccessful 1956 revolt of the Hungarian people against their Soviet-supported communist government includes numerous photos.

1777. Hintz, Martin. Hungary. (Enchantment of the World). Childrens Press, 1988. 128 p. ill. $23.

Gr 7-9. B 85: Feb 15 1989. Hungary's history, economy, government, geography, politics, and problems of the late 1980s are covered in this overview that is enriched by photos and maps.

1778. Lengyel, Emil. Land and People of Hungary. Rev. ed. (Portraits of the Nations Series). Harper, 1972. 160 p. ill. $12.

Gr 5-9. Metzner. Illustrations and maps enrich this introduction to Hungary's history, geography, resources, culture, and people.

1779. Lye, Keith. Take a Trip to Hungary. Watts, 1986. 32 p. ill. $10.

Gr 2-5. B 82: May 15 1986. Photos on each page and a brief, informative text introduce Hungarian history, geography, industry, and cities.

Hungary–Biographies

1780. Finkelstein, Norman H. Theodor Herzl. (Impact Biography). Watts, 1987. 128 p. ill. $12.

Gr 6+. B 84: Mar 1 1988. BR 6: Jan/Feb 1988. SLJ 34: Jan 1988. VOYA 11: Jun 1988. Angered by anti-Semitic actions throughout Europe, Herzl, a noted Hungarian author, devoted his life to laying the groundwork for the establishment of a Jewish nation, a dream that was realized 44 years after his death.

1781. Gurko, Miriam. Theodor Herzl: The Road to Israel. Jewish Publication Society, 1988. 89 p. ill. $13.

Gr 4-8. B 85: Mar 15 1989. + - SLJ 35: Jul 1989. Although he died almost 50 years before Israel became a nation, Herzl devoted his life to its creation because he saw anti-Semitism all over Europe. His personal and political life is presented in this illustrated work.

Hungary–Fiction

1782. Hamori, Laszlo. Dangerous Journey. Harcourt, 1962; 1966. 190 p. ill. Pb $2.

Gr 4-6. Metzner. * B 58: May 1 1962. * HB 38: Jun 1962. + - LJ Jun 15 1962. This fast-moving and dramatic story is about 2 boys who seek to escape from communist Hungary to safety in Sweden.

Iceland

1783. Berry, Erick. Land and People of Iceland. Rev. ed. (Portraits of the Nations Series). Harper, 1960; 1972. 128 p. ill. $12.

Gr 5-9. Metzner. B 56: Jan 15 1960. * LJ 84: Dec 15 1959. Berry's readable, illustrated introduction to Iceland covers the nation's culture, social life, economy, geography, and history to the early 1970s.

1784. Lepthien, Emilie U. Iceland. (Enchantment of the World). Childrens Press, 1987. 127 p. ill. $20.

Gr 4-6. B 84: Oct 15 1987. SLJ 34: Feb 1988. Colorful photos and a section of factual information are included in this well-organized account of Iceland's history, industry, culture, geography, government, and notable persons.

Ireland

1785. Fairclough, Chris. We Live in Ireland. (Living Here). Bookwright Press; dist. by Watts, 1986. 60 p. ill. $11.

Gr 4-7. B 83: Jan 15 1987. + - BC 40: Jan 1987. Colorful photos and a map supplement this work that briefly introduces Irish history and geography but emphasizes interviews with persons from various walks of life, showing living conditions in contemporary Ireland.

1786. Fradin, Dennis B. Republic of Ireland, The. (Enchantment of the World). Childrens Press, 1984. 128 p. ill. $13.

Gr 4-9. B 81: Sep 1 1984. SLJ 31: Dec 1984. Famous people, past and present, are included in this illustrated overview that covers history, culture, customs, geography, and politics.

1787. Hodges, Michael. Ireland. (Living Through History). David & Charles, 1988. 72 p. ill. $18.

Gr 9+. BR 7: Sep/Oct 1988. On Easter Monday, 1916, an uprising began in Ireland that led to civil war. As a result the Republic of Ireland was formed, free from British rule. Quotes show the situation from many points of view and photos support the text.

1788. Kee, Robert. Ireland: A History. Little, Brown, 1982. 256 p. ill. $20.

Gr 9+. B 78: Apr 15 1982. LJ 107: Apr 15 1982. Kee's well-written and illustrated survey of Irish history reveals details of those events that have been significant in the development of the current situation in Ireland and Northern Ireland.

1789. Loughrey, Patrick. People of Ireland, The. New Amsterdam, 1989. 208 p. ill. $25.

Gr 9+. B 85: May 15 1989. The diverse ethnic groups that comprise the Irish people are explored in this book based on a BBC series.

1790. Meyer, Kathleen Allen. Ireland: Land of Mist and Magic. (Discovering Our Heritage). Dillon Press, 1983. 143 p. ill. $10.

Gr 4-8. B 79: Jul 1983. SLJ 29: Aug 1983. Ireland's history, geography, social life, culture, folklore, and holidays are covered in this work that includes photos, a map, and a glossary.

1791. Nowlan, Nora. Shannon: River of Loughs and Legends. (Rivers of the World). Garrard, 1965. 96 p. ill. $4.

Gr 4-7. Metzner. The Shannon, a navigable river that flows through central Ireland, has been of historical importance in the development of the nation. Nowlan discusses the history and culture of the people who have lived on its banks.

1792. O'Brien, Elinor. Land and People of Ireland. Rev. ed. (Portraits of the Nations Series). Harper, 1953; 1972. 128 p. ill. $12.

Gr 5-9. Metzner. B 50: Feb 1 1954. LJ 79: Jan 15 1954. Photos and bits of poetry enrich this introduction to Ireland and its history.

Ireland—Biographies

1793. Boylan, Henry. Dictionary of Irish Biography, A. Barnes & Noble, 1978. 385 p. $25.

Gr 9+. + - B 76: Jan 1 1980. Notable Irish persons of all occupations from ancient times to 1977 are covered.

1794. MacNamara, Desmond. Eamon De Valera. (World Leaders Past & Present). Chelsea House, 1988. 107 p. ill. $17.

Gr 9+. + - BR 7: Nov/Dec 1988. + - VOYA 12: Apr 1989. De Valera led Ireland's struggle for independence and became prime minister and president. This chronological presentation clarifies his influence on history.

1795. Wallace, Martin. 100 Irish Lives. Barnes & Noble, 1983. 184 p. ill. $18.

Gr 9+. B 80: Feb 1 1984. These brief biographies of notable Irish and Anglo-Irish persons are chronologically arranged. Photos and an index enhance their usefulness.

Ireland—Fiction

1796. Langford, Sondra Gordon. Red Bird of Ireland. Atheneum, 1983. 175 p. $11.

Gr 6-9. * SE 48: May 1984. SLJ 30: Nov 1983. The repression by absentee English landlords and the devastation of the potato famine in the late 1840s provide the setting for this story of Aderyn and her family.

1797. Stolz, Mary. Pangur Ban. Harper, 1988. 182 p. ill. $14.

Gr 6+. + - B 85: Nov 1 1988. BC 42: Oct 1988. + - SLJ 35: Nov 1988. A 9th-century Irish artist lives the quiet life of a monk. When word comes that Viking invaders are coming he hides his book, an illuminated life of St. Patrick, in a cave, where it is found 3 centuries later.

Italy

1798. Caselli, Giovanni. Florentine Merchant, A. (Everyday Life of). Peter Bedrick, 1986. 30 p. ill. $10.

Gr 4-7. BR 5: Mar/Apr 1987. SLJ 33: Dec 1986. Numerous illustrations enhance this account of the home of Messer Francesco, a merchant who lived near Florence in the 14th century. Based on accounts and letters.

1799. Coppa, Frank J. Dictionary of Modern Italian History. Greenwood, 1985. 496 p. $55.

Gr 9+. B 82: Apr 1 1986. Italian personalities, history, institutions, events, and problems from the 18th century to the 1980s are included in this well-indexed reference work.

1800. DiFranco, Anthony. Italy: Balanced on the Edge of Time. (Discovering Our Heritage). Dillon Press, 1983. 127 p. ill. $10.

Gr 4-8. B 79: Jul 1983. * BR 2: Nov/Dec 1983. SLJ 29: Aug 1983. A summary of useful reference material is followed by an overview of Italian geography, history, culture, and information on Italian immigrants to the United States. Photos and a glossary are included.

1801. Hibbert, Christopher. Rome: The Biography of a City. Norton, 1985. 387 p. ill. $25.

Gr 9+. B 81: Jun 15 1985. LJ 110: Jun 15 1985. In this illustrated overview of Rome from ancient times to the end of World War II, Hibbert emphasizes the social life and customs of its people.

1802. James, Ian. Inside Italy. Watts, 1988. 32 p. ill. $12.

Gr 3-5. B 85: Jan 15 1989. Colorful photos and maps supplement this brief introduction to Italian history, geography, cities, culture, and resources.

1803. Nowlan, Nora. Tiber: The Roman River. (Rivers of the World). Garrard, 1967. 96 p. ill. $4.

Gr 4-7. Metzner. The Tiber, flowing southward the length of Italy and through Rome, has been of historical importance in the development of the nation. Nowlan discusses the history and culture of the people who have lived on its banks.

1804. Stein, R. Conrad. Italy. (Enchantment of the World). Childrens Press, 1984. 127 p. ill. $15.

Gr 4-8. B 81: May 15 1985. SLJ 31: Aug 1985. Maps, photos, and a section of facts augment this account of Italian geography, culture, economy, and the nation's history since ancient times.

1805. Ventura, Piero. Venice: Birth of a City. Putnam, 1988. 36 p. ill. $14.

Gr 3-7. B 84: Jul 1988. BC 41: Jul 1988. HB 64: Sep/Oct 1988. * SE 53: Apr/May 1989. + - SLJ 35: Sep 1988. This pictorial history of Venice from 300 B.C. to the 1980s concludes with a 4-page fold-out showing the city today.

Italy–Biographies

1806. Haney, John. Cesare Borgia. (World Leaders Past & Present). Chelsea House, 1987. 112 p. ill. $16.

Gr 6-10. B 83: Aug 1987. Life in Renaissance Italy is pictured in this biography of Cesare Borgia, a politician who attempted to gain control of Italy by any means, including cruelty and exploitation. Illustrations and maps are included.

1807. Harris, Nathaniel. Leonardo and the Renaissance. (Life and Times). Bookwright Press; dist. by Watts, 1987. 47 p. ill. $12.

Gr 5-7. B 84: Dec 15 1987. SE 52: Apr 1988. Following a brief introduction to da Vinci is a colorful account of everyday life during the Renaissance.

1808. Hartenian, Larry. Benito Mussolini. (World Leaders Past & Present). Chelsea House, 1988. 112 p. ill. $17.

Gr 6-10. B 84: Jun 1 1988. Captioned illustrations augment this biography that traces the development of Mussolini's political philosophy, his rise to power, alliance with Hitler, and death.

1809. Provensen, Alice. Leonardo da Vinci: The Artist, Inventor, Scientist in Three-Dimensional Movable Pictures. Viking, 1984. 12 p. ill. $15.

Gr 1-8. * B 81: Jan 15 1985. * BC 38: Jan 1985. * SE 49: Apr 1985. + - SLJ 31: Jan 1985. Life in Florence, Italy in 1492 is portrayed in this pop-up book that introduces the many facets of da Vinci's genius.

1810. Vinke, Herman. Giuseppi Garibaldi. (World Leaders Past & Present). Chelsea House, 1987. 112 p. ill. $17.

Gr 6-10. B 84: Nov 15 1987. SLJ 34: Mar 1988. Numerous illustrations enhance this account of Garibaldi's leadership in Italian revolutionary activities. He sought social justice and inspired loyal followers in the mid-1800s.

1811. Viotti, Andrea. Garibaldi: The Revolutionary and His Men. Blandford; dist. by Sterling, 1980. 236 p. ill. $20. Lib. ed. $16.

Gr 9+. B 76: May 15 1980. - LJ 105: Apr 15 1980. Numerous photos and a chronology augment Viotti's account of the political and military activities of Garibaldi, 3 generations of his family, and the military force that he founded, which attained national unity for Italy.

Italy–Fiction

1812. Anno, Mitsumasa. Anno's Italy. Collins, 1980. 48 p. ill. $9. Lib. ed. $9.

Gr K+. B 76: Apr 1 1980. * BC 33: May 1980. HB 56: Jun 1980. HB 57: Jan/Feb 1981. SLJ 26: May 1980. As a lone horseman travels across Italy, the past and present, real and imagined events all merge. Suitable for all ages.

1813. O'Dell, Scott. Road to Damietta, The. Houghton, 1985. 230 p. $15.

Gr 8+. + - BC 39: Dec 1985. * SE 50: Apr/May 1986. SLJ 32: Dec 1985. * VOYA 8: Feb 1986. Life in Italy in the 13th century and the events of the 5th Crusade are shown in this fictionalized biography of St. Francis of Assisi.

Netherlands

1814. Fradin, Dennis B. Netherlands, The. (Enchantment of the World). Childrens Press, 1983. 128 p. ill. $12.

Gr 5-7. B 79: Aug 1983. + - SLJ 30: Sep 1983. This introduction to the Netherlands covers history, geography, cities, industry, customs, and notable persons. Photos and a ready-reference section are included.

Gr 5-9. B 82: Jan 15 1986. SLJ 32: Apr 1986. Basic historical and other information is included, but the emphasis of this work is on the daily lives of 3 citizens. Colorful photos, maps, and a glossary are included.

Netherlands–Fiction

1816. Holland, Cecelia. Sea Beggars, The. Knopf, 1982. 305 p. $14.

Gr 10+. BR 1: Jan/Feb 1983. The rebellion of the Netherlands against Spain during the Inquisition (16th century) is the setting of this thoughtful and action-filled novel that features teenage siblings.

1817. Krasilovsky, Phyllis. First Tulips in Holland, The. Doubleday, 1982. 28 p. ill. $13. Lib. ed. $14.

Gr K-3. B 78: May 15 1982. + - BC 35: Jun 1982. + - SLJ 28: Mar 1982. Richly colored illustrations embellish this fictionalized account of how tulips came to Holland.

Norway

1818. Burks, John B. Norway in Pictures. Rev. ed. (Visual Geography Series). Sterling, 1980. 64 p. ill. $5. Pb $3.

Gr 4-6. + - SLJ 27: Mar 1981. Burks' brief overview of Norwegian history, geography, culture, and economy includes photos and a map.

1819. Hintz, Martin. Norway. (Enchantment of the World). Childrens Press, 1982. 126 p. ill. $10.

Gr 4-8. B 79: Apr 1 1983. SLJ 29: Apr 1983. Full-color photos enhance this introduction to the people of Norway, their history, culture, and folklore. Also covered are geography, industry, and agriculture.

1820. Lye, Keith. Take a Trip to Norway. Watts, 1985. 32 p. ill. $9.

Gr 2-4. B 81: May 15 1985. Photos on each page and a brief informative text introduce Norwegian history, geography, industry, and cities.

Norway–Kings, Queens, Rulers, etc.

1821. Greve, Tim. Haakon VII of Norway: The Man and the Monarch. Hippocrene, 1983. 212 p. ill. $25.

Adult. B 82: Dec 1 1985. Haakon VII, who was born a Danish prince, was chosen king by the Norwegian people and parliament at the time of independence in 1905. His biography explores his leadership to the time of his death in 1957.

Poland

1822. Donica, Ewa. We Live in Poland. (Living Here). Bookwright Press; dist. by Watts, 1985. 60 p. ill. $11.

Gr 5-9. + - B 82: Jan 15 1986. + - SLJ 32: Apr 1986. In separate interviews an architect, a farmer, and two journalists discuss their life and work in Poland and the nation's culture, history, geography, and politics.

1823. Greene, Carol. Poland. (Enchantment of the World). Childrens Press, 1983. 126 p. ill. $12.

Gr 4-6. + - B 79: Aug 1983. + - SLJ 30: Sep 1983. Colorfully illustrated, this introduction to Poland covers the nation's history, geography, notable persons, resources, culture, and economy.

1824. Leslie, R. F. History of Poland Since 1863, The. Cambridge University Press, 1980. 494 p. $45.

Gr 11+. HT 14: Aug 1981. LJ 106: Feb 1 1981. This balanced history covers Polish cultural, economic, political, and social developments since 1863.

1825. Lye, Keith. Take a Trip to Poland. Watts, 1985. 32 p. ill. $9.

Gr 2-4. B 81: May 15 1985. Photos on each page and a brief, informative text introduce Polish history, geography, industry, and cities.

1826. Obojski, Robert. Poland in Pictures. Rev. ed. (Visual Geography Series). Sterling, 1981. 64 p. ill. $5. Pb $3.

Gr 7+. + - SLJ 28: May 1982. Obojski's introduction to Polish history, geography, culture, and economy includes numerous photos.

1827. Pfeiffer, Christine. Poland: Land of Freedom Fighters. (Discovering Our Heritage). Dillon Press, 1984. 175 p. ill. $10.

Gr 4-8. B 80: Jul 1984. SLJ 30: Aug 1984. Photos, a map, and a glossary supplement this introduction to Poland's history, geography, economy, and customs. Polish immigrants to the United States and their famous descendants are also discussed.

1828. Sandak, Cass R. Poland. (First Book). Watts, 1986. 88 p. ill. $10.

Gr 5+. B 82: Jun 15 1986. BR 5: Nov/Dec 1986. SLJ 33: Sep 1986. This brief overview of the highlights of Polish history to 1985 also covers geography and resources. Included are lists of noted persons and major cities, and a pronunciation guide.

1829. Sharman, Tim. Rise of Solidarity, The. (Flashpoints). Rourke, 1987. 78 p. ill. $11.

Gr 7-10. + - SLJ 33: Aug 1987. Sharman's overview of Polish trade unionism from the end of World War II to the mid-1980s shows the impact of the nation's economic problems and the leadership of Lech Walesa.

1830. Tene, Benjamin. In the Shade of the Chestnut Tree. Jewish Publication Society, 1981. 136 p. ill. $9.

Gr 4-9. * B 78: Oct 1 1981. BC 35: Jan 1982. Each of 12 chapters is an anecdote from the author's memories of growing up in the Jewish ghetto in Warsaw between the two world wars.

1831. Worth, Richard. Poland: The Threat to National Renewal. (Impact Book). Watts, 1982. 87 p. ill. $8.

Gr 7+. B 78: Jul 1982. VOYA 6: Feb 1983. The political history of Poland over the past 30 years is the emphasis of this illustrated work.

Poland–Biographies

1832. Ascherson, Neal. Book of Lech Walesa, The. Simon & Schuster, 1982. 203 p. $13. Pb $5.

Poland–Biographies

1832. Ascherson, Neal. Book of Lech Walesa, The. Simon & Schuster, 1982. 203 p. $13. Pb $5.

Gr 10+. B 78: Aug 1982. BR 2: May/Jun 1983. LJ 107: Jul 1982. These 10 essays, which focus on various aspects of the life and career of Lech Walesa, conclude with an interview with him. A chronology of Polish history is included.

1833. Craig, Mary. Lech Walesa and His Poland. Continuum; dist. by Harper, 1987. 336 p. ill. $19.

Gr 9+. + - B 84: Oct 1 1987. LJ 112: Sep 15 1987. A brief history of Poland for the past 40 years is provided in order to set the context for the biography of Walesa, a Nobel Prize winner who fought for workers' rights in the 1980s.

1834. Eringer, Robert. Strike for Freedom! The Story of Lech Walesa and Polish Solidarity. Dodd, 1982. 157 p. ill. $12.

Gr 9+. B 79: Nov 15 1982. LJ 107: Nov 15 1982. + - SLJ 29: Feb 1983. A brief summary of Polish history sets the stage for this chronicle of the Solidarity movement, and its leader Lech Walesa, in its early days (1980-1981).

1835. Kaye, Tony. Lech Walesa. (World Leaders Past & Present). Chelsea House, 1989. 112 p. ill. $17.

Gr 7+. B 86: Oct 1 1989. BR 8: Nov/Dec 1989. SLJ 35: Oct 1989. Walesa's role in Poland's history before the fall of the communist government is examined in this illustrated, balanced work.

1836. Madison, Arnold. Polish Greats. McKay, 1980. 114 p. $8.

Gr 4-8. B 77: Sep 1 1980. + - BC 34: Jan 1981. SLJ 27: Mar 1981. This collection of concise and readable biographies of 13 notable Poles emphasizes the last 150 years.

1837. Singer, Isaac Bashevis. Day of Pleasure: Stories of a Boy Growing Up in Warsaw. Farrar, 1969. 227 p. ill. Pb $6.

Gr 6-8. B 82: Sep 15 1985. Stories of Singer's childhood in Warsaw are illustrated with old photos.

1838. Singer, Isaac Bashevis. In My Father's Court. Fawcett, 1966. 307 p. Pb $3.

Gr 9+. B 82: May 15 1986. This warm and humorous memoir of growing up as the son of a rabbi in early 20th-century Warsaw provides a wealth of detail about social customs.

1839. Walesa, Lech. Way of Hope, A. Holt, 1987. 325 p. ill. $20.

Gr 9+. B 84: Dec 1 1987. BR 7: May/Jun 1988. LJ 113: Jan 1988. SLJ 34: Mar 1988. + - VOYA 11: Apr 1988. Walesa's account of the Solidarity labor movement encompasses the history of Poland in the 1980s.

Poland–Fiction

1840. Kelly, Eric P. Trumpeter of Krakow. Macmillan, 1929; 1966. 224 p. ill. $14. Pb $4.

Gr 7+. Metzner. B 25: Dec 1928. Fifteenth-century Poland is the setting for this dramatic story of the Tarnov crystal. The story is enriched by rich detail of medieval life.

1841. Mark, Michael. Toba: At the Hands of a Thief. Bradbury; dist. by Macmillan, 1985. 136 p. $12.

Gr 8+. B 81: May 15 1985. * SE 49: Apr 1985. VOYA 8: Feb 1986. Life in a warm Jewish family in 1913 Poland is seen through this story of Toba whose mother wants to send her to America to join her sister.

1842. Michener, James A. Poland. Random, 1983. 556 p. $18.

Gr 10+. B 79: Jul 1983. LJ 108: Sep 1 1983. Michener's saga presents Polish history through the story of 3 families whose lives have centered around the village of Buk from 1200 to 1980.

Portugal

1843. Cross, Esther. Portugal. (Enchantment of the World). Childrens Press, 1986. 127 p. ill. $20.

Gr 4-6. B 82: Aug 1986. SLJ 33: Oct 1986. This well-organized, illustrated introduction to Portuguese history, geography, culture, economy, and government includes a brief reference section.

1844. Lye, Keith. Take a Trip to Portugal. Watts, 1986. 32 p. ill. $10.

Gr 2-4. B 83: Oct 15 1986. SLJ 33: Feb 1987. Photos on each page and a brief informative text introduce Portuguese history, geography, industry, and cities.

Romania

1845. Carran, Betty B. Romania. (Enchantment of the World). Childrens Press, 1988. 128 p. ill. $22.

Gr 4-8. B 84: Aug 1988. SLJ 35: Oct 1988. Current political conditions are discussed in this introduction to Romania that also covers history, geography, social life, and culture.

Rome

1846. Biel, Timothy Levi. Pompeii. (World Disasters). Lucent Books; dist. by Greenhaven Press, 1989. 64 p. ill. $12.

Gr 4-6. + - SLJ 35: Sep 1989. Illustrations and quotes from eyewitnesses augment this book about Pompeii, which covers the history of the city and its destruction.

1847. Caselli, Giovanni. Roman Soldier, A. (Everyday Life of). Peter Bedrick, 1986. 30 p. ill. $10.

Gr 4-7. BR 5: Mar/Apr 1987. SLJ 33: Dec 1986. Numerous illustrations enhance this account of the experiences of a new recruit in the 3rd-century Roman army serving in Britain.

1848. Connolly, Peter. Hannibal and the Enemies of Rome. Silver Burdett, 1980. 77 p. ill. Lib. ed. $7.

Gr 6-8. B 76: Apr 15 1980. The accomplishments of the Roman army as it fought the Etruscans, Celts, and Hannibal's Carthaginians are clarified by maps, charts, diagrams, and drawings.

1849. Connolly, Peter. Roman Army, The. Silver Burdett, 1980. 77 p. ill. Lib. ed. $7.

Gr 6-9. B 76: Apr 15 1980. + - BC 33: Jun 1980. The accomplishments of the Roman army in Macedonia and Europe

1850. Corbishley, Mike. Roman World, The. Warwick; dist. by Watts, 1986. 94 p. ill. $14.

Gr 5-9. B 83: Dec 15 1986. + - SLJ 33: Feb 1987. In addition to an introductory overview of the history of the Roman empire, Corbishley presents information on food, education, crafts, sports, and religion.

1851. Cornell, Tim. Atlas of the Roman World. Facts on File, 1982. 240 p. ill. $35.

Gr 11+. B 79: Nov 15 1982. B 79: May 1 1983. LJ 107: Oct 15 1982. Over 50 maps, over 250 illustrations, and a concise narrative convey historical and geographical information about the Roman Empire.

1852. Gibbon, Edward. Gibbon's Decline and Fall of the Roman Empire. Abridged ed. Rand McNally, 1980. 256 p. ill. $20.

Gr 9+. B 76: Jun 1 1980. Selections from Gibbon's masterpiece are combined with attractive pictures to tell the story of the splendors of Rome.

1853. Goodenough, Simon. Citizens of Rome. Crown, 1979. 192 p. ill. $15.

Gr 9+. B 76: Feb 1 1980. LJ 105: Jan 15 1980. SLJ 26: Feb 1980. This lively and well-illustrated account of life in ancient Rome covers the social system and family life in addition to political and legal concerns, economics, religion, the military, and urban problems.

1854. Hamilton, Edith. Roman Way. Avon, 1932; 1981. 281 p. Pb $3.

Gr 7+. Metzner. B 29: Nov 1932. Hamilton's classic work presents a lively and balanced account of life in ancient Rome.

1855. Hughes, Jill. Imperial Rome. Rev. ed. (Civilization Library). Gloucester Press; dist. by Watts, 1985. 32 p. ill. $10.

Gr 5-7. SLJ 32: Mar 1986. This simple introduction to the political structure of ancient Rome includes a map.

1856. Millard, Anne. Welcome to Ancient Rome. Usborne; dist. by National Textbook, 1981. 64 p. ill. Pb $4.

Gr 6-9. * BR 3: Sep/Oct 1984. Millard's profusely illustrated work introduces the history and customs of the people of ancient Rome.

1857. Miquel, Pierre. Life in Ancient Rome. (Silver Burdett Picture Histories). Silver Burdett, 1981. 64 p. ill. $8.

Gr 5-9. B 77: Jul 15/Aug 1981. + - SLJ 28: Jan 1982. Miquel provides a broad historical perspective of ancient Rome along with unusual facts, key dates, a glossary, and numerous illustrations.

1858. Pluckrose, Henry. Romans. (Small World). Gloucester Press; dist. by Watts, 1982. 28 p. ill. $8.

Gr 2-4. B 78: Jul 1982. SLJ 29: Oct 1982. The military and building accomplishments of the ancient Romans are emphasized in this colorful overview.

1859. Robinson, Charles Alexander. Ancient Rome. Rev. ed. (First Book). Watts, 1984. 64 p. ill. $9.

Gr 5-9. B 80: Aug 1984. SLJ 30: May 1984. Robinson's chronological introduction to the history of Rome includes photos and a map. Special chapters on daily life in Rome and art in the Augustan age are included.

1860. Ross, Stewart. Roman Centurion, A. (How They Lived). Rourke, 1987. 32 p. ill. $9.

Gr 4-7. SLJ 33: Jun/Jul 1987. This illustrated introduction to the life of a Roman centurion covers weapons, food, and clothing. It presents a picture of life at that time.

1861. Simkins, Michael. Warriors of Rome: An Illustrated Military History of the Roman Legions. Blandford; dist. by Sterling, 1989. 160 p. ill. $25.

Gr 9+. B 85: Apr 15 1989. The history of the formidable Roman Legions is covered in this illustrated work.

1862. Wilkes, John. Roman Army. (Cambridge Topic Book). Lerner, 1977. 51 p. ill. $9.

Gr 5-10. Metzner. SLJ 24: Apr 1978. Photos, charts, maps, diagrams, and other illustrations enrich this account of the everyday activities of the Roman army.

1863. Windrow, Martin. Roman Legionary, The. (Soldier Through the Ages). Watts, 1985. 32 p. ill. $11.

Gr 5-10. B 81: Apr 15 1985. BR 4: Mar/Apr 1986. SLJ 32: Sep 1985. Large, colorful drawings enhance the concise text that introduces the Roman soldier, his training, weapons, tactics, promotion, and retirement. Background information on the empire is included.

Rome–Biographies

1864. Bowder, Diana. Who Was Who in the Roman World: 753 BC-AD 476. Cornell University Press, 1980. 256 p. ill. $25.

Gr 7+. LJ 106: Feb 15 1981. LJ 107: May 15 1982. VOYA 7. Feb 1985. Over 900 biographical entries, a chronology, glossary, family trees, numerous illustrations, and maps are included in this useful reference work.

1865. Connolly, Peter. Tiberius Claudius Maximus: The Cavalryman. (Rebuilding the Past). Oxford University Press, 1989. 32 p. ill. $13.

Gr 5-10. SLJ 35: May 1989. Numerous illustrations and maps enrich this brief account of the techniques, weapons, and routine of life in the Roman army.

1866. Connolly, Peter. Tiberius Claudius Maximus: The Legionary. (Rebuilding the Past). Oxford University Press, 1989. 32 p. ill. $13.

Gr 5-10. SLJ 35: May 1989. Details of daily life in the Roman army are revealed in this brief introduction to Roman history.

1867. Kittredge, Mary. Marc Antony. (World Leaders Past & Present). Chelsea House, 1987. 112 p. ill. $17.

Gr 6+. B 84: Jan 15 1988. BR 7: Nov/Dec 1988. SLJ 34: Mar 1988. The military, political, and social climate of the last years of the Roman Republic provide the setting for the biography of Marc Antony, a brave and resourceful leader who failed because he could not control himself.

1868. Powers, Elizabeth. Nero. (World Leaders Past & Present). Chelsea House, 1987. 112 p. ill. $17.

1868. Powers, Elizabeth. Nero. (World Leaders Past & Present). Chelsea House, 1987. 112 p. ill. $17.

Gr 6-10. B 84: Jan 15 1988. A chronology and photos enhance this biography of Nero, emperor of Rome from 54 to 68 A.D.

Rome–Fiction

1869. Anderson, Paul Lewis. Pugnax the Gladiator. Biblio, 1939. 296 p. ill. $12.

Gr 7-11. Metzner. This lively story of a prisoner who becomes a gladiator presents an accurate picture of Roman life.

1870. Anderson, Paul Lewis. Slave of Catiline. Biblio, 1930. 255 p. ill. $15.

Gr 7-11. Metzner. In his absorbing story of a young slave who became a famous gladiator, Anderson presents an authentic picture of everyday life and politics in Rome.

1871. Anderson, Paul Lewis. With the Eagles. Biblio, 1929. 280 p. ill. $15.

Gr 7-11. Metzner. Anderson's account of Caesar's conquest of Gaul as seen by a young legionary is readable and dramatic.

1872. Bradshaw, Gillian. Beacon at Alexandria, The. Houghton, 1986. 376 p. maps. $18.

Gr 9+. B 83: Sep 1 1986. LJ 111: Sep 1 1986. Disguised as a eunuch, a noblewoman studied medicine at Alexandria and became a famous physician. This effective novel of 4th-century Europe explores its attitudes toward women and medicine.

1873. Bradshaw, Gillian. Imperial Purple. Houghton, 1988. 324 p. $19.

Gr 9+. B 85: Nov 1 1988. LJ 114: Nov 15 1988. SLJ 35: Feb 1989. Demetrius, a weaver living in the Eastern Roman Empire in the early 5th century, is commissioned to weave a purple cloak. She soon finds herself in the midst of a conspiracy to overthrow the emperor.

1874. Church, Alfred J. Lucius: Adventures of a Roman Boy. Biblio, 1885; 1960. 341 p. $15.

Gr 7-11. Metzner. Originally published in 1885, this story of a Roman boy's adventures remains popular today.

1875. Wells, Reuben F. On Land and Sea with Caesar; Or Following the Eagles. Biblio, 1926. 326 p. ill. $12.

Gr 7-11. Metzner. Since its original publication in 1926 this has been a popular story of adventure with the Roman legions.

1876. Wells, Reuben F. With Caesar's Legions. Biblio, 1923; 1951. 336 p. ill. $16.

Gr 7-11. Metzner. This adventure story concerns two Roman youths who were with Caesar's army during the conquest of Gaul.

1877. Wood, Barbara. Soul Flame. Random, 1987. 372 p. $19.

Gr 9+. + - B 83: Feb 1 1987. LJ 112: Mar 15 1987. Selene, raised and trained by a healer-woman, followed her craft through Persia, Jerusalem, Alexandria, and Rome. Ancient medical lore and religion are interwoven in this historical novel.

1878. Yarbro, Chelsea Quinn. Locadio's Apprentice. Harper, 1984. 219 p. $12. Lib. ed. $12.

Gr 6-9. B 81: Dec 15 1984. + - SLJ 31: Nov 1984. VOYA 7: Feb 1985. This story of an apprentice doctor, set in ancient Pompeii, provides rich detail of the social life and medical practice of the time.

Rome–Kings, Queens, Rulers, etc.

1879. Bruns, Roger. Julius Caesar. (World Leaders Past & Present). Chelsea House, 1987. 112 p. ill. $17.

Gr 6+. B 84: Nov 15 1987. BR 7: Sep/Oct 1988. + - SLJ 34: Dec 1987. VOYA 11: Oct 1988. This highly illustrated biography includes numerous quotes, and shows how Caesar used his personal contacts and military conquests to gain political power.

1880. Massie, Allan. Caesars, The. Watts, 1984. 233 p. ill. $17.

Gr 9+. B 80: May 1 1984. + - BR 3: Sep/Oct 1984. VOYA 7: Oct 1984. The personal and political lives of Rome's first 12 emperors are covered in this illustrated text.

1881. Matthews, Rupert. Julius Caesar. Bookwright Press; dist. by Watts, 1989. 32 p. ill. Lib. ed. $12.

Gr 3-8. B 85: May 1 1989. SLJ 35: Sep 1989. A timeline and glossary supplement this illustrated introduction to the life and reign of Julius Caesar.

1882. May, Robin. Julius Caesar and the Romans. (Life and Times). Bookwright Press; dist. by Watts, 1985. 59 p. ill. $11.

Gr 4-7. B 82: Sep 1 1985. - SLJ 32: Sep 1985. A glossary and a chronology are included in this broad introduction to Roman history, its culture, and its leaders.

1883. Suetonius Tranquillus, Gaius. Twelve Caesars, The. Rev. ed. Penguin, 1979. 287 p. ill. Pb $15.

Gr 10+. B 76: Apr 1 1980. Color plates and a glossary enhance this edition of a standard biography of the Caesars that tells their strengths, weaknesses, and vices.

1884. Walworth, Nancy Zinsser. Augustus Caesar. (World Leaders Past & Present). Chelsea House, 1988. 112 p. ill. $17.

Gr 9+. B 85: Dec 1 1988. BR 8: May/Jun 1989, Sep/Oct 1989. SLJ 35: Feb 1989. VOYA 12: Feb 1989. The political and social history of Rome are revealed in this account of the personal and public life of Augustus Caesar.

Rome–Social Life and Customs

1885. Andrews, Ian. Pompeii. (Cambridge Topic Book). Lerner, 1980. 51 p. ill. $5.

Gr 4-7. B 76: Jul 1 1980. SLJ 27: Mar 1981. This comprehensive introduction to life in Pompeii at the time of its destruction covers public life, occupations, religion, and buildings. It includes maps and diagrams.

1887. Corbishley, Mike. Romans, The. (History as Evidence). Warwick; dist. by Watts, 1984. 37 p. ill. $10.

Gr 5+. B 80: May 1 1984. + - BC 38: Sep 1984. BR 3: Sep/Oct 1984. SLJ 30: Aug 1984. Living conditions in the cities and farms of ancient Rome are described, along with an explanation of how conquered areas were changed as they became part of the empire. Photos, maps, and drawings are included.

1888. Goor, Ron. Pompeii: Exploring a Roman Ghost Town. Harper, 1986. 118 p. ill. $12. Lib. ed. $12.

Gr 5-10. * B 83: Dec 15 1986. BC 40: Nov 1986. * BR 5: Mar/Apr 1987. HB 63: Jan 1987. HB 63: Nov 1987. * SE 51: Apr/May 1987. * SLJ 33: Dec 1986. Goor's attractive account of what the excavations of lava-covered Pompeii have revealed about its cultural, social, political, and religious life includes recipes, graffiti, photos, and drawings.

1889. Lamprey, Louise. Children of Ancient Rome. (Roman Life and Time Series). Biblio, 1922; 1961. 262 p. ill. $15.

Gr 7-11. Metzner. Lamprey's classic is a detailed account of what it was like to be a child in ancient Rome.

1890. Lewis, Brenda Ralph. Growing up in Ancient Rome. Batsford, 1980. 72 p. ill. $15.

Gr 4+. + - SLJ 27: Feb 1981. This brief, illustrated introduction to Roman life emphasizes what life was like for children.

1891. Rutland, Jonathan. Roman Town, A. (See Inside). Warwick; dist. by Watts, 1986. 32 p. ill. $11.

Gr 4-8. BR 6: May/Jun 1987. BC 40: Nov 1986. SLJ 33: Feb 1987. Cutaway pictures reveal life in an ancient Roman town, showing the effects of social class. Entertainment and religion are also covered, and a glossary is included.

1892. Tingay, G. I. F. These Were the Romans. Dufour, 1987. 193 p. ill. Pb $13.

Gr 9+. * BR 6: May/Jun 1987. Illustrations and quotes enhance this social history of the Roman people that makes clear their contributions to western civilization.

Rome–Technology and Civilization

1893. Hamey, L. A. Roman Engineers, The. (Cambridge Topic Book). Lerner, 1982. 51 p. ill. $6.

Gr 6-10. B 78: Feb 1 1982. BC 35: Mar 1982. SLJ 28: Apr 1982. The impressive Roman roads, bridges, buildings, and aqueducts are described as well as the methods of construction and the materials and tools used. Photos of ruins still existing are included.

1894. Harris, Jacqueline L. Science in Ancient Rome. Watts, 1988. 72 p. ill. $11.

Gr 5-7. B 85: Dec 15 1988. The Romans' masterful application of scientific principles in the construction of buildings, roads, and bridges is emphasized in this well-illustrated, lively text.

Soviet Union

1895. Anderson, Madelyn Klein. Siberia. Dodd, 1988. 148 p. ill. $14.

Gr 5-9. B 84: Apr 1 1988. BC 41: May 1988. SLJ 34: Jun/Jul 1988. Anderson's readable survey of the history, politics, and geography of Siberia includes photos.

1896. Boyette, Michael. Soviet Georgia. (Places and Peoples of the World). Chelsea House, 1988. 104 p. ill. $13.

Gr 5-7. B 85: Feb 15 1989. SLJ 35: Feb 1989. Soviet Georgia, which lies between the Black and Caspian seas, is prosperous and independent, by Soviet standards. Boyette introduces Georgia's history, culture, economy, government, and people.

1897. Freemantle, Brian. KGB. Holt, 1982. 192 p. ill. $15.

Gr 9+. B 79: Jan 15 1983. LJ 107: Dec 15 1982. The history and methods of the KGB are explained.

1898. Gillies, John. Soviet Union: The World's Largest Country. Dillon Press, 1985. 159 p. ill. $11.

Gr 4-8. B 82: Dec 1 1985. SLJ 32: Oct 1985. Following historical information is a lively, balanced, and illustrated account of life in the Soviet Union, including holiday celebrations, schooling, sports, family life, food, and money.

1899. Jackson, W. A. Douglas. Soviet Union. (Fideler/Gateway Global Community Series). Gateway Press, 1988. 160 p. ill. $17.

Gr 5-9. B 85: Dec 1 1988. Soviet history, geography, government, culture, social life, economy, resources, transportation, communication, and people are covered in this overview.

1900. Keeler, Stephen. Passport to the Soviet Union. Watts, 1988. 48 p. ill. $12.

Gr 4-9. B 84: May 15 1988. + - SLJ 34: Aug 1988. Colorful photos and the brief text present an overview of the Soviet Union, including history, geography, and many aspects of social life.

1901. Kort, Michael. Soviet Colossus: A History of the USSR. Scribner, 1985. 324 p. $20.

Gr 10+. B 81: Mar 1985. + - LJ 109: Nov 15 1984. Kort examines 20th-century Russia as an extension of traditions, including the continuation of aristocratic leadership and the economic exploitation of the peasants. His history covers events since the 1917 revolution.

1902. Lawson, Don. K.G.B., The. (Spy Shelf). Messner; Wanderer, 1984. 191 p. $9. Pb $4.

Gr 5+. B 80: Mar 1 1984. VOYA 7: Feb 1985. Within the context of Soviet history Lawson describes the work of the KGB, which serves as a secret police force within the Soviet Union and as an international espionage agency.

1903. Maclean, Fitzroy. Portrait of the Soviet Union. Holt, 1988. 230 p. ill. $24.

Gr 9+. + - BR 7: Jan/Feb 1989. SLJ 35: Sep 1988. Maclean clearly explains the history, geography, and culture of the 15 republics within the Soviet Union and their relation to the central government as he compares the Russia of the late 1980s with the Russia he knew 50 years ago.

1903. Maclean, Fitzroy. Portrait of the Soviet Union. Holt, 1988. 230 p. ill. $24.

Gr 9+. + - BR 7: Jan/Feb 1989. SLJ 35: Sep 1988. Maclean clearly explains the history, geography, and culture of the 15 republics within the Soviet Union and their relation to the central government as he compares the Russia of the late 1980s with the Russia he knew 50 years ago.

1904. Mandel, William M. Soviet But Not Russian. The 'Other' Peoples of the Soviet Union. Ramparts, 1985. 383 p. ill. $20.

Gr 9+. + - B 81: Apr 1 1985. + - LJ 110: Apr 15 1985. Mandel covers the ethnic groups that are a part of the Soviet population, using both historical accounts and personal interviews.

1905. Paxton, John. Companion to Russian History. Facts on File, 1983. 503 p. maps. $22.

Gr 9+. B 81: Oct 15 1984. BR 4: Mar/Apr 1986. LJ 109: Mar 1 1984. Over 2500 concise entries cover Russian art, ballet, politics, notable persons, events, and ideas. A chronology and maps are included.

1906. Perkovich, George. Thinking About the Soviet Union. Educators for Social Responsibility, 1989. 245 p. Pb $25.

Gr 10+. * BR 8: Sep/Oct 1989. VOYA 12: Aug 1989. A variety of viewpoints present background information on Soviet economy, government, foreign policy, human rights, and culture.

1907. Rickard, Graham. Chernobyl Catastrophe, The. (Great Disasters). Bookwright Press; dist. by Watts, 1989. 32 p. ill. $11.

Gr 3-6. B 85: May 15 1989. SLJ 35: May 1989. Numerous drawings and photos clarify the brief text that explains the Chernobyl disaster.

1908. Riordan, James. Soviet Union: The Land and Its People. Rev. ed. (Silver Burdett Countries). Silver Burdett, 1987. 43 p. ill. $15.

Gr 4-6. SLJ 33: Aug 1987. Attractive drawings and photos enhance this revised introduction to the Soviet Union, its history, geography, art, education, food, government, industry, leisure, and sports.

1909. Rodimeza, Irina. Kremlin and Its Treasures, The. Rizzoli, 1987. 356 p. ill. $75.

Gr 9+. LJ 113: Aug 1988. SLJ 35: May 1988. Large attractive photos show the architecture and decoration of the Kremlin buildings as well as historical collections of jewelry, weapons, vestments, and art dating from the 11th century.

1910. Seaton, Albert. Soviet Army: 1918 to the Present. New American Library, 1987. 292 p. ill. $20.

Gr 9+. B 83: Mar 1 1987. This compact history of the Soviet army since 1918 shows the impact of political considerations and traditional values on its effectiveness.

1911. Shoemaker, M. Wesley. Soviet Union and Eastern Europe 1983, The. (World Today Series). Stryker-Post, 1983. 119 p. ill. Pb $4.

Gr 7+. B 80: Mar 1 1984. The first half of this work is an overview of Soviet social and political history. The second half profiles nations in the Soviet bloc: Albania, Bulgaria, Czechoslovakia, East Germany, Hungary, Poland, Romania, and Yugoslavia.

1912. Smith, Samantha. Journey to the Soviet Union. Little, Brown, 1985. 122 p. ill. $20. Pb $12.

Gr 3-7. B 81: Aug 1985. BC 38: Apr 1985. Numerous photos illustrate Samantha Smith's account of her visit to the Soviet Union at the invitation of the Soviet president.

1913. Ustinov, Peter. My Russia. Atlantic; dist. by Little, Brown, 1983. 224 p. ill. $20.

Gr 10+. B 79: Apr 1 1983. BR 2: Jan/Feb 1984. LJ 108: Apr 15 1983. Ustinov traces the history of Russia since ancient times, showing how a quest for security has led to defensiveness, isolation, and fear of foreigners. A readable and well-illustrated introduction.

Soviet Union–0–1917

1914. Ignatieff, Michael. Russian Album, The. Viking, 1987. 185 p. ill. $19.

Gr 10+. B 83: Aug 1987. LJ 112: Jul 1987. Based on the experiences of his family, who were leaders in Czarist Russia, Ignatieff discusses life before and during the 1918 revolution.

1915. Resnick, Abraham. Russia: A History to 1917. (Enchantment of the World). Childrens Press, 1983. 127 p. ill. $13.

Gr 5-8. B 80: Mar 1 1984. + - SLJ 30: May 1984. Color photos, a list of notable persons, and a chronology enhance this history of Russia before the 1917 revolution.

1916. Rogger, Hans. Russia in the Age of Modernization and Revolution 1881-1917. (Longman History of Russia). Longman, 1983. 323 p. Pb $16.

Gr 12+. HT 20: Nov 1986. For the advanced student, a synthesis of Soviet economic, political, and social trends in the 36 years that culminated in the revolution.

1917. Tessendorf, K. C. Kill the Czar: Youth and Terrorism in Old Russia. Atheneum, 1986. 128 p. ill. $13.

Gr 7+. B 82: Aug 1986. BC 39: Apr 1986. HB 63: Jan/Feb 1987. * SE 51: Apr/May 1987. SLJ 33: Sep 1986. + - VOYA 9: Feb 1987. In 1881 five young terrorists were hanged for the assassination of Czar Alexander II. Although the czar's policies were comparatively liberal, and the young people sought to force greater reforms, their acts resulted in greater repression.

Soviet Union–0–1917–Fiction

1918. Appel, Allen. Time After Time. Carroll & Graf, 1985. 373 p. $17.

Gr 9+. B 82: Oct 1 1985. A riveting time-travel adventure in which Alex tries to rescue the czar and his family from the Red Army.

1919. Borovsky, Natasha. Daughter of the Nobility, A. Holt, 1985. 480 p. $17.

Gr 9+. B 82: Sep 15 1985. + - LJ 110: Sep 1 1985. SLJ 32: Oct 1985. This romantic novel, written in the form of a memoir, is full of rich detail about life in Russia during the reign of the last czar, Nicholas II.

1920. Doig, Ivan. Sea Runners, The. Atheneum, 1982. 288 p. map. $14,

Gr 9+. B 79: Sep 1 1982. B 85: Nov 1 1988. LJ 107: Sep 1 1982. In 1853 4 indentured Swedish laborers rebelled against their Russian masters and tried to escape in a handmade canoe, fighting storm and starvation as they traveled from Russian Alaska toward Oregon. Based on a true story.

1921. Fisher, Leonard Everett. Russian Farewell, A. Four Winds, 1980. 133 p. ill. $10.

Gr 5-8. B 77: Feb 15 1981. BC 34: May 1981. SLJ 27: Jan 1981. This story of the Shapiro family shows the rise of anti-Semitism in Russia following the 1905 war with Japan and the role of the new railroad in bringing more persecution and in making escape to the United States more possible.

1922. Malamud, Bernard. Fixer, The. Farrar; Washington Square Press, 1966. 335 p. $18. Pb $3.

Gr 11+. B 82: May 15 1986. LJ 91: Jul 1966, Oct 15 1966. This tragic story is based on a true account of anti-Semitism in czarist Russia. It concerns a Jewish odd-job man who is accused of a murder in order to discredit all Jews.

1923. Pitt, Nancy. Beyond the High White Wall. Scribner, 1986. 135 p. $12.

Gr 6-9. B 82: Aug 1986. BC 40: Sep 1986. HB 62: Sep/Oct 1986. + - SLJ 32: Aug 1986. VOYA 9: Dec 1986. Until she witnessed a murder, Libby had felt secure in her loving Jewish home, but anti-Semitism was strong in 1903 czarist Russia. Based on experiences of the author's family.

Soviet Union–1917-1953

1924. Campling, Elizabeth. How and Why: The Russian Revolution. (Weighing Up the Evidence). Batsford; dist. by David & Charles, 1987. 64 p. ill. $16.

Gr 8+. SLJ 33: Apr 1987. Enrichment material for students with some background on the revolution, this includes excerpts from letters, speeches, and newspapers; photos; brief biographies; and a glossary.

1925. Campling, Elizabeth. Russian Revolution, The. (Living Through History). Batsford; dist. by David & Charles, 1985. 72 p. ill. $15,

Gr 7+. + - B 82: Dec 1 1985. + - BR 4: Mar/Apr 1986. SLJ 32: Feb 1986. Quotes enhance these profiles of 15 American, British, and Russian observers of the revolution. Suitable to provide a varied perspective for students who have some background on the revolution, this includes a chronology and a glossary.

1926. Riaboff, Alexander. Gatchina Days: Reminiscences of a Russian Pilot. Smithsonian, 1986. 183 p. ill. $20.

Gr 9+. + - BR 5: Jan/Feb 1987. + - LJ 111: Aug 1986. Riaboff reminisces about his experiences as a Russian pilot during World War I and the Russian revolution and civil war.

1927. Ross, Stewart. Russian Revolution, The. Bookwright Press; dist. by Watts, 1989. 64 p. ill. Lib. ed. $13.

Gr 7+. B 85: Jun 1 1989. SLJ 35: Aug 1989. This succinct, illustrated work presents the highlights of Soviet history from 1914 to 1924. A glossary and brief biographies of notable persons are included.

Soviet Union–1917-1953–Fiction

1928. Holman, Felice. Wild Children, The. Scribner, 1983. 149 p. $12.

Gr 6+. * B 80: Sep 15 1983. BC 37: Dec 1983. HB 59: Dec 1983. * SE 48: May 1984. SLJ 30: Nov 1983. * VOYA 7: Apr 1984. World War I and the Russian revolution left thousands of homeless and starving children roaming in bands trying to survive. Through Alex and his friends, Holman tells their little-known story.

1929. Koestler, Arthur. Darkness at Noon. Macmillan; Bantam, 1941. 254 p. $16. Pb $4.

Gr 10+. B 37: Jun 15 1941. B 82: May 15 1986. LJ 66: May 1 1941. In 1930 Rubashov, one of the last of the original Central Committee of the Communist Party, is accused of incredible crimes, tortured, and executed, in a story based on the experiences of many people in the notorious Moscow Trials.

1930. Pasternak, Boris. Doctor Zhivago. Pantheon; Ballantine, 1958. 558 p. $18. Pb $4.

Gr 10+. B 55: Oct 15 1958. B 82: May 15 1986. + - LJ 83: Sep 15 1958. Zhivago, an intellectual physician, is the focus of this lengthy novel about the Russian revolution and its aftermath.

1931. Posell, Elsa. Homecoming. Harcourt, 1987. 230 p. $15.

Gr 6-9. B 84: Dec 1 1987. BC 41: Jan 1988. HB 64: Mar/Apr 1988. SLJ 34: Dec 1987. * VOYA 11: Apr 1988. Olya's Jewish family was well-to-do because her father worked for the czar, but the Bolshevik revolution put them in danger. Father fled and mother and children were left without resources. Based on the experiences of the author's family.

1932. Rybakov, Anatoli. Children of the Arbat. Little, Brown, 1988. 685 p. $20.

Gr 12+. B 84: Apr 1 1988. - BR 7: Nov/Dec 1988. + - LJ 113: Aug 1988. After suppression for 20 years, this novel of life in Moscow under Stalin was released. It concerns Sasha, an eager young communist who is exiled to Siberia; Vanya, a pleasure-seeking woman; and Yuri, an opportunist.

1933. Solzhenitsyn, Alexander. One Day in the Life of Ivan Denisovich. Bantam, 1963. 160 p. Pb $3.

Gr 10+. B 82: May 15 1986. LJ 88: Feb 1 1963. A realistic and graphic account of a day in the life of an inmate of a forced labor camp in Siberia.

Soviet Union–1953-1999

1934. Beloff, Nora. Inside the Soviet Empire: The Myth and the Reality. Times Books, 1980. 188 p. $10.

Gr 9+. B 76: Jun 15 1980. - LJ 105: Jun 1 1980. In her travels through the Soviet Union, Beloff examined how regional nationalities were being assimilated, and reveals a militaristic, change-resistant government that discriminates against nationalist groups.

1935. Bernards, Neal. Soviet Union, The. (Opposing Viewpoints Series). Greenhaven Press, 1987. 251 p. ill. $14. Pb $7.

Gr 7+. B 84: Feb 15 1988. SLJ 34: Feb 1988. Selected from articles, interviews, reports, and speeches are opposing points of view concerning Soviet economic problems, discrimination, foreign policy, human rights, and other contemporary issues.

1936. Gorbachev, Mikhail. Perestroika: New Thinking for Our Country and the World. Harper, 1988. 254 p. $20.

Gr 9+. B 84: Jan 15 1988. + - BR 7: Nov/Dec 1988. * LJ 113: Feb 15 1988. Gorbachev's detailed presentation of the reforms he proposes includes a plea for support from the Soviet people and western leaders.

1937. Kerblay, Basile. Gorbachev's Russia. Pantheon, 1989. 156 p. ill. Pb $9.

Gr 9+. B 85: Mar 1 1989. LJ 114: Apr 1 1989. Kerblay clearly explains the political, social, and economic implications of Gorbachev's reforms.

1938. Nagorski, Andrew. Reluctant Farewell. Holt, 1985. 291 p. $17.

Gr 9+. B 82: Dec 1 1985. LJ 110: Dec 1985. * VOYA 9: Apr 1986. Nagorski was Moscow bureau chief for Newsweek magazine. He reports his impressions of Moscow society and Russian politics.

1939. Soviet Union, The. 2nd ed. (Congressional Quarterly). Congressional Quarterly, 1986. 383 p. $16.

Gr 9+. * BR 5: Jan/Feb 1987. This balanced reference on the Soviet Union has chapters on such topics as history, Khrushchev, Brezhnev, foreign policy, the military, economy, and culture. Maps, charts, biographies, and a chronology are included.

1940. Walker, Martin. Waking Giant: Gorbachev's Russia. Pantheon, 1987. 298 p. $18.

Gr 9+. B 83: Jan 15 1987. Walker, a British journalist, presents the Soviet Union of the late 1980s as a waking giant that is instituting wide-reaching political and social changes.

Soviet Union–1953-1999–Fiction

1941. Bograd, Larry. Kolokol Papers, The. Farrar, 1981. 196 p. $10.

Gr 7+. + - B 78: Feb 1 1982. + - BC 35: May 1982. SLJ 28: Mar 1982. VOYA 5: Jun 1982. The son of a dissident, Leo must learn to deal with the realities of life under a repressive regime as well as the natural problems of an adolescent.

1942. Sevela, Ephraim. Why There Is No Heaven on Earth. Harper, 1982. 205 p. $10. Lib. ed. $10.

Gr 7+. B 78: Jul 1982. + - BC 36: Nov 1982. + - BR 1: Sep/Oct 1982. HB 58: Aug 1982. + - SLJ 28: Apr 1982. The narrator tells about the adventures of his mischievous but loving Jewish friend. Set in a Russian village shortly before the beginning of World War II.

1943. Sherman, Eileen Bluestone. Monday in Odessa. Jewish Publication Society, 1986. 164 p. $11.

Gr 5-9. * SE 51: Apr/May 1987. SLJ 33: Jan 1987. The story of 12-year-old Marina shows the prejudice faced by Soviet Jews, which causes many of them to endure the difficult process of applying for an exit visa. Based on a true story.

Soviet Union–1953-1999–Social Life and Customs

1944. Rywkin, Michael. Soviet Society Today. M. E. Sharpe, 1989. 235 p. $35. Pb $13.

Gr 9+. B 85: Aug 1989. + - LJ 114: Jul 1989. Rywkin presents a clearly written exploration of contemporary Soviet cultural and political life, ethnic groups, and economic concerns.

Soviet Union–Biographies

1945. Ali, Tarik. Trotsky for Beginners. (Pantheon Documentary Comic Book). Pantheon, 1980. 173 p. ill. Pb $3.

Gr 9+. SLJ 27: Dec 1980. Cartoons and quotes introduce Leon Trotsky, a major leader of the Russian revolution.

1946. Baker, Nina. Lenin. Vanguard, 1945. 257 p. ill. $13.

Gr 7-9. Metzner. B 42: Jan 15 1946. Baker's balanced account of Lenin's life clarifies the role he played in Soviet politics.

1947. Butson, Thomas. Mikhail Gorbachev. (World Leaders Past & Present). Chelsea House, 1986. 116 p. ill. $16.

Gr 8+. B 83: Feb 15 1987. + - SLJ 33: Feb 1987. Quotes and illustrations enhance this chronological account of Gorbachev's rise to power. It provides an overview of Soviet political history since the 1930s.

1948. Caulkins, Janet. Picture Life of Mikhail Gorbachev. Rev. ed. Watts, 1989. 64 p. ill. Lib. ed. $11.

Gr 2-6. B 85: May 1 1989. + - SLJ 34: Jun 1989. A timeline, glossary, and photos of Gorbachev and his family augment this concise, informative introduction to the Soviet leader and his policies.

1949. Clark, Ronald W. Lenin. Harper, 1988. 576 p. ill. $28.

Gr 9+. B 85: Nov 15 1988. LJ 113: Dec 1988. Lenin's private life was instrumental in shaping his political philosophy. Clark's distinguished biography presents a clear picture of the man and his influence on world history.

1950. Conquest, Robert. Stalin and the Kirov Murder. Oxford University Press, 1989. 164 p. $17.

Gr 9+. SLJ 35: Oct 1989. The assassination of Sergei Kirov cleared the way for Stalin to become the unquestioned dictator of the Soviet Union. This account is based on interviews and documents.

1951. Dovlatov, Sergei. Ours. Weidenfeld & Nicholson, 1989. 105 p. $16.

Gr 9+. B 85: Mar 1 1989. LJ 114: Mar 1 1989. Dovlatov presents revealing and humorous anecdotes about 4 generations of his well-to-do family, and the reasons he was forced to emigrate to the United States.

1952. Feinberg, Barbara Silberdick. Marx and Marxism. Watts, 1985. 122 p. $10.

Gr 6-10. B 82: Jan 1 1986. BR 4: Mar/Apr 1986. SLJ 32: Aug 1986. Part I focuses on the life of Karl Marx and shows how events in his life influenced his economic and political philosophy. Part II is a clear, basic explanation of his theories.

1953. Haney, John. Vladimir Ilich Lenin. (World Leaders Past & Present). Chelsea House, 1988. 112 p. ill. $17.

Gr 6-10. B 84: Apr 1 1988. Haney's biography of Lenin shows how his personal goals and the political events of the time brought about his leadership of a revolution that changed world history.

1954. Hunter, Nigel. Karl Marx. (Great Lives). Bookwright Press; dist. by Watts, 1987. 32 p. ill. $11.

Gr 4-7. SLJ 34: Mar 1988. This colorful introduction presents the highlights of Marx' life and beliefs.

1955. Kort, Michael. Nikita Khrushchev. (Impact Book). Watts, 1989. 160 p. ill. $13.

Gr 7+. B 86: Nov 1 1989. SLJ 35: Nov 1989. In recounting Khrushchev's political successes and failures, Kort also presents Soviet history of the time. Photos and quotes augment the work.

1956. Levchenko, Stanislav. On the Wrong Side: My Life in the KGB. Pergammon-Brassey; dist. by Kampmann, 1988. 244 p. $19.

Gr 9+. B 84: Mar 15 1988. Levchenko was a high ranking KGB expert in Japan who defected to the United States in 1979. This is his account of his espionage activities, his rise to power, and his decision to defect.

1957. Marrin, Albert. Stalin: Russia's Man of Steel. Viking, 1988. 202 p. ill. $14.

Gr 9+. B 85: Dec 15 1988. * BR 8: Sep/Oct 1989. HB 65: Mar/Apr 1989. * SLJ 35: Nov 1988. Photos and numerous quotes augment this political and personal biography of the Russian dictator.

1958. Medvedev, Roy. Khrushchev. Anchor/Doubleday, 1983. 292 p. ill. $18.

Gr 9+. B 79: Apr 1 1983. + - LJ 108: May 1 1983. This balanced account of the life of the Soviet leader who succeeded Stalin emphasizes his public life.

1959. Navazelskis, Ina L. Leonid Brezhnev. (World Leaders Past & Present). Chelsea House, 1987. 112 p. ill. $17.

Gr 6+. + - B 84: Oct 15 1987. * BR 7: Sep/Oct 1988. VOYA 11: Oct 1988. The history of Russia since the 1917 revolution is seen in this biography of Brezhnev, who led the Soviet Union for 18 years.

1960. Oleksy, Walter. Mikhail Gorbachev: A Leader for Soviet Change. Childrens Press, 1989. 152 p. ill. Lib. ed. $15.

Gr 4-6. B 85: Aug 1989. SLJ 35: Nov 1989. Oleksy's illustrated biography of Gorbachev is a balanced account of the Soviet leader's personal and political life.

1961. Rawcliffe, Michael. Lenin. (Reputations). Batsford; dist. by David & Charles, 1989. 62 p. ill. $20.

Gr 7+. SLJ 35: May 1989. A profusion of quotes presents conflicting views about Lenin's politics and leadership. Maps and photos are included.

1962. Resnick, Abraham. Lenin: Founder of the Soviet Union. (People of Distinction). Childrens Press, 1988. 132 p. ill. $13.

Gr 5-9. B 84: Jun 1 1988. + - SLJ 34: Aug 1988. Resnick explains why and how Lenin came to lead the 1917 Bolshevik revolution, his dictatorial leadership style, and his continuing importance to the Soviets.

1963. Sadler, Catherine Edwards. Sasha: The Life of Alexandra Tolstoy. Putnam, 1982. 138 p. ill. $10.

Gr 9+. B 79: Oct 15 1982. + - BC 36: Nov 1982. BR 2: Sep/Oct 1983. SLJ 29: Jan 1983. VOYA 5: Dec 1982. As the daughter of Leo Tolstoy, Alexandra had a lonely, aristocratic childhood. As an adult she worked to help refugees and the down-trodden. Her biography describes life in Russia during and after the revolution.

1964. Sullivan, George. Mikhail Gorbachev. Messner; Silver Burdett, 1988. 132 p. ill. Lib. ed. $10. Pb $6.

Gr 5-10. B 84: Aug 1988. BR 8: May/Jun 1989. SLJ 34: Aug 1988. + - VOYA 11: Oct 1988. Gorbachev's rise to political power and his policies are the focus of this illustrated biography.

1965. Topalian, Elyse. V. I. Lenin. (Impact Biography). Watts, 1983. 122 p. ill. $9.

Gr 7+. B 79: Aug 1983. BR 2: Nov/Dec 1983. SLJ 30: Oct 1983. Although he grew up a privileged youth, Lenin spent his life working for the revolution. Topalian shows the chaos in Russia at the turn of the century and how events dictated policy.

Soviet Union–Espionage and Spies

1966. Brook-Shepherd, Gordon. Storm Birds: Soviet Postwar Defectors. Weidenfeld & Nicholson, 1989. 386 p. $20.

Gr 10+. B 85: Jun 15 1989. + - LJ 114: Jun 15 1989. In discussing the Soviet spies who defected to the west, Brook-Shepherd discusses their all-too-human motives and their weaknesses, presenting an unusual view of the world of espionage.

1967. Yost, Graham. KGB: The Russian Secret Police from the Days of the Czars to the Present. (World Espionage). Facts on File, 1989. 160 p. ill. $17.

Gr 8+. B 86: Oct 1 1989. + - SLJ 35: Nov 1989. There has been a secret police force in the Soviet Union since the days of Ivan the Terrible. Yost places the KGB in context and examines its role inside the U.S.S.R. and in international politics.

Soviet Union–Fiction

1968. Herman, Charlotte. House on Walenska Street, The. Dutton, 1989. 80 p. $11.

Gr 3-6. B 86: Nov 1 1989. SLJ 35: Dec 1989. Leah is a young Jewish girl growing up in Russia at the turn of the 20th century. Her widowed mother tries to care for the family and protect them from the pogroms, while letters from cousins in America tell of the wonders there.

1969. Shusterman, Neal. Dissidents. Little, Brown, 1989. 183 p. $14.

Gr 6-10. + - B 85: Aug 1989. BC 42: Jun 1989. * BR 8: Nov/Dec 1989. + - SLJ 35: Oct 1989. As son of the United States ambassador, Derek finds his life excessively restrictive. When he has a chance to help a Russian girl rescue her father, a Soviet dissident, he becomes involved in a dangerous adventure.

Soviet Union–Kings, Queens, Rulers, etc.

1970. Alexander, John T. Catherine the Great: Life and Legend. Oxford University Press, 1988. 352 p. $25.

Gr 9+. B 85: Oct 1 1988. Catherine was a German princess who became the Empress of Russia and ruled for 34 years. Alexander chronicles her reign and shows her political genius.

1971. Baker, Nina. Peter the Great. Vanguard, 1943. 310 p. ill. $13.

Gr 7+. Metzner. B 40: Jan 1 1944. This entertaining, fictionalized biography of Peter the Great presents his story against a colorful background of life and events in 18th-century Russia.

1972. Bobrick, Benson. Fearful Majesty: The Life and Reign of Ivan the Terrible. Putnam, 1987. 384 p. ill. $20.

Gr 10+. LJ 112: Aug 1987. This biography of the czar's personal and political life describes Moscow society and Ivan's relations with other monarchs.

1973. Butson, Thomas. Ivan the Terrible. (World Leaders Past & Present). Chelsea House, 1987. 112 p. ill. $17.

Gr 6+. B 84: Nov 15 1987. BR 7: Nov/Dec 1988. + - SLJ 34: Dec 1987. Early in his reign Ivan initiated many beneficial policies, but he is remembered for the cruelty of his last years. The harsh truth of these complex times is presented.

1974. De Jonge, Alex. Fire and Water: A Life of Peter the Great. Coward, McCann, 1980. 278 p. $13.

Gr 9+. B 76: Jun 15 1980. LJ 105: Jun 15 1980. SLJ 27: Sep 1980. This readable profile of the flamboyant Russian czar shows his efforts to modernize his nation, and the extremes in both the nation and its ruler.

1975. Grabbe, Alexander. Private World of the Last Tzar: In the Photographs and Notes of General Count Alexander Grabbe. Little, Brown, 1985. 191 p. ill. $25.

Gr 9+. B 81: Mar 1 1985. LJ 110: Mar 1 1985. These photos of Nicholas II, the czar of Russia, and his family were taken by the head of his military escort. Editing and the addition of background materials was done by the photographer's son and daughter-in-law.

1976. Longworth, Philip. Alexis: Tsar of All the Russias. Watts, 1984. 305 p. ill. $19.

Gr 11+. B 81: Sep 15 1984. B 82: Dec 1 1985. Longworth examines the life and work of Alexis and shows that he began many of the reforms that were credited to his son, Peter the Great.

1977. Massie, Robert. Nicholas and Alexandra. Atheneum; Dell, 1967. 584 p. ill. $25. Pb $5.

Gr 10+. B 82: Dec 1 1985. B 82: Jan 1 1986. LJ 92: Nov 15 1967. An intimate account of the last days of the Russian empire and the personal tragedy of the family of the emperor.

1978. Massie, Robert. Peter the Great: His Life and World. Knopf; dist. by Random, 1980. 864 p. ill. $20.

Gr 11+. * B 77: Sep 1 1980. B 82: Dec 1 1985. LJ 105: Sep 15 1980. This readable and accurate biography presents detail of the life of an energetic Russian emperor and shows how his controversial reforms affected Russian culture and history.

1979. Stanley, Diane. Peter the Great. Macmillan, 1986. 32 p. ill. $13.

Gr 2-7. B 83: Oct 1 1986. BC 40: Oct 1986. HB 63: Jan/Feb 1987. * SE 51: Apr/May 1987. + - SLJ 33: Nov 1986. Stanley's attractive, full-color picture biography shows the youth of the Russian emperor and the highlights of his reign.

1980. Troyat, Henri. Alexander of Russia: Napoleon's Conqueror. Dutton, 1983. 356 p. ill. $18.

Gr 10+. LJ 108: Feb 15 1983. Alexander I led his nation against Napoleon's advances and helped establish the Holy Alliance to preserve peace in Europe, but he is believed to have spent his last days as a hermit.

1981. Troyat, Henri. Catherine the Great. Dutton, 1980. 377 p. ill. $18.

Gr 9+. B 76: Jun 15 1980. LJ 105: Nov 1 1980. Troyat's lively biography of a naive German princess who became the empress of Russia includes a chronology.

1982. Troyat, Henri. Ivan the Terrible. Dutton, 1984. 283 p. ill. $19.

Gr 9+. B 80: Jun 1 1984. B 82: Dec 1 1985. + - LJ 109: May 15 1984. SLJ 31: Nov 1984. The fierce personality of Russia's first czar is clearly seen in this biography.

1983. Troyat, Henri. Peter the Great. Dutton, 1987. 432 p. ill. $23.

Gr 9+. B 83: Jul 1987. + - LJ 112: Jul 1987. The difficulties of the czar's childhood, his accomplishments, and the violence of his reign are graphically portrayed.

1984. Vogt, George. Nicholas II. (World Leaders Past & Present). Chelsea House, 1987. 116 p. ill. $16.

Gr 7+. B 83: May 1 1987. SLJ 34: Sep 1987. Profusely illustrated and enhanced by quotes, this is the story of the well-meaning but inept last czar of Russia.

Soviet Union–Kings, Queens, Rulers, etc.–Fiction

1985. Almedingen, E. M. Crimson Oak, The. Coward, McCann, 1983. 112 p. $10.

Gr 5-9. + - B 79: Apr 15 1983. + - BC 36: Apr 1983. HB 59: Aug 1983. + - SLJ 30: Nov 1983. In 18th-century Russia peasants were forbidden to read, and Peter's efforts to learn landed him in jail. Vivid details of peasant life enrich the story.

Soviet Union–Persecution and Political Prisoners

1986. Gilbert, Martin. Shcharansky. Viking, 1986. 467 p. ill. $25.

Gr 9+. B 82: Jun 1 1986. BR 5: Jan/Feb 1987. LJ 111: Jun 1 1986. This biography of Anatoly Shcharansky also provides a rich account of the life lived by dissident Soviet Jews who try to emigrate.

1987. Hautzig, Esther. Endless Steppe: Growing Up in Siberia. Crowell, 1968; 1987. 256 p. $14. Pb $3.

Gr 7+. Metzner. B 84: Mar 1 1988. HB 44: Jun 1968. LJ 93: Oct 15 1968. SLJ 34: Apr 1988. The author and her family were sentenced to 5 years in exile in Siberia in 1941 when she was 10 years old. She tells of the minutiae of their daily hardships without bitterness.

1988. Jerusalem Post. Anatoly and Avital Shcharansky: The Journey Home. Harcourt, 1986. 263 p. ill. $16.

Gr 9+. B 83: Nov 1 1986. LJ 111: Dec 1986. The efforts of Anatoly and Avital Shcharansky to leave the Soviet Union became an international affair. This dramatic account of their lives includes photos.

1989. LeVert, Suzanne. Sakarov File: A Study in Courage. Messner, 1986. 128 p. ill. $10.

Gr 6+. + - B 82: Jun 15 1986. BC 40: Sep 1986. * SE 51: Apr/May 1987. - SLJ 33: Oct 1986. LeVert summarizes Soviet history and government policy to provide the context for the world renowned human rights activity of Sakharov, a Soviet nuclear physicist. Includes photos.

1990. Ratushinskaya, Irina. Grey Is the Color of Hope. Knopf, 1988. 368 p. $19.

Gr 9+. B 85: Oct 1 1988. * LJ 113: Oct 15 1988. For writing poetry considered to be anti-Soviet, Ratushinskaya spent years in a closely guarded Soviet prison. Her moving account of daily events records heroism, wit, and determined humanity.

1991. Rubenstein, Joshua. Soviet Dissidents: Their Struggle for Human Rights. Beacon, 1980. 304 p. $13.

Gr 9+. BR 1: Nov/Dec 1982. SLJ 27: Dec 1980. This clear account of the price paid by dissident Soviet citizens is based on numerous interviews with emigrants.

1992. Stajner, Karlo. Seven Thousand Days in Siberia. Farrar, 1988. 400 p. $30.

Gr 9+. B 84: Jan 15 1988. LJ 113: Jan 1988. Stajner presents an understated and moving account of the 20 years he spent in a Soviet Gulag in Siberia after he went to the Soviet Union in 1932 to help build a socialist nation.

1993. Wiesel, Elie. Jews of Silence: A Personal Report on Soviet Jewry. Schocken, 1987. 160 p. Pb $9.

Gr 9+. B 83: Apr 15 1987. Wiesel's 1966 edition of this work provided an account of Soviet Jews at a time when they were forbidden to emigrate. This expanded edition recounts the changes in Soviet policy over the past 20 years.

Soviet Union–Social Life and Customs

1994. Blum, Dieter. Russia: The Land and People of the Soviet Union. Abrams, 1980. 187 p. ill. $45.

Gr 9+. B 77: Sep 1 1980. LJ 105: Jul 1980. This richly diverse collection of photos shows Russian agriculture, industry, sports, and culture at their best.

1995. Day in the Life of the Soviet Union, A. Collins; dist. by Harper, 1987. 240 p. ill. $40.

Gr 9+. B 84: Oct 15 1987. LJ 112: Nov 15 1987. In May 1987, 100 photographers took over 100,000 photos, from which 275 were selected to illustrate life in the Soviet Union.

1996. Farb, Nathan. Russians, The. Barron's, 1980. 79 p. ill. Pb $15.

Gr 9+. LJ 105: Jul 1980. At an exhibit of American photos held in Novosibirsk, Farb took photos of the Russian people who attended, and he presents 79 of these photos of ordinary Soviet citizens.

1997. Kaiser, Robert. Russia from the Inside. Dutton, 1980. 186 p. ill. $18. Pb $11.

Gr 9+. B 77: Sep 15 1980. LJ 105: Jul 1980. This collection of photos taken by former Soviet citizens provides a candid view of the social and political lives of ordinary persons. The text provides a good introduction to Soviet culture.

1998. Lee, Andrea. Russian Journal. Random, 1981. 239 p. $14.

Gr 9+. SLJ 28: Feb 1982. The author and her husband lived among the ordinary people in Moscow and Leningrad in 1978-1979. They spoke Russian and made many friends. She presents a perceptive report on their experiences.

1999. Schecter, Jerrold. Back in the U.S.S.R: An American Family Returns to Moscow. Scribner, 1989. 384 p. ill. $23.

Gr 9+. B 85: Jan 1 1989. LJ 114: Feb 1 1989. Schecter's family lived in Moscow in the 1960s and recorded their experiences in An American Family in Moscow. Attracted by glasnost and perestroika they returned in 1987, renewed old acquaintances, and record here the changes they observed.

2000. Shipler, David K. Russia: Broken Idols, Solemn Dreams. Times Books, 1983. 392 p. $18.

Gr 9+. B 79: Aug 1983. LJ 108: Sep 1 1983. SE 49: May 1985. The author interviewed many Soviet citizens to compile this account of the bleak life lived by ordinary Soviet people in the late 1970s.

2001. Wachtel, Andrew. At the Dawn of Glasnost: Soviet Portraits. Proctor Jones; dist. by Publishers Group West, 1988. 136 p. ill. Pb $20.

Gr 9+. B 85: Dec 15 1988. Interviews and over 200 photos show the daily lives of ordinary people, including a fire chief, a grape grower, bakers, and a jazz musician.

2002. Young, Cathy. Growing Up in Moscow: Memories of a Soviet Girlhood, 1963-1980. Ticknor & Fields, 1989. 352 p. $19.

Gr 9+. B 05: May 15 1989. LJ 114: May 1 1989. Young grew up in Moscow and presents a lively account of customs, social conditions, and everyday events in the Soviet capital in the 1970s.

Soviet Union–Ukraine

2003. Oparenko, Christine. Ukraine, The. Chelsea House, 1988. 96 p. ill. $13.

Gr 4-6. B 85: Apr 1 1989. Photos and maps augment this clear account of Ukrainian history, geography, culture, people, and problems.

Soviet Union–Uzbekistan

2004. Wilkins, Frances. Uzbekistan. Chelsea House, 1988. 95 p. ill. $13.

Gr 4-6. B 85: Apr 1 1989. Colorful photos and maps augment this introduction to the history, geography, and daily life of Uzbekistan, a republic in the Soviet Union.

Spain

2005. Cross, Esther. Spain. (Enchantment of the World). Childrens Press, 1985. 127 p. ill. $20.

Gr 4-6. B 82: Mar 1 1986. Spanish history, geography, culture, industry, and people are introduced in this illustrated work.

2006. Miller, Arthur. Spain. (Places and Peoples of the World). Chelsea House, 1989. 120 p. ill. $13.

Gr 4-6. B 85: Apr 1 1989. SLJ 35: May 1989. VOYA 12: Aug 1989. Miller's introduction to Spain's history, geography, culture, people, and contemporary problems includes colorful photos.

2007. Unstead, R. J. Galleon, A. (See Inside). Warwick; dist. by Watts, 1986. 32 p. ill. $11.

Gr 4-8. BR 6: May/Jun 1987. SLJ 33: Feb 1987. Cutaway pictures show the design and construction of the great vessels of the Spanish Armada. Famous battles and life on board are also covered. Includes glossary.

2008. Woods, Geraldine. Spain: A Shining New Democracy. (Discovering Our Heritage). Dillon Press, 1987. 166 p. ill. $13.

Gr 4-8. B 84: Oct 1 1987. SLJ 34: Oct 1987. Full-color photos supplement this survey of Spanish history. Also covered are crafts, agriculture, education, geography, government, recreation, and holidays.

2009. Yokoyama, Masami. Spain. (Children of the World). Gareth Stevens, 1987. 63 p. ill. $13.

Gr 3-7. B 83: Jun 1 1987. SLJ 33: Aug 1987. Following an introduction to the life of a young Spanish child is information on Spanish history, culture, agriculture, geography, and resources.

Spain–0-1935

2010. Anderson, David. Spanish Armada, The. Hampstead Press; dist. by Watts, 1988. 48 p. ill. $12.

Gr 5-9. B 85: Jan 15 1989. * SLJ 35: Apr 1989. Concise and highly illustrated, Anderson's introduction to the Armada describes the battle's causes, events, and results, and daily life in England and Spain in 1588.

2011. Connatty, Mary. Armada, The. Warwick; dist. by Watts, 1988. 48 p. ill. $14.

Gr 5+. B 84: Apr 1 1988. SLJ 35: May 1988. Portraits, maps, and illustrations enhance this lively and impartial account of the power struggle that led Spain to launch her mighty armada against England, and the culminating battle.

2012. Finkelstein, Norman H. Other 1492: Jewish Settlement in the New World. Scribner, 1989. 96 p. ill. $13.

Gr 6+. B 86: Nov 1 1989. BC 43: Dec 1989. The time of Columbus' exploration (which was heavily financed by Jewish backers) was also the time of the Spanish Inquisition that forced Jews to abandon their faith or leave the country. Many of these persons came to the New World and settled in North and South America.

2013. Garnett, Henry. Know About the Armada. Dufour, 1967. 60 p. ill. $14.

Gr 7+. Metzner. This brief, illustrated overview of the Armada covers the causes and events of a memorable battle between the English and the Spanish in the English Channel.

2014. Harris, Nathaniel. Armada: The Decisive Battle. (Day That Made History). Batsford; dist. by David & Charles, 1987. 64 p. ill. $17.

Gr 6-10. * BR 6: Nov/Dec 1987. + - SLJ 34: Mar 1988. This clearly written work with archival illustrations analyzes the causes of the war between Spain and England and the impact of this battle on history.

2015. Howarth, David. Voyage of the Armada: The Spanish Story. Viking, 1981. 255 p. ill. $14.

Gr 9+. * B 77: Jul 1 1981. LJ 106: Sep 1 1981. SLJ 28: Jan 1982. In 1588 Spain sent the largest fleet ever assembled to fight against the English. Told from the Spanish point of view, this account shows clearly why the Armada was doomed before it sailed.

2016. Martin, Colin. Spanish Armada, The. Norton, 1988. 296 p. ill. $28.

Gr 9+. B 85: Sep 1 1988. LJ 113: Sep 1 1988. This large-format, illustrated account of the Armada is chronologically arranged. It covers political conflicts, military issues, and the details of building and manning the ships.

2017. McDowall, David. Spanish Armada, The. (Living Through History). Batsford; dist. by David & Charles, 1988. 72 p. maps. $18.

Gr 8+. BR 7: Nov/Dec 1988. - SLJ 35: Mar 1989. The causes for the enmity between the British and Spanish that led to the development of the Armada are explained, along with the way the sailors lived. Quotes, illustrations, and brief biographies are also included.

Spain–0-1935–Fiction

2018. Aiken, Joan. Teeth of the Gale, The. Harper, 1988. 308 p. $15. Lib. ed. $15.

Gr 7+. B 85: Sep 15 1988. BC 42: Nov 1988. BR 8: May/Jun 1989. HB 64: Nov/Dec 1988. SLJ 35: Nov 1988. * VOYA 11: Dec 1988. Spies, political intrigue, romance, and adventure are part of this historical novel set in Spain in 1820. This sequel to Go Saddle the Sea and Bridle the Wind concludes with an afterword that clarifies the historic background.

2019. De Trevino, Elizabeth Borton. I, Juan de Pareja. Farrar, 1965. 180 p. $10.

Gr 7-10. B 82: Dec 1 1985. LJ 90: Jul 1965. A slave who served Velazquez, a famous 17th-century artist, tells the story of their lives and provides a fine account of life in Spain during the reign of King Phillip IV.

2020. Gidley, Charles. Armada. Viking, 1988. 437 p. $20.

Gr 9+. B 84: Jan 1 1988. LJ 113: Jan 1988. This historical adventure concerns Tristan Pascoe, a Cornish fisherman's son, who is at various times a sailor, a slave, a fugitive, a lover, and a spy for Elizabeth I as the battle of the Armada draws near.

2021. Von Canon, Claudia. Inheritance, The. Houghton, 1983. 212 p. $11.

Gr 9+. B 79: Jun 1 1983. * BC 37: Sep 1983. BR 2: Sep/Oct 1983. HB 59: Aug 1983. * SE 48: May 1984. + - SLJ 30: Sep 1983. + - VOYA 6: Dec 1983. The horrors of the Spanish Inquisition in the late 16th century provide the setting for this story about Miguel, who learns that his father has committed suicide and that his inheritance is being held by the Great Inquisitor.

Spain–1936-1999

2022. Katz, William Loren. Lincoln Brigade: A Picture History. Atheneum, 1989. 96 p. ill. $15.

Gr 7+. + - B 85: Jul 1989. + - BC 43: Sep 1989. BR 8: Nov/Dec 1989. HB 65: Nov/Dec 1989. SLJ 35: Sep 1989. An abundance of photos augments this account of the Spanish civil war and the Americans of the Lincoln Brigade who fought against fascism there.

2023. Lawson, Don. Abraham Lincoln Brigade: Americans Fighting Fascism in the Spanish Civil War. Harper, 1989. 176 p. ill. $12. Lib. ed. $12.

Gr 7+. B 85: May 15 1989. BC 43: Sep 1989. BR 8: Nov/Dec 1989. HB 65: Nov/Dec 1989. * SLJ 35: Jul 1989. * VOYA 12: Oct 1989. The political and military issues of the Spanish civil war of the 1930s are clarified in this account of the activities of American volunteers who fought for the democracy.

2024. Miller, John. Voices Against Tyranny: Writing of the Spanish Civil War. Scribner, 1986. 231 p. $17. Pb $8.

Gr 9+. B 82: Aug 1986. This anthology of essays and stories commemorates the Spanish civil war and show its duality.

2025. Mitchell, David. Spanish Civil War, The. Watts, 1983. 208 p. ill. $19.

Gr 9+. B 79: Apr 15 1983. LJ 108: Apr 1 1983. This effectively illustrated, topical depiction of the civil war incorporates excerpts from eyewitness accounts. A chronology and a glossary are included.

2026. Preston, Paul. Spanish Civil War, 1936-39, The. Grove; dist. by Random, 1986. 184 p. ill. $20.

Gr 9+. B 83: Sep 15 1986. LJ 111: Sep 15 1986. Preston analyzes the causes of the Spanish civil war within the context of Spanish history. Photos and a glossary are included.

2027. Smolan, Rick. Day in the Life of Spain, A. Collins; dist. by Harper, 1988. 220 p. ill. $45.

Gr 9+. B 84: Jun 1 1988. One hundred photojournalists took thousands of pictures of Spain and its people on one day and from these selected photos that present a fresh picture of post-Franco Spain.

2028. Spanish Civil War: A History in Pictures. Norton, 1986. 192 p. ill. $30.

Gr 10+. LJ 111: Sep 15 1986. This photo-history of the Spanish civil war (1936-1939) includes archival photos and reproductions of posters and other propaganda materials from both the Loyalist and Franco camps.

Spain–1936-1999–Fiction

2029. Griffiths, Helen. Last Summer: Spain 1936. Holiday, 1979. 151 p. ill. $8.

Gr 5-10. B 76: Jan 1 1980. HB 56: Apr 1980. SLJ 26: Dec 1979. + - VOYA 2: Feb 1980. The Spanish civil war had not affected Eduardo when he and his father went to their country estate for the summer. But the disappearance of his father and the death of two servants left the boy alone with an elderly horse to cross the war-torn plain to find his mother.

2030. Watson, James. Freedom Tree, The. Victor Gollancz; dist. by David & Charles, 1986. 160 p. $17.

Gr 5-10. + - B 83: Nov 1 1986. + - SLJ 33: Feb 1987. Two young runaways go to Spain to join the international brigade fighting the fascists. They see trench warfare and the bombardment of Guernica in this fast-moving story that includes vivid descriptions.

Spain–Biographies

2031. Garza, Hedda. Francisco Franco. (World Leaders Past & Present). Chelsea House, 1987. 112 p. ill. $17.

Gr 6-10. B 83: Aug 1987. SLJ 34: Nov 1987. * VOYA 12: Jun 1989. Garza details the events of Franco's life and shows how he analyzed the Spanish political situation in order to gain and retain power. The events of the Spanish civil war and the role of Americans and the United States government are also shown.

2032. Snellgrove, Laurence Ernest. Franco and the Spanish Civil War. McGraw-Hill; Longman, 1968; 1980. 118 p. ill. Pb $5.

Gr 9+. Metzner. LJ 93: Sep 15 1968. Some persons felt that Franco was an opportunistic dictator, while others felt that he saved Spain from communism. In examining both points of view Snellgrove explores the historical and political reasons for the civil war.

Spain–Kings, Queens, Rulers, etc.

2033. McKendrick, Melveena. Ferdinand and Isabella. (Horizon Caravel Book). Harper, 1968. 151 p. ill. $16.

Gr 7+. Metzner. D 65: Oct 1 1968. This well-illustrated work examines the lives of the royal pair and the methods they used to unite the nation and retain their power.

2034. Stevens, Paul. Ferdinand and Isabella. (World Leaders Past & Present). Chelsea House, 1987. 111 p. ill. $17.

Gr 6-10. B 84: Mar 1 1988. Stevens' illustrated biography is well researched. It discusses the positive results of Ferdinand and Isabella's efforts to modernize Spain, and the tragic effects of the Inquisition.

Sweden

2035. Bjener, Tamiko. Sweden. (Children of the World). Gareth Stevens, 1987. 63 p. ill. $13.

Gr 3-7. B 83: Jun 1 1987. SLJ 34: Dec 1987. One part of this book covers Swedish history, government, agriculture, geography, social life, and industry. The other part is an introduction to the life of a typical child from a well-to-do family.

2036. Hintz, Martin. Sweden. (Enchantment of the World). Childrens Press, 1985. 125 p. ill. $20.

Gr 4-6. B 82: Mar 1 1986. Hintz's illustrated introduction to Swedish history, economy, culture, government, and geography includes maps and a reference section.

2037. Olsson, Kari. Sweden: A Good Life for All. (Discovering Our Heritage). Dillon Press, 1983. 144 p. ill. $10.

Gr 4-8. B 79: Jul 1983. BC 36: May 1983. SLJ 29: Aug 1983. This introduction to Swedish history and geography, customs, education, and sports includes a discussion of current political problems. Photos, a pronunciation guide, and a map are included.

Sweden–Fiction

2038. Kullman, Harry. Battle Horse, The. Bradbury, 1981. 183 p. $9.

Gr 6-8. BC 35: Oct 1981. VOYA 4: Dec 1981. This runner-up for the 1980 Hans Christian Andersen Medal reveals the inequities in Swedish social structure 50 years ago. Action centers in a school where the upper class boys are "knights" and the lower class boys are honored to be their "horses."

Switzerland

2039. Hintz, Martin. Switzerland. (Enchantment of the World). Childrens Press, 1986. 127 p. ill. $15.

Gr 4-6. B 83: Apr 1 1987. SLJ 33: May 1987. Colorful photos augment the text that covers Swiss history, culture, geography, industry, and people.

2040. Schrepfer, Margaret. Switzerland: The Summit of Europe. (Discovering Our Heritage). Dillon Press, 1989. 142 p. ill. $13.

Gr 3-7. B 85: Jul 1989. + - SLJ 35: Oct 1989. Swiss history, culture, economy, government, and the daily lives of the people are covered in this illustrated overview that includes a map and a glossary.

Switzerland–Biographies

2041. Bawden, Nina. William Tell. Lothrop, 1981. 28 p. ill. $9. Lib. ed. $9.

Gr 1-4. B 78: Nov 15 1981. B 83: Mar 1 1987. + - BC 35: Feb 1982. HB 58: Feb 1982. SLJ 28: Feb 1982. This account of the legendary William Tell provides the setting for an account of the Swiss movement for independence in 1300.

2042. Brown, Pam. Henry Dunant. (People Who Have Helped the World). Gareth Stevens, 1989. 68 p. ill. $13.

Gr 9+. B 85: Aug 1989. SLJ 35: Nov 1989. A chronology, glossary, maps, photos, drawings, and quotations enrich this introduction to the Swiss founder of the International Red Cross.

Switzerland–Fiction

2043. Buff, Mary M. Apple and the Arrow: The Legend of William Tell. Scholastic, 1951. 80 p. $3.

Gr 4-6. Metzner. B 48: Sep 1 1951. * HB 27: Sep 1951. * LJ 76: Sep 1 1951. The Swiss struggle for freedom climaxed in 1291 with the courageous deeds of William Tell and his son, Walter, who is the narrator of this account.

Vikings

2044. Atkinson, Ian. Viking Ships, The. (Cambridge Topic Book). Lerner, 1980. 51 p. ill. $5.

Gr 4-9. B 76: Jul 15 1980. SLJ 27: Mar 1981. This introduction to the explorations of the Norsemen in Europe ca. 900 A.D. includes diagrams of ships, photos, and maps.

2045. Caselli, Giovanni. Viking Settler, A. (Everyday Life of). Peter Bedrick; dist. by Harper, 1986. 30 p. ill. $10.

Gr 4-7. BR 5: Mar/Apr 1987. + - SLJ 33: Dec 1986. Numerous illustrations enhance this account of a Viking family settling in Denmark in the 10th century.

2046. Gibb, Christopher. Viking Sailor, A. (How They Lived). Rourke, 1987. 32 p. maps. $9.

Gr 4-7. SLJ 33: Jun/Jul 1987. Colorful drawings, photos, and maps enrich this account of the daily life of a Viking sailor.

2047. Hughes, Jill. Vikings. Rev. ed. (Civilization Library). Gloucester Press; dist. by Watts, 1984. 32 p. ill. $9.

Gr 3-6. B 81: Sep 1 1984. + - SLJ 31: Oct 1984. Colorful photos and a glossary augment this introduction to Viking history and culture.

2048. Martell, Hazel. Vikings, The. (History as Evidence). Warwick; dist. by Watts, 1986. 37 p. ill. $11.

Gr 4-8. B 82: May 15 1986. BC 39: Jul/Aug 1986. SLJ 33: Dec 1986. Maps, a glossary, photos, and colorful drawings enhance this lively account of Viking history and culture.

2049. Simpson, Jacqueline. Everyday Life in the Viking Age. Putnam, 1967; 1987. 208 p. ill. $18.

Gr 7-9. Metzner. This illustrated account of Viking daily life and customs includes maps and plans.

2050. Windrow, Martin. Viking Warrior, The. (Soldier Through the Ages). Watts, 1985. 32 p. ill. $11.

Gr 4-6. B 81: Aug 1985. SLJ 32: Sep 1985. Large, colorful drawings enhance the concise text that introduces the Vikings and explains the reasons for their explorations. Viking culture, ships, military practices, and trade are also covered.

Vikings–Biographies

2051. Janeway, Elizabeth. Vikings. (Landmark Book). Random, 1951; 1981. 175 p. ill. Lib. ed. $9. Pb $5.

Gr 7-9. Metzner. + - LJ 76: Oct 15 1951. This readable, fictionalized biography of Eric the Red and his son Leif the Lucky covers their explorations in Iceland, Greenland, and Vinland.

2052. Schiller, Barbara. Eric the Red and Leif the Lucky. (Adventures in the New World). Troll, 1979. 48 p. ill. $5. Pb $2.

Gr 5-8. SLJ 26: Jan 1980. The political and social climate is accurately portrayed in this brief introduction to the noted Norse father and son who explored Iceland and Greenland circa 1000 A.D.

Vikings–Fiction

2053. Haugaard, Erik Christian. Leif the Unlucky. Houghton, 1982. 206 p. $9.

Gr 6-10. B 78: Apr 1 1982. BC 35: Jul/Aug 1982. HB 58: Aug 1982. SLJ 28: Mar 1982. The increasingly cold climate and extended isolation from the Norse homeland threaten the survival of the Viking settlement in Greenland, and a leadership struggle ensues.

2054. Treece, Henry. Viking's Dawn. S. G. Phillips, 1956. 252 p. ill. $15.

Gr 7-9. Metzner. B 53: Nov 1 1956. + - LJ 81: Dec 15 1956. As Harald, the son of an outcast lord, travels with the Vikings to Britain, he recounts their adventures and realistic details of their lives.

Yugoslavia

2055. Greene, Carol. Yugoslavia. (Enchantment of the World). Childrens Press, 1984. 128 p. ill. $13.

Gr 4-8. B 81: Sep 1 1984. + - SLJ 31: Oct 1984. Greene's colorfully illustrated introduction to Yugoslavia covers history, geography, culture, politics, and customs.

2056. Lye, Keith. Take a Trip to Yugoslavia. Watts, 1987. 32 p. ill. $10.

Gr 2-5. B 83: Apr 15 1987. SLJ 33: Aug 1987. A brief, informative text and photos on each page introduce Yugoslav history, geography, industry, and cities.

2057. Yokotani, Takako. Yugoslavia. (Children of the World). Gareth Stevens, 1988. 64 p. ill. $13.

Gr 2-4. B 85: Dec 15 1988. Colorful photos complement the text that introduces the life of a Yugoslav family. A brief section provides facts on the nation's history, government, culture, and cities.

Yugoslavia–Biographies

2058. Maclean, Fitzroy. Tito: A Pictorial Biography. McGraw-Hill, 1980. 127 p. ill. $15. Pb $10.

Gr 10+. B 77: Jan 15 1981. LJ 106: Jan 15 1981. Prolifically illustrated, this readable biography traces Tito's personal life and his leadership of Yugoslavia from 1939 to his death in 1980.

2059. Schiffman, Ruth. Josip Broz Tito. (World Leaders Past & Present). Chelsea House, 1987. 112 p. ill. $17.

Gr 6+. B 83: Jun 15 1987. SLJ 33: Aug 1987. This clearly written and highly illustrated biography shows Tito's outstanding military leadership during World War II and his leadership of communist Yugoslavia, which was strong enough to stay outside the Soviet bloc.

North America

General

2060. Georges, D. V. North America. (New True Book). Childrens Press, 1986. 44 p. ill. $12.

Gr 2-4. SLJ 33: May 1987 A short history is included in this colorful work that covers North American geography, resources, wildlife, industry, technology, and people.

General–Caribbean

2061. Carroll, Raymond. Caribbean: Issues in U.S. Relations. (Impact Book). Watts, 1984. 104 p. map. $10.

Gr 6+. + - B 81: Dec 1 1984. * BR 4: May/Jun 1985. SLJ 31: May 1985. * VOYA 8: Apr 1985. This well-organized examination of the history of each nation in the Caribbean includes extensive information on the region's relationship with the United States and current political conditions.

2062. Griffiths, John C. Caribbean in the Twentieth Century, The. (Twentieth Century World History). Batsford; dist. by David & Charles, 1985. 71 p. ill. $15.

Gr 7+. B 81: Jun 15 1985. The last 100 years of the history of the Caribbean nations, and their relations with the United States, are examined from the British point of view in this heavily illustrated work.

General–Caribbean–Fiction

2063. Michener, James A. Caribbean. Random, 1989. 672 p. $23.

Gr 9+. B 86: Sep 1 1989. Michener's saga of the history of the Caribbean ranges from ancient to modern times.

2064. O'Dell, Scott My Name Is Not Angelica. Houghton, 1989. 144 p. $15.

Gr 6-8. + - SLJ 35: Oct 1989. * VOYA 12: Dec 1989. Raisha, a Senegalese girl, is captured and sold into slavery on the Island of St. John. When a slave rebellion is defeated, all the slaves throw themselves from a cliff except Raisha who elects to save her unborn child.

General–Central America

2065. Cheney, Glen Alan. Revolution in Central America. (Impact Book). Watts, 1984. 90 p. ill. $9.

Gr 7+. B 80: May 15 1984. BR 3: Nov/Dec 1984. SLJ 30: Aug 1984. SLJ 32: Dec 1985. * VOYA 7: Dec 1984 A country-by-country account of recent history is included in this balanced overview of the problems of Central America.

2066. Griffiths, John C. Crisis in Central America, The. (Flashpoints). Rourke, 1988. 77 p. ill. $12.

Gr 6-9. SLJ 35: Feb 1989. The causes for the crisis in Central America and the impact of these events on international politics are examined in Griffiths' balanced work.

2067. Karen, Ruth. Land and People of Central America, The. Rev. ed. (Portraits of the Nations Series). Harper, 1965; 1972. 160 p. ill. $12.

Gr 5-9. Metzner. LJ 90: Sep 15 1965. This readable, illustrated introduction to the geography and history of Central America covers from the time of the Maya to the early 1970s.

2068. Langley, Lester D. Central America: The Real Stakes. Crown, 1985. 288 p. $16.

Gr 9+. B 81: Jun 1 1985. LJ 110: May 1 1985. Langley's collection of essays and speeches from Latin studies conferences held at the University of Kentucky in 1983 and 1984 explores the history of relations between Latin American countries and the United States and suggests alternatives to current policies.

2069. Lye, Keith. Take a Trip to Central America. Watts, 1985. 32 p. ill. $10.

Gr 2-4. B 82: Jan 1 1986. + - SLJ 32: Apr 1986. This introduction to the history, geography, economy, and culture of 7 Central American nations includes colorful photos, maps, and a page of illustrations of stamps and currency.

2070. Markun, Patricia Maloney. Central America and Panama. Rev. ed. (First Book). Watts, 1983. 86 p. ill. $9.

Gr 4-8. B 79: May 15 1983. B 82: Dec 1 1985. SLJ 29: Apr 1983. The history, geography, and culture of Belize, El Salvador, Guatemala, Costa Rica, Honduras, Nicaragua, and Panama, and their relations with the United States, are introduced.

2071. Nuccio, Richard A. What's Wrong, Who's Right in Central America? A Citizens Guide. Facts on File, 1986. 136 p. ill. $15.

Gr 9+. B 83: Dec 15 1985. Nuccio's balanced examination of the history of the political situations in El Salvador, Costa Rica, Guatemala, Honduras, and Nicaragua includes an assessment of the role of the United States in the region.

2072. Schooley, Helen. Conflict in Central America. (Keesing's International Studies). Longman; dist by St. James Press, 1987. 326 p. maps. $45.

Gr 10+. B 84: Oct 15 1987. Essays discuss the political, social, and economic history of each Central American nation and the situation there in the mid-1980s. A list of acronyms is included, along with numerous tables and maps.

General–Central America–Mayas

2073. Beck, Barbara L. Ancient Maya, The. Rev. ed. (First Book). Watts, 1983. 64 p. ill. $9.

Gr 5-7. B 79: Apr 1 1983. SLJ 29: Apr 1983. This introduction to the sophisticated Mayan society speculates on the causes for the collapse of their culture. Photos and maps are included.

2074. Gallenkamp, Charles. Maya: The Riddle and Rediscovery of a Lost Civilization. 3rd rev. ed. Viking, 1985. 222 p. ill. $23.

Gr 9+. B 81: Jun 15 1985. A brief history of the Mayan people is included in this account of recent discoveries concerning Mayan life. Over 100 photos enrich the text.

2075. McKissack, Patricia. Mayas, The. (New True Book). Childrens Press, 1985. 45 p. ill. $8.

Gr 2-3. + - SLJ 32: Apr 1986. This brief introduction to Mayan history and culture includes illustrations.

2076. Meyer, Carolyn. Mystery of the Ancient Maya, The. Atheneum, 1985. 93 p. ill. $12.

Gr 6+. B 81: Mar 15 1985. B 82: Dec 1 1985. BC 38: Jul/Aug 1985. * SE 50: Apr/May 1986. * SLJ 31: May 1985. This readable and well-illustrated account of the Mayan civilization covers its origins, accomplishments, and culture.

General–Central America–Mayas–Fiction

2077. Peters, Daniel. Tikal: A Novel about the Maya. Random, 1983. 422 p. $17.

Gr 9+. B 80: Sep 1 1983. LJ 108: Sep 1 1983. Rich detail of Mayan customs, religious ceremonies, and politics enhances this novel that speculates on the reasons for the evacuation of Tikal, a major city.

General–West Indies

2078. Anthony, Suzanne. West Indies. (Places and Peoples of the World). Chelsea House, 1989. 128 p. ill. $13.

Gr 5-8. B 85: Jul 1989. * BR 8: Sep/Oct 1989. + - VOYA 12: Oct 1989. The history, geography, politics, economy, and culture of the West Indies are covered in this illustrated work.

Antigua

2079. Kincaid, Jamaica. Small Place, A. Farrar, 1988. 81 p. $14.

Gr 9+. B 84: Jun 15 1988. LJ 113: Jul 1988. Kincaid introduces the history of Antigua and its political and economic conditions and shows that independence has not closed the economic gap between the haves and the have nots.

Canada

2080. Brickenden, Jack. Canada. (Countries of the World). Bookwright Press; dist. by Watts, 1989. 48 p. ill. Lib. ed. $13.

Gr 4-8. B 85: May 15 1989. SLJ 35: May 1989. This colorfully illustrated work introduces daily life in Canada as well as its history, geography, government, climate, and economy.

2081. Canada. (Library of Nations). Time-Life; dist. by Silver Burdett, 1987. 160 p. ill. $19.

Gr 9+. * BR 6: Mar/Apr 1988. Coats of arms, photographic essays, maps, and graphs enrich this detailed and well-organized narrative on Canadian history, people, government, economy, and resources.

2082. Duggan, William Redman. Our Neighbors Upstairs: The Canadians. Nelson-Hall, 1979. 366 p. maps. $17. Pb $9.

Gr 9+. B 76: Feb 1 1980. HT 11: Feb 1981. This thoughtful work on Canadian history and culture is clearly written and includes maps.

2083. Ferguson, Linda. Canada. Scribner, 1979. 242 p. ill. $10.

Gr 6+. B 76: Jan 15 1980. HB 56: Apr 1980. * SE 44: Apr 1980. + - SLJ 26: Feb 1980. Ferguson traces the history of Canada from the days of the native people to the 1970s. Also covered are Canadian geography, economy, politics, and culture.

2084. Hanmer, Trudy J. St. Lawrence, The. (First Book). Watts, 1984. 60 p. ill. $9.

Gr 5-8. B 81: Dec 15 1984. SLJ 31: Nov 1984. Photos augment this introduction to the history and geographical importance of the St. Lawrence River and the surrounding area.

2085. Heritage of Canada. 1st Canadian ed. Reader's Digest (Canada); dist. by Norton, 1978. 376 p. ill. $25.

Gr 9+. B 77: Oct 15 1980. Each of the 42 chronologically arranged chapters concerns a site of historical significance. Maps and illustrations enhance the essays, which were written by experts.

2086. Jacobs, Jane. Question of Separatism: Quebec and the Struggle over Sovereignty. Random, 1980. 134 p. $9.

Gr 9+. B 77: Sep 15 1980. LJ 105: Oct 1 1980. Jacobs' analysis of the economic, cultural, and political issues of the proposed separation of Quebec from the rest of Canada argues in favor of separation.

2087. Lambie, Beatrice R. Mackenzie: River to the Top of the World. (Rivers of the World). Garrard, 1967. 96 p. ill. $4.

Gr 4-7. Metzner. In this illustrated introduction to the Mackenzie River, which flows north through central Canada to Mackenzie Bay, Lambie discusses the history and culture of the people who have lived on its banks and the importance of the river to them.

2088. Lim, Sing. West Coast Chinese Boy. Tundra; dist. by Scribner, 1979. 64 p. ill. $13.

Gr 3-7. B 76: Feb 15 1980. BC 33: Mar 1980. HB 56: Apr 1980. SLJ 26: Apr 1980. The artist-author tells of his boyhood as a young Chinese boy in Vancouver. He speaks of everyday experiences, festivals, relatives, joy, and sorrow.

2089. MacDonald, Ervin Austin. Rainbow Chasers, The. Salem House; dist. by Merrimack Publishers' Circle, 1984. 272 p. maps. $9.

Gr 9+. B 80: May 1 1984. MacDonald's family were pioneers in the Canadian west. He presents a lively account of the hazards they endured in settling the new land.

2090. Marsh, James H. Canadian Encyclopedia, The. Hurtig, 1985. 2089 p. ill. $175.

Gr 9+. B 82: May 15 1986. * LJ 110: Dec 1985. This 3-volume encyclopedia covers all aspects of Canadian life and includes biographies of noted persons.

2091. Poynter, Margaret. Gold Rush! The Yukon Stampede of 1898. Atheneum, 1979. 91 p. ill. $7.

Gr 5-9. SE 44: Apr 1980. SE 44: Oct 1980. Poynter's balanced and illustrated account of the 1898 gold rush to the Yukon shows the greed, courage, and endurance of the thousands who risked everything for wealth.

2092. Ross, Frances Aileen. Land and People of Canada, The. Rev. ed. (Portraits of the Nations Series). Harper, 1964. 152 p. ill. $12.

Gr 5-9. Metzner. LJ 90: Jan 15 1965. This clear and balanced account covers Canadian political, social, and historical development through the early 1960s.

2093. Shepherd, Jenifer. Canada. (Enchantment of the World). Childrens Press, 1988. 144 p. ill. $22.

Gr 4-7. B 85: May 15 1988. + - SLJ 34: Aug 1988. Canadian history, geography, government, economy, and society are introduced in this colorful overview.

2094. Thompson, Wayne C. Canada 1985. (World Today Series). Stryker-Post, 1985. 119 p. ill. Pb $5.

Gr 7+. B 82: Feb 1 1986. Maps and photos add to this well-organized paperback which surveys Canada's history, political system, geography, culture, and people.

2095. Wartik, Nancy. French Canadians, The. (Peoples of North America). Chelsea House, 1989. 112 p. ill. $17.

Gr 5-10. B 85: Apr 1 1989. SLJ 35: Jun 1989. VOYA 12: Aug 1989. Photos, drawings, and maps augment this chronology of 400 years of French Canadian history, including the separatist movement.

2096. Watson, Jane W. Canada: Giant Nation of the North. Garrard, 1968. 111 p. ill. $8.

Gr 3-6. Metzner. The nation's history, geography, government, culture, and legends are included in Watson's overview of Canada.

2097. White, Anne T. St. Lawrence: Seaway of North America. (Rivers of the World) Garrard, 1961. 96 p. ill. $4.

Gr 4-7. Metzner. The waterway provided by the St. Lawrence and the Great Lakes has been of critical importance in the development of eastern Canada. White discusses the history and culture of the people who have lived on its banks.

Canada–Biographies

2098. Wallace, W. Stewart. Macmillan Dictionary of Canadian Biography, The. 4th rev. ed. Macmillan of Canada, 1978. 914 p. $50.

Gr 9+. B 76: Feb 1 1980. These reliable, concise biographical sketches of over 5000 notable Canadians from all fields cover persons who died before 1976.

Canada–Espionage and Spies

2099. Callwood, June. Emma: A True Story of Treason. Beaufort, 1985. 272 p. $17.

Gr 9+. B 81: Mar 15 1985. Canada's first convicted woman spy was found guilty of giving secrets to the Russians in 1946. Her story is unusual because the government's efforts to make an example of her violated Canadian law.

Canada–Fiction

2100. Alderson, Sue Ann. Ida and the Wool Smugglers. Douglas & McIntyre, 1987. 32 p. ill. $12.

Gr K-3. B 84: Nov 15 1987. B 84: Mar 1 1988. HB 64: May 1988. SLJ 34: Aug 1988. British Columbia in the late 19th century is the setting for this lively picture-book story of a little girl who rescues her sheep herd from smugglers.

2101. Anderson, Margaret J. Journey of the Shadow Bairns, The. Knopf; dist. by Random, 1980. 152 p. $8. Lib. ed. $8.

Gr 5-8. B 77: Nov 1 1980. + - BC 34: Feb 1981. HB 57: Apr 1981. SLJ 27: Jan 1981. In 1903 orphaned Elspeth (age 13) and Robbie (age 4) left Scotland to find an aunt in Canada. Details of their journey and frontier life enhance the story.

2102. Bond, Nancy. Another Shore. Macmillan, 1988. 316 p. $16.

Gr 7+. B 85: Sep 1 1988. BC 42: Oct 1988. * BR 8: May/Jun 1989. HB 65: Mar/Apr 1989. SLJ 35: Oct 1988. * VOYA 11: Dec 1988. Modern Lyn, working as a guide to a colonial coffeehouse, suddenly finds herself transported to Nova Scotia in 1744 and must learn to live according to the social ideas of the time. Bond's time-travel story is rich in historical detail.

2103. Downie, Mary Alice. Last Ship, The. (Northern Lights). Peter Martin, 1980. 32 p. ill. $7.

Gr 2-3. SLJ 27: May 1981. Watercolor illustrations embellish this story of 17th-century life in New France as seen from a child's point of view.

2104. Doyle, Brian. Angel Square. Bradbury, 1986. 136 p. $10.

Gr 4-6. + - SLJ 33: May 1987. Life in Ottawa at the end of World War II, with its ethnic strife and wintry weather, are shown in this story about Tommy, who tries to solve the mystery of an attack on a Jewish nightwatchman.

2105. Hamilton, Mary. Sky Caribou, The. (Northern Lights). Peter Martin, 1980. 32 p. ill. $7.

Gr 2-3. SLJ 27: May 1981. This story based on Canadian history tells how the son of a Chipewyan chief helped Samuel Hearne discover the Coppermine River.

2106. Hamilton, Mary. Tin-Lined Trunk, The. Kids Can Press, 1981. 63 p. ill. Pb $3.

Gr 5-7. SLJ 28: Sep 1981. Over 80,000 orphaned or poor children were sent from British slums to live in Canada between 1868 and 1925. Hamilton based her story of Polly and Jack on the actual experiences of these children.

2107. Hudson, Jan. Sweetgrass. Philomel, 1989. 159 p. $14.

Gr 5-9. * B 85: Apr 1 1989. BC 42: Apr 1989. BR 8: Sep/Oct 1989. * SLJ 35: Apr 1989. - VOYA 12: Jun 1989. The story of the rite-of-passage of Sweetgrass includes a great amount of detail about life of 19th-century Canadian Blackfeet.

2108. Lunn, Janet. Shadow in Hawthorn Bay. Scribner, 1987. 180 p. $13.

Gr 5-10. B 83: Jun 1 1987. BC 40: Jun 1987. * BR 6: Nov/Dec 1987. HB 63: Sep/Oct 1987. SLJ 34: Sep 1987. VOYA 10: Aug/Sep 1987. Realistic details of pioneer life in Canada in 1815 and good characterizations enrich this story of a Scottish girl who crosses the ocean to find her cousin after receiving a supernatural plea from him.

2109. McSweeney, Susanne. Yellow Flag, The. (Northern Lights). Peter Martin, 1980. 32 p. ill. $7.

Gr 2-3. SLJ 27: May 1981. The story of Irish immigrants in upper Canada is seen through the experiences of a mother and her daughter.

2110. Neilan, Sarah. Paradise. St. Martin's, 1982. 345 p. $14.

Gr 9+. B 79: Oct 1 1982. + - LJ 107: Oct 1 1982. This lively romance, set in the Canadian wilderness during the War of 1812, shows the problems of pioneer life.

2111. Rawlyk, George. Streets of Gold. (Northern Lights). Peter Martin, 1980. 32 p. ill. $7.

Gr 2-3. + - SLJ 27: May 1981. The British siege of the French fort of Louisbourg is told from the point of view of an underage recruit who looked for adventure.

2112. Smith, T. H. Cry to the Night Wind. Viking, 1986. 160 p. $12.

Gr 6-9. BR 5: Mar/Apr 1987. SE 51: Apr/May 1987. SLJ 33: Feb 1987. On a trip to survey British Columbia in the 1790s, an 11-year-old sea captain's son is captured by the Indians. He befriends a seal pup, who helps him escape in a lively adventure.

2113. Tanaka, Shelley. Michi's New Year. (Northern Lights). Peter Martin, 1980. 32 p. ill. $7.

Gr 2-3. SLJ 27: May 1981. The stories in this series relate events in Canadian history from a child's point of view. Michi is a new immigrant who came to Canada from Japan in 1900.

2114. Webster, Jan. Muckle Annie. St. Martin's, 1986. 299 p. $17.

Gr 9+. B 82: Dec 1 1985. SLJ 32: May 1986. The pioneering spirit of settlers in British Columbia in the late 1850s is seen in these adventures of a determined young woman who travels from Scotland to Canada seeking the man she has promised to marry.

Costa Rica

2115. Costa Rica in Pictures. Rev. ed. (Visual Geography Series). Lerner, 1987. 64 p. ill. $10.

Gr 4+. B 83: Aug 1987. SLJ 33: Jun/Jul 1987. This well-organized and heavily illustrated work explores the history, land, people, government, and economy of Costa Rica. Maps are included.

2116. Rolbein, Seth. Nobel Costa Rica: Waging Peace in Central America. St. Martin's, 1988. 288 p. $17.

Gr 9+. B 85: Nov 15 1988. LJ 113: Dec 1988. SLJ 35: Mar 1989. The past 40 years of Costa Rican political and social development are discussed in this readable work that also presents a colorful description of the land and people.

Cuba

2117. Lindop, Edmund. Cuba. (First Book). Watts, 1980. 64 p. ill. $7.

Gr 5-8. B 76: Jul 1 1980. B 82: Dec 1 1985. Following a brief overview of Cuban geography and history is a balanced account of the political, social, and cultural development of Cuba since Castro attained power in 1959.

2118. Lye, Keith. Take a Trip to Cuba. Watts, 1987. 32 p. ill. $10.

Gr 2-4. B 83: Apr 15 1987. SLJ 33: Aug 1987. A brief, informative text and photos on each page introduce Cuban history, geography, industry, and cities.

2119. Vazquez, Ana Maria B. Cuba. (Enchantment of the World). Childrens Press, 1988. 127 p. ill. $21.

Gr 4-7. B 84: May 15 1988. SLJ 35: Jan 1989. Photos enrich this well-organized presentation of Cuban history, geography, culture, government, and religion.

Cuba–Biographies

2120. Bourne, Peter G. Fidel: A Biography of Fidel Castro. Dodd, 1986. 352 p. ill. $20.

Gr 9+. B 82: Jun 15 1986. BR 5: Jan/Feb 1987. This insightful biography of the Cuban dictator includes information on Cuban social and political history and on international affairs.

2121. Griffiths, John C. Castro. (World Leaders in Context). Batsford; dist. by David & Charles, 1981. 90 p. ill. $15.

Gr 6+ + - B 78: Mar 15 1982. - SLJ 28: May 1982. This account of Castro as a revolutionary and political leader is based primarily on his statements in speeches and interviews.

2122. Vail, John J. Fidel Castro. (World Leaders Past & Present). Chelsea House, 1987. 113 p. ill. $17.

Gr 6-10. SLJ 33: May 1987. VOYA 12: Jun 1989. Numerous quotes and illustrations highlight this biography of Cuba's communist dictator. It emphasizes Castro's political activities.

Dominican Republic

2123. Creed, Alexander. Dominican Republic. Chelsea House, 1987. 92 p. ill. $12.

Gr 6-9. SLJ 34: Mar 1988. Creed's well-illustrated introduction to the history, geography, culture, economy, and people of the Dominican Republic includes maps.

2124. Haverstock, Nathan A. Dominican Republic in Pictures. (Visual Geography Series). Lerner, 1988. 64 p. ill. $10.

Gr 5+. B 84: Apr 15 1988. SLJ 34: Apr 1988. This introduction to the Dominican Republic covers history, economy, geography, government, and people. Maps and photos enhance the text.

El Salvador

2125. Adams, Faith. El Salvador: Beauty Among the Ashes. (Discovering Our Heritage). Dillon Press, 1986. 135 p. ill. $12.

Gr 3-7. B 82: Mar 1 1986. BC 39: Feb 1986. + - BR 5: Sep/Oct 1986. + - SLJ 32: Mar 1986. Adams covers the history, culture, and religion of El Salvador and examines how the civil war affects the economy and daily life. Photos are included.

2126. Cheney, Glenn Alan. El Salvador, Country in Crisis. (Impact Book). Watts, 1982. 90 p. ill. $8.

Gr 7+. B 78: Jul 1982. SLJ 28: Aug 1982. This objective examination of the background of the recent bloody conflict in El Salvador considers the political and economic issues involved and the role of the United States.

2127. Dilling, Yvonne. In Search of Refuge. Herald Press, 1984. 288 p. ill. $10.

Gr 10+. + - BR 3: Sep/Oct 1984. LJ 109: Aug 1984. Dilling sets the historical background of the violent political situation in El Salvador and provides a graphic account, with vivid photos, of the horrors suffered by the people.

2128. Haverstock, Nathan A. El Salvador in Pictures. Rev. ed. (Visual Geography Series). Lerner, 1987. 64 p. ill. $11.

Gr 4-9. B 83: Jun 15 1987. B 83: Aug 1987. SLJ 33: Jun/Jul 1987. History, economy, government, land, and people are all covered in this highly illustrated and balanced introduction to El Salvador.

2129. Sanders, Renfield. El Salvador. (Places and Peoples of the World). Chelsea House, 1988. 104 p. ill. $12.

Gr 4-6. B 85: Dec 15 1988. This illustrated introduction to El Salvador covers history, economy, government, geography, social life, and current problems. A glossary is appended.

Grenada

2130. Eisenberg, Joyce. Grenada. (Places and Peoples of the World). Chelsea House, 1988. 88 p. ill. $12.

Gr 4-8. BR 7: Sep/Oct 1988. + - SLJ 34: Aug 1988. A reference section and maps supplement this introduction to Grenada. Covered are history, social life and customs, and current political concerns.

Guatemala

2131. Anderson, Marilyn. Granddaughters of Corn: Portraits of Guatemalan Women. Curbstone; dist. by Talman, 1988. 124 p. ill. $35. Pb $20.

Gr 9+. B 85: Oct 15 1988. LJ 113: Nov 15 1988. Through personal narratives Guatemalan women tell of the systematic political oppression that is destroying their villages. Their story is accompanied by moving photos of these women and their children and by lists of the names of women who have "disappeared."

2132. Guatemala in Pictures. Rev. ed. (Visual Geography Series). Lerner, 1987. 64 p. ill. $10.

Gr 4-9. B 83: Aug 1987. SLJ 33: Jun/Jul 1987. This clear and balanced illustrated introduction to Guatemalan history, government, economy, and resources includes photos and maps.

2133. Perl, Lila. Guatemala: Central America's Living Past. Morrow, 1982. 157 p. ill. $8.

Gr 5-9. B 78: Aug 1982. + - SLJ 28: Aug 1982. Guatemalan history, economics, politics, and ecology, are covered. An extensive section on contemporary living conditions emphasizes the Indians and the poor. Photos are included.

Haiti

2134. Anthony, Suzanne. Haiti. (Places and Peoples of the World). Chelsea House, 1989. 110 p. ill. $13.

Gr 5+. B 85: Jul 1989. * BR 8: Nov/Dec 1989. VOYA 12: Dec 1989. Haitian history, geography, politics, economy, and culture are covered in this illustrated work.

2135. Haiti in Pictures. Rev. ed. (Visual Geography Series). Lerner, 1987. 64 p. ill. $10.

Gr 4-9. B 83: Aug 1987. + - BC 41: Sep 1987. SLJ 34: Oct 1987. Photos, maps, and graphs enhance this introduction to Haitian history, economy, government, land, and people.

2136. Hanmer, Trudy J. Haiti. (First Book). Watts, 1988. 96 p. ill. $10.

Gr 4-8. B 84: Mar 1 1988. + - BC 41: Mar 1988. SLJ 35: Jun/Jul 1988. The nation's history and contemporary problems are the focus of this illustrated introduction to Haiti.

Haiti—Biographies

2137. Condit, Erin. Francois and Jean-Claude Duvalier. (World Leaders Past & Present). Chelsea House, 1989. 112 p. ill. $17.

Gr 6+. B 85: Aug 1989. BR 8: Sep/Oct 1989. * VOYA 12: Dec 1989. The poverty of Haiti and its violent history are revealed in this introduction to Francois Duvalier and his son Jean-Claude, both of whom were presidents. Photos are included.

Honduras

2138. Honduras in Pictures. Rev. ed. (Visual Geography Series). Lerner, 1987. 64 p. ill. $10.

Gr 4-9. B 83: Aug 1987. SLJ 33: Jun/Jul 1987. This well-illustrated and well-organized introduction to the history, resources, culture, economy, and government of Honduras includes photos.

Honduras—Biographies

2139. Alvarado, Elvia. Don't Be Afraid, Gringo: A Honduran Woman Speaks from the Heart. Institute for Food and Development Policy, 1987. 167 p. ill. Pb $10.

Gr 9+. B 84: Dec 1 1987. Born to a peasant family, Alvarado led in the struggle for land and political reform. In telling her story she shows the effects of foreign influence on events in Honduras.

Jamaica

2140. Lye, Keith. Take a Trip to Jamaica. Watts, 1988. 32 p. ill. $11.

Gr 2-4. B 85: Nov 1 1988. - SLJ 35: Jan 1989. A concise commentary and large photos introduce facts about Jamaican history, geography, politics, and social life.

Mexico

2141. Casagrande, Louis B. Focus on Mexico: Modern Life in an Ancient Land. Lerner, 1986. 96 p. ill. $15.

Gr 4-9. * B 82: Jul 1986. B 83: Jun 15 1987. SLJ 32: Aug 1986. A brief overview of Mexican history is followed by an introduction to 4 young Mexicans who represent the nation's diverse cultures. Numerous photos are included.

2142. Casasola, Agustin Victor. Tierra y Libertad!: Photographs of Mexico, 1900-1935. Universe Books, 1986. 104 p. ill. $15.

Gr 8+. LJ 111: May 1 1986. VOYA 11: Jun 1988. Selected photos from the Casasola archive show the political and social struggles of the Mexican people from 1910 to 1935.

2143. Constable, George. Mexico. (Library of Nations). Time-Life; dist. by Silver Burdett, 1985. 160 p. ill. $14.

Gr 7+. * BR 4: Mar/Apr 1986. Emphasis is on the people of Mexico in this introduction to Mexico, its land, people, and history. Photos and helpful graphs are included.

2144. De Trevino, Elizabeth Borton. Here Is Mexico. Farrar, 1970. 256 p. $11.

Gr 7+. Metzner. B 67: Sep 1 1970. + - BC 24: Nov 1970. - LJ 95: Jun 15 1970. De Trevino lived in Mexico for years. Her introduction to her adopted country includes anecdotes and personal comments along with history and geography. Lists of presidents and important dates are included.

2145. Epstein, Sam. Mexico. Rev. ed. (First Book). Watts, 1983. 64 p. ill. $9.

Gr 4-8. B 79: May 15 1983. SLJ 29: Mar 1983. SLJ 30: Nov 1983. The history of Mexico from ancient times is introduced. Also considered are Mexican politics, government, economy, resources, and tourist attractions. Photos and a map are included.

2146. Jacobsen, Karen. Mexico. (New True Book). Childrens Press, 1982. 45 p. ill. $7.

Gr 1-4. B 79: Mar 1 1983. SLJ 30: Sep 1983. SLJ 31: Apr 1985. Colorful photos, diagrams, and maps enhance this introduction to Mexico and its people.

2147. Johnson, Raymond. Rio Grande, The. (Rivers of the World). Silver Burdett, 1981. 69 p. ill. $8.

Gr 5-8. B 78: Sep 1 1981. SLJ 28: Nov 1981. The history and economic importance of the Rio Grande River and the surrounding area are introduced in this colorful work.

2148. Knowlton, MaryLee. Mexico. (Children of the World). Gareth Stevens, 1986. 63 p. ill. $13.

Gr 3-6. + - BC 40: Mar 1987. - SLJ 34: Sep 1987. This brief introduction to the history and people of Mexico includes photos, a map, and a section of factual information.

2149. Larralde, Elsa. Land and People of Mexico, The. Rev. ed. (Portraits of the Nations Series). Harper, 1968. 160 p. ill. $12.

Gr 5-9. Metzner. LJ 90: Feb 15 1965. This introductory overview of Mexican history from ancient times to the 1960s includes photos and a map.

2150. Matthews, Rupert. Eruption of Krakatoa, The. (Great Disasters). Bookwright Press; dist. by Watts, 1989. 32 p. ill. $11.

Gr 3-6. SLJ 35: May 1989. The disaster of the eruption of Krakatoa and its impact on Mexico are covered in this brief, illustrated work.

2151. Mexico in Pictures. Rev. ed. (Visual Geography Series). Lerner, 1987. 64 p. ill. $10.

Gr 4-9. B 83: Aug 1987. SLJ 33: Aug 1987. This colorful and well-organized introduction to Mexican history, government, economy, ecology, resources, and culture includes numerous photos.

2152. Miller, Robert Ryal. Mexico: A History. University of Oklahoma Press, 1985. 414 p. ill. $20.

Gr 10+. B 82: Sep 1 1985. LJ 110: Jun 1 1985. Miller's balanced account of the cultural, economic, political, and social history of Mexico from the time of the Aztecs includes statistical tables and a glossary.

2153. Riding, Alan. Distant Neighbors; Portrait of the Mexicans. Knopf, 1985. 368 p. $19.

Gr 9+. B 81: Jan 1 1985. * LJ 110: Jan 1985. Following a brief historic overview that shows Mexico's diverse heritage, Riding explores Mexico's current problems and what these mean to the United States.

2154. Rodman, Selden. Short History of Mexico, A. Rev. ed. Stein & Day, 1981. 177 p. ill. $15.

Gr 9+. B 77: Jun 15 1981. A name index and chronology enhance this concise account of Mexican history that ranges from pre-Aztec times to 1980.

2155. Smith, Eileen Latell. Mexico: Giant of the South. (Discovering Our Heritage). Dillon Press, 1983. 159 p. ill. $10.

Gr 3-8. B 80: Oct 1 1983. B 83: Jun 15 1987. + - SLJ 30: Nov 1983. Mexican history, geography, culture, sports, noted persons, and emigration to the United States are all covered in this illustrated work. A glossary is included.

2156. Stein, R. Conrad. Mexico. (Enchantment of the World). Childrens Press, 1984. 126 p. ill. $13.

Gr 4-8. B 80: Aug 1984. B 82: Dec 1 1985. Current problems are examined in this well-illustrated and balanced account of Mexico's history, geography, politics, and economics.

Mexico–Aztecs

2157. Beck, Barbara L. Aztecs, The. Rev. ed. (First Book). Watts, 1983. 64 p. ill. $9.

Gr 5-8. B 79: Apr 1 1983. SLJ 29: Apr 1983. This introduction to the Aztecs describes their rise to power and their daily lives. Photos, drawings, and a map are included.

2158. Beck, Barbara L. First Book of the Aztecs, The. Watts, 1966. 72 p. ill. $9.

Gr 4-6. B 82: Dec 1 1985. Beck's simple and authentic introduction to the Aztec civilization is enriched by excellent photos.

2159. Berdan, Frances. Aztecs, The. Chelsea House, 1988. 112 p. ill. $17.

Gr 6-10. B 85: Mar 1 1989. The arts and crafts of the Aztec people are seen in this introduction to Aztec history and culture.

2160. Bray, Warwick. Everyday Life of the Aztecs. Putnam, 1969; 1987. 240 p. ill. $18.

Gr 7-11. Metzner. LJ 94: Jul 1969. This well-illustrated account of the culture and history of the Aztecs covers family life, occupations, religion, and politics.

2161. Fagan, Brian M. Aztecs, The. Freeman, 1984. 322 p. ill. $28. Pb $15.

Gr 9+. B 80: Aug 1984. Numerous photos and maps augment this account of the origin, rise, and fall of the Aztec empire, its culture, and political elements.

2162. Fisher, Leonard Everett. Pyramid of the Sun, Pyramid of the Moon. Macmillan, 1988. 32 p. ill. $14.

Gr 4-6. * B 85: Oct 1 1988. BC 42: Sep 1988. SLJ 35: Sep 1988. A chronology, map, and illustrations enhance this concise account of the pyramids at Teotihuacan which were sacred to ancient civilizations.

2163. Hughes, Jill. Aztecs. Rev. ed. (Civilization Library). Gloucester Press; dist. by Watts, 1986. 32 p. ill. $10.

Gr 3-5. B 83: Dec 15 1986. This profusely illustrated introduction to Aztec history and culture includes a pronunciation guide.

2164. Karen, Ruth. Feathered Serpent: The Rise and Fall of the Aztecs. Four Winds, 1979. 184 p. ill. $9.

Gr 9+. SLJ 27: Oct 1980. This examination of Aztec history and culture considers art, diet, dress, housing, manners, politics, and slavery. Full-page photos are included.

2165. Marrin, Albert. Aztecs and Spaniards: Cortez and the Conquest of Mexico. Atheneum, 1986. 144 p. ill. $13.

Gr 7+. * B 82: Apr 15 1986. BC 39: Apr 1986. HB 62: Sep/Oct 1986. * SE 51: Apr/May 1987. * SLJ 32: Aug 1986. Marrin's dramatic and graphic account of Aztec culture and its destruction by Cortes includes photos of artifacts and drawings based on primary sources.

2166. McKissack, Patricia. Aztec Indians. (New True Book). Childrens Press, 1985. 48 p. ill. $8.

Gr 1-3. B 82: Dec 1 1985. + - SLJ 32: Apr 1986. Colorful photos, drawings, and diagrams enrich this brief introduction to Aztec history and culture.

2167. Steel, Anne. Aztec Warrior, An. (How They Lived). Rourke, 1988. 32 p. ill. $13.

Gr 3-6. B 85: Nov 15 1988. SLJ 35: Jun 1989. The way of life of the Aztec warrior and the government of his people are introduced in this profusely illustrated work.

Mexico–Aztecs–Fiction

2168. Highwater, Jamake. Sun, He Dies: A Novel about the End of the Aztec World. Lippincott, 1980. 319 p. ill. $12.

Gr 9+. B 76: Jul 1 1980. LJ 105: May 1 1980. SLJ 27: Oct 1980. VOYA 3: Oct 1980. VOYA 5: Jun 1982. Nanautzin, of humble origins, rose to the high position of Chief Orator for Montezuma. Through his story the reader sees all levels of Aztec culture and its destruction by the Spaniards.

2169. O'Dell, Scott. Captive, The. Houghton, 1979. 224 p. $9.

Gr 7+. B 76: Nov 1 1979. BC 33: Mar 1980. + - HB 55: Dec 1979. * SLJ 26: Nov 1979. Rich in action and historical detail, this story of the conquistadors among the Mayas and the Aztecs is told by an idealistic young priest who succumbs to the desire for power. This is a prequel to The Feathered Serpent.

2170. O'Dell, Scott. Feathered Serpent, The. Houghton, 1981. 216 p. $10.

Gr 7+. B 78: Oct 1 1981. BC 35: Dec 1981. HB 58: Feb 1982. SLJ 28: Oct 1981. A young Spanish seminarian was accepted by the Mayans as a god in The Captive, a prequel to this work. In The Feathered Serpent he travels to the Aztec empire to learn how to rule and is caught up in the tragic conflict between Montezuma and Cortes.

Mexico–Bibliographies

2171. Robbins, Naomi C. Mexico. (World Bibliographical Series). Clio Press, 1984. 165 p. $35.

Gr 9+. B 81: Sep 1 1984. This selective bibliography includes material on all aspects of Mexican life.

Mexico–Biographies

2172. Baker, Nina. Juarez, Hero of Mexico. Vanguard, 1942. 316 p. ill. $13.

Gr 7-9. Metzner. B 39: Nov 1 1942. HB 18: Nov 1942. LJ 67: Oct 15 1942. This balanced biography of the Indian who was president of Mexico in the 1860s shows how Benito Juarez' land and economic reforms and political integrity made him a national hero.

2173. De Trevino, Elizabeth Borton. Juarez, Man of Law. Farrar, 1974. 142 p. $6.

Gr 4-8. + - B 71: Jan 15 1975. B 82: Dec 1 1985. LJ 99: Nov 15 1974. A lawyer, president of Mexico, and national hero, Benito Juarez did much to improve the welfare of his countrymen, though many called him a dictator. This simple biography includes fictionalized scenes.

2174. Ragan, John David. Emiliano Zapata. (World Leaders Past & Present). Chelsea House, 1989. 112 p. ill. $17.

Gr 6+. B 85: Aug 1989. BR 8: Sep/Oct 1989. SLJ 35: Oct 1989. VOYA 12: Dec 1989. This heavily illustrated biography places in historical context the life of Mexico's revolutionary leader, who promoted land reform and the causes of the nation's poor.

2175. Rosenblum, Morris. Heroes of Mexico. Fleet Press, 1969. 144 p. $9.

Gr 5-8. B 83: Jun 15 1987. Famous Mexican men and women since the time of the Aztecs are included in this collective biography that covers all fields.

2176. Wepman, Dennis. Benito Juarez. (World Leaders Past & Present). Chelsea House, 1986. 116 p. ill. $16.

Gr 6+. B 83: Feb 15 1987. + - SLJ 33: Feb 1987. VOYA 11: Jun 1988. An insightful look at Mexico in the mid-19th century is presented in this biography of a Zapotec Indian peasant whose struggles to fight injustice elevated him to the presidency of Mexico.

Mexico–Exploration and Explorers

2177. Diaz del Castillo, Bernal. Cortez and the Conquest of Mexico by the Spaniards in 1521. Abridged ed. Shoe String, 1942; 1988. 165 p. ill. $18.

Gr 7+. VOYA 11: Feb 1989. Diaz was a soldier with Cortes' army. This abridged edition of his memoirs provides a reliable account of the conquest of Mexico. Drawings enhance the text.

2178. Wilkes, John. Hernan Cortes, Conquistador in Mexico. (Cambridge Topic Book). Lerner, 1977. 51 p. ill. $7. Pb $4.

Gr 5-8. B 82: Sep 15 1985. SLJ 24: Apr 1978. Photos, maps, and illustrations augment the readable text that describes

Cortes' exploration and his destruction of the Aztec civilization.

Mexico—Fiction

2179. De Trevino, Elizabeth Borton. Guero: A True Adventure Story. Farrar, 1989. 99 p. ill. $13.

Gr 4-9. B 86: Sep 1 1989. BC 42: Jun 1989. HB 65: Sep/Oct 1989. + - SLJ 35: Sep 1989. Events in Mexico late in the 19th century provide the setting for this novel of a judge and his family who were sent into exile after he was deposed by a coup.

2180. Hennessy, Max. Crimson Wind, The. Atheneum, 1985. 247 p. $14.

Gr 9+. B 81: May 15 1985. + - LJ 110: May 1 1985. The politics and battles of the 1911 Mexican revolution are clarified in this novel about the adventures of a British journalist.

Nicaragua

2181. Adams, Faith. Nicaragua: Struggling with Change. (Discovering Our Heritage). Dillon Press, 1987. 149 p. ill. $13.

Gr 3-8. B 83: May 15 1987. + - SLJ 33: Aug 1987. Colorful photos augment this discussion of Nicaraguan history, geography, the culture of its diverse peoples, and the struggle between the Sandinistas and the Contras.

2182. Angel, Adriana. Tiger's Milk: Women of Nicaragua. Seaver Books; dist. by Holt, 1987. 142 p. ill. $19.

Gr 9+. B 84: Dec 1 1987. SLJ 34: Jan 1988. Nicaraguan women of all ages and social groups discuss the current political situation in Nicaragua and the effects of foreign influence.

2183. Cabezas, Omar. Fire from the Mountain: The Making of a Sandinista. Crown, 1985. 221 p. $14.

Gr 9+. B 81: Jul 1985. B 82: Jan 15 1986. + - LJ 110: Jul 1985. Cabezas' earthy memoir of his experiences as a youthful recruit in the Sandinista rebel forces in the early 1970s was a best seller in Nicaragua.

2184. Davis, Peter. Where Is Nicaragua? Simon & Schuster, 1987. 349 p. $19.

Gr 9+. B 83: Aug 1987. LJ 112: Apr 15 1987. LJ 113: Jan 1988. In his clear account of Nicaraguan history, culture, politics, and personalities, Davis emphasizes the Sandinista/Contra struggle and the complexities of the role of the United States in that struggle.

2185. Gelman, Rita Golden. Inside Nicaragua: Young People's Dreams and Fears. Watts, 1988. 198 p. ill. $14.

Gr 6+. * B 84: Jul 1988. BC 41: Jul 1988. + - BR 7: Nov/Dec 1988. + - SLJ 34: Jun/Jul 1988. VOYA 11: Oct 1988. + - VOYA 12: Jun 1989. Gelman's vivid account shows how people lived in Nicaragua during the mid-1980s when the nation was torn by the civil war between the Contras and the Sandinistas.

2186. Gentile, William Frank. Nicaragua. Norton, 1989. 131 p. ill. $35.

Gr 9+. B 85: Jul 1989. An introduction to Nicaragua's history is followed by colorful photos showing various aspects of life in a nation that has been torn by war for 10 years.

2187. Hanmer, Trudy J. Nicaragua. (First Book). Watts, 1986. 66 p. ill. $9.

Gr 6-8. B 82: May 15 1986. BC 40: Sep 1986. BR 5: Nov/Dec 1986. + - SLJ 33: Oct 1986. Hanmer presents an introduction to the land, climate, history, and customs of Nicaragua and a balanced examination of the Somoza dictatorship and the Sandinista regime.

2188. Lye, Keith. Take a Trip to Nicaragua. Watts, 1988. 32 p. ill. $11.

Gr 2-4. B 85: Nov 1 1988. + - SLJ 35: Jan 1989. A concise commentary and large photos introduce facts about Nicaraguan history, geography, politics, and social life.

2189. Rosset, Peter. Nicaragua: Unfinished Revolution, the New Nicaragua Reader. Grove, 1986. 505 p. ill. $23. Pb $13.

Gr 9+. B 83: Mar 15 1987. Rosset's partisan presentation of historical and political information on Nicaragua includes an interview with President Daniel Ortega and excerpts from numerous documents.

Nicaragua—Biographies

2190. Cruz, Arturo. Memoirs of a Counter-Revolutionary. Doubleday, 1989. 288 p. $19.

Gr 10+. B 86: Sep 15 1989. LJ 114: Sep 1 1989. Cruz supported the Sandinistas in the early days of their rule, but his disillusionment caused him to become a spokesman for the Contras. Here he tells of his experiences during the struggle.

Panama

2191. Markun, Patricia Maloney. Panama Canal, The. Rev. ed. (First Book). Watts, 1979. 66 p. ill. $9.

Gr 3-6. B 82: Dec 1 1985. SLJ 26: Apr 1980. The political and engineering history of the canal are presented along with a description of a typical trip through it.

2192. Panama in Pictures. Rev. ed. (Visual Geography Series). Lerner, 1987. 64 p. ill. $10.

Gr 4-9. B 83: Aug 1987. SLJ 34: Oct 1987. Information on the construction and operation of the canal is included in this work that covers Panamanian history, geography, economy, and government.

2193. St. George, Judith. Panama Canal: Gateway to the World. Putnam, 1989. 114 p. ill. $16.

Gr 5+. B 85: Apr 15 1989. HB 65: Jul/Aug 1989. SLJ 35: Apr 1989. VOYA 12: Aug 1989. A balanced history of the building of the Panama Canal is presented in this well-illustrated work.

South America

General

2194. Georges, D. V. South America. (New True Book). Childrens Press, 1986. 44 p. maps. $12.

Gr 2-4. SLJ 33: May 1987. A short history is included in this colorful work that covers South American geography, resources, wildlife, industry, technology, and people.

General—Amazon River

2195. Cheney, Glenn Alan. Amazon, The. (First Book). Watts, 1984. 59 p. ill. $9.

Gr 6-8. B 81: Dec 15 1984. SLJ 31: Dec 1984. Readers journey down the Amazon and investigate the societies that live on its shores, gaining historical, cultural, economic, and ecological insight.

General—Indians of South America

2196. Morrison, Marion. Indians of the Andes. (Original Peoples). Rourke, 1987. 48 p. ill. $13.

Gr 3-6. B 84: Jan 15 1988. - SLJ 34: Apr 1988. Morrison's introduction to the history, culture, and religion of the indigenous peoples of the Andes includes photos and a glossary.

Argentina

2197. Argentina in Pictures. (Visual Geography Series). Lerner, 1988. 64 p. ill. $10.

Gr 5-8. B 84: Apr 15 1988. + - SLJ 35: May 1988. This volume on Argentine history, geography, culture, religion, education, and health includes photos, maps, and charts.

2198. Hintz, Martin. Argentina. (Enchantment of the World). Childrens Press, 1985. 127 p. ill. $20.

Gr 4-6. B 82: Mar 1 1986. + - SLJ 32: May 1986. Colorful photos augment this text that covers Argentine history, culture, geography, industry, and people.

2199. Lye, Keith. Take a Trip to Argentina. Watts, 1986. 32 p. ill. $10.

Gr 2-4. B 83: Oct 15 1986. SLJ 33: Feb 1987. Photos on each page and a brief informative text introduce Argentine history, geography, industry, and cities.

Argentina—Biographies

2200. DeChancie, John. Juan Peron. (World Leaders Past & Present). Chelsea House, 1987. 111 p. ill. $17.

Gr 6+. B 84: Nov 15 1987. + - SLJ 34: Feb 1988. Peron's important influence in Argentine history is clearly presented. Photos, quotes, and a timeline augment the balanced text.

2201. Fraser, Nicholas. Eva Peron. Norton, 1981. 192 p. ill. $15.

Gr 9+. B 77: Jun 1 1981. SLJ 28: Jan 1982. LJ 106: May 1 1981. Photos and illustrations enhance this objective account of Eva Peron's private and political life.

Bolivia

2202. Bolivia in Pictures. Rev. ed. (Visual Geography Series). Lerner, 1987. 64 p. ill. $10.

Gr 5-9. B 84: Oct 15 1987. * SE 52: Apr/May 1988. SLJ 34: Jan 1988. This balanced introduction to Bolivian history, geography, government, economy, and people includes colorful photos.

2203. Morrison, Marion. Bolivia. (Enchantment of the World). Childrens Press, 1988. 128 p. ill. $23.

Gr 4-9. B 85: Feb 15 1989. SLJ 35: Mar 1989. The contemporary concerns of Bolivia are covered, along with its history, government, geography, economy, politics, and culture in this illustrated work.

Brazil

2204. Brazil. (Children of the World). Gareth Stevens, 1988. 64 p. maps. $13.

Gr 3-5. + - SLJ 35: Sep 1988. In addition to a brief section on Brazilian history, geography, resources, and similar topics, an account is given of the daily life of a wealthy child.

2205. Carpenter, Mark L. Brazil: An Awakening Giant. (Discovering Our Heritage). Dillon Press, 1987. 125 p. ill. $13.

Gr 5+. B 84: Feb 15 1988. BR 7: May/Jun 1988. SLJ 34: Mar 1988. This survey of Brazilian history and culture includes information on myths, holidays, food, and sports, and is enhanced by color photos.

2206. Cross, Wilbur. Brazil. (Enchantment of the World). Childrens Press, 1984. 127 p. ill. $15.

Gr 5-7. B 81: May 15 1985. SLJ 31: Aug 1985. Cross' coverage of Brazilian history, geography, culture, and economy includes maps, photos, and a reference section that covers statistical information, notable people, and dates.

2207. Haverstock, Nathan A. Brazil in Pictures. Rev. ed. (Visual Geography Series). Lerner, 1987. 64 p. ill. $10.

Gr 4-9. B 83: Aug 1987. SLJ 33: Aug 1987. Haverstock's colorful introduction to Brazilian history, government, land, and people includes maps and photos.

2208. Levine, Robert M. Historical Dictionary of Brazil. (Latin American Historical Dictionaries). Scarecrow, 1979. 297 p. $13.

Gr 9+. B 76: Apr 15 1980. Emphasis is on Brazilian culture in this work that includes a classified bibliography of English-language books and articles on Brazil. Number 19 of the series.

Chile

2209. Garcia Marquez, Gabriel. Clandestine in Chile: The Adventures of Miguel Littin. Holt, 1987. 114 p. ill. $14.

Gr 9+. B 83: May 15 1987. * LJ 112: Jun 15 1987. SLJ 33: Aug 1987. Life in Chile under the Pinochet regime was documented in a secret film made by Miguel Littin, a Chilean exile who risked death to record this account of national fear and repression.

2210. Haverstock, Nathan A. Chile in Pictures. (Visual Geography Series). Lerner, 1988. 64 p. ill. $10.

Gr 5-8. B 84: Apr 15 1988. SLJ 35: Oct 1988. Chile's history, economy, culture, resources, and government are introduced in this work that includes numerous photos, maps, and charts.

2211. Huber, Alex. We Live in Chile. (Living Here). Watts, 1986. 60 p. ill. $11.

Gr 5-8. B 82: May 15 1986. Ready reference information about Chile is appended to an interview with a Chilean ski instructor, who tells about life in Chile and brings in aspects of the nation's history, geography, and economy.

2212. Timerman, Jacobo. Chile: Death in the South. Knopf, 1987. 130 p. $16.

Gr 9+. B 84: Dec 15 1987. LJ 113: Jan 1988. VOYA 12: Jun 1989. This clearly written report on the human rights violations of Pinochet's dictatorship in Chile ends each chapter with the testimony of someone who has been a victim, as was the author.

Chile-Biographies

2213. Garza, Hedda. Salvador Allende. (World Leaders Past & Present). Chelsea House, 1989. 112 p. ill. $17.

Gr 6+. BR 8: May/Jun 1989, Sep/Oct 1989. SLJ 35: Aug 1989. VOYA 12: Aug 1989. The personal and political life of Allende and relations between Chile and the United States are covered in this illustrated work.

Ecuador

2214. Ecuador in Pictures. (Visual Geography Series). Lerner, 1987. 64 p. ill. $10.

Gr 4-7. B 84: Jan 1 1988. + - SLJ 34: Mar 1988. The history, government, economy, land, and people of Ecuador are introduced in this heavily illustrated work.

2215. Lepthien, Emilie U. Ecuador. (Enchantment of the World). Childrens Press, 1986. 127 p. ill. $20.

Gr 4-8. B 82: Jul 1986. B 83: Jun 15 1987. Colorful photos enhance this work on Ecuador's history, economy, culture, geography, resources, and people.

French Guinea–Biographies

2216. Laye, Camara. Dark Child. Farrar, 1954. 188 p. $6.

Gr 9+. B 51: Dec 15 1954. B 82: May 15 1986. * LJ 79: Nov 1 1954. In this sensitive autobiography Laye tells of growing up in the traditional way in a village in French Guinea and his later education in France. He presents an intimate view of the customs, habits, and superstitions of a simple society.

Guyana

2217. Guyana in Pictures. (Visual Geography Series). Lerner, 1988. 64 p. ill. $10.

Gr 5-8. B 84: Apr 15 1988. Numerous photos, maps, and charts augment this account of Guyanan history, geography, resources, cities, government, and culture.

Paraguay

2218. Haverstock, Nathan A. Paraguay in Pictures. (Visual Geography Series). Lerner, 1988. 64 p. ill. $10.

Gr 5-8. B 84: Apr 15 1988. + - SLJ 35: May 1988. Photos, charts, and maps augment this introduction to Paraguayan history, geography, resources, culture, and government.

Peru

2219. Crosby, Alexander L. Rimac: River of Peru. (Rivers of the World). Garrard, 1965. 96 p. ill. $4.

Gr 4-7. Metzner. In presenting information on the Rimac River, Crosby discusses the history and culture of the people who have lived on its banks.

2220. Lye, Keith. Take a Trip to Peru. Watts, 1987. 32 p. ill. $10.

Gr 2-4. B 84: Nov 15 1987. Photos on each page and a brief, informative text introduce Peruvian history, geography, industry, and cities.

Peru–Incas

2221. Beck, Barbara L. Incas, The. Rev. ed. (First Book). Watts, 1983. 64 p. ill. $9.

Gr 5-8. B 79: Apr 1 1983. SLJ 29: Apr 1983. This introduction to Inca life covers their history, culture, and social structure. Photos, a chronology, and a map are included.

2222. Blassingame, Wyatt. Incas and the Spanish Conquest, The. Messner, 1980. 192 p. ill. $9.

Gr 6-8. SLJ 27: Sep 1980. SLJ 28: Sep 1981. Blassingame explores the culture and actions of both the Incas and their Spanish conquerors in detail.

2223. Burland, Cottie A. Inca Peru. (Great Civilizations). Dufour, 1957; 1975. 93 p. ill. $7.

Gr 4-8. Metzner. B 82: Dec 1 1985. Burland's brief, illustrated overview of life among the Incas covers clothing, architecture, education, industry, and culture.

2224. Gemming, Elizabeth. Lost City in the Clouds: The Discovery of Machu Picchu. (Science Discovery Book). Coward, McCann, 1980. 75 p. ill. Lib. ed. $6.

Gr 4-8. B 76: Jun 1 1980. B 82: Dec 1 1985. BC 34: Sept 1980. * SE 45: Apr 1981. SLJ 26: May 1980. Information on Incan history and culture is included in this account of the 1911 discovery of Machu Picchu, a well-preserved mountain city.

2225. Marrin, Albert. Inca & Spaniard: Pizarro and the Conquest of Peru. Atheneum, 1989. 211 p. ill. $14.

Gr 7-10. * B 86: Oct 15 1989. SLJ 35: Nov 1989. VOYA 12: Dec 1989. Marrin presents a realistic introduction to Incan history and culture, and to Pizarro and his conquest of the Inca nation. Line drawings based on the work of an Indian artist enhance the work.

2226. McKissack, Patricia. Inca, The. (New True Book). Childrens Press, 1985. 45 p. ill. $8.

Gr 2-3. SLJ 32: Apr 1986. This brief introduction to Inca history and culture includes photos, a map, and a glossary.

2227. Millard, Anne. Incas, The. Warwick; dist. by Watts, 1980. 44 p. ill. $10.

Gr 5-10. B 82: Dec 1 1985. Many colorful photos and drawings enhance this readable account of Inca history.

2228. Morrison, Marion. Atahuallpa and the Incas. (Life and Times). Bookwright Press; dist. by Watts, 1986. 59 p. ill. $11.

Gr 5-7. BC 40: Dec 1986. + - SLJ 33: Nov 1986. The development, growth, and conquest of the Inca civilization are emphasized in this introductory work that also provides information on Atahuallpa, the illegitimate son of Huayma Capac, the Inca emperor.

2229. Morrison, Marion. Inca Farmer, An. (How They Lived). Rourke, 1988. 32 p. ill. $13.

Gr 3-6. B 85: Nov 15 1988. SLJ 35: Jun 1989. In this introduction to the daily life of an Inca peasant, Morrison presents information on Inca history, religion, medicine, government, social life, and housing.

Suriname

2230. Beatty, Noelle B. Suriname. (Places and Peoples of the World). Chelsea House, 1987. 96 p. ill. $12.

Gr 6-8. B 84: Feb 1 1988. Beatty's illustrated introduction to Suriname presents a balanced look at its history, geography, politics, culture, and economy.

Uruguay

2231. Dobler, Lavinia. Land and People of Uruguay. Rev. ed. (Portraits of the Nations Series). Harper, 1972. 160 p. ill. $12.

Gr 5-9. Metzner. Dobler's overview covers the history, geography, government, economy, people, and customs of Uruguay, the smallest country in South America.

2232. Haverstock, Nathan A. Uruguay in Pictures. (Visual Geography Series). Lerner, 1987. 64 p. ill. $10.

Gr 4-8. B 84: Jan 1 1988. + - SLJ 34: Mar 1988. VOYA 12: Jun 1989. Full-color photos and political and physical maps complement this overview of the history, economy, government, land, and people of Uruguay.

Venezuela

2233. Morrison, Marion. Venezuela. (Enchantment of the World). Childrens Press, 1989. 128 p. ill. $23.

Gr 5-7. B 85: Aug 1989. Colorful photos enrich this overview of Venezuela's history, economy, culture, and geography.

2234. Venezuela in Pictures. (Visual Geography Series). Lerner, 1987. 64 p. ill. $10.

Gr 4-7. B 84: Jan 1 1988. SLJ 34: Mar 1988. This pictorial introduction to Venezuela covers history, geography, government, and the people. The impact of the petroleum industry is included in the discussion of the Venezuelan economy.

Author Index

Title Index

Subject Index

Jews–Bibliographies

Jews–Biographies

Jews–Fiction

Series Index

Weighing Up the Evidence

Why They Became Famous

Windows on the World

Witness History Series

Women History Makers

Women in World Area Studies

Women of Our Time

Work Throughout History Series

World at War

World Bibliographical Series

World Disasters

World Espionage

World Landmark Books

World Leaders in Context

World Leaders Past & Present

World of Change

World of Knowledge

World of Science

World Today Series

World War II

Grade Level Index

5-10

5-11

5-Adult

8-10

8-Adult

9-10

9-11

9-Adult

10-Adult

11-Adult

12-Adult

Adult